Best Places to Stay in Florida

The Best Places to Stay Series

Best Places to Stay in America's Cities
Kenneth Hale-Wehmann, Editor

Best Places to Stay in Asia
Jerome E. Klein

Best Places to Stay in California
Anne E. Wright

Best Places to Stay in the Caribbean
Bill Jamison and Cheryl Alters Jamison

Best Places to Stay in Florida
Christine Davidson

Best Places to Stay in Hawaii
Kim Grant

Best Places to Stay in Mexico
Bill Jamison and Cheryl Alters Jamison

Best Places to Stay in the Mid-Atlantic States
Kent Steinriede

Best Places to Stay in the Midwest
John Monaghan

Best Places to Stay in New England
Christina Tree and Kim Grant

Best Places to Stay in the Pacific Northwest
Marilyn McFarlane

Best Places to Stay in the Rockies
Roger Cox

Best Places to Stay in the South
Carol Timblin

Best Places to Stay in the Southwest
Anne E. Wright

Best Places to Stay in Florida

Christine Davidson

Bruce Shaw, Editorial Director

Sixth Edition

HOUGHTON MIFFLIN COMPANY

BOSTON • NEW YORK

Sixth Edition

ISSN: 1048-5430
ISBN: 0-618-00534-X

Printed in the United States of America

Maps by Charles Bahne
Design by Robert Overholtzer
This book was prepared in conjunction with Harvard Common Press.

QUM 10 9 8 7 6 5 4 3 2 1

To my favorite traveling companions:
Chip, Mike, and Jen

Acknowledgments

Books are not just the result of the author's research and writing, but also a reflection of the aid and encouragement of a number of people. This has been particularly true of *Best Places to Stay in Florida*, which depended on the interest of so many.

My thanks first to researchers who visited places included in the first five editions, most of which are also in this edition: Jeff Bernstein, Ruth and Bob Davidson, Corbie Morrison, Linda Prior, Marcella Schaible, Linda Durgin, Suzan Helgerson Pruiett, and Pamela Steele.

For this edition, I would also like to thank Susan Jimison, Beverly Butterworth, Kay Loudenslager, and Dawn Higgins. Many thanks to the various tourism and visitors' bureaus of Florida counties, the Florida Department of Natural Resources, and members of Florida Bed & Breakfast Inns. My greatest appreciation goes to my family for their support and encouragement.

Contents

Introduction

Best Places to Stay in Florida is a gleaning of the best Florida has to offer out of hundreds of hotels, inns, B&Bs, motels, condos, and resorts.

This book includes a map showing the regions into which we've broken the state, some travel tips, and a brief history on the early development of Florida as a resort. At the beginning of each regional chapter is a brief description of the history, geography, and attractions of that section of the state. Notice, too, that there is a listing of the "best" of several specific types of accommodations, such as Beachside, Budget Finds, Eclectic Finds, etc. These designations are for those who wish to stay in a place that has a particular ambience or location.

In describing the various accommodations, we have tried to describe objectively the intentions and successes of a place. Obviously, the criteria for judging a "best" Budget Find will differ from those for a "best" Spa. The primary standards are distinct atmosphere, cleanliness, and the palpable presence of outstanding management. In some cases, the latter may be a hotel corporation with high standards; in another, it may be a retired school principal running a B&B who lends her books out to guests to read at night. Under no circumstances can anyone pay to be included in *Best Places to Stay*.

The majority of accommodations in *Best Places to Stay in Florida* were seen personally by the author. A few inns and hotels were initially seen or were rechecked by a researcher, and some establishments were seen twice, once by a researcher and a few months later by the author. The researchers were charged with the task of viewing places — usually anonymously — with the same criteria that the author used. In addition, the opinions and experiences of relatives and friends living in a particular area of Florida were often solicited. All the places described in the book have been operating successfully for at least one year. While there's always an attempt to keep personal values and interests out of the selections, some biases have certainly crept in. We are not exactly ashamed of these biases and believe that many other modern travelers share them.

No doubt there have been some oversights, either for lack of time or because an excellent resort or inn was new. This is particularly true of some B&Bs in Key West and St. Augustine, where so many places have opened recently that it has been difficult to see them all. If you know of a "great place" that you think we may not be aware of, please write. On the last page of this book you'll find information about sending in a Best Places Report.

All accommodations listed in the book have air conditioning — not an unimportant consideration in Florida. Nearly all guest rooms described have private baths. The few exceptions are in B&Bs and Budget Finds where most rooms have private baths but a few share a bath—ideal for those on a tight budget. Several historic B&Bs have bathrooms with old clawfoot tubs; a showerhead and metal surround for the shower curtain are rigged up above. Some of these work pretty well and some do not. If it's important for you to have a bathroom with a real shower stall or fixed enclosure, ask about bathroom choices when making reservations. Some of the larger B&Bs and inns have both an old-fashioned tub for soaking and a new shower stall in a modern tile bathroom.

We made an effort to avoid including places that are overpriced, crowded with tour groups, across a busy road from the water or an attraction for children, or decorated with plastic furniture. Very few chain hotels or high-rises are included. The most important criterion for all who researched accommodations was, Would I want to stay here?

Our one regret is that a good many of the recommendations are expensive. As everywhere in the world, you get what you pay for, and in Florida you pay quite a bit, especially during the winter season. But there are ways to get around this — you might consider visiting a plush resort in November, when skies are gloomy in Cleveland or New York but gorgeous in Naples or Boca Raton. Or come to South Florida during the height of the winter season but stay at a Victorian B&B instead of a costly resort. Or rent a condo that may initially appear expensive but will offer savings in meals prepared in the kitchen. A good travel agent can advise you on ways to save on air travel during certain seasons and times of the week.

Best Places to Stay is not just for people with a great deal of disposable income, who can take a vacation whenever they feel the need. In fact, it is because most travelers to Florida are not part of this lucky elite that a book like this is so important. One way or another, traveling to Florida from another part of the country and staying for a long weekend or several days is costly. Each year thousands of people come back from Florida disappointed and disillusioned after a honeymoon, getaway golf weekend, or trip to Disney World. The hotel was glitzy and overpriced. The beach was half a mile away across a hot asphalt highway. The motel was an hour from Disney World. . . . Such experiences can sour even the good times on a Florida vacation.

Most of these too-typical experiences are undergone by travelers who have saved for months to visit Florida. When they finally go, they enjoy splurging a little. But no one enjoys wasting money, even those who have a lot of it. Vacationers to Florida want to feel good about the environment they're staying in, to get their money's worth, and to come as close as possible to the kind of vacation they've fantasized about. Therefore, our final criterion was, Is this place worth it? The answer was a definite "yes" for those accommodations described in this book.

Planning for Florida

Getting There

It is possible to drive from the Northeast or the Midwest and arrive in Florida within 24 hours. College students do it all the time on spring breaks. But unless you've got the endurance of a college kid, it's unwise to start a Florida holiday this way. The alternatives are to drive and stay at motels along the way, take a series of buses or trains, or fly. The latter choice is preferred by most vacationers, who have limited time in Florida and want to get there as soon and as painlessly as possible.

A travel agent is the best source of information on what flights are the least expensive. Buying tickets several weeks in advance or flying in the middle of the week can lead to substantial savings. Agents can consult computer listings to find the best deals, as can you, on the Internet.

Organizations such as group travel clubs, AAA, AARP, and American Express also have some very good deals. These organizations charge a fee for membership. If you belong to an airline's frequent flyer club, have senior citizen "getaway" tickets, or belong to a college alumni group that can obtain group fares, you can also save.

The quality of airports varies in Florida, although most are very good. The most crowded is Miami International Airport, largely because of all the people who come through on their way somewhere else: a Caribbean cruise or a flight to South America or the islands. If you're planning on a vacation to southeast Florida or the Keys, consider flying to Fort Lauderdale's airport 40 minutes north of Miami and then driving to your destination. The 40 extra minutes is worth it; besides, you could be delayed at the Miami airport for at least 40 minutes just because of the crowds or a lost bag.

Driving in Florida

Many of the larger hotels in Florida either offer shuttle service to and from the airport or have agents for rental car companies working out of their hotels. Some vacationers prefer to take the shuttle to their accommodation and, after a couple of days of enjoying their hotel's amenities, rent a car from an agent for the remainder of their stay. Rates vary depending on the season in Florida. Winter rates are higher throughout the state, even in the north, where winter is actually the low season. It's always best to reserve a car in advance, particularly in southern Florida in winter.

There are a number of rental agencies in Florida. Which ever you choose, be certain it has road service. A couple of the bargain companies don't provide this service and may not tell you that — until you call from a roadside phone for help. All agencies provide minimal insurance and optional collision insurance that they urge you to get. The latter is quite costly and is necessary only if your own insurance policy doesn't cover you for collision in a rental car. Be advised, however, that you will usually be responsible for the deductible portion on your policy and will probably have to pay for any damages immediately, with your insurance company reimbursing you later.

It's important to remember several things when driving in Florida. The state is full of tourists — many of them driving unfamiliar rental cars and not knowing exactly where they're going. Many drivers travel in the left lane at snail-slow speeds, particularly in the Orlando/Disney World area, and on roads where there is no median strip or there are frequent crossways on the median strip. This is because there are so many attractions and accommodations on the left side of the street. With only a name or street number to go by, people will inch along until they figure out where to cross.

The situation is complicated by the number of elderly drivers in the state. Many of them haven't been in Florida for long, either, and may be forgetful. They, like tourists, will often drive at extremely slow speeds in the left-hand lane — or any lane — of a major highway. They may also slow down nearly to a stop before making a right or left-hand turn. For some reason, drivers in Florida, old and young, use directional signals sparingly. Or they turn on a directional signal to go left and then leave the signal on for miles — what Jerry Seinfeld calls the "eventual left." In short, you have to drive defensively, purchase clearly marked street maps, and get precise directions for any destination so you don't contribute to the problem or become involved in an accident.

For the most part, Florida's roads are well maintained and well marked. In some areas, there seems to be construction all the time, and the road work causes delays. But the state makes an effort to have most of the work done by the start of the winter season.

The most heavily traveled highways run north to south. Old Route 1, constructed on the roadbed of Flagler's railway, runs along the Atlantic coast. This is a great highway for sightseeing, especially from Boca Raton to Palm Beach. Often only one lane wide, it's congested in the Miami area and has an almost rural feel north of St. Augustine and Ponte Vedra.

Interstate 95 runs almost parallel to Route 1 and is a faster road. It, too, can get congested, particularly from Miami to Fort Lauderdale. It is often better to pay the toll and take the Florida Turnpike, which runs from Florida City, just south of Miami, to the junction with Interstate 75 northwest of Orlando.

The Gulf coast equivalent of I-95 is I-75; it is usually less traveled than 95. Florida's other interstate highway is I-10, which runs from Jacksonville to the Alabama border and beyond. A huge network of state highways crisscrosses the middle of the state from 10 south. A few, like Highways 27 and 41 (the Tamiami Trail), are narrow and old but are favored by many for their lack of congestion and the interesting sights along the way.

Rates

Many hotels in Florida have high and low seasons and in-between periods called shoulder season or value season; the range of rates in one year can be enormous. The person who sees the rates for a resort in a fall magazine article may be in for a shock when making reservations for the same place in February. However, almost all of the resorts and hotels in this book have group rates and special packages. Hotels in cities sometimes have discount rates on weekends, while places in tourist spots may have lower rates during the week.

Unless money is no object, always ask for detailed information about the range of rates. Many hotel reservationists will initially quote you a price for a superior or deluxe room. You may have to request specifically the price of a standard room.

You probably will have to ask for information about any packages or specials, too. But once you begin to ask questions and establish your interest in "values," as the industry calls them, you'll find that most personnel taking reservations will be extremely helpful in giving you the information you need to save money.

Unless a hotel has only one type of room and one standard rate for that room year-round, *Best Places to Stay in Florida* gives a range, from low to high. In other words, we list the lowest rate at low season and the highest rate at high season. If suites, apartments, or cottages are available, we do the same for each of those. Rates usually go up about $10 each year for a room and a little higher for suites. Some B&Bs and inns may not raise prices for two or three years.

With the exception of a few urban hotels, rates listed are for double occupancy. Some city hotels that cater to corporate executives traveling alone list only single rates and then add a charge for an "extra person" when a couple occupies the room. Many hotels that do not list corporate rates in the data do, in fact, have them. Deciphering the rates for spas may be tricky because the spa may quote a rate as "double occupancy," but the rate is still "per person." Some spas include nearly all treatments in the per-person rate, while others charge separately for them.

Taxes and Other Added Charges

Visitors sometimes are confused by the room and meal taxes in Florida, particularly when resorts in the same town quote different taxes. The state has a sales tax on all hotel rooms. Sometimes this is figured into the price of a room; sometimes it isn't. In many cases, various local and county taxes are added onto the basic state tax. We have made every effort to provide you with all tax charges in the data above each entry. But because taxes keep going up and the reporting of taxes can be inconsistent from hotel to hotel, the information we provide may not be the total tax liability. When making reservations, be certain to ask what the total tax charges will be in addition to the basic room rate.

Most hotels and resorts also have a fee for any "extra person" or "extra adult" in the room above its stated capacity. In other words, if you are a family of four and have a grandparent traveling with you who plans to sleep on a rollaway in a room with

two double beds, there will be a charge. In some places the hotel may advise you to book a suite with a capacity for six people. Every place is different, so it is wise to ask ahead when
making reservations.

Most hotels and resorts in Florida do not take pets. A few
family vacation cottages and B&Bs have a tradition of allowing
small animals for a fee. Even these are beginning to change
former policies and are simply pointing guests to the nearest
boarding kennel. The few places in the book that will take pets
are listed under "Pets Allowed" in the chapter called "What's
What" at the back of the book.

Some resorts have a no-tipping policy; gratuities are figured
into the room rate. At others, a service charge is added to your
bill. Again, be sure to inquire about all fees and charges, especially if you're on a tight budget.

Payment

Payment is almost always by credit card in Florida, though
some hotels will accept a personal check with proper identification (one or two major credit cards). Many hotels also require
credit card identification with traveler's checks. In any case, it's
difficult to vacation in Florida without plastic of some sort.
The exceptions to this are a few small inns and B&Bs that will
not take credit cards and prefer a check or cash.

Late Check-out

Be sure you know check-in and check-out times and the policy
on extended check-out. Some hotels have a liberal policy about
using their pool and changing rooms after check-out; others do
not. Policies sometimes change according to season even in the
most laid-back resorts.

Traveling with Children

Florida is a great place to vacation with kids. Most hotels and
resorts allow children to stay with parents at no charge. The
ages at which they allow this vary, however, so it's important
to take note of this in the information at the beginning of each
entry in this book.

The personnel at the hotels, resorts, and various attractions in Walt Disney World bend over backwards to accommodate families. If you have young or handicapped children, inquire about high chairs, strollers, cribs, or wheelchairs, so you can avoid having to bring them along. If you stay at a hotel or resort owned by Disney World, ask about the various Family Plans — these combine the price of accommodations, attraction tickets, and meals (including tip), making for a more carefree vacation in Disney World.

Bugs and Other Florida Wildlife

It goes without saying that anyone traveling to Florida should bring lots of sunblock and maybe a wide-brimmed hat. But many people forget to bring insect repellent, and beautiful Florida is home to plenty of insects that bite and sting. Many of the least populated regions of Florida are so lovely you'll want to just sit for hours and take it all in, watching a troop of ducks or the pelicans diving for fish. If you do, you'll be a sitting duck yourself. Insect repellent is imperative. In areas that have biting ants, spiders, or sand fleas, you should keep repellent — or shoes and socks — on your feet at all times.

In some coastal regions of Florida, signs are posted on the beach warning of sea lice. These are small critters in the ocean who love to hide in the elastic bands of swimsuits. They are not a big problem as long as you do not sit around in a wet suit. You should take off your swimsuit immediately after getting back to your hotel and rinse it a couple of times in tap water, as well as thoroughly soaping up and showering yourself.

Many jokes circulate outside of Florida about golfers seeing alligators lounging on a golf course green or waddling onto a resort's front lawn. These cases are rare. Alligators tend to be shy. However, their protection by the law has resulted in some overpopulation and aggressiveness over food sources. What an alligator considers a "food source" can be pretty disturbing. There have been incidents in recent years of hungry alligators going after pet dogs and children in Boynton Beach and along the Loxahatchee River. Anyone who wants to play Crocodile Dundee should forget it in Florida. Alligators are magnificent creatures, but they should be avoided except on supervised tours.

General Safety

There has been some concern in recent years regarding human predators and the safety of tourists in Florida, especially in Miami. As in any large city, it is wise not to be an easy mark. Avoid driving in poorly lighted areas at any time of night. If you are at an airport parking lot late at night, pay the extra money to get a burly porter for your luggage, or ask for security, if available. Always stay in well-lighted areas near people, and pay attention to any intuitive negative feelings about groups of kids hanging around or a loitering lone stranger.

When renting a car, make sure you know exactly where you are going before leaving the airport. In general, it is always best to stop driving shortly after sundown and to bring enough money so that you can stay in a secure hotel, rather than sleeping by the side of the road or at a rest stop. After the murder of a tourist who had been sleeping at a rest stop near Tallahassee, 24-hour security was mandated at all highway rest stops, which has made both Floridians and out-of-state visitors feel safer. But it is uncertain how long this will continue.

Always keep one credit card, a few dollars, and quarters in a skirt or pant pocket just in case you are parted from your wallet. Don't be obvious about using a map when you are sightseeing — this identifies you as a stranger, especially if you get out of the car to make a phone call at a public phone by the side of the road. There have been instances of purse snatching or pocket picking while tourists were distracted making a call.

People who would watch their wallet on a crowded city street or be suspicious of a stranger following them in New York or Washington, D.C., often unwind so thoroughly on a Florida vacation that they forget to be careful in the state's large urban areas. Taking standard precautions should be enough to avoid robbery or injury.

Area Code Changes

Because of its rapid growth, Florida area codes change frequently. If you have a problem when calling for reservations, call Directory Assistance.

Things to Do

There's an enormous range of things to do and see in Florida. Most towns have visitor centers and tourism associations with lots of information on area attractions, and many hotels have racks of promotional materials. The number of offerings can be so overwhelming that first-time visitors may see the well-advertised attractions that don't appeal to them and miss the places that would genuinely interest them.

The concierge or someone at the front desk will usually recommend area attractions, beaches, and parks. The innkeepers at B&Bs are usually great resources for what to see in a particular area. You may want to do a little reading ahead of time and ask friends who have been to Florida for suggestions. Many cities and towns have tourist bureaus and chambers of commerce that are more than happy to send you free information before a trip.

Finding the Real Florida

The Early Development of Florida

At the end of the 19th century, Henry Flagler, John D. Rocke-feller's partner in Standard Oil, retired early from the oil business and began to develop the east coast of Florida as a resort mecca accessible via railroad. He, of course, would own the railroad, and perhaps grow rich. He never became wealthy from his hotel and railroad building, but he did do a great service to Floridians then struggling to survive — and to the millions living elsewhere in the nation who would enjoy the sunshine and beauty of this state.

Initially, Flagler improved only the existing railroad to St. Augustine, the settlement he had earlier visited with an invalid wife and found lacking in upscale amenities. Besides the unpleasant hotel he and his family stayed in, there were only a few public buildings, some huts made of scrub palm, and the salt-weathered farmhouses of struggling settlers. So Flagler built a spectacular hostelry in St. Augustine, the Ponce de Leon, and a less imposing one across the street to accommodate the spillover. Eventually, Flagler erected hotels up and down his Atlantic Ocean rail route that offered the luxury his wealthy friends and colleagues were accustomed to.

However, once guests arrived, there was little to do, save fish or swim or change clothes three times a day and promenade the hotel verandahs. This could become a bore a few weeks into the season. So Flagler created resorts around a number of recreation activities: shuffleboard, swimming, croquet, and golf — a game imported from Scotland and played for the first time in Florida on a course Flagler built in 1897. Thus was born the tradition of the Florida "destination resort" and the "golf resort."

By 1912, Flagler's railroad and string of resort hotels reached from St. Augustine to Key West, an incredible achievement at the time, since much of Florida was jungle and swamp. The railroad bridges to Key West, one of them traversing a seven-mile-long expanse of water, were considered in their day an engineering marvel to rival the Panama Canal.

Flagler's arena of development was principally the east coast, with a few forays into agricultural central Florida. On the Gulf coast, Henry Plant, a wealthy rival of Flagler's, was also building a railroad system. He had first come to Florida as a land speculator, and he returned after the Civil War to purchase several narrow-gauge railroads that ran from Savannah, Georgia, to Jacksonville. From Jacksonville he turned to Tampa and the Gulf coast.

Like Flagler, he had his triumphs. Plant's engineers created the port of Tampa by constructing a causeway and piers in the deep waters of the bay. During the Spanish-American War, the U.S. War and Navy departments moved troops and supplies through Tampa — rather than Flagler's Miami — because the harbor could accommodate larger ships. Though the Gulf coast did not offer quite the challenge that the keys did, building a railroad was not easy here, either, for the Gulf coast was also swampy, with dense jungle and a plethora of mosquitoes and other stinging, biting wildlife. Tampa became Plant's base, and it was here that he built in 1891 what many consider his greatest achievement: the Tampa Bay Hotel, a fantastical gingerbread and Moorish brick palace that is now part of the University of Tampa. Rooms went for the unheard-of price of $75 a night. When the hotel was completed, Plant invited Flagler to the grand opening. Flagler wired back asking how he would find Tampa. Plant is reputed to have wired back, "Just follow the crowd, Henry."

As the years passed, the Gulf coast towns of Naples and St. Petersburg were developed and became popular. F. Scott Fitzgerald and his family frequented the Don CeSar, a pink stucco palace majestically sited on St. Petersburg Beach and the Gulf of Mexico. Writers and artists journeyed on the railroad to the Casa Marina in Key West, Flagler's last grand resort. The Vanderbilts, du Ponts, Colliers, and Lindberghs preferred the serenity of the barrier islands of the Gulf coast, then accessible only by boat.

In the early days of Florida development, few people owned winter homes, so most stayed at one of the elegant watering holes. Many of these were made of wood, and some of the most elegant eventually burned down. In their place, Spanish-style hotels were built in the 1920s of shellstone and stucco. Some of the fantastic hotels built by Flagler and Plant and a 1920s visionary, Addison Mizner, have fortunately survived. The Ponce de Leon in St. Augustine and the Tampa Bay Hotel in Tampa now house colleges. The Boca Raton, an eclectic stucco palace built by self-taught architect Mizner, is still thriving as a resort hotel, as is the Breakers, which was originally built as an annex to the Royal Poinciana but thrived on its own.

Of all the resort towns that Flagler created along his railroad, Palm Beach became the most exclusive and the most desirable. The oceanfront Royal Poinciana Hotel, which opened in 1894, was the largest resort hotel in the world and became the place for the powerful and wealthy to spend the season. Later, beautiful mansions and "cottages" were built in Palm Beach in lavish but exquisite taste.

Many showed an appreciation for Florida's Spanish heritage and for the building materials native to the area, most notably coquina and coral stone. Coquina is a shellstone made of thousands of tiny shells that congeal over the centuries with sand and are then cut into masonry blocks that are enduring and beautiful. The best examples of coquina buildings are in St. Augustine, where there was a ready supply of stone from nearby Anastasia Island. Sometimes used as a basic building material to be plastered over with stucco, coquina is most arresting when the stone is left in its natural state.

Coral stone, or key stone, is even more lovely. When cut, the pores and wavy tendrils of the once-live coral become visible; often little spiral shells are perfectly preserved in cavities of the coral. Addison Mizner used a great deal of coral stone as embellishment for archways and window frames in his buildings. Some of the mansions this eccentric designed can still be seen on Palm Beach's Worth Avenue residential area and shopping district.

For all its natural beauty and exciting architecture, Palm Beach was considered unbearably snobby in the 1920s and 1930s, and people who didn't have the right last name were often frozen out socially in the balmiest of weather. Miami was initially developed as an orange-growing region, but it soon became the common man's answer to Palm Beach. It was created in the 1890s by Flagler and a young widow from Cleveland named Julia Tuttle, who hoped to make a fortune for herself and her children. She died at 49 before this could happen, and in the last years of her life gave Flagler more than a hundred acres to build a hotel on, along with half of her other land holdings, figuring that a railroad and hotel would greatly increase the value of her property. In Miami, Flagler built the Royal Palm, the first of many hotels in Miami.

The vegetation in Miami and its barrier islands across Biscayne Bay grew so luxuriantly that, in the 1890s and for years after, no one thought too much of cutting down trees and shrubs. Some of these trees were coconut palms that had been imported by the Spanish and Americans; others were oranges, limes, bananas, and guavas. There were also various palm trees and thickets of mangroves. Miami Beach was mostly swamp in the 1890s, filled with biting insects, snakes, cabbage palm, and Spanish bayonet, a vicious form of yucca.

Miami Beach Development in the Twentieth Century

By the 1920s, Miami was a civilized and exciting city that was more open and welcoming than Palm Beach had ever been. A sandbar and marshy area in Biscayne Bay that had been filled in when the Miami River was dredged to create a canal was now called Miami Beach, and it was becoming a resort playground. The principal area developed for tourists and retirees during the first half of the century was South Beach: lower Collins Avenue, Ocean Drive, and neighborhoods just east of Biscayne Bay. Some of the most innovative development occurred during the 1930s and 1940s, resulting in what is now known as the art deco district.

Though it is difficult to devise an all-encompassing description of this architectural and decorative style, the buildings were usually of stucco, with smooth, streamlined exteriors on corners and entryways. Art deco architects used their fancy in devising decorative plaster ornaments on these buildings, and often introduced modernistic decorative friezes and borders on the exteriors. The hotels and apartment buildings were painted in bright pinks, lemon yellows, and sherbet pastels. Contrasting colors were used to accentuate different sculpted decorative lines and protrusions.

At the time, art deco was considered up-to-date and chic. Elegant shops and restaurants were built and the entire area became fashionable. Soon this area became the playground of the wealthy upper middle class of New York and other northern cities, particularly of Jews and others who had been denied access to Palm Beach. Many people retired here and moved into elegant apartment buildings.

But in the 1950s and 1960s, art deco began to look silly. Flat, utilitarian buildings came into vogue, and lower Collins Avenue, which had been so fashionable, began to decline. Developers moved to upper Collins Avenue to build new hotels and residential apartment buildings, and the South Beach neighborhood deteriorated still further.

The developers on upper Collins Avenue maximized profits on their expensive plots of oceanfront land by packing as many people into the hotels as possible. The high-rise hotels they built were much bigger than anything the lower Collins section of Miami Beach had ever seen. Today, this congested forest of hotels looks as if it was built by a homesick midtown Manhattanite. Many still consider the area quite fashionable, but it has a decidedly urban feel except when you are actually on the beach.

Preserving natural areas or sharing the beach was the last thing developers were thinking about. The high-rises obliterate any view of the beautiful beach unless you're inside one of the overpriced rooms or suites. In the South Miami Beach neighborhood you can get to the beach from Ocean Drive, which runs parallel to lower Collins Avenue, but on upper Collins Avenue, unless you're staying at a Collins Avenue hotel, you cannot get to the beach without walking down a side street. Collins Avenue north of 44th Street is wall-to-wall hotels and condos — the beach is behind the lobbies and boutiques of the concrete and glass buildings. Fortunately, there are still some public beaches just north and south of the high-rise stretch, at the side streets of 21st, 46th, 65th, 75th, and 81st.

In fairness to the developers, it must be said that many tourists coming to Florida from the North were used to skyscrapers and concrete and demanded nothing better of the hoteliers. The sunshine and the ocean were enough to make them feel they were on vacation. There were restaurants and jazz clubs and other night life nearby or across the bay in Miami, one of the most beautiful cities in the United States. So thousands of people found — and still find — their experience in a high-rise on Miami Beach perfectly satisfactory. But others have taken their honeymoon or family vacation in Miami Beach and have been greatly disappointed.

The beach behind the big hotels on upper Collins Avenue is lovely, with wide sweeps of pale sand and good-sized waves. There's a pleasant raised boardwalk on the beach with railings and good lighting that's safe to walk even in the evening. Biscayne Bay, on the other side of Collins Avenue, is also a lovely stretch of water, but the high-rises of upper Collins Avenue are most unbeachlike. There are some notable exceptions; in general, Miami Beach is best for people who want the specific combination of urban development and beach.

Central Florida and Disney

After World War II, the average worker began to earn enough to afford a modest winter vacation in Florida, and the state opened up to the average traveler rather than the average millionaire. Hundreds of hotels and motels opened their doors. The ability of many older people to sell their homes after retirement and buy one in Florida also spurred the tourist boom. Most of these retirees had children and grandchildren who would want to take a break from chill northern winds to visit. There wasn't always room for them with Mom and Dad, so more motels and hotels were built.

The majority of these families, as well as the wealthy who had come for decades, still came only for the winter. They stayed mainly on the east and west coasts of south Florida that Flagler and Plant had tamed. Tallahassee, in the middle of northern Florida, was chilly in the winter and concentrated on passing the laws of the state and educating its young people. The rest of northern Florida had more in common with the Georgia countryside than it did with Palm Beach. Central Florida was given over primarily to agriculture, especially the growing of citrus fruits. For decades, citrus growing was the region's economic mainstay, rather than tourism and winter residency.

One exception to this was the Orlando area, southwest of Daytona Beach. In the middle of this century, the city of Orlando was still a sleepy southern town. Prosperous families and elderly widows who preferred the beautiful lakes and fragrance of orange blossoms to the faster-paced activity of the coasts would come to Orlando and nearby Winter Park and Mount Dora every winter. Mansions and more modest bungalows curved around the lakes, and the pace of life beneath moss-draped oaks was very slow. But developers from Anaheim, California, changed all that.

For many years, farmers in the central Florida region had had to deal with the devastating effects of frosts in the winter that could destroy a citrus crop. Some farmers found that they could do much better financially by selling their groves to large developers for housing. When farmers in Kissimmee and Lake Buena Vista, just south of Orlando, were approached by anonymous developers from Disney, most sold their land.

Since Disney World opened in 1971, the Orlando area hasn't been the same. There are still the lovely lakes in and around Orlando and some stately old homes and oak-lined streets. Certainly, the purchase and development by the Disney people of agricultural land in Lake Buena Vista and Kissimmee helped the area economically. But it also created a boom that still continues — and that the highways of Orlando and surrounding towns cannot always handle.

The Magic Kingdom, patterned after California's Disneyland, opened first, followed by EPCOT, an Experimental Prototype Community Of Tomorrow, and Disney-MGM Studios. Although these attractions are several miles south of Orlando, the city and surrounding communities have experienced enormous growth in the last two decades. An amazing number of shopping centers, housing developments, hotels, and motels have mushroomed near Disney World, as well as many secondary tourist attractions: Flea World, Xanadu, Sea World, Fort Liberty, King Henry's Feast, Mardi Gras, Water Mania, Citrus Circus, Great American Fun Factory, Shell World, Jungle Falls, and the Elvis Presley Museum. Some of these, such as Sea World, are wonderful; others are tacky and tasteless. None has a low admission price.

The Other Florida

One result of Disney World and the subsequent development of Orlando is that people now come to Florida throughout the year, rather than just in winter. Today, more people come to central Florida than to the coasts. The Orlando area has changed from an agricultural economy to a thriving metropolis where large corporations have their national headquarters and distribution centers.

But with prosperity have come problems of congestion and a strain on services and highways. The growth has also made Orlando and Disney World almost synonymous with the word Florida. Not everyone is happy about this, especially old-timers and jaded travel writers. Disney World, EPCOT, and Sea World are wonderful places to visit, and it is to the credit of their developers that they are beautifully landscaped and maintained.

Orlando is an exciting city with restaurants, clubs, museums, cultural events, and commerce. But Orlando and the east coast of Florida have been overdeveloped, and they certainly don't represent all that is Florida.

Comfortable accommodations and modern transportation were never meant to destroy the natural beauty, character, or heritage of Florida. But in the last four decades, development and overdevelopment on both coasts have nearly succeeded in doing that. In the 1950s and 1960s, the gracious lines of Spanish-style architecture, as well as the traditional tin roofs and bungalow styles of the Old Florida domestic architecture, were replaced by a modern style that reflected none of Florida's heritage. Florida became the sort of place where finding wooden furniture rather than plastic in a hotel room was unusual. Rooms that had ceiling fans and windows and doors for cross-ventilation were replaced by sealed, air-conditioned boxes where you couldn't open a window to get a sea breeze. Native trees were destroyed and many species of wildlife threatened. Novelist Joy Williams describes with fitting anguish what has happened to the state in her guidebook, *The Florida Keys:* "Florida, that splendid, subtle, once fabulous state, has been exploited, miscomprehended and misused, drained and diked, filled in and paved over. The values of man have been imposed with a vengeance."

Anyone with a little knowledge of the state's history and wildlife is apt to ask, where is the real Florida? Where are the natural white beaches, the hammocks of Florida hardwoods, the haunts of pirates and conquistadors? Where are the Cuban cigar factories, the streets of canopied oaks draped with Spanish moss, the wood-framed Victorian homes and Southern mansions, the old train depots? Most of it is still here. One purpose of this book is to present some of what is best and rarest in the state, and to enable visitors to see the diversity, uniqueness, and wild beauty that is Florida.

Florida's Intracoastal Waterway

The series of channels, inlets, lakes, and rivers between the mainland shore of Florida and its barrier islands is a region unto itself, the Intracoastal Waterway. The Intracoastal is not unique to Florida; it runs from northern Maine down the Atlantic coast, past the Carolinas and Georgia, around southern Florida, up the Gulf coast between the mainland and gulf islands, and ends in Brownsville, Texas. In Florida, an inland route crosses the mainland. Most boaters start this route north of Palm Beach at the St. Lucie River, navigating the river canal west to Lake Okeechobee, crossing the lake to the Caloosahatchee River, then following the river west to the Gulf of Mexico. Along the route of both the inland and coastal Waterway are some state parks where it's pleasant to stop and picnic.

If you are lucky, you may see dolphins dipping in and out of the water or manatees (sea cows) lumbering through the Intracoastal and its canals. Manatee protection zones are marked by white signs along the Waterway, particularly in Fort Lauderdale. In these areas, boaters must run dead slow from mid-November to mid-March.

You can sometimes swim with manatees in canals off the Intracoastal and on the keys if your boating party has stopped for a while. They're gentle mammals who eat marine plants and are found in fresh water as well as salt. In fact, they are the state freshwater mammal, while dolphins are the state saltwater mammal. If there's a garden hose handy, you can turn it on to make an arc over where the manatees are swimming, and they'll raise their heads to get a swallow. Manatees do not have teeth and will not hurt you. However, you can hurt them, so do not swim on their backs or play rough. If you see plastic netting on an adult or baby, swim with them to gain their confidence and then take the net off. This plastic netting has been responsible for the killing and maiming of many manatees and other marine animals.

Like manatees, dolphins are willing to swim with humans, but this is not as easy to do in the wild as it is with manatees, who move a good deal more slowly. If you should have the opportunity to swim with a dolphin, do so gently. They appear to like humans, and some swimmers try to do tricks with them, play piggyback, or hold onto their fins for a ride. These stunts, done in shows with trained animals, can hurt wild dolphins. It's better just to pat them gently or swim close by.

The Real Florida

Finding the real Florida is, of course, a rather personal quest. To the families who flock to Seaside on the Emerald Coast, it may mean an old-style clapboard cottage on the Gulf of Mexico. To a retired couple looking for a winter retreat, it may mean sharing a duplex with friends for a few days on Palm Island or staying at a grand old resort, with the ghost of F. Scott Fitzgerald walking the elegant corridors. To others, the real Florida may be a secluded fishing shack on a canal in the keys, with herons and pelicans the only rivals for the fish.

For most travelers who develop an interest in finding the real Florida, a vacation means seeing Florida's native wildlife and rich vegetation, learning about the state's Native American and Latin heritage, and discovering an architecture influenced by many elements in the state's history. To offer what is genuine in *Best Places to Stay in Florida*, an effort has been made to choose accommodations for their authenticity and integrity. As often as possible, places have been selected for their natural beauty and for a sense of intimacy and quiet. Beach, destination, and golf and tennis resorts have been chosen with an eye to their respect for the environment and success in making a large resort seem small. Even in the cities that Flagler and Plant first developed, there are still owners and managers of urban hostelries who maintain a respect for Florida's exotic greenery, lovely beaches, and eclectic mix of cultures.

At the beginning of each regional section is a list of the best accommodations in each category, for example, "Best B&Bs" or "Best Island Getaways." These categories are a help to people who want to focus on a specific *type* of place to stay, satisfying a particular recreational, business, atmospheric, or budgetary preference.

Definitions

art deco: A style of architecture and interior design popular in Miami Beach in the 1930s and '40s that was streamlined, decorative, and modernistic. Most examples are in the South Miami Beach neighborhood of Ocean Drive and Collins Avenue. See the information on art deco hotels in "Finding the Real Florida."

chikee hut: A shelter with a roof of thatched palm fronds built by Florida Indians and the early Spanish and American settlers. Adaptations are used throughout Florida today as everything from beach shelters to bars. Some of the best examples are found at Seminole Indian villages.

conch: Pronounced "conk." A marine mollusk with a sweet, flavorful meat used in chowders, fritters, and other Florida dishes. At one time, the spiral, pink shells were used by Native

Americans to call people home or announce a celebration. Slang: a native of the Florida Keys.

Conch Republic: A nickname for Key West.

coquina: Spanish for shellstone; a white stone made up of congealed marine shells cut to form masonry blocks.

coral stone: Cut coral, used as a decorative veneer or in blocks. Sometimes called key stone or coquina. The most beautiful is composed of fan-shaped coral, with small shells or fragments of shells trapped in the crevices of the coral.

Florida room: A screened or glassed-in porch, usually on the back of a house.

hammock: A hardwood forest or thicket of native trees and shrub.

key lime: A small, round, yellow lime used in key lime pie and other Florida desserts and dishes.

Old Florida architecture: A style popular in the 1920s in domestic or public buildings that includes crimped tin roofs, wood clapboards, double-hung windows, and porches with overhangs. The term sometimes refers to an eclectic mix of architecture that includes Mediterranean, Italian, Moorish, Victorian, and Old South styles. It can also refer to an interior design typical of Old Florida buildings.

tabby: Concrete made from sand, lime, and shellstone dust or chips.

Florida

Pensacola
Tallahassee
Panhandle
Jacksonville
Gainesville
Central
Florida
Daytona Beach
Cedar Key
Orlando
Northeast
Coast
Tampa
Lake Wales
Gulf Coast
Sarasota
Jupiter
Palm Beach
Naples
Southeast Coast
Flamingo
Miami
The Keys
Key Largo
Key West

The Northeast Coast

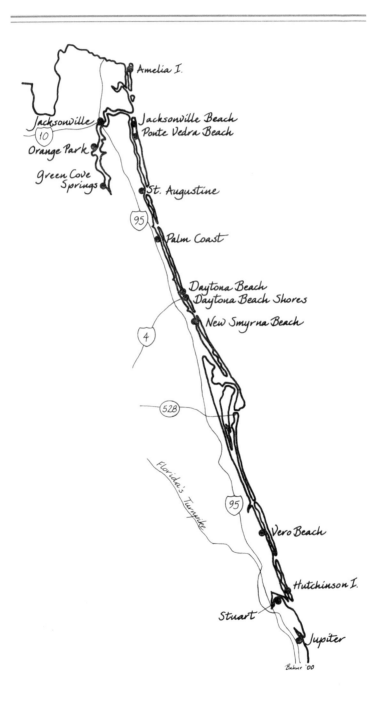

Amelia I.

Jacksonville
10
Orange Park
Green Cove
Springs

Jacksonville Beach
Ponte Vedra Beach

St. Augustine

95

Palm Coast

Daytona Beach
Daytona Beach Shores
New Smyrna Beach

4

528

Florida's Turnpike

95

Vero Beach

Hutchinson I.

Stuart

Jupiter

Bahne '00

Best B&Bs

Amelia Island
Addison House, 34
Bailey House, 39
The Fairbanks House, 44
Walnford Inn , 53
Daytona Beach
Coquina Inn B&B, 55
Green Cove Springs
River Park Inn, 61
Jacksonville
Cleary-Dickert House B&B, 66
House on Cherry Street, 68
Plantation Manor Inn, 72
New Smyrna Beach
Night Swan Intracoastal B&B , 83
Riverview Hotel, 85
St. Augustine
Carriage Way B&B, 97
Casa de la Paz, 99
Casa de Solana, 101
Casa de Suenos B&B, 104
Casablanca Inn on the Bay, 106
Castle Garden, 108
The Cedar House Inn Victorian B&B , 109
Centennial House B&B , 112
The Kenwood Inn, 116
Old Powder House Inn, 120
St. Francis Inn, 122
The Secret Garden Inn , 123
Victorian House, 125
Westcott House, 127
Stuart
HarborFront Inn B&B, 129

Best Beachside Accommodations

Amelia Island
Elizabeth Pointe Lodge, 41
1735 House, 51

Jacksonville Beach
  Pelican Path B&B, 75
Jupiter
  Jupiter Beach Resort, 77
  Jupiter Reef Club, 79
Ponte Vedra Beach
  The Lodge & Club, 92
  Ponte Vedra Inn & Club, 94

Best Budget Finds

Daytona Beach
  Sunny Shore Motel, 60
Jupiter
  Jupiter Waterfront Inn, 81
St. Augustine
  International Haus, 114

Best City Stop

Jacksonville
  Omni Jacksonville Hotel, 70

Best Eclectic Find

Vero Beach
  The Driftwood Resort, 133

Best Island Getaway

Hutchinson Island
  Indian River Plantation Marriott Resort, 63

Best Resorts and Spas

Amelia Island
  Amelia Island Plantation, 36
  Ritz-Carlton, Amelia Island, 49

Daytona Beach
  Indigo Lakes Holiday Inn, 57
Palm Coast
  Palm Coast Golf Resort, 90
Ponte Vedra Beach
  Sawgrass Marriott Resort, 96
Stuart
  Pirates Cove Resort and Marina, 131

Best Small Hotels, Inns, and Motels

Amelia Island
  Florida House Inn, 46
Daytona Beach
  Live Oak Inn, 58
New Smyrna Beach
  Riverview Hotel, 85
Orange Park
  The Club Continental on the St. Johns, 87
St. Augustine
  Old City House Inn, 118

The northeasternmost corner of Florida is within whistling distance of Georgia. Not surprisingly, the summer resorts of **Amelia Island** attract many people from Atlanta and other southern cities and towns. The island, named after the daughter of King George II, has both an Old South and a beachside ambience. The island has a varied heritage and is the only place in the United States to have been under eight different flags, among them the "Amelia Island Patriots," a ragtag American group. Amelia Island was fought over for years by nations and pirates because of its strategic location until it found stability under the U.S. flag. During the late 19th and early 20th centuries it enjoyed prosperity as a resort.

Today, it is again becoming popular for its charm and natural beauty. There are some interesting B&Bs here, as well as Amelia Island Plantation, a large coastal resort, and the Ritz-Carlton. In making reservations, bear in mind that in April some resorts have tennis tournaments that can drive the rates up almost to the summer high. Other hotels and B&Bs in northern Florida offer the same rate year-round.

The largest town on Amelia Island is Fernandina Beach. The old section of Fernandina, developed in the late 19th century, has a neighborhood of Victorian homes and turn-of-the-century public buildings that are highlights of a self-directed walking tour. Fernandina's Historic District is listed in the National Register of Historic Places and should not be missed. There are some interesting pubs, restaurants, and boutiques in the fine old buildings that line Centre Street, which ends at the historic shrimp docks on the Intracoastal Waterway.

The largest city in Northeast Florida is **Jacksonville.** Approximately 30 miles west from the coast, it is a lively river city that has enjoyed a recent cultural and economic revival. This area has both a coastal atmosphere and, especially just outside the city proper, a Panhandle country feel. The Riverside-Avondale section of town has a variety of historic properties, some of which have recently been made into B&Bs.

Northeast Florida, like Central Florida, has real *towns.* Getting excited about this is something that people from New England and the Midwest — with their town squares and Main Streets — cannot entirely understand. Most municipalities in Florida are unfortunately just a grid of highways with shopping centers, mobile home parks, and housing developments strung out along that grid — no real town center and not much community spirit.

So when a town is a real, recognizable *town,* it's a big deal. Such places are often referred to as "historic," yet when an outsider rolls into town he may see just a bunch of old clapboard or Spanish-style dwellings and some businesses with 1920s architecture. This is not a big deal to outsiders, but to Floridians, it means a piece of the state's heritage has actually been preserved instead of being torn down to make room for something bigger and flashier with no connection to the past. The state has an extremely interesting and varied heritage dating back to Spanish explorers, and the architecture in some Old Florida towns reflects this, with a mix of Spanish, Victorian, Bahamian, and even Moorish styles.

The oldest town in the state (and the oldest continuously settled city in the United States) is **St. Augustine,** located on Matanzas Bay, part of the Intracoastal Waterway. Most of the city's fine old buildings, some dating from Spanish possession, have been lovingly preserved. East of the city proper, on a sandbar accessible by St. Augustine's graceful Bridge of Lions, is a nice beach.

To find out about the history of the town and get oriented, most first-time visitors take advantage of the Information Center on San Marco Avenue. In addition, there are sightseeing trolleys and horse-drawn carriage tours — more expensive than the trolleys but more fun. There are some tourist traps, but for most visitors, it is enough simply to walk the narrow streets and take in a few of the attractions in a self-guided walking tour after going on a trolley ride.

Most people start at the fort, Castillo San Marcos, and the Spanish Quarter and then explore the side streets off King Street. Be certain to get a look at King Street's Flagler College, the former Ponce de Leon Hotel built in 1887 by Henry Flagler, with early stained-glass windows by Louis Tiffany. Across the street is the Lightner Museum, which was once the other Flagler hotel in town, the Alcazar. The "Oldest House in the United States," a few streets southeast of the Alcazar, is also worth seeing.

There are many more interesting sights along the northeast coast. Just south of the white beaches of **Daytona** is Cape Canaveral. It may not seem that there's much going on here, particularly if a shuttle isn't due to go up, but there are some space exhibits and a national wildlife refuge that should not be missed. Most of the accommodations are motel and hotel chains, though some people venture farther south to stay in **Stuart.**

South of Cape Canaveral and the John F. Kennedy Space Center are beaches, state recreational areas, and the attractive Old Florida town of Melbourne. Just off the coast of Stuart is beautiful **Hutchinson Island,** accessible by bridges over the Indian River. Strict zoning laws here protect the wonderful mangrove swamps along the water. The House of Refuge, built in 1875 as a rescue station for sailors, is now a historical museum and the site of green sea turtle research and preservation work.

Residents of the island and nearby Stuart are mindful of the delicate ecology of the area. Each year in late spring and early summer, the turtles migrate to the beach to lay their eggs. During the nesting season, there are expeditions to nearby beaches to see the wild turtles. After the eggs are laid, the sites of the buried eggs are labeled with small wooden signposts so beachcombers can avoid damaging the nests. Also on Hutchinson Island, the Elliott Museum commemorates the life of inventor Sterling Elliott and includes displays of Indian artifacts, a typical Victorian parlor and dining room, a smithy, antique automobiles and motorcycles, and a number of Elliott's own inventions.

Farther south are fashionable **Vero Beach** and the quiet town of **Jupiter,** which home-boy Burt Reynolds put on the map with his dinner theater (now under new ownership) and acting institute. A number of wealthy, influential people live a serene life on the Intracoastal in Jupiter and nearby Hobe Sound, rather than in the limelight of Palm Beach or Miami. This area has become a desirable destination for those who want to avoid glitz and large crowds.

Amelia Island

Addison House

614 Ash Street
Amelia Island, FL 32034
800-943-1604
904-277-1604
www.addisonhousebb.com

> **Three houses that back
> onto a private garden
> courtyard in Amelia Island's
> historic district**

Innkeepers: John, Donna, and Jennifer Gibson. **Accommodations:** 14 rooms. **Rates:** $99–$165. **Included:** Full breakfast, afternoon refreshments. **Minimum stay:** 2 nights for weekends; 3 nights for holidays and special events. **Added:** 9% tax; $20 for rollaway bed for extra person in room (please request at time of making reservation). **Payment:** Major credit cards, traveler's checks. **Children:** Older children welcome. **Smoking:** Not allowed on property. **Open:** Year-round.

➤   **Most of the bathrooms have a whirlpool tub; all but one of the Garden House rooms have a two-person whirlpool. According to Donna, for each bathroom, "we'd get the biggest Jacuzzi that we could fit into the space."**

The original 1876 Addison home is located on the corner of 7th and Ash Streets. The old house had very spacious side and back yards, where the owners of this B&B resourcefully built two reproduction Victorians. If you didn't know that these buildings are only a few years old, you would never guess it, so seamlessly do they blend with the original. All have verandas and railed porches, with just a touch of gingerbread here and there. All are painted a pale lime green, with soft ivory trim and peach doors.

Best of all, the three back up to a brick courtyard with ferns and fountains and crescents of flower beds. This area is beautiful during the moist early morning, when guests often take their breakfast on the back porches; throughout the day, when this becomes the best possible spot for reading or napping; and certainly in the evening, when the fountains and gardens are softly lit and this becomes an extremely romantic spot.

The Addison House is immaculately cared for. This comes at a price for anyone who does not appreciate a smoke-free environment. All guests, upon check-in, must sign an agreement that they understand that the B&B is a completely smoke-free facility and that they will pay a cleaning fee of $100 if they violate the agreement. Guests must also agree to pay for any damage to "furniture, bathroom fixtures and linens that exceeds normal wear."

Having said that, it might seem that the Gibsons would be unfriendly hosts, but they are pleasant, gentle folk who simply want to have a B&B that is quiet and well ordered. Donna and John got the idea for running a B&B toward the end of a long stint in Mexico, where John worked for an international company. With the imminent prospect of a return to the States, they bought the original house and Donna and their daughter Jennifer moved to Amelia Island to hire carpenters, with the expectation that John would soon be joining them. A long year later, he finally did. Meanwhile, Donna kept busy overseeing the construction and decoration of the guest rooms and common rooms.

The result is impressive. As in most B&Bs, each guest room is quite individual. One room might have a garden motif with soft yellow walls, filmy white drapings over the Shaker four-poster bed, and floral swags at the windows, while another room might have an extremely ornate iron bedstead with frilly pillows and lavender-tinted walls. All of the rooms have pine floors with pretty area rugs. The beds are queen- or king-size with extra-thick pillow-top mattresses. In the main house, five rooms have fireplaces. The bathrooms are large for a B&B, and it is so nice that the Addison House Web site includes details about them in a room chart.

When making reservations, be sure to ask for details about each room. The Addison House includes a corporate room and a first-floor handicapped-accessible room. Most rooms have nice views of the garden, but, again, ask for details.

All guest rooms have access to a communal porch or veranda or have their own private balcony. The view from most of these outdoor spaces is of the courtyard, which passersby cannot see from the street. Although many people who come to Addison House comment on how similar this B&B is to guest houses in Key West, the back yards of which create a private garden courtyard, the Gibsons were influenced by their years in Mexico. "Our idea was of a hacienda centered around a secret garden," says Donna. In fact, the Gibsons brought the three-tiered stone fountain that is the garden's centerpiece from Mexico, as well as a carved wooden bench in the main house and other small decorative pieces that individualize spaces.

The full breakfast is served at a polished table in the dining room or out on the porch at small tables. At the Addison House you can get acquainted with other guests or spend time alone — or a little of both. Long conversations at the breakfast table and "the B&B

Experience" are not forced. The room rate includes refreshments in the afternoon. With advance notice, the Gibsons will prepare a picnic lunch, honeymoon or anniversary packages, or special desserts. Good restaurants, some in interesting historic buildings, are within easy walking distance.

Amelia Island Plantation

Fernandina Beach
Amelia Island, FL 32034
800-874-6878
904-261-6161

A resort and residential community on 1,200 acres

Accommodations: Several hundred rooms and villas. **Rates:** $160–$700 (varies according to season); packages and group rates available; midweek package discounts. **Minimum stay:** With some packages and during holidays. **Added:** 9% tax. **Payment:** American Express, Visa, MasterCard, Discover. **Children:** Free in room with parents; some charges with recreational packages. **Smoking:** Nonsmoking units available. **Open:** Year-round.

➤ **The sense of timelessness at Amelia Island Plantation is nowhere more evident than on the boardwalk in the salt marsh. You look out over acres of marsh grass and quiet water. Far out on a point of land, you may see a solitary white heron standing still as a statue.**

It is understandable why people come back to Amelia Island Plantation year after year. In fact, there is so much to do and see here that some people give up trying after twenty years or so, and simply buy a house or villa on the property and move in. Occasionally, the sales pitch is a little heavy for those who only want to come here to relax and use resort or conference facilities, rather than buy a summer place.

Amelia Island is only 30 minutes from the Jacksonville airport, but when you come through the security gates you enter a world of lush forests of myrtle, live oak, magnolia, and pine; acres and acres of undulating marsh grass; exotic tropical birds that stalk the lagoons; and long stretches of white beach with sand dunes rising beyond.

It takes the sound of someone laughing or whacking a tennis ball to remind you that this is also a busy resort. Amelia Island has a staggering array of activities: tennis, golf, swimming, biking, jogging, working out, hiking, fishing, and boating, as well as horseback riding and historic sightseeing.

The resort is probably most famous for golf and tennis. The challenging Amelia Links, designed by Pete Dye, has 27 holes that break down into three distinctive "nines": Oceanside, bordering the Atlantic and the dunes; Oakmarsh, featuring challenging holes near the edge of the marsh; and Oysterbay, with marsh hazards and twisting fairways. Amelia Island's newest course, designed by Tom Fazio, is Long Point. The natural beauty of the marshland, dunes, and woods has been masterfully incorporated.

The tennis settings are just as impressive. There are 25 tennis courts: 19 clay, four Omni (grass), and two Deco-Turf hard courts. There is a well-supplied pro shop and excellent instruction for both adults and children. Activity centers around Racquet Park, a beautiful facility nestled among live oak trees dripping with Spanish moss. Racquet Park also houses a fitness center and a glass-enclosed pool. On a cool spring or fall day, swimming in this large heated pool feels like being in a big glass house in the jungle.

Racquet Park also has a well-appointed conference center, a 6,000-square-foot meeting space with four rooms that hold up to 125 people. The center has its own restaurant, hotel rooms, and suites.

A larger facility is the 22,500-square-foot Executive Meeting Center, with five seminar rooms and a 6,000-square-foot ballroom that can be divided into smaller rooms. The Amelia Inn, just a few yards away, has soundproof meeting rooms that can accommodate groups of 100 or more. Services offered include a message and copy center, call-service buttons in each meeting room, round-the-clock conference planning, a banquet kitchen, audiovisual assistance, multimedia presentation equipment, and secretarial service.

There is a tremendous variety of accommodations for families, groups, and couples, including full-size houses in the rental pool. Inquire about the intricacies of seasonal rates and the Plantation's special packages and group rates when making reservations. Rooms and villas on the ocean, while expensive, often have dramatic views of the rolling dunes and the Atlantic.

All of the accommodations are attractively decorated and well furnished. Each rental villa is rated every year; any villa that falls below the resort's high standards is taken out of the rental pool.

All villas have well-equipped kitchens, but there is a variety of restaurants at the resort. The most romantic overlooks the oceanside golf links and the dunes. The Beach Club Sports Bar & Grill has a big-screen TV, pool, and electronic games and serves grilled seafood and steaks for lunch and dinner. For breakfast, lunch, and snacks, there are a number of other restaurants throughout the property. Three lounges serve drinks, and the informal Seaside Sweets serves ice cream concoctions.

Although Amelia Island is a great place for family togetherness, the resort makes it easy for parents to get away from their children and vice versa. A babysitting service is available, and there is also a wonderful children's program for kids aged three to twelve. Available during the spring and summer and for special holidays, it includes supervised recreation on the playgrounds, including one on its own little island, field trips, special projects, hikes, sports, and games. There is swimming instruction at the kiddie pool and tennis instruction for older children. The Beach Club has an unobtrusive electronic game arcade. The Club also rents out body boards, beach chairs and umbrellas, rubber rafts, and boats. Paddleboats are available for exploring the Plantation's natural lagoons and narrow tributaries.

Both kids and adults enjoy fishing at the stocked lagoons on the property. There is also fishing and crabbing in the Intracoastal Waterway. Farther out in the Atlantic are tarpon, marlin, and kingfish. The Amelia Angler, at the Beach Club, will arrange deep-sea charter boats for guests.

The Plantation itself is worth exploring, starting with the Sunken Forest Trail, actually a boardwalk through a ravine of ancient myrtle and oak. Some of the smaller myrtle trees are reminiscent of the twisted, ancient olive trees that grow on Tuscan hillsides — and they are just as old, if not older.

A stay at Amelia Island Plantation inspires many guests to take an interest in the island and its history. The area was home to the Timuquan Indians for centuries until the Spanish and the English discovered it. From then on, it had a rather bloody and unstable history, until well into the 19th century. Altogether, Amelia Island has been under the flags of eight different nations and has had many names. The name that finally stuck was that of the winsome, never-married daughter of George II.

Bailey House

28 South 7th Street
Fernandina Beach
Amelia Island, FL 32034
800-251-5390
904-261-5390
Fax: 904-321-0103
www.bailey-house.com

> A B&B in a residential
> neighborhood of other
> historic houses near
> downtown Fernandina
> Beach

Innkeepers: Tom and Jenny Bishop. **Accommodations:** 10 rooms. **Rates:** $115–$175; weekly rates available. **Included:** Full breakfast. **Minimum stay:** 2 nights on most weekends; 3 nights on holiday weekends. **Added:** 9% tax; $20 for extra person in room. **Payment:** Major credit cards, traveler's checks. **Children:** Older children welcome. **Smoking:** Outside only. **Open:** Year-round.

➤ **Fernandina Beach is one of the few communities along either Florida coast with extant Victorian homes. These wood-frame houses are replete with gingerbread and gables, leaded and stained glass, fishtail shingling, turrets and towers — and Bailey House is one of the most wonderful examples on Amelia Island. Its 19th-century features are accented with contrasting colors of tan and teal, ivory and red. A new addition to the left of the house, which provides spacious Carriage House accommodations, blends in beautifully with the rest of this fine old home.**

The Bailey House was built on a corner lot between 1892 and 1895 by Effingham W. Bailey, an agent for a steamship company on the island. Bailey's occupation has led to speculation that the heartpine woodwork of the house was probably executed by ship's carpenters. In any case, the decision to create an elegant, beautifully crafted home on the lot given to Bailey and his bride as a wedding present was that of Bailey's wife. She had the choice of either a small house, which could be completely furnished or a more palatial residence, which the newlyweds would furnish over the years. Fortunately for everyone, she chose the latter. Members of the Bailey family lived in the house until 1963 — more than enough time to collect all of the furnishings necessary for the mansion.

Today, a white picket fence encloses the large corner lot and a brick walkway leads up to a wraparound porch furnished with wicker. Inside is a large front hallway with a handsome fireplace, one of six. The floors are polished pine and are covered with Oriental rugs. One of the most distinctive features of this spacious entryway is the stained-glass window on the stairway wall. Adjacent to the graceful entrance is an elegant front parlor with lace curtains at the bay windows.

Three bedrooms for guests are on the first floor and the rest are on the second floor. Innkeepers Tom and Jenny Bishop live on the third floor. A polished banister with intricately carved newel posts leads upstairs. All of the rooms are individually decorated with fine old bedsteads, armoires, marble-topped tables, and tulip and Tiffany-style lamps. Some have working marble fireplaces. One of the downstairs rooms, the Amelia, is wheelchair accessible. All of the rooms have either a queen- or king-size bed. The Rose Room and the Victorian Room also have a single bed, and the Amelia Room and Marie's are spacious enough to have two additional single beds.

All of these guest rooms, as well as the parlor and formal dining room, are furnished with antiques, many of them crafted in the Eastlake or late Victorian style, with burled woods, ornate carvings, and dark polished veneers. The bedrooms are almost able to transport guests to an earlier time. The private bathrooms are a nice mix of modern conveniences and old-fashioned features. Many of the bathrooms have a separate shower as well as a clawfoot or slipper tub. The French Garden Room and the Carriage House Suite have a two-person whirlpool tub and a separate shower. All rooms have a direct-dial telephone and cable TV.

Guests are treated to a full breakfast each morning in the elegantly appointed dining room. The Bishops change their hot entree daily so that long-term guests can enjoy a variety of gourmet morning feasts: stuffed french toast, banana pancakes, eggs, or a casserole. Jenny makes homemade granola and always includes fresh fruit and juices, as well as hot tea and coffee.

After breakfast, the town of Fernandina Beach awaits. It's fun to stroll through with nothing else in mind but taking in the old houses and the pretty gardens, which display both subtropical and Old South vegetation: ferns and palms coupled with camellias and magnolias. Bailey House has bicycles for those who would rather ride than walk. Golf is available less than 5 minutes away by car at a municipal course. Tennis and horseback riding are nearby, as are the pleasures of the beach.

Elizabeth Pointe Lodge

98 S. Fletcher Avenue
Amelia Island, FL 32034
904-277-4851
www.ElizabethPointeLodge.com

A B&B with old-fashioned appeal

Innkeepers: David and Susan Caples. **Accommodations:** 25 rooms and suites. **Rates:** Rooms $140–$285; suites vary, ask for rates. **Included:** Full breakfast and morning newspaper. **Minimum stay:** For special events. **Added:** 9% tax; $20 additional person. **Payment:** Major credit cards, personal checks. **Children:** Welcome; children 5 and under free in room with parent. **Smoking:** On the porch only. **Open:** Year-round.

➤ **Staff members seem to genuinely enjoy themselves, in spite of their often hectic pace, and there is a sense of everyone being part of one big, happy, hard-working family.**

Innkeepers David and Susan Caples built Elizabeth Pointe Lodge in 1991 after successfully operating the 1735 House, another B&B on Amelia Island, in addition to a rental business. Susan spent childhood summers on the New Jersey shore, and both loved the look and the feel of old-fashioned summer places. They envisioned a shingled, Nantucket-style cottage on the beach with furnishings that would look as if they'd been there forever and where people would walk in and think, "I'm home." With cleverness and professionalism (both studied at the Cornell's hotel management school), they succeeded admirably.

The lodge they created with architect David Beer has the best of both the old and new. Although there are none of the disadvantages of a genuinely old inn — no water stains on the ceiling or whistling drafts from oceanfront windows — there is the lazy comfortableness of an old place.

The center of activity is the lounge in the middle of the house, called the library. A rough stone fireplace dominates one wall, while a cushioned window seat runs beneath a long row of small-paned windows. In the corner is a bay window with a round oak table where people play cards or visit. Floor-to-ceiling bookcases fill two walls, and the Capleses encourage guests to lounge on the library's sofa and read whatever they fancy. This is a place where guests can really settle in.

Outside is a wraparound porch with white wicker rockers and chaises. Near the bay window, the porch widens enough to hold two tables with chairs where guests can take meals or just read. The view here is wonderful, with softly sloping sand dunes covered with flowering vines and sea oats and the sea roaring in on the harder sand below. Bicycles are available for those who wish to ride into the historic village of Fernandina Beach.

In the afternoon, the staff always sets out fresh lemonade, and in the evening there is complimentary wine. Limited but delicious menus are available for lunch and dinner for those who don't wish to go out. Guests can also buy homemade muffins and cookies throughout the day and scrumptious desserts in the evening. They can eat on the porch, in the library, or in the big dining room or Sun Room, where breakfast is served each morning.

The staff is efficient and patient, there to help anyone who needs it. They are a very good group, made up of old-timers who have been with the Caples family for years, energetic young people in their twenties, and members of the Capleses' B&B seminars who learn innkeeping by serving in various roles at Elizabeth Pointe Lodge. In the summer, the Capleses' daughters, Katie and Beth Ann (for whom the inn was named), devise activities for kids staying at the lodge.

The full breakfasts are worth writing home about. Biscuits are oversize and fluffy, and fruit muffins are loaded with fruit. A typical breakfast starts with three kinds of cold juice dispensed from old-fashioned glass milk bottles, a choice of packaged cereals, creamy grits, an egg dish such as scrambled eggs with dill, muffins or biscuits (or both), fresh fruit salad, brewed coffee, and an assortment of teas. Everything is laid out at 7:30 A.M. on a long buffet from which guests help themselves till 9:30. Most people sit together at big oak tables, but honeymooners sometimes sit out on the romantic back porch.

The dining room doubles as a conference room for seminars the Capleses hold on B&B management and marketing for potential B&B owners. The couple also serves lunch here, though this is not advertised. The Capleses also rent out Miller Cottage, Harris Lodge, and other houses and condos. Among these is Katie's Light, a replica of a Chesapeake Bay lighthouse, named after the couple's older daughter.

Even with all they have going on, Susan and David have found time to gradually individualize the guest rooms at Elizabeth Pointe Lodge. All rooms have pine woodwork and floors, and windows overlooking the ocean or island. Furnishings are simple, with reproduction sleigh beds and four-posters, wicker rockers, and armoires.

Number 8 is a small oceanfront room with a king-size four-poster bed, an old armoire, and a wonderful view from its three windows overlooking the water. The throw rugs on the pine floors fit right in. The faux marble whirlpool tub in the bathroom is oversize.

All of the rooms have the look and feel of those of an inn on the New England coast. Some rooms are almost austere-looking, with their pine floors and wooden furniture. For example, a canopy Shaker-style four-poster bed might not have a lace or crocheted canopy. As Susan says, "I didn't want any fluff."

All bathrooms have oversize faux marble tub-showers (a few with Jacuzzis) and brass fixtures that look a hundred years old. A brass and glass shelf above the sink might hold a small vase of daisies or sea heather and wild asters, and there's always another vase of flowers in the bedroom. The oceanfront kings and queens are the most desirable accommodations at the lodge, although decorative touches in the other rooms compensate for their less dramatic views. Fourth-floor rooms have bead board paneling and lots of interesting angles — and there's an elevator. All rooms contribute to the quiet rejuvenation of the spirit that is part of being a guest at Elizabeth Pointe Lodge.

The Fairbanks House

227 South 7th Street
Amelia Island, FL 32034
800-261-4838
904-277-0500
Fax: 904-277-3103

An industrial baron's palace where, amazingly, everybody makes you feel at home

Innkeepers: Theresa and Bill Hamilton. **Accommodations:** 6 rooms, 3 suites, 3 cottages. **Rates:** $125–$225; golf and romance packages. **Included:** Full breakfast. **Minimum stay:** 2 nights for nonholiday weekends; 3 nights for holiday and special-event weekends. **Added:** 9% tax; $50 for extra person in room. **Payment:** Major credit cards, traveler's checks. **Children:** Older children welcome. **Smoking:** Not allowed on property. **Open:** Year-round.

➤ **The best part of staying here is that everyone is so nice. The owners and their staff are not interested in intimidating anyone, and the place is very, very comfortable.**

Listed on the National Register of Historic Places, the Fairbanks is one of the most spectacular examples of 19th-century Italianate architecture on the East Coast. Painted in contrasting colors of green, ivory, and brick red, the house has everything this baroque style of residential architecture could dish out: Italianate archways, balustrades, balconies, dormers, verandas, bay windows, and even a four-story tower. It is a great treat to stay in this amazing and beautiful building.

The Fairbanks B&B is situated on a one-acre lot on a quiet street a few blocks from Centre Street. Part of the side yard has been given over to parking, but the rest of the lot is quite beautiful. A white picket fence separates the front lawn from a flower-bordered courtyard. Stairs lead up to an arched loggia, where many guests have breakfast in the morning and then sit out and relax in the afternoon. Just beyond the brick courtyard are the patio and swimming pool — the Fairbanks is the only B&B on the island that has a pool. At one end of the patio are umbrellaed tables and chairs, and at the other end is a vine-covered arbor.

Inside the house are 12-foot ceilings with elegant moldings, heart-pine floors, tall bookcases made of orangewood from the groves of the original owners, wooden archways and fluted columns, fireplaces tiled with scenes from Shakespeare, and a mahogany spool staircase with an elaborately carved newel post. Furnishings in the parlors and dining room are very Victorian, right down to the Victorian kitsch of two vanilla-colored ceramic cocker spaniels on the fireplace mantel. Period wallpapers, Oriental rugs, chandeliers, and potted palms all add to the look.

A gourmet breakfast is served in the dining room each morning at the big mahogany table — or you can go out to little tables on the loggia overlooking the garden and courtyard. There's always a hot entree like quiche or orange pecan French toast, sweet breads, fresh fruit, juice, coffee, and assorted teas. There are also complimentary refreshments in the evening.

All of the rooms are gorgeous, some very Victorian and ornate and others less so. Be certain to ask for details about the rooms when making reservations, or see the Fairbanks's Web site. Rooms number 3 and 4 have the best views from private porches; six of the accommodations have working fireplaces. The woman who previously owned the Fairbanks was a wizard with fabric. She made all of the drapes, swags, and curtains at the long windows in rich designer fabrics.

One of the prettiest rooms is number 5, with soft blue plaster walls, a queen-size and a twin bed covered in white Battenberg lace, a sitting area by the windows, a small kitchen, and a clawfoot tub in the bathroom. The Tower Suite is worth reserving if you are traveling with another couple and would also like to cook some of your own meals. Climbing the stairway is a little like climbing up a steep ladder, but the view is fantastic and the rooms are spacious and imaginatively decorated. There are two bedrooms with a shared bath and a living/dining/kitchen area with an open concept floor plan, interesting angles on the ceiling, and a skylight. The Fairbanks also has cottage accommodations, originally built for servants, that are beautifully decorated and very comfortable.

The surrounding neighborhood is great for walking, and the Fairbanks is a popular stopping place for those on walking tours of the historic district. Nearby Centre Street offers antiquing and shopping. The best place to spend a day on the beach on Amelia Island is Fort Clinch State Park, a 5- or 6-minute drive from the Fairbanks.

Florida House Inn

2022 South Third Street
Amelia Island, FL 32034
800-258-3301
904-261-3300
www.floridahouse.com

> A rambling inn and
> restaurant in a historic
> district

Innkeepers: Jeanine Rowe, Karen and Bob Warner. **Accommodations:** 14 rooms. **Rates:** Rooms $70–$135, suite $145. **Included:** Full breakfast. **Minimum stay:** 2–3 nights for weekends. **Added:** 9% tax; $10 extra person in room. **Payment:** Major credit cards, personal checks. **Children:** Welcome. **Smoking:** On veranda and in pub only. **Open:** Year-round.

➤ **The restaurant at the Florida House serves lunch and dinner and is open every day except Monday. The boarding house tables encourage folks to get to know each other. Sunday brunch is popular with island residents as well as hotel guests and includes fried chicken, eggs, ham, butter beans or black-eyed peas, sausage gravy, and cornbread.**

The Florida House Inn looks just the way the state's oldest extant hotel should: a turn-of-the-century clapboard structure painted deep green, with louvered shutters, white-railed verandas, gingerbread brackets upstairs and down, a big oak tree in the back yard, and a picket fence out front.

But it wasn't always like this. Owners Bob and Karen Warner spent a year restoring the Florida House after decades of neglect had left it a town eyesore. Now listed on the National Register of Historic Places, the inn looks just right; the heart-pine floors, plaster walls, and fireplaces have all been brought back to life. While the restoration focused on saving the original whenever possible, there was also a sensible response to 20th-century guests' needs for modern bathrooms, telephones, TVs, and other amenities.

Guests enter the inn by the front veranda and a paneled wood door. Inside is a typical 19th-century entryway with a stairway in the middle of the hall, a front parlor to the left, and a room on the right that's been made into a pub with a dartboard, a fine old fireplace, and British ambience. The small parlor has a paneled fireplace, a sofa, and a table with magazines.

At the back of the long hallway, there is a door to a large brick courtyard and the entrance to the restaurant. Here, overnight guests eat breakfast at long tables, boarding-house style: orange juice, fruit, pancakes, eggs, and breakfast meats. Every day it's a little different. Afterwards, guests can linger at the table and talk with others, rock on the veranda, or sit out in the courtyard among the camellias.

The Florida House is an "inn" in the traditional sense of a lodging that serves three meals a day. In addition to the full southern breakfast served from 8:15 to 9:30 A.M. (with coffee starting at 7:30), there are hearty meals at lunch and dinner that include platters of country-fried chicken, mashed potatoes, southern cornbread, old-fashioned desserts like apple crisp and lemon meringue pie, and plenty of iced tea. The friendly conversations with those sitting at the same table include locals as well as inn guests, since the Florida House is a popular place to eat for islanders, too. When meals are not being served, the dining room can double as a conference room for businesses that hold retreats or meetings here.

Each of the rooms and suites is individually decorated, with quilts and ruffled shams and pillows on the four-poster beds, rustic-looking rugs on the pine floors, and armoires. Room 2, in the main house, is especially nice, with a queen-size bed and large tile bath with shower, as well as a spacious porch. Room 9 has a king-size bed and a tub against one wall. A toilet and tiny corner sink are in a separate closet-size room. Another standout is number 10, with a queen-size bed, a paneled fireplace that was diligently stripped and refinished to reveal the natural wood, and a tile bath that has a whirlpool.

The newest rooms at the Florida House are on "Tree House Row" in a second-floor addition on the back of the inn under the spreading limbs of a huge live oak. All of those rooms have separate outdoor entrances, king-size beds, pine floors, working fieldstone fireplaces, large bathrooms, and two windows looking out onto the oak tree and furnished deck. Karen and Bob and their staff outdid themselves in furnishing and decorating these rooms.

"French Country" is done up in exuberant blue and yellow fabrics that Karen bought in France. The four-poster spool bed has a thickly woven coverlet of yellow and blue flowers, with matching shams, a bedskirt, a canopy ruffle, and decorative pillows in complementary patterns. White mesh Eiffel Tower table lamps and framed French prints complete the look — charming but not overdone. The armoire, small writing desk, and the floors are light pine. The tiled bathroom has a combination tub and two-person shower with a shower head on each wall and an oversize whirlpool tub. The floor and walls are sheathed in earth-tone tile.

The other three rooms have an outdoors theme. Number 14 has a red stained floor, a bedstead made of logs and curving branches, and a floor-to-ceiling stone chimney. The bedspread and curtains are a rich green and red plaid. A red afghan is draped across the back of the comfortable easy chair. Number 15 is even more woodsy, with split logs on the walls and another bedstead of thick aspen made by Bob and his carpentry crew. Room 16 has wainscoting of pecky cypress on one wall and a handsome red Navaho rug.

All of the bathrooms in these new accommodations run the length of the room, so they're extra large. They include unusual vanities created from country-style bedroom bureaus, with a sink set in the bureau top. There are plenty of drawers in the bathroom vanity for those at the inn for a long stay. The floors and walls of the bathrooms have distinctive tile work in green and tan or deep brown. Each bathroom is also individualized with terrycloth towels that have a pattern of deer or pine trees or some other scene that fits in with the theme of the room. Louvered wooden doors separate the bathroom and bedroom. Chambray cotton robes hang in the cedar-lined closets.

Guests often spend a good deal of time just relaxing at the inn, but there is certainly a great deal to do in Fernandina Beach and elsewhere on Amelia Island. The Florida House Inn is just off Centre Street, the main street of town. Numbered streets run perpendicular to Centre and streets with tree names run parallel to it, so it's quite easy to find one's way around. The historic district covers about 30 blocks, from the Intracoastal Waterway and the shrimp docks at the foot of Centre to the edge of the town proper. On the edge of town is Fort Clinch, a state park and popular beach.

Most of the buildings on Centre Street are brick or masonry and include the turn-of-the-century Nassau Courthouse and a Greek Revival Methodist church where the bells play a carillon every afternoon at 4:00. The residential homes fanning out from Centre Street are mostly clapboard Victorians with gingerbread details. Trolley tours leave from the shrimp dock, but it's also fun to take a self-directed walking tour of old homes, using the map for sale at the chamber of commerce, located in the old depot near the docks.

Fernandina Beach calls itself the "birthplace of the shrimping industry." It's interesting to sit on a bench on the dock and watch the shrimp boats with their wide wings of nets go out each day or to see people coming back with their catches after a day of fishing. Charter fishing boats do a brisk business here. Rental boats are available for a pleasure cruise up the Intracoastal. Brett's Waterway Café, next to the shrimp dock, is an excellent restaurant for seafood for either lunch or dinner.

Guests have access to most of the verandas at Florida House, which are furnished with comfortable chairs and rockers. There's also room to spread out in the beautifully landscaped courtyard, where white iron lawn chairs are arranged around tables on the brick pavement. This courtyard, shaded by the oak tree, has become a favorite place for wedding receptions in Fernandina.

The Ritz-Carlton, Amelia Island

4750 Amelia Island Parkway
Amelia Island, FL 32034
800-241-3333
904-277-1100
Fax: 904-261-9063

A sophisticated island retreat

Accommodations: 404 rooms, 45 suites. **Rates:** Rooms $179–$249, suites $249–$359; $1,500 for presidential suite; packages available. **Minimum stay:** With some packages. **Added:** 9% tax. Payment: Major credit cards. **Children:** 18 and under free in room with parents. **Smoking:** Nonsmoking rooms available. **Open:** Year-round.

➤ **The outdoor pool is shaped like a lagoon with landscaped islands of palms and tropical greenery; the elegant indoor pool has floor-to-ceiling windows and looks out over the outdoor pool and the sand dunes.**

The Ritz-Carlton, Amelia Island provides an escape to beauty and luxury. The beach is lovely here, with sea oats and flowering vines growing on the gentle slopes. Nearby, thick woods and quiet marshes serve as sanctuaries for waterfowl and other animals. There's also a golf course, serpentine swimming pool, and a hotel of towers and porticoes filled with marble and brocade. It may seem a little showy, but perhaps because Amelia Island has been a family vacation spot for so long, it's also a place where you can relax and enjoy yourself — the patrons who come here haven't forgotten that this is the beach.

This particular beach is part of the Summer Beach Resort and Country Club. It is obvious that the Ritz-Carlton is part of a country club as soon as you turn into the landscaped drive. To the left is the Summer Beach Clubhouse, golf shop, and the golf course. Beyond it is the eight-story Ritz-Carlton, its ornate Victorian fountain spraying water in front of the porte cochere and uniformed bellmen at the door. Inside are patterned marble floors, fine antiques of inlaid wood, oil paintings, Audubon prints, brocade wall hangings, and, as always, a highly trained staff to satisfy a guest's every need and whim.

The hotel is built in a compact U shape. The conference facilities and tennis center are in one wing, a fitness center and indoor pool are in the other. The Lobby Lounge and the reception and concierge desks are in the main area connecting the wings. The far end of the lounge forms a semicircle overlooking the ocean. Planters filled with bromeliads, orchids, and tropical greenery divide the large room into three spaces. On one side is a long marble bar and a small lounge; at the other is a cozy sitting room with a fireplace. In between is the main lounge, where afternoon tea is served.

The Grill Room serves dinner only, while the more informal Café serves three meals a day. Though service is occasionally on the slow side at the Café, the food is excellent, as it is at all the restaurants. And traditional Key lime pie is an event in itself: no simple wedge of pie here, but a small individual pie swimming in a pool of vanilla Anglaise, edged with loops of raspberry and mango sauce and garnished with mint leaves. It's a good thing so much recreation is available.

Apart from the obvious choice of golf on the Summer Beach course, there is tennis on 11 lighted courts, including a banked court for spectators and both hard and clay surfaces. Swimming is a special pleasure here: the Atlantic is only a few hundred feet from the back door, and there are two swimming pools. The Fitness and Recreation Centers are near the indoor pool.

Horseback riding is offered at the other end of the island at Seahorse Stables. The stables are near the bridge to Little Talbot Island, where locals often fish. Amelia Island is unusual in that riding is allowed on the beach. Boats can be chartered at the shrimp docks in Fernandina Beach.

Spend some time exploring the charming, historic town of Fernandina Beach. The Chamber of Commerce, in a railroad depot near the docks on Front Street, sells maps that can be used as a guide for a walking tour. There are wonderful examples of Victoriana in the houses and public buildings of the 30-block historic district; ornate embellishments show the influence of Moorish, Queen Anne, Chippendale, and Carpenter styles, which combined make one grand architectural statement. Especially fun is the "C House" on the corner of Beech and 8th streets and Fairbanks Folly on 7th Street.

During a stay on Amelia Island, one is struck by contrasts. The Parkway just off A1A is rather wooded, with ancient myrtle and live oak trees draped with Spanish moss. It's hard to believe that the city of Jacksonville is only 25 minutes away; this could be rural Georgia. The turnoff into the Summer Beach Resort has a much tamer, landscaped look, with wedges of green lawn and flower beds planted along the road. The manicured golf course and Mediterranean-style Ritz-Carlton loom beyond.

Although northerners often think of all of Florida as a winter resort, Amelia Island is at its best in summer and in the temperate months of fall and spring. In July and August, the Ritz-Carlton attracts southerners who come to the northeast Florida coast to escape the heat. In the winter months, the Ritz hosts a number of business meetings in its conference center. Although it's easy to get to the island from the airport and I-95, it's fun to take the ferry from Mayport, especially if you have children along.

1735 House & Amelia Island Lodging System

584 S. Fletcher
Amelia Island, FL 32034
800-872-8531
904-261-4148
www.1735house-bb.com
www.amelialodgings.com

A nautical-themed B&B

Innkeeper: William L. Auld. **Accommodations:** 5 suites in 1735 House; number in Amelia Island Lodging System varies. **Rates:** 1735 House, $100–$160; Amelia Island Lodging System, $82–$180; weekly/monthly rates available. **Included:** Continental breakfast. **Minimum stay:** None. **Added:** 9% tax. **Payment:** Major credit cards, personal checks. **Children:** Welcome. **Smoking:** On porches only. **Open:** Year-round.

The sand here is very fine, and the green-blue surf is warm. There's usually a nice Atlantic breeze to cool the air. The days are made for lying on the beach or taking long walks along the dunes.

The 1735 House, built in 1938, was the first B&B to open on Amelia Island. Because it is right on the ocean, is reasonably priced, and has charming rooms, it is still one of the most popular B&Bs on the island.

In 1735, Englishman James Oglethorpe, governor of Georgia, "discovered" Amelia Island and named it after the daughter of George II. Amelia Island soon became a pirates' hideout, and there are still many local legends of buried treasure. In keeping with local history, the suites resemble captains' quarters — small, with an efficient use of space. Each has an attractive bath, a compact master bedroom, and a narrow room with bunk beds. Furnishings are in wicker, wood, or rattan. Oceanfront suites have a living/dining area with a table and chairs. All suites have kitchenettes, and all have color TVs. Walls are of knotty pine, with various nautical brass fittings and antiques for decoration.

Breakfast is a generous meal of pastries, fresh fruit and juice, and coffee or tea, which comes to your room in a wicker basket with the morning newspaper. There is no dining room here, but there are lots of places for lunch and dinner in the nearby seaport town of Fernandina Beach. Ice, juice, and sodas are available in the galley. Amenities include telephones in the rooms, mini-lines for drying clothes, and plastic bags for storing wet swimsuits.

The front of the 1735 House faces South Fletcher, or Route A1A, the beach's main road. The house is close to the road, with parking at the front door. A minor drawback for country inn perfectionists is that, despite its charming interior, the facade of the 1735 House is unprepossessing. The inn is a squarish, New England-style house with practical white vinyl clapboard siding and black shutters and awnings.

A brick patio overlooking the ocean runs the length of the back of the house. It is furnished with chairs and tables and, although it's for everybody to enjoy, is directly accessible from the first-floor Captain's Suite — ideal for a family with children who love the beach.

The Aulds and their staff also operate the Amelia Island Lodging System, a reservation service listing a variety of vacation accommodations, from a large log cabin to a bungalow in the woods to a resort with more than 100 rooms and villas.

One favorite is the lighthouse at 736 South Fletcher. It has four stories: a bedroom and sunken shower bath on the first floor, a gal-

The Northeast Coast

ley and living room on the second, a master bedroom with a queen-size captain's bed on the third, and an observation deck on the top floor. A reproduction of the original Amelia Island Lighthouse, its wooden floors and ceilings and old brass fixtures are true to the original. The Lodging System has two other lighthouses and a lighthouse-keeper's cottage.

Also offered by Lodging System is a newly renovated four-bedroom home right on the ocean. It has a dining room table that seats 10, a full kitchen, a utility room, a covered breezeway with a Ping-Pong table, and a screened-in porch overlooking the water.

There is tremendous variety in price and style in the listings; write for a brochure or call for a rundown on the places that would suit you best. It's a good idea to keep in mind the dynamics of the island when renting a place. The narrow southern end, near the Ritz-Carlton and Amelia Island Plantation Resort, is the trendier, wealthier end of the island, where private residences are usually large and well kept. Farther north, the houses are smaller and don't have the manicured landscaping that houses near the Ritz have. These are real Florida summer places, where you can come in from the beach with a little sand on your feet and not feel that you'll destroy the decor. Most families with young children would probably be more relaxed in these imperfect little houses on or near the beach.

Walnford Inn

102 South 7th Street
Fernandina Beach
Amelia Island, FL 32034
800-277-6660
904-277-6660
www.walnford.com

A comfortable house in the island's historic district that is full of unusual antiques

Innkeepers: Linda and Bob Waln. **Accommodations:** 8 rooms; 1 suite. **Rates:** $85–$155. **Included:** Full breakfast. **Minimum stay:** During some weekends and special events; 2–3 nights for special packages. **Added:** 9% tax. **Payment:** Major credit cards, traveler's checks. **Children:** Older children welcome. **Smoking:** Outside only. **Open:** Year-round.

➤ **Linda Waln started out years ago as an innkeeper by taking the spill-over from a neighborhood B&B nearby whose owners hated to turn away guests when their place was full. Later, without even a sign out front, she**

rented out rooms in the attractive house she bought next door. Linda enjoyed having guests so much that she decided to run a B&B full-time. She now has the Walnford Inn, the house next door for *her* spillover, and two resort condos on the other side of Amelia Island available to guests.

The house is just one block from Centre Street, the focus of 19th-century Fernandina Beach. Numbered streets running perpendicular to Centre were saved from destruction in the 20th century largely because the area had such a severe economic decline that there was no money for rehabilitation. As a result, 19th-century brick buildings along Centre Street and wooden clapboard family homes on the side streets like 7th have been untouched for a century — fortunately for us!

The Walnford Inn is an understated Victorian, with pale yellow siding with white trim and green shutters, lacy balustrades, and bracketed pillars on the front veranda. The grassy corner lot is enclosed in a white picket fence. The guest house next door, which is part of the inn, is very similar in architecture and decor.

Both houses have interesting antiques that Linda and her family have collected over the years. In Monica, a first-floor room in the main house, there's a carved wooden armoire made from an enclosed Brittany bed that looks as if Joan of Arc might have slept in it. Solomon, a second-floor room, has a mirrored headboard framed with intricately carved brass. Some of the rooms have the original wood and tile fireplace and, in the bathroom, an old-fashioned clawfoot tub with a hand-held shower. Other rooms have wonderful modern amenities, such as a two-person marble whirlpool soaking tub and separate shower.

All of the rooms have a telephone (with local calls free) and cable TV; some have a VCR. The walls are painted soft neutral colors rather than papered, which creates a nice backdrop for the wooden antiques and keeps the guest rooms from looking too fussy. Some of the guest rooms have a fireplace or a private balcony. Orientals and other attractive area rugs are on the pine floors. The very private Penthouse Suite, on the third floor of the main house in what was once an attic, has a king-size bed, a sunny sitting area, a 27-inch color TV with VCR, and a two-person corner whirlpool tub in the bathroom.

In the downstairs of the main house are the sitting room, the library, and the dining room, where the Walns serve their famous breakfasts: stuffed French toast one day, an egg dish the next, raspberry pancakes the day after. Guests always comment on the great breakfast, which can also be taken in your room or out on the porch in warm weather. The dining room set is very different from the antiques that are on the first floor of the main house: a glass table with pink chairs upholstered right down to the legs, a somewhat jarring contemporary look that doesn't quite fit with the mirrored antique buffet that's adjacent.

Little extras that can be arranged ahead of time at the Walnford Inn include a bottle of wine or champagne on arrival (nonalcoholic available), flowers and chocolate-covered strawberries in the room (part of the B&B's Getaway package), a carriage ride through the historic district, or the ministrations of a masseuse or masseur. The Walns have bicycles that are available for guests' use, and they are happy to make arrangements for golfing and kayaking trips. Shrimp boats are often tied up at the dock at the end of Centre Street, and up and down Centre are boutiques, galleries, and restaurants.

Daytona Beach

The Coquina Inn B&B

544 S. Palmetto Avenue
Daytona Beach, FL 32114
904-254-4969
800-805-7533
coquinaBnB@aol.com
www.coquinaInnDaytonaBeach.com

> **An inn featuring early-20th-century Florida architecture**

Innkeepers: Ann Christoffersen and Denis Haight. **Accommodations:** 4 rooms. **Rates:** Rooms $80–$110. **Included:** Full breakfast, evening sherry or port wine. **Minimum stay:** 5 nights during Race and Bike Week. **Added:** 11% tax. **Payment:** MasterCard, Visa, American Express, Discover. **Children:** Older children allowed. **Smoking:** Limited. **Open:** Year-round.

➤ **Breakfast, served in the Coquina's colorful dining room, is spectacular. A typical meal might be homemade breads and fruits from the local farmers' market followed by thick slices of French toast, an omelette, eggs Benedict, or an eggs Foxworthy.**

Although the Coquina Inn is on a main thoroughfare of Daytona Beach and just minutes from Halifax Harbor Marina and the ocean, the atmosphere is residential and quiet. In the historic district, where fine old homes line streets with names like Magnolia, Orange, and Cedar, the inn is one of the finest examples of Florida architecture in this gracious neighborhood. It was meticulously restored and updated by the previous owners, with restoration and careful maintenance continued by the present owners, Ann and Denis.

Built in 1912, the inn derives its name from the coquina shellstone on its facade and in the distinctive coquina fireplaces. It is a beautifully proportioned house, with arched windows in front and in the sun porch, a Spanish tile roof, and casement windows. The oak floors in the drawing room and the Mexican tiles in the sun porch are original. Brass sconces on the walls and fans on the high ceilings complete the gracious mood of these two rooms, joined by French doors. The dining room is "southern comfort," as Ann and Denis put it, with salmon walls and built-in cupboards. There are always flowers on the small tables, which are set for a full breakfast. The graceful windows here and throughout the house are made more beautiful by gauzy curtains above narrow wooden shutters or richly draped curtains.

The four guest rooms are on the second floor and are named for Florida flowers: Azalea, Magnolia, Hibiscus, and Jasmine. The latter was originally the master bedroom. It has a mahogany queen-size bed, a coquina fireplace, and soft peach walls. The bathroom has the original old tub and an oak floor. Jasmine is furnished with 1920s mahogany furniture and a seven-foot-tall queen-size canopy bed draped in a light, airy netting. The room can be joined with the Hibiscus for a family. The Hibiscus has a wicker queen-size bed and a sitting area with a wicker settee and coffee table, a large bath, and an outdoor deck accessible by French doors.

Magnolia has an old double four-poster and a twin daybed. The view from the window seat is of the garden. Magnolia's adjoining bathroom has a clawfoot tub and old brass and porcelain fixtures. The beautifully decorated Azalea is done in rich, rosy florals and has lots of fancy pillows on the full-size water bed. Azalea's bathroom is at the end of a quirky little hallway within the room.

All of the rooms have fresh-cut flowers, a teddy bear, cable TV, and a private bathroom.

Indigo Lakes Holiday Inn

2620 W. International Speedway Blvd.
Daytona Beach, FL 32114
800-223-4161 in Florida
904-258-6333
Fax: 904-254-3611

A quiet retreat near the speedway

Accommodations: 151 rooms and kitchenette suites. **Rates:** $85–$120, higher during Daytona Race Week; packages available. **Minimum stay:** With some packages. **Added:** 11% tax; $10 extra adult. **Payment:** Major credit cards, personal checks. **Children:** Under 12 free in room with parents. **Smoking:** Nonsmoking rooms available. **Open:** Year-round.

➤ **The conference facilities are among the best in Florida. The 2,200 square feet of meeting space can accommodate up to 200 people and was designed for small meetings; there is none of the crowded, impersonal feeling of large convention hotels.**

It's hard to believe that Indigo Lakes, with its 4,000 acres of woodlands, ponds, marshlands, and lagoons, is just five minutes from Daytona Regional Airport and the International Speedway. There are several acres of beautifully landscaped lawns and gardens surrounding the main buildings, and great herons stand guard in the marshes. Throughout, an effort is made to bring the outside indoors, with rich wood paneling and large windows overlooking the woods and greenery. This is a very upscale Holiday Inn.

Accommodations include rooms and kitchen suites; the best overlook the pool. All inn rooms are attractively decorated and have a patio or balcony, TV, bedside television and light controls, phones, and work areas. Rooms are furnished with king-size beds or two doubles. A few suites have kitchenettes.

The inn has a handsome reception area and lobby, where it's pleasant to read or watch the passing scene. The carpet of deep indigo follows a color scheme carried out in many of the common rooms. Standard accommodations are spacious and include a small refrigerator and coffeemaker. The landscaping is attractive and conscientiously maintained. Rooms overlook landscaped areas and the pool or the parking lot, so ask about the view when making reservations.

Facilities include a fully equipped fitness club, a six-lane Olympic-size pool, and excellent golf and tennis. Indigo Lakes has a full-service golf shop, putting and chipping greens with a practice sand trap, and a 400-yard driving range. The attractive tennis center has 10 all-weather courts lighted for night play and a pro shop.

Live Oak Inn

444–448 S. Beach Street
Daytona Beach, FL 32114
800-881-4667
904-252-4667
Fax: 904-239-0068

A historic inn in Old Daytona

Innkeepers: Jessie and Del Glock. **Accommodations:** 12 rooms. **Rates:** $90 on weekends, $80 Monday through Thursday; reduced rates for packages and longer stays; higher rates for special events. **Included:** Beverage on arrival, expanded Continental breakfast. **Minimum stay:** 5 nights during special events. **Added:** 11% tax; $10 extra person. **Payment:** MasterCard, Visa, personal checks, cash. **Children:** Young children discouraged because of antiques. **Smoking:** On porch, deck, and veranda only. **Open:** Year-round.

➤ **The spirit of the early Daytona era has been beautifully preserved here in the choice of antiques and other appointments, but also in the atmosphere the innkeeper has created.**

The Live Oak Inn is not part of the Daytona beach scene, although that famous strip of sand is easily accessible. The inn harks back to a gentler time in this part of the world. Old Daytona is on the mainland, while Daytona Beach and Daytona Beach Shores are on a barrier island across the Intracoastal Waterway. (Guests arriving by boat can dock at the marina and simply walk across the street.) The Live Oak Inn comprises two historic buildings — one built in 1871, the other in 1881, making them Daytona's oldest houses. Both are listed on the National Register of Historic Places. The inn is also reputed to be the site of the founding of Daytona by town father Mathias Day.

The main house has four guest rooms and sits impressively on the corner, surrounded by attractive gardens and a picket fence. Ancient oak trees, festooned with Spanish moss, shade the old clapboard building. An old-fashioned wraparound porch is furnished with rockers. As one would expect at a "real Florida inn," many guests sit out here reading or gazing out at the marina and Intracoastal across the street. A heavy wooden door leads into a formal 19th-century entryway and the reception area. Lots of windows let the sun shine in.

Adjoining this building is a house built in 1871 and recently refurbished, with a total of eight guest rooms, half with a Jacuzzi in the bathroom and half with views of the marina. An effort is made to educate guests with a light hand about Old Daytona, including naming rooms after people who contributed prominently to the history of Florida and the Daytona region.

The bedrooms are decorated with late-19th-century antiques, iron bedsteads, and period color schemes. Bathrooms are small to moderate-size. All guest rooms have telephones, TVs, and VCRs. Some of the rooms have enclosed porches, and three have balconies. The Foster Room is especially appealing, with sky blue plaster walls, a white iron bedstead, and a balcony. The Rogers Room — named after Dr. Josie Rogers, Daytona's first woman doctor and its only woman mayor — has polished maple floors, period antique furnishings, and a black iron bedstead. The bathroom floor has original black and white tiles.

The chef of the Live Oak Inn is making a name for himself in this century. He teaches cooking classes at the local college as well as operating the Live Oak Inn Restaurant. Restaurant guests eat at tables and chairs set up in the front parlors. There is also outside dining on the large deck joining the two houses. In only a few years, the Live Oak Inn has become well known in the area for delicious food. It has also proved itself to be a wonderful place to stay for those who are wary of the sometimes honky-tonk beach scene across the bridge.

Daytona Beach Shores

Sunny Shore Motel

2037 S. Atlantic Avenue
Daytona Beach Shores, FL 32118
800-874-2854
904-252-4569

A well-maintained budget motel on the beach

Owner: Vicki Ogle. **Accommodations:** 34 rooms, suites, and efficiencies. **Rates:** Rooms $40–$58, suites $72–$101, efficiencies $44–$65; weekly rates available. **Minimum stay:** 5 nights. **Payment:** Discover, MasterCard, Visa. **Added:** 11% tax; $5 extra adult; $3 for cribs and rollaways. **Children:** Under 12 free in room with parents; no students unaccompanied by adult. **Smoking:** Allowed. **Open:** Year-round.

➤ **Sunny Shore is immaculate, inside and out. Rooms have modern furniture and are designed with the vacationing family in mind. Baths have a separate vanity area, which eases morning crowding. Most families choose an efficiency with two double beds and a small kitchen.**

Daytona Beach is overrun by wild college crowds in winter and spring. Therefore, if you're planning a vacation on this famous — and infamous — beach, it's important to choose your accommodations carefully. Families and adult couples are usually happiest at places like the Sunny Shore, which doesn't allow students without their parents. Though Sunny Shore is oriented to vacationing families, groups and couples are welcome, as long as they are quiet and turn out the lights early.

All the rooms have recently been redecorated with blue carpeting and new vinyl kitchen floors. The best rooms are at the back of the motel, especially 211 and 212, which have small balconies overlooking the ocean. Although the motel is on busy Atlantic Avenue, guests are here for the beach and the reasonable prices. They can park their cars in front of their rooms and usually leave them there all day. From the parking lot, it's just a few steps to the pool and the beach beyond. Groceries are available at the supermarket just down the street.

Daytona Beach is wide and gorgeous, and the surf is warm, with a variety of wave heights that depend on the time of day, the weather, and the season. You can body surf or swim or just wade along the shore.

Watch out for cars on the beach. Residents and visitors are still allowed to drive right on the beach, so parents of small children cannot go to sleep in the sun, no matter how far from the surf their children are playing.

Summer is the high season here, and a family can get a very good rate in the winter, fall and spring — except for Race Week, when the place is extremely crowded.

Green Cove Springs

River Park Inn

103 South Magnolia Avenue
Green Cove Springs, FL 32043
888-417-0363
904-284-2994
www.riverparkinn.com

> **Attractive, reasonably priced rooms in a house built in 1887**

Innkeepers: Pat Sickles Garlinghouse and Dale Garlinghouse. **Accommodations:** 4 rooms. **Rates:** $65–$100. **Included:** Full breakfast. **Minimum stay:** Some weekends and special events. **Payment:** Cash, checks, major credit cards, traveler's checks. **Children:** Allowed. **Smoking:** Allowed on porch and upstairs veranda. **Open:** Year-round.

➤ **The Victorian ornateness is tempered with the openness and informality of Pat and her husband, Dale, for whom this is home year-round.**

Green Cove Springs is about half an hour west of St. Augustine and the northeast coast beaches. The neighborhood in which the River Park Inn is located is just off a "miracle mile" section of Route 17 that is rimmed with car dealerships for almost the entire mile. But once you turn off, you are in the historic district of the town. Several 19th- and early-20th-century houses here have been restored, and a few more are in the first stages of this process.

The River Park Inn is vintage Victorian, painted charcoal gray and deep burgundy, with louvered shutters at the small-paned windows and verandas on both the first and second floors. The crimped tin roof and third-floor dormer are typical of the Old Florida style of architecture.

Just inside is a parlor furnished with Victorian pieces. Ornate, formal-looking swags are at the large windows. The dining room is decorated in a similar Victorian style, yet innkeeper Pat's roomy kitchen is also visible. A typical breakfast is generous and delicious: fresh fruit, juice, grits, scrambled eggs or French toast, and bacon, followed by plenty of hot coffee.

The guest rooms are both downstairs and upstairs. The decor of the rooms is a mix of Victorian and country: often the windows have quilted valances that match or complement the beautiful quilts on the bed. Lace curtains, matelasse bedspreads, antique bureaus, and sprays of dried flowers further individualize each room. Transoms, those narrow, old-fashioned windows above doors that were opened to let hot air escape from a room, are above nearly every door. Guest room floors are fully carpeted in soft broadloom.

The Master Suite was originally two bedrooms and includes a sitting room furnished with an upholstered fainting couch. The romantic (but nonworking) fireplace, one of several in the house, has a solid fire screen handpainted in a "primitive country" style. In the bathroom there's both a whirlpool tub and a shower. All of the private baths at the River Park Inn are new and have fresh-looking ceramic tile.

The wide, second-story veranda has a sofa and chairs and, best of all, a large hot tub, which any guest is invited to soak in. From the veranda, there's a view of the riverside and park, which are diagonally across the street. Guests visit with each other on this veranda and the downstairs porch, which is furnished with a porch swing, a double rocker, and chairs. It's easy to get into a redolent, southern mood here and spend much of the day reading and rocking.

Just across the street is Spring Park, which has the town's municipal swimming pool, fed by a natural mineral spring — thus the name. Just beyond the playground and pool is the bank of the St. John's River. Although the river is wonderful to look at, only expert swimmers try to swim in it; the current is quite strong here. A gentle tributary of the St. Johns, Governor's Creek, is just up the road. The Green Cove Springs Marina is also close by. A couple of good restaurants are within walking distance of the River Park Inn.

Recreation is in St. Augustine to the east, Jacksonville to the north, Gainesville to the west, and Orlando and Disney World to the south. There are plenty of nice beaches up and down the coast. There's also much to be said for staying close to home. The River

Park Inn is listed on the National Register of Historic Places and is on the Green Cove Springs walking tour of historic buildings.

There is quite a lot of Florida history in this town. A favorite of Native Americans because of the mineral springs and the fishing, the area was later developed by whites in the early 1800s when a saw mill was erected under a Spanish land grant. It also became a center for growing citrus and for lumbering and, by the end of the 19th century, was a warm-weather destination for tourists who came here on river steamboats. The town suffered a decline after a citrus freeze in 1895, and Flagler's railroad bypassed the town as he expanded south to the warmer Palm Beach/Miami area. So the town has had its ups and downs. But if you want a peaceful, pleasant B&B with Victorian ambiance and modern extras like the veranda hot tub, you can't do better than the River Park Inn.

Hutchinson Island

Indian River Plantation Marriott Resort

555 N.E. Ocean Boulevard
Hutchinson Island
Stuart, FL 34996
800-775-5936
561-225-3700

| **A true destination resort**

Accommodations: 200 hotel rooms, 70 1-bedroom suites and studios; 28 1- and 2-bedroom oceanfront condos. **Rates:** Hotel rooms $129–$210, 1-bedroom suites $180–$340, studios $140–$265; packages available. **Minimum stay:** 2 or 3 nights with some packages. **Added:** 6% tax. **Payment:** Major credit cards. **Children:** Under 17 free in room with parents. **Smoking:** Nonsmoking rooms available. **Open:** Year-round.

➤ **The marina is one of the most beautiful in Florida — a full-service, 77-slip facility. Along with a fuel dock and utility and telephone hook-ups, there are washers and dryers, showers, lockers, and a well-equipped ship's store. The marina staff is cordial and helpful. Mariners should make reservations well in advance of arrival time, especially in season.**

Stuart, Florida, is a city of inlets and rivers, with the Atlantic Ocean surging just beyond the Indian River and Hutchinson Island.

Indian River Plantation Resort is easily accessible by bridges, but with its location on quiet A1A, the resort has an insular feeling.

The resort's marina is located two miles north of the St. Lucie Inlet on the Indian River stretch of the Intracoastal Waterway. The land along the marina is rimmed by mangroves. Guests walk from their boats down a wooden pier and through a small forest of these trees to reach the plantation's hotel. Those arriving by car cross picturesque bridges over the Indian River to the island. In the lobby, white ceiling fans revolve lazily and a cool peach marble floor is underfoot. On a platform in the center of the lobby guests can sit surrounded by large planters of green plants. Just outside is a waterfall.

After registering, hotel guests take the elevator to rooms above the lobby or walk across a courtyard under huge white latticework archways to the accommodations in the other wing. (Larger villa accommodations are at the other end of the resort.) The 200 hotel rooms are all a bit larger than the average standard hotel room, with thick carpeting and quilted spreads. Amenities include hair dryers, remote control cable TV, and private balconies.

The hotel is adapted from the Old Florida style: gray roof and clapboards, white trim and latticework, and touches of pale peach on the terraces. Although the style is carried out not with the traditional tin and wood but in sturdy vinyl and other practical materials, none of it looks cheap or flimsy.

In addition to the standard rooms at the resort's new hotel, there are also spacious suites and one- and two-bedroom villas on the beach. Located in mid-rise buildings, these accommodations are particularly sought after by families and those here for longer stays. They have fully equipped kitchens and attractively furnished bedrooms and living/dining areas. Most have spectacular views of the ocean and dunes. From the top floors of the open-air hallways in some of the villas, you can look out at the Atlantic on one side and the Indian River on the other.

Apart from ocean swimming and beaching, there is an impressive array of recreation at Indian River Plantation. There are 13 tennis courts, seven of which are lighted for night games. The tennis center provides excellent instruction, clinics, and tournaments for guests and club members of all ages, as well as equipment rentals and an excellent pro shop. Golf is on two excellent 18-hole courses.

The resort has four swimming pools, and water sports like Jet Skiing and water skiing are available. The marina rents boats and arranges deep-sea fishing excursions and sunset cruises along the

Intracoastal Waterway. Indian River Plantation also has bicycling and jogging trails and a fitness facility.

The convention center includes an impressive grand ballroom and a number of breakout rooms and hospitality suites. The Elliott Amphitheater has a modern stage, a floor-to-ceiling projection screen, an audiovisual system, and cushioned armchairs arranged in tiers, with individual lighting and writing space for each conference participant. These facilities, coupled with the resort's natural beauty and recreation, make it popular with business, professional, and environmental groups.

A year-round supervised activities program for kids includes snorkeling, bike rides, movies, parties, and lots of time on the beach. A camp program in the summer offers children tennis, golf, and swimming lessons, fishing trips, arts and crafts sessions, and field trips to nearby attractions.

The resort's restaurants, lounges, and bars must take some of the credit for its popularity. Of the four restaurants, Scalawags is the largest and most elegant, with both indoor and terrace dining. All the delicious pastries and pies are made from scratch at the plantation. The Inlet is the resort's small, formal restaurant and serves only dinner. The Porch, overlooking the tennis courts, serves three meals daily. The Emporium, with its old-fashioned decor, serves meals all day and has an ice cream parlor. Although the food is not up to the standards of the other three restaurants, its informality and proximity to the gift shop and marine store make it a good place for families with children.

For a change of pace, the county beach is just a few minutes away, with very warm water, lovely natural vegetation, and just enough shells to be interesting. Families will enjoy the area's other nearby attractions; these are not glitzy commercial lures. The House of Refuge, for example, built in 1875 as one of seven coastal rescue stations, is now a museum of marine artifacts and 19th-century living quarters, and houses a research facility for the study of the life cycle of green sea turtles. They say that when the resort was being built, a turtle's nest was found on the property and all construction was halted on that site until the nesting season was over. This is typical of the attitude at the plantation and in the town of Stuart. Guests at the resort have the privilege of enjoying carefully preserved natural beauty while indulging their love of recreation and sport.

Jacksonville

Cleary-Dickert House B&B

1804 Copeland Street
Jacksonville, FL 32204
904-387-4762
Fax: 904-387-4003
info@cleary-dickert.com
www.cleary-dickert.com

Elegant and friendly

Innkeepers: Betty Sue Dickert and Joe Cleary. **Accommodations:** 10 suites. **Rates:** $89–$199. **Included:** Full breakfast. **Minimum stay:** 2 nights on some weekends and special events. **Added:** 12.5% tax; $20 for extra person in room. **Payment:** Major credit cards, traveler's checks. **Children:** In Magnolia accommodations only. **Smoking:** Outside only. **Open:** Year-round.

➤ **The Cleary-Dickert House B&B should perhaps be called the Cleary-Dickert House and Garden B&B.**

This spacious, early-20th-century family home is on a corner lot in the Avondale/Riverdale historic district, just one house from the St. John's River. The Cleary-Dickert B&B is surrounded by gardens on three sides, and inside are rooms that overlook the garden or are gardenlike themselves. A vine-covered bower leads into the front garden, where there are lawn chairs and a wooden swing. Even though this garden is unfenced and faces Copeland Street, there is some privacy here because the vegetation is thick.

A pathway curves from here into the side garden. An arched iron gate in a repeating rose and tendril design leads to a brick-walled garden. Here there are tile and brick fountains, some tasteful statues, and flowerbeds and pots of azaleas, impatiens, ivy, bamboo, palms, and ferns. In the house, the formal dining room, parlor, and sun porch overlook these gardens, as do many of the guest rooms. The sun porch is lovely, with a sofa and love seat in a muted floral print. Vines grow along the window outside, and vines of ivy are stenciled on the walls of the sun porch, so it is as if the curling vines have come inside.

Many of the guest suites have a garden theme, as one would expect. A typical suite might have floral-patterned wallpaper, an ornate French provincial queen-size bedstead with a quilted spread, and flowered shams, bed ruffle, sheets, and pillows. Curtains and swags are lacy white or in a print that complements the wallpaper or bedspread. Some of the decor is very Victorian and frilly, but there is also a nod to the graciousness of Old Florida and the South. Two suites have private entrances from the courtyard or front drive; these are nice if you want extra privacy. All suites have a sitting room as well as the bedroom itself and a nice private bathroom. And, naturally, flowers cut from the garden are everywhere.

In addition to the suites in the brick and stucco main house, there are "family accommodations" in Magnolia, a house of the same era just across St. Johns Avenue that has been divided into apartments. The place has a somewhat musty smell, and the accommodations are not of the caliber of those in the main house. The stucco interior walls are painted in glossy colors, the wood around a door might be chipped, or the kitchen might have an old, scratched sink. These are good if you are staying in the Jacksonville area for an extended period and want to cook, or if you have children. Adults can still spend time in the main house, where the number of fine furnishings makes it inappropriate for kids.

Breakfast can be served in your suite by special request, but most guests eat beneath the crystal chandelier at the long, polished mahogany table in the formal dining room. A typical breakfast begins with freshly brewed coffee or English tea, fruit cup and orange juice, and homemade muffins or sweet bread with jams and jellies, followed by a hot dish like eggs Benedict. Recipes are influenced by both southern cooking and traditional English cuisine. With advance notice, Betty Sue will also prepare a breakfast for special diets.

The Cleary-Dickert House is run by innkeepers Betty Sue Dickert and Joe Cleary, who are southern and English, respectively. Joe's influence is seen in the traditional English tea that is served every afternoon; there's also wine and cheese. Betty Sue's influence is seen in the elegance and graciousness of the house. Both Betty Sue and Joe enjoy the Avondale/Riverdale neighborhood and are happy to recommend excellent restaurants within walking distance and further afield.

Concerning things to do, all of the cultural offerings of the city of Jacksonville are within easy driving distance, as is Jacksonville Beach. The Avondale/Riverdale area is romantic to walk in during early evening hours, especially along the Italianate balustrade that borders the St. Johns River.

House on Cherry Street

1844 Cherry Street
Jacksonville, FL 32205
904-384-1999
Fax: 904-384-5013

A B&B that feels like a
friend's home

Innkeeper: Carol Anderson. **Accommodations:** 5 rooms. **Rates:** $79–$109. **Included:** Continental breakfast; hors d'oeuvres and wine in evening. **Minimum stay:** 2 nights during special events. **Added:** 12.5% tax. **Payment:** MasterCard, Visa, American Express, personal checks. **Children:** 10 and older welcome. **Smoking:** Only in common room and on porches. **Open:** Year-round; occasionally closed for two or three days.

➤ In the evening, Carol offers guests wine and two or three of her superlative hors d'oeuvres, served on the porch or in the living room. This is a beautifully appointed front parlor with pale aqua walls and brocade wing

chairs. To keep the room from looking too elegant, Carol has covered almost every available surface with a piece from her duck decoy collection.

Carol Anderson is an extremely congenial host who seems to truly enjoy all those who stay with her. Her house looks more New England than Florida, with square-rigger architecture and small-paned lights on each side of the sturdy door. The street the B&B is named after ends at a little neighborhood park and the St. Johns River. Cherry Street is part of the Avondale/Riverdale historic district, one of the most desirable sections of Jacksonville. This "reservations only" inn is a wonderful place to rest and feel at home, and it is also within easy driving distance of many area attractions and walking distance from elegant shopping and dining.

A large grandfather clock stands by the entryway. In the spacious foyer, some old wooden decoys are displayed; most of the collection is in the living room. Several of the antique woven spreads that Carol also collects are draped over wooden blanket racks in the hall.

The guest rooms are decorated with more decoys, four-poster beds, and antiques. Although some of the wonderful bedsteads are antiques, the queen-size mattresses are firm and new. The rooms are carpeted or have area rugs on the light pine floors. Windows afford views of the St. Johns River or of gardens. Baths are modern, though one or two are on the small side.

A newly opened accommodation is a large, long room on the second floor that has several windows overlooking the river. A stenciled border in soft blues and greens runs along the top of the wall just below the high ceiling. The understated four-poster bed has a crocheted lace canopy and another one of Carol's richly colored woven coverlets. The bathroom is a bit small for the size of the room but has a full bathtub with a shower head and what appears to be the original white ceramic tile. A large walk-in closet is just to the right of the bathroom door. At the other end of the room is a sitting room that has a comfortable sofa and rocker, small TV, antique chest, and large-paned windows overlooking the back yard and the river. Built-in shelving along one wall holds books and a collection of decoys and porcelain.

In a hallway nook on the second floor is a small refrigerator with complimentary soda and beer. Ice is downstairs in the kitchen. Guests can relax with a drink in the sitting room or parlor or out on the porch. Carol has her own active life as a mom and grandmother and as a tennis pro who officiates at regional and national games. But she enjoys getting to know guests and is very helpful in recommending local sights and excellent restaurants.

Carol serves a Continental breakfast in the morning; it's light but delicious. A typical meal offers fresh fruit and juice, rolls, breads, yogurt, and cereals, including homemade granola. If you have dietary restrictions or prefer low-calorie food, Carol will accommodate you. Still, it's a mistake to miss out on a real Anderson breakfast. Guests can enjoy an extra cup of coffee on the screened porch overlooking the backyard and the St. Johns River.

Omni Jacksonville Hotel

245 Water Street
Jacksonville, FL 32202
800-THE-OMNI
904-355-OMNI

| A downtown hotel near trendy Jacksonville Landing |

General Manager: John Remmers. **Accommodations:** 354 rooms. **Rates:** Rooms $149–$189, Omni Club rooms $189; packages and discount weekend rates available. **Minimum stay:** With some packages. **Added:** 12.5% tax. **Payment:** Major credit cards. **Children:** Under 17 free in room with parents. **Smoking:** Nonsmoking rooms available. **Open:** Year-round.

➤ **The Omni is a convenient business hotel and also a wonderful place to mix business with pleasure: the entire Jacksonville Landing area is hopping day and night.**

The Omni Jacksonville is one of the few top-notch hotels in downtown Jacksonville. Why they're so scarce in a town that has had a major urban rehabilitation is hard to say; perhaps the hotel business just hasn't caught up with the resurgent city.

The Omni is near Jacksonville Landing, a harbor development with dozens of trendy shops and some lively restaurants. The St. Johns River and Intracoastal Waterway are adjacent, so guests can take river-taxi rides, cruise on a big replica paddle wheeler, and stroll along the Riverwalk.

The Omni is a popular convention hotel for companies from out of town and is also a meeting place for smaller Jacksonville-area businesses. The entrance off busy Water Street is impressive, with light marble floors, massive veneered pillars, and Oriental art. The reception area is spacious enough to handle registering convention groups, and the staff remains polite and unruffled even when working with large groups.

The second-floor conference rooms include the Florida Ballroom, which can be subdivided. Just off the ballroom is a big sitting area for taking a break between meetings or lingering for informal discussions.

Juliette's, the hotel's restaurant, is named after Juliette DuBois, a 19th-century city resident who was famous as a cook on her father's riverboat. Juliette's serves three meals a day and is located in a smashing four-story atrium. The food has improved recently and includes a nice brunch on Sundays. Juliette's Lounge is popular with both the Jacksonville business community and visitors from out of town.

Rooms at the Omni are a bit larger than the average standard accommodation. Some of the rooms overlook city streets and parking lots, but the best expose a slice of the busy St. Johns River. The rooms have been recently renovated and have thick wall-to-wall carpeting and attractive wooden furniture. The baths have ceramic tile and marble sinks.

Nearby are the beaches of the northeast Florida coast, just as wide as Daytona but less crowded. St. Augustine, the oldest established city in the United States, and Fort Caroline, the first European colony, are both within easy driving distance. Marineland, one of Florida's oldest and most worthwhile attractions, is 40 minutes away. Golf, museums, and shopping are also close by.

Residents of Jacksonville fondly refer to their city as "Jax" — there is a feeling of vitality and strong community pride here. After a stay at the Omni, you may find that the mood of Jax is catching.

Plantation Manor Inn

1630 Copeland Street
Jacksonville, FL 32204
904-384-4630

A B&B with Old South hospitality

Innkeepers: Jerry and Kathy Ray. **Accommodations:** 9 rooms. **Rates:** Rooms $120–$160, suites: $135-$175. **Included:** Full breakfast. **Minimum stay:** None. **Added:** 12.5% tax. **Payment:** American Express, MasterCard, Diners Club, Visa, personal checks. **Children:** 12 and over welcome. **Smoking:** Only on porches. **Open:** Year-round.

➤ **All the rooms on the second and third floors have access from the second-floor hallway to the veranda. This is furnished with white iron lawn furniture cushioned with big pillows and is shaded by large old trees.**

Jerry and Kathy Ray were not exaggerating when they named their B&B Plantation Manor. The three-story house is very southern, very much the manor. It sits on a slight rise on a corner lot in the city's most attractive historic neighborhood. The two Doric columns flanking the entryway are massive. Slightly smaller columns support the second-floor veranda that wraps around the imposing house. Built in 1905 and occupied by a number of successful Jacksonville citizens, it began to deteriorate by the middle of the century. After the Rays bought the place, Jerry and a team of workers undertook the arduous task of renovating the house. It took a year to complete the new roof and four-foot overhangs outside, and eight months to strip the cypress woodwork of layers of paint in the interior, to say nothing of spackling and painting and decorating — Kathy's domain.

The finished house has high ceilings, patterned pine floors, plastered or papered walls, and an elegant wooden banister. Furnishings include 19th-century antiques, gilded French provincial reproductions, and contemporary pieces. Guests enter the wide formal entry and first see the ornate living room, which has a semicircular sofa before a paneled and tiled fireplace.

On the opposite side of the entry hall is a room that was probably a formal dining room in the original house and is now an attractive boardroom for businesspeople who hold executive retreats and conferences at Plantation Manor. A large table has space to spread out, and large double doors close off the room from the rest of the Manor. A fax machine sits in the corner.

In the middle of the house is what was probably a back parlor in 1905 and is now a dining room. Here Kathy serves breakfast at whatever time guests request it. A typical morning meal might consist of a ham omelette, homemade breads and pastries, fresh fruit and juice, coffee and tea.

A side door leads to a small porch and several steps down to a brick patio and a swimming pool. Furnished with benches, lawn chairs, and chaises, the area is surrounded by flowerbeds and has become a favorite for weddings and receptions in Jacksonville. It would be easy to feel like a southern belle in such a setting. Wisteria grows over the porch arbor and Grecian columns flank the pool.

Not surprisingly, a favorite bedroom at the Manor is the Honeymoon Suite, which has bright green walls, a four-poster bed, tiled fireplace, walk-in closet, a loveseat in the sitting area, and an Oriental rug on the natural pine floors. The bathroom has a pedestal sink, brass and porcelain fixtures, built-in drawers original to the house, and a spanking new shower as well as an old tub. The large bathroom also has a bay window with a padded window seat decorated with white embroidered pillows. The one very modern note in the Honeymoon Suite is the 52-inch TV opposite the four-poster, which the Rays seem to feel guests expect today.

The Louie Room, down the second-floor hallway from the Honeymoon Suite, is furnished with a full bedstead in tiger maple, an armoire with a beveled glass mirror, and an Oriental rug on the natural wood floor. Bouquets of false flowers decorate some surfaces, evidence of a slight fussiness in the house that is perhaps part of the southern Victorian look.

The third floor has three private suites, where Kathy has made the most of interesting angles created by the eaves. Here, original matchstick paneling has been painted in soft colors, and the focus of the rooms is often the unusual bedsteads. The beds have a pretty Battenberg lace coverlet or a richly figured spread. Plush carpeting covers the floor.

All of the suites and rooms have private baths that nicely combine new and old features, as well as telephones and TVs — usually large-screen models.

Though Kathy and Jerry could play the role of lord and lady of the manor, they are down-to-earth southerners who came late to the pleasures of antique collecting and historic homes. They stand ready to make a visit as pleasurable and, for their business clients, as efficient, as possible.

Jacksonville Beach

Pelican Path B&B

11 North 19th Avenue
Jacksonville Beach, FL 32250
888-749-1177
904-249-1177
Fax: 904-346-5412
ppbandb@aol.com
www.pelicanpath.com

**A California-style beach
house overlooking the
Atlantic**

Innkeepers: Joan and Tom Hubbard. **Accommodations:** 4 rooms. **Rates:** $80–
$175; rates lower Monday–Thursday; $20 for extra person in room; special
packages; corporate and extended-stay rates available. **Included:** Full
breakfast. **Added:** 12.5% tax. **Minimum stay:** During some holidays and special
events. **Payment:** Major credit cards, traveler's checks. **Children:** Adults only.
Smoking: Outside only. **Open:** Year-round.

➤ **Innkeepers Tom and Joan Hubbard have two names for their B&B:
Pelican Path and *Lieu de Loisir* (French for "a place of leisure"). Both
names are extremely appropriate for this beachside getaway. Tom and
Joan have made every effort to provide a relaxing adults-only retreat.**

The house itself is a square-rigger style with an exterior of tabby
cement stones on the first floor and vinyl siding on the second and
third floors. The place is patterned after the San Francisco hillside

houses that Joan and Tom admired on a West Coast trip they took shortly before designing and building their B&B.

Built in 1998, Pelican Path sits astride a long narrow lot, with a large shingled house a few feet from it on the left and the town's Oceanfront Park pavilion on the right. A narrow street, almost like a private drive, runs past it, on which there are other large beach houses. Parking is easy here because adjacent to the Hubbards' driveway and garage is the parking lot for the town's small Ocean-front Park. This northern end of Jacksonville Beach is more upscale than the southern end, with some newly constructed, fairly expensive houses built right on the beach. But all of Jax Beach, as it is fondly called, is pretty down-to-earth, no matter what the price tag of the houses.

The heart of the Pelican Path B&B is the first-floor great room, furnished in informal bamboo. A full breakfast is served here every morning from 7:30 till 9 at tables overlooking the water. After breakfast and in the evening, the tables serve as places for board games, puzzles, and impromptu card games. If it's a chilly evening, a fire burns in the fireplace opposite the comfortable couch. It is in this space that guests have what Joan and Tom call the Pelican Path's "indoor experience." For an outdoor experience, sliders open onto a furnished deck and a short flight of steps leads out to a small grassy back yard furnished with lawn chairs and a table and then to sand dunes and sea grass and the booming Atlantic beyond.

It is quite acceptable to stay here for a long weekend and do absolutely nothing at all. But if you're game, there are fishing and boating nearby, a day trip to Amelia Island on the ferry, visits to revitalized downtown and harborside Jacksonville, bicycling on bikes provided by Joan and Tom, and swimming a few steps from the back door. There's also wonderful bird-watching.

The presence of water birds is so pleasantly ubiquitous here that the Hubbards have named each of their four guest rooms after shore birds. Royal Tern and Skimmer are oceanfront rooms with sliders to private balconies. The railed balconies are furnished with cushioned PVC chairs and chaise longues. The rooms have a king-size bed, VCR, and a whirlpool tub in the modern bathroom. Mini-blinds are on the contemporary-style windows rather than curtains or drapes. Colors are light, with ivory plaster walls, bleached bamboo furniture, and white and brass paddle fans above.

The other two rooms, Ruddy Turnstone and Sanderling, have the same light color scheme with white wicker furniture, a queen-size bed, and a modern-style bay window that gives a sidelong view of the ocean. If you can afford it, the oceanfront rooms are worth the extra expense. Off-season (November to February) the prices on all guest rooms are reduced, and there's a further reduction on week-day evenings. All rooms have a small refrigerator, coffee maker, hair dryer, telephone, and cable TV.

The breakfast that is included in the room rate is filling and very good: an entree of eggs, waffles, or egg casserole with bacon or ham, and plenty of homemade sweet bread, fruit juice, and fresh fruit to complete the meal. In the evening, Joan and Tom can direct you to some excellent restaurants within easy driving distance of their B&B.

When you're looking forward to a vacation on the beach, it is sometimes easy to forget that Jacksonville is Florida's largest city, and traffic going out of both the downtown area and the airport can be fast and heavy. If you're not in a hurry, consider taking Route 90/212 east to Jacksonville Beach, rather than Route 202, also called J. T. Butler Boulevard. Butler/202 is a fast, busy highway and, on one of the entries to it from Jacksonville, it's easy to get side-tracked if you get caught in the right lane during rush hour. Route 90/212 has some traffic lights and a couple of tacky "miracle miles," but there are also some nice stretches. In general, it's a more "beachy" and less hectic route to the ocean. Once you're here, the beach and birds encourage a feeling of leisure and peace, and you can forget that cities even exist.

Jupiter

Jupiter Beach Resort

5 North A1A
Jupiter, FL 33477
800-228-8810
561-746-2511
Fax: 561-744-1741

A pleasant retreat on uncrowded Jupiter Beach

Manager: Christine Clifford. **Accommodations:** 148 rooms and 45 suites. **Rates:** Rooms $115–$360, suites $125–$450, penthouse suites $400–$1,000; packages available; $15 charge for rollaway; no charge for crib. **Minimum stay:** With some packages and high-season weekends. **Added:** 10% tax. **Payment:** Major credit cards. **Children:** 17 and under free in room with parent. **Smoking:** Non-smoking rooms available. **Open:** Year-round.

➤ **An elevated boardwalk meanders from the pool patio down to the breezy beach. Sea oats, sea grapes, and many wildflowers and vines grow on the dunes.**

Compared with other towns in Palm Beach County, Jupiter is little known. Jupiter Inlet Colony and Jupiter Island have now become more exclusive than the town of Palm Beach. Once a small fishing village, Jupiter has grown enormously in the past twenty-five years; however, there is still an uncrowded, nautical feel to the area, and it's possible to find a place to park your car near the beach even on the weekends.

At the Jupiter Beach Resort, however, you need not worry about parking. You can do it yourself or ask the valet. The hotel is luxurious but informal. The decor and atmosphere often remind visitors of a Caribbean resort. Staff members make you feel at home, and their name tags, with their hometown included, remind you that lots of people here are from someplace else.

A variety of accommodations is available, from standard rooms (lower floors overlook the parking lot, but higher floors have good views) to deluxe oceanfront suites. Furnishings are wicker and bamboo, and an armoire holds a stocked mini-bar and cable TV (with interactive services like bill review and video checkout). Other amenities include in-room message system, coffeemaker, complimentary coffee, cotton robes, and a newspaper delivered to your door in the morning. Bed choices are two doubles, a queen, or a king. The color scheme is Caribbean and gauzy mosquito netting hangs above the bed. The new marble bathrooms feature pedestal sinks and oversize mirrors; the usual toiletries are blessed with the helpful addition of beach-tar remover. Balconies are tiny, even on the expensive Oceanview rooms, with just enough room for two wicker chairs. But the views are super: Jupiter Inlet and Jupiter Island, the Intracoastal Waterway, and the Atlantic beyond.

Most people eat at festive Sinclair's Ocean Grill or on the patio outside overlooking the pool. Food is more than adequate, and the Sunday brunch is especially good. Cuisine is a combination of Caribbean and Pacific Rim with a little traditional Floridian, such as fresh grouper and yellowtail snapper. Main dishes are complemented by native vegetables. Desserts are often flavored with native fruits and nuts.

Other restaurants include a café and an ice cream parlor. The Cabana is a friendly bar by the lobby where you can get anything from healthful fruit drinks to rum drinks to hearty meals. Service is friendly and efficient. Those on an extended stay who wish to venture out to area restaurants might try Ruth's Chris Steakhouse in North Palm Beach or Nick's Tomato Pie for Italian cuisine.

Jupiter Beach Resort is the site of a number of meetings and conferences for area businesses. The conference staff tries to make such business events productive and pleasant. For the most part they succeed, though there is a problem with understaffing during some business dinners. If the evening is scheduled to begin with cocktails at 6:30 and dinner at 7, it may be 8:30 before everyone is served an entrée. Business services include multiparty conference calling and fax services. Also helpful is the multilingual concierge. Meeting rooms are at the far end of the resort, away from the beach and Sinclair's Grill. In between are the spacious lobby and lounge, where soft music is played on a grand piano. Both resort guests and residents of nearby communities enjoy relaxing here.

The back of the resort is organized around the beach and the patio and pool. There's also tennis, a game room, and a fitness center with cardiovascular equipment and weight machines. At nearby marinas, sailing, windsurfing, snorkeling, boating, and fishing are available by the hour or by the day.

Jupiter Reef Club

1600 So. A1A
Jupiter, FL 33477
561-747-7788, ext. 1
Fax: 561-743-0577

A restful getaway on a breezy turquoise ocean

Manager: Kathi Poteet. **Accommodations:** 31 condos (22 1-bedroom/1 bath, 5 2-bedroom/1 bath, 4 2-bedroom/2 bath). **Rates:** $105–$225. **Minimum stay:** 2 nights. **Added:** 10% tax. **Payment:** Visa, MasterCard, traveler's checks, personal checks. **Children:** Free in condo with parent; $25 weekly crib rental. **Smoking:** Allowed. **Open:** Year-round.

➤ **The Jupiter Reef Club definitely caters to people who enjoy the out-of-doors.**

The Jupiter Reef Club is a club, a time-share, a resort. Rentals are available to the general public for as short a time as two nights, though most people come here for a long weekend or more. The atmosphere is very relaxed.

The Club is located on the main beach drag in Jupiter, narrow Highway A1A. But because this is upscale Jupiter, that fact does not mean there are hot dog stands and dive shops crammed along the road. The Club's neighbors are a few condo high rises, some private homes, and several exclusive developments with architecture reminiscent of Key West Victorian mansions. There *is* some traffic on the road, as well as cars parked along the side, since parking lots for beachgoers fill up by noon, but the traffic is minimal compared with other beach towns in Florida.

When visitors first arrive at the Jupiter Reef Club, they park in one of the private lots just off A1A and then take steps down to the units and the recreational area overlooking the ocean — so there's a feeling of being sheltered and "away from it all."

The exterior of the rustic-looking building is sided with stained cedar and accented with "Harmony Stone." The generous use of these irregular chunks of tan and pumpkin-colored stone on the face of the building, in landscaping walls, the barbecue grills, and the terrace give the Club a solid, handsome visage. Landscaping is quite natural, with native Florida plants and beach grasses and, in between concrete pathways and stone steps, some lawn and flowers.

The Club is a U-shaped building with one-story condo units on the sides and a block of two-story, two-bedroom condos in the center. The most expensive condos have a living/dining area, bath, and kitchen on the first floor and two bedrooms and a bath on the second. Other two-bedroom units have all the rooms on one floor, either the first or second. Most accommodations are one-bedrooms with a one-person kitchen. All accommodations have at least a small patio on the first floor, and some two-bedroom units have a railed deck on the second floor as well. Most units have at least a partial ocean view.

The living/dining area of each type of accommodation is attractively furnished with a sofa and easy chair as well as a dining table for four. If the terrace is too windy, guests usually eat inside. But even in a strong ocean breeze, a great many people take their meals outside. The terrace has a pool and Jacuzzi, a large gazebo, umbrella-shaded tables near the barbecue grills, and a ring of comfortable chaises and deck chairs around the terrace. Steps lead down to the beach and the ocean. The beach is a little narrow here, but you can walk north or south for a wider beach.

The terrace is very private — just members of the Club and overnight guests — but the atmosphere does not seem cliquey. People are quite sociable and amiably share grills. Yet you can also just sit in the sun by yourself and talk to no one if you prefer. Either way, there's no pressure. Most people are here to swim and relax, perhaps take a long walk on the beach in the evening. But there is recreation and entertainment close by, fishing and boating at the marinas, golfing on municipal courses, canoe trips down the Loxahatchee River, polo games in Wellington, and shopping on Worth Avenue in Palm Beach and at the nearby Gardens mall. Still, once you get into the rhythm of lazy days at the Jupiter Reef Club, it's pretty hard to leave.

Jupiter Waterfront Inn

18903 S.E. Federal Highway
Jupiter, FL 33469
561-747-9085

A budget suite motel on the Intracoastal

Accommodations: 36 suites. **Rates:** Jacuzzi suites $109–$199, 2-queen suites $99–$179; weekly and monthly rates available. **Included:** Continental breakfast. **Minimum stay:** None. **Added:** 7% tax; $8 extra adult depending on season and day of week. **Payment:** Major credit cards. **Children:** 13 and under free in room with parents. **Smoking:** Nonsmoking rooms available. **Open:** Year-round.

➤ **For water sports and boating, there are marinas just down the road where visitors can also get information about the best places for fishing.**

The Jupiter Waterfront Inn is an upscale motel located just off Route 1, also called Federal Highway. Although Route 1 is congested and lined with dozens of gas stations and shopping malls farther south, the stores and the traffic thin significantly in Jupiter. By the time the highway winds up the coast to this motel, there are only trees and dunes on the west side of the road and houses and marinas on the east side. The Jupiter Waterfront Inn fits right in, with its coral-colored siding and Florida-style tin roof. The motel is set back a bit and, in spite of being on a highway, there is little noise this far from the town center.

Guest rooms face the Intracoastal and a newly landscaped patio and pool. It's pleasant to sit out here night or day: this stretch of the Intracoastal is especially beautiful. The view extends over a wide strip of water, a small island, then more water and Jupiter Island, and finally the Atlantic. It's not heavily populated, and manatees and many waterfowl come to feed here. There are boats and jet skis on the water, especially on the weekends, so it would be inaccurate to say this is a remote, untouched area, but it is peaceful in spite of the recreational activity. A wooden pier stretches out over the water, with stairs that lead down to a small beach (though most guests choose to swim in the pool). A tiled Jacuzzi wreathed in green plants is built a few feet above the pool so that guests have a slightly elevated view of the waterway while they soak. Each room has a small patio or balcony with vinyl furniture.

In addition to the outdoor Jacuzzi available for all guests to use, several of the suites have Jacuzzis right in the room. These accommodations cost a bit more than the two-queen suites during the off-season, but they're the same price during high season, so request a Jacuzzi suite when you make your reservations. Further reductions in the room rates are available for extended stays in the high season if you call two or more months in advance. The Jacuzzi suites have a sitting area with a foldout couch, coffee table, a small square table, and sliders to a small patio or balcony with a water view. The kitchenette has a Formica countertop and sink with a little refrigerator beneath, and the bedroom has a queen- or king-size bed. Except for the Jacuzzi, there is no tub, but the shower is oversize and includes a little seat.

Furniture in the guest rooms looks like blond oak but is actually a good imitation in Formica. Families with older children or couples traveling together can request rooms with connecting doors.

The regular or "Queen" suites are similar in decor to the Jacuzzi suites but have two beds instead of one and are therefore more economical for a family. The bathrooms have a tub shower. One or two more kids can be bedded down on a foldout couch in the sitting area overlooking the patio, though you'd want to spend a lot of time outside to avoid feeling too cramped. These suites also have a small countertop and a sink with cupboards beneath, although there is no fridge. There's also a small square table with two chairs. Some units have begun to look a bit worn recently, with paint peeling above the kitchen counter and rusty areas around the doors.

On the patio near the pool is a small barbecue grill. Simple meals can be prepared if you're in a Jacuzzi suite with a refrigerator, but most guests eat in Jupiter or nearby Tequesta, where there are several reasonably priced restaurants and pizza places. In the morning, the motel has a complimentary Continental breakfast of orange juice, coffee, tea, cereal, bagels, and pastries. These are served at a long counter in the reception center where there are two round kitchen tables. Some folks take breakfast back to their rooms or eat on their patio.

There is a small laundry room by the reception area, and dry-cleaning establishments and supermarkets in Jupiter and Tequesta.

Nearby attractions include the Jupiter Lighthouse, a dinner theatre, and peaceful Jonathan Dickenson State Park. Hobe Sound, just up the highway, has a nice walking beach. Forty minutes farther up the coast is the town of Stuart, which looks like any other overdeveloped Florida town until you get to the northern end. Just east of Federal Highway is a small regional theater and a historic district with some interesting little shops and restaurants — a real town, a rarity in modern Florida. A visit here is of greater interest to adults than kids, though there is a wonderful shop called Rare Earth Pottery where the potters will make stoneware plates incorporating the impressions of small hands.

New Smyrna Beach

Night Swan Intracoastal B&B

512 South Riverside Drive
New Smyrna Beach, FL 32168
800-465-4261
904-423-4940
www.NightSwan.com

A homey B&B that affords beautiful views of the Intracoastal by day and restful sleep by night

Innkeepers and owners: Chuck and Martha Nighswonger. **Accommodations:** 16 rooms. **Rates:** $85–$160. **Included:** Full breakfast. **Minimum stay:** 2–7 nights during holiday and special events. **Payment:** Major credit cards, personal checks, traveler's checks. **Children:** Welcome with watchful parents. **Smoking:** Allowed on open porches. **Open:** Year-round.

➤ **Chuck and Martha Nighswonger are friendly, kind people who have run their B&B for several years, and, yes, their name does mean "Night Swan" — in Swiss German.**

The Night Swan is now made up of three houses: the original B&B on the corner of Anderson Street and Riverside Drive, a small cottage behind it on Anderson Street, and another house of similar architecture next door that shares the grassy lawn between. Both of the houses are solid, turn-of-the-century family homes that have porches (some open, some enclosed), dormers, a mix of clapboards and fishtail shingles, and substantial brick chimneys. The little cottage behind the main house is a bungalow and shares a big oak tree with it.

The three houses are not actually on the Intracoastal Waterway — few houses on this section of it are — but are just across from it. So guests do have to cross the street to get to the B&B's dock, though traffic is pretty light. The neighborhood is part of the historic part of New Smyrna Beach; the beach itself is a short distance over a bridge. Some of the beach area is a little like Daytona and overbuilt; some of it is funky and charming. Hotels and B&Bs on the waterway have a more peaceful atmosphere than those on the beach, so the Night Swan is a good choice if that's the ambiance you want, and it is certainly close to everything.

Besides going to the beach, you can rent boats for sailing, charter a deep-sea vessel, and go golfing nearby. The Night Swan's dock is a nice place to laze around and watch water birds and dolphins, as are the front porches. The B&B is located in a pleasant family neighborhood, so there's also much to be said for a good old-fashioned walk along the tree-lined streets.

Martha and Chuck are good cooks and give guests a choice of having a full breakfast in the dining room or a Continental one on the porch, the dock, or in their room. The full breakfast might be stuffed French toast one day and an egg casserole the next. Martha prides herself on not repeating the same meal twice during a week-long stay. Portions are generous, but for those on a diet, Martha has some low-cholesterol breakfast entrées, too.

With three houses to choose from, there is a good deal of variety in guest rooms. The walls are generally painted or papered in soft colors; the large attic rooms on the third floor of the main house have natural wood bead board. The period wooden bedsteads in all of the rooms are covered with quilts or chenille or woven spreads. Curtains at the double hung windows look homemade. A room might have a desk or a trunk or slipcovered wing chair; each is decorated a little differently, as in a family home. A private bath complements the room's decor, and each comes in a variety of sizes and shapes. Views are of the waterway; the treetops of magnolias, old oaks, or palms; or the broad lawn that runs between the two houses on Riverside Drive.

The living room in the main house is a gathering place at the B&B, especially in the winter. Wing chairs and an old-fashioned mahogany and brocade sofa are on each side of the brick fireplace. In one corner is a baby grand piano and, as Chuck says, "piano players are welcome." On each side of the fireplace are wooden bookcases, and guests are free to peruse the selections during their stay. Pull up a chair and make yourself at home.

Riverview Hotel

103 Flagler Avenue
New Smyrna Beach, FL 32069
904-428-5858

A historic B&B with old-fashioned comfort

Owners: Christa and Jim Kelsey. **Accommodations:** 18 rooms and suites. **Rates:** Rooms $80–$100, suites $130–$150; cottage $200; corporate rates available Sunday-Thursday. **Included:** Expanded Continental breakfast. **Minimum stay:** None, except on special event weekends. **Added:** 10% tax; $10 extra person. **Payment:** Major credit cards. **Children:** Well-behaved children welcome; under age 5 free in room with parent. **Smoking:** Discouraged. **Open:** Year-round.

➤ **Nightly turndown service includes chocolates on the pillow, dimmed lights, and terry robes on the bed. In the morning, guests are given breakfast in bed: warm pastries, bowls of fresh fruit, cereal, juice, and coffee, along with a newspaper. Many guests enjoy their breakfast on their private patio or balcony.**

The beautifully restored Riverview Hotel stands near a bridge over the Indian River, part of the Intracoastal Waterway. The house is architecturally Old Florida, with a gray tin roof, pink wooden clapboards, and lots of railed verandas. The house is two stories in some sections, three in the older sections. Old-fashioned cloth awnings shade the verandas on the second and third floors.

Originally the home of the bridge-tender, the Riverview was built in 1886 and restored in the 1980s by Cissie and John Spang, who earlier refurbished the Park Plaza Hotel in Winter Park. They did an excellent job here, restoring the old pine floors and covering them with fine Oriental rugs. Much of the furniture in common rooms and guest rooms is natural or painted wicker. There are good reproductions and some antiques. In the large common room by the reception area, French doors open onto a brick patio.

The guest rooms have wood ceilings and paddle fans, wicker and oak furniture, wood blinds, and antique embellishments. Baths are modern, with an old-fashioned feel. French doors on the first floor open to the patio and pool. Balconies on the second floor overlook the pool; these rooms are very romantic. The patio is pretty, with wicker baskets and clay pots of flowers on the brick pavement and an ivy-covered fence offering a screen from the street and bridge. The pool is kept very clean and has a colorful Italian tile border. Brown Jordan chaises are placed around the pool.

Poolside rooms and veranda rooms have wicker chairs or love-seats just outside the French doors. Guests can have their breakfast served here or in their rooms. There is no dining room in the hotel, so most guests have lunch at the Eurocafe next door or at one of the little places on the beach. Riverview Charlie's, the restaurant adjacent to the hotel, is great for seafood at dinner. Built of 100-year-old brick and old beams, Riverview Charlie's has docking facilities and covered dining.

The hotel now has an adjoining two-bedroom cottage that includes a two-person Jacuzzi. The cottage sleeps four for no additional charge and has all of the amenities of the hotel.

The Riverview is on Flagler Avenue, with a circular drive and a brick sidewalk in front. The owners have seen to it that there is ample parking. New Smyrna Beach is similar to Daytona (a little tacky but with a wide sandy beach), and the shops and boutiques in the old part of the town are fun to poke around in. Many guests love staying in the middle of this more historic area, with the sound of cars bumping over the Indian River Bridge and the clang of the alarm as the drawbridge is raised. But if you're a light sleeper, request one of the rooms at the far end of the hotel.

Orange Park

The Club Continental on the St. Johns

2143 Astor Street
Orange Park, FL 32073
800-877-6070
904-264-6070
Fax: 904-215-9503

> **Luxury Italian Renaissance accommodations at a budget price**

Owners: The Massee family. **Accommodations:** 22 suites. **Rates:** Rooms $65–$110, 1-room suites $110–$160, 2-room suites $145, tower apartment $1,600 monthly; other discounts available. **Included:** Continental breakfast. **Minimum stay:** None. **Added:** 10% tax. **Payment:** Major credit cards. **Children:** Welcome. **Smoking:** Nonsmoking rooms available. **Open:** Year-round.

➤ **The peaceful waters of the St. Johns River are a presence everywhere at the Club Continental. The estate is located on the widest part of the river, so it is almost like looking out over a small lake. A romantic stone balustrade that runs along the river is a lovely place to walk in the evening.**

The Club Continental was built as a private summer home in 1923 by Caleb Johnson, heir to the Johnson (later Palmolive) Soap Company fortune. At the time, Orange Park had no electricity or paved streets. Johnson and his family loved the remoteness of the country and named their Mediterranean estate Miro Rio. (Today, the Club is an easy 15 miles south of the metropolis of Jacksonville.) Eventually, the estate came down to Margaret Johnson Massee's son, Jon, who had the idea of making the estate into a private club in the 1960s. Renamed Club Continental, the place became synonymous with fine dining, Mediterranean elegance, and southern graciousness. Jon's son, Caleb Massee, his sisters Karrie and Jeanne, and mother, Frederica, now manage the club. It is a combination private dining and country club, a resort, and an inn with surprisingly reasonable rates.

Guests turn off busy Orange Park streets into residential Astor Street and pass through the lacy iron gates of the Continental Club into what seems like a different era and perhaps a different country. Magnolias and huge live oaks shade the parklike grounds. A circular drive curves up to a fountained courtyard and then to the arched doorway of the vine-covered mansion. The architecture and interior decor are Mediterranean, with ornate columns, coffered ceilings, leaded windows, carved stone reliefs, wrought-iron filigreed lamps, and lovely archways.

For all its elegance, the place has a lived-in feel. The stucco in the original building is a bit stained. The walls of the foyer have never been painted and have a mellow patina. Leaves that fall in the courtyard are not swept away immediately by an overly efficient gardener. Flowers that begin to fade are not always replaced right away — all part of the relaxed Continental ambience. This is not an immaculately manicured resort but a family home and club still lovingly cared for by the Massees. Karrie or Jon Massee is often at the reception desk, on hand to describe the history of the place or to help with checkout.

Just beyond the elegant staircase is the club lounge, originally the mansion's morning room, now decorated with family photos. Archways lead to what was once the drawing room, now frequently used for dining and for wedding receptions. Ornate black wrought-iron rods hold the drapes at the French windows that lead to a vine-covered loggia. Leaded-glass windows flank a carved stone fireplace. At the other end of the house is another loggia that Jon Massee enclosed to create a club dining room overlooking the garden and the St. Johns River. Another smaller room in back is furnished with pieces that Frieka Massee found in the attic: an antique European tapestry and an old marble table with intricate iron and brass embellishments.

The dining room, open only to club members and overnight guests, is well known in the area for its Continental and American cuisine. A typical dinner might begin with Parmesan oysters or a creamy onion soup flavored with white wine and ginger, then proceed to Norwegian salmon or a rich veal Continental, followed by pecan torte. It may be difficult to get dinner reservations on a Saturday night if there is a wedding reception scheduled, but this is almost made up for by the excellent Sunday brunch, which includes offerings such as creamy shrimp and artichoke soup, eggs Benedict, and soft-shell crabs. The daily complimentary Continental breakfast for guests usually includes homemade pastries, an assortment of cereals, and fruit.

Overlooking the river outside the dining room loggia is a landscaped terrace that wraps around the side of the house to the swimming pools and kids' wading pool. Just beyond the drive are the tennis courts. The tennis pro is quite popular here, and the facilities include seven courts, two of which are lighted for night play. On a sandy spot under the oaks just in front of the tennis courts is a volleyball net for pickup games. A few hundred feet away is a marina with 85 slips available for guests' boats, with advance request. The club can also arrange for sailboat charters.

Expansive river views are part of the experience in most of the rooms. The original mansion has four rooms and two suites on the second floor and an apartment on the third, called the Inn at Club Continental. Room names like the Mexican Room or the English Room reflect the origin of furnishings that were brought back from the Massees' travels. The tower apartment has been recently refurbished and has a well-equipped kitchen, a living room with cushioned bamboo sofas, French doors to a newly tiled balcony, a king-size bed and a daybed, and a private bathroom with the original ceramic tile still intact. The apartment is a good choice for a family or for anyone planning a long stay.

Also appropriate for extended stays are the suites in the Winterbourne, another mansion on the grounds, which was built in 1870 and restored by Mrs. Massee in the 1950s. There is no maid service here, so these accommodations are really like renting a small home. All have period furnishings and private baths. Most suites have views of the water, though any view of the grounds is attractive. The spacious drawing room is often the site of weddings and receptions. A pillared porch runs along the front of the house, and a wide lawn sweeps down to the river.

The newest accommodations are in a two-story, balustraded building that beautifully matches the Mediterranean architecture of the club, down to the texture and color of the stucco. These rooms, called Continental suites, have a king- or queen-size bed, spacious private baths (some with Jacuzzis), tiled balconies, and river views. Room 201 is wheelchair-accessible and one of three rooms that have two queen-size beds. Room 204 has an antique fireplace, a king-size bed, a spacious sitting area, reproduction and antique furniture, and a hand-painted mural in the large bathroom. The fireplace and Jacuzzi suites here are an amazing bargain: reasonable on winter weekends and even less expensive Sunday through Thursday or off-season.

Next door to the Continental Suites is the River House Pub, an Old Florida-style cottage with white clapboards and a tin roof that could be straight out of Key West. Used as a golf clubhouse after the Civil War, it is reputed to be the oldest clubhouse in Florida. It was destined for demolition until Frederica Massee bought the old place and had it moved here by the river. Now a smoky little game club and pub, the River House is popular with a mix of blue-collar workers and wealthy sages who love to come here to shoot the breeze, listen to the live entertainment, and play poker. Jeanne Massee Patterson and her husband, Bill, run the place as an informal complement to the Continental's dining club. Outback is a wonderful multilevel deck that has a pool table, subtropical plantings, wood swings, plenty of room for parties, and a superlative view of the St. Johns.

The Massees are a resourceful and interesting family, and they run the Club as a labor of love. If there is a disadvantage to having the third and fourth generations of a family run such an enterprise, it is that occasionally there seems to be some confusion as to the division of labor among the Massees; perhaps the place is too much like home. For example, sometimes no one is at the reception desk when a guest wants to check in or out, and it is unclear who was supposed to be there. However, this is a small price to pay for old-world ambience, excellent dining, and bargain suites.

Palm Coast

Palm Coast Golf Resort

300 Clubhouse Drive
Palm Coast, FL 32037
800-654-6538
904-445-3000

A large, lush resort complex on the Intracoastal

Accommodations: 154 rooms. **Rates:** Rooms $85–$140; rates lowest on weeknights, packages available. **Minimum stay:** With some packages. **Added:** 9% tax. **Payment:** Major credit cards. **Children:** Under 17 free in room with parents. **Smoking:** Nonsmoking rooms available. **Open:** Year-round.

➤ **The big draws here are the views and the sporting activities. The beach and the club are just a few minutes away by shuttle. The ocean is warm, and the waves are big enough for some body-surfing but not so big that they overwhelm children.**

All guest rooms at the Palm Coast Golf Resort overlook the water — either the Intracoastal or the resort's marina. The Palm Coast is part of a residential resort community sculpted out of 42,000 acres of scrub palm and pine forests by ITT several years ago. It has become a popular place for golf, tennis, and boating and is now under new ownership and management.

Guest rooms have king-size beds or two doubles, and rooms are spacious enough for a family. The appointments are basic oak hotel furniture, but the bedspreads and coordinating drapes are attractive and the carpets are thick underfoot.

For freshwater swimming, there are three pools as well as whirlpool spas. Fishing rods, boats, and bicycles, including tandems, can be rented. The resort is also easy driving distance to the beach.

Golf is excellent, with four 18-hole courses. Arnold Palmer designed the challenging Matanzas Woods and Pine Lakes, a long course with lots of water and sand hazards, and Gary Player designed Cypress Knoll. Pretty Palm Harbor has native oaks and palms and fairways that pros describe as "testy." Tennis here is world-class, with three surfaces: clay, hard, and grass. There are 16 courts, with some lit for night play. The Players Club tennis complex includes a clubhouse restaurant and a pro shop.

Many companies hold small meetings and conferences here. The resort's seven meeting and banquet rooms can accommodate groups from 10 to 300. An open-air, waterfront pavilion of natural wood is pleasant for outdoor parties. A conference staff attends to the details, from banquets to audiovisual needs to transportation.

The resort's restaurant serves breakfast, lunch, and dinner, and a generous buffet on Sundays. Cocktails and after-dinner drinks are served in the lounge, where there is live entertainment. Like the restaurant, this has a lovely view of the pool and marina at night. The marina (at Marker 803 on the Intracoastal Waterway) has 80 slips — enough to accommodate you if you call ahead and small enough to be friendly.

Ponte Vedra Beach

The Lodge & Club

607 Ponte Vedra Boulevard
Ponte Vedra Beach, FL 32082
800-243-4304
904-273-9500

**A Mediterranean-style
beach and fitness club**

Accommodations: 66 rooms and suites. **Rates:** Rooms $160–$335, suites $230–$365; packages available; daily service charge in lieu of gratuities. **Minimum stay:** Two nights with packages. **Added:** 9% tax. **Payment:** Major credit cards. **Children:** Under 17 free in room with parents. **Smoking:** Nonsmoking rooms available. **Open:** Year-round.

➤ **The patio, paved with brick and tabby, has a beautifully tiled Mediter-ranean-style fountain and courtyard. Tiered flowerbeds, bordered in tiles with a shell motif, rise above the main swimming pool, which overlooks Ponte Vedra Beach.**

The town of Ponte Vedra is rather upscale; the oceanside homes north and south of the lodge are some of the most attractive in Florida. The Lodge & Club at Ponte Vedra Beach reflects both the exclusive clubbiness of the area and its sporting informality. Those who know the Lodge consider it a special place. The rates are far more reasonable than they are at points farther south, and the crowds are thinner.

The low-rise buildings of the lodge are buff-colored stucco. The arched windows sport blue-green awnings. The Mediterranean de-tails and Spanish red-tile roofs give it the aura of a 1920s country club. Guests enter the resort through leaded-glass double doors to a terra-cotta-tiled entryway. Upstairs, there's a spectacular dining room with lots of windows overlooking the ocean.

Conference rooms are found in this upstairs area and also down-stairs. The meeting space includes 2,500 square feet indoors and 4,000 square feet outside, ideal for outdoor banquets and recep-tions. All the meeting space overlooks the ocean. One reason the club is so successful for meetings as well as vacations is the serv-ice. There is a great sensitivity to guests' needs here. A maid qui-etly sweeps the terra cotta tiles outside a conference room while a meeting takes place, rather than vacuuming. Staff members pride themselves on having "five-star spirit."

The rooms also deserve five stars. Every accommodation has at least one balcony — many have two. The furniture is bleached oak. All bathrooms are very large and have a long vanity counter, Jacuzzi, shower, robes, safes, and mini-bars.

The oceanfront suite is the lodge's most expensive accommodation. It features a full kitchen with aqua tile counters and bleached oak cabinets. The living room has a balcony and a fireplace flanked by comfortable sofas. Another balcony is just off the bedroom. All accommodations have a cushioned window seat and a king- or queen-size bed. The bathroom has a small TV and a makeup mirror in addition to the standard luxuries. The Superior Corner rooms, with two queen-size beds and two balconies, are the best value for a family. These are actually the lodge's standard rooms, but they are a cut above the usual hotel standard.

The decor throughout the hotel includes lovely artwork. Many of the public areas have vaulted wooden ceilings and detailed stonework. The attention to design is found in all the outdoor recreational areas, too. Masonry walls around the fitness center and pool area are bordered with aqua tiles. Windows have little wells beneath them for flowers and Mediterranean detailing above.

The Lodge has a children's pool, an adult pool that is heated year-round, and a big whirlpool partially enclosed by a tiled wall — a lion's head at its center spouts water. A renovation in 1996 created an expanded aerobics room, a larger exercise room with additional state-of-the-art equipment, and direct access to the lap pool from these rooms. From the pool, one can look out to the Atlantic.

The beach is accessible via wooden stairways over the low sand dunes and vegetation. In summer, especially, the beach is a favorite gathering place for adults and children of all ages. The water is warm, and there's always a cool breeze. For those who seek other activity, there are several excellent tennis courts and golf courses nearby.

Ponte Vedra Inn & Club

200 Ponte Vedra Boulevard
Ponte Vedra Beach, FL 32082
800-234-7842
904-285-1111

| **A gracious club with luxury accommodations on the ocean** |

General Manager: Dale Haney. **Accommodations:** 222 rooms and suites. **Rates:** Rooms $160–$295, suites $200–$395; meal plans and packages available. **Minimum stay:** 2 or 3 nights with some packages. **Added:** 9% tax. **Payment:** Major credit cards. **Children:** Under 16 free in room with parents. **Smoking:** Nonsmoking rooms available. **Open:** Year-round.

➤ **There is plenty to do here besides swimming and sunbathing. It is a delight simply to walk the grounds: there are several varieties of palms, massive beds of bright annuals, and lush green lawns. A lagoon meanders through the property, with a golf island in the middle and a small dock.**

The Ponte Vedra Inn & Club was founded in 1928 as a private club. The rooms in the original inn have been converted into executive offices, so guests no longer stay in the old building, but the new buildings are some of the most tastefully decorated accommodations in Florida. They are directly on the beach, along with the fitness center and spa. The various club amenities — the original inn, the golf course, the tennis courts and racket club, the conference center, the restaurants — are on the other side of Ponte Vedra Boulevard beside a subtropical lagoon.

The rooms and suites are tucked into low-rise stucco buildings with names like Beach House, Ocean House, and Summer House. These are set back a bit from the boulevard, with a lawn and parking out front and the ocean and beach in the back. The wide range of accommodations includes standard suites, presidential suites, superior oceanside suites, and large and small deluxe suites.

Although winter is the low season, only one or two days (or no days) of a week's stay may see rain or overcast skies, so it's worthwhile to consider coming then. The resort also offers golf, tennis, spa, and holiday packages. A standard suite has a terrace and large windows overlooking the ocean, a living/dining area, and a charming kitchen with a breakfast bar.

Some bedrooms have padded bentwood bedsteads. Others have four-poster beds. Sliding glass doors call attention to the ocean view. Step outside and you're on a beach of bright, clean sand. The water is deep blue and pleasantly warm. There are usually couples walking along the beach and lots of kids and their parents swimming or playing in the sand. Just a few minutes away on Route A1A is a more dramatic beach with high dunes that sweep down to the ocean. It is worth hiking up to see them, though visitors should stay off the fragile dunes.

For golfers, there's the Golf Club, a pro shop, the Golf Club Restaurant, and two spectacular championship courses — the Lagoon Course and the Ocean Course. Both have enough bunkers and water hazards to keep you busy. Tennis is just as exciting, with 15 Har-Tru courts overlooking the lagoon, seven lighted for night play. Individual instruction is hardly inexpensive here, but the group rate (for a minimum of six players) is affordable at $15.00 per hour. The resort offers some good tennis packages.

The resort's luxury spa, 10,000 square feet in size, is north Florida's largest. More than 100 personal pampering services are available, including massages, facials, fango wraps, body polishes, manicures, and pedicures. Spa packages are also available which include lodging, services, and meals. The fitness center has a complete Cybex circuit, treadmills, stationary bikes, and free weights. Aerobics classes are held throughout the day, and there's a steam room and sauna to relax in.

Ponte Vedra staff members take seriously the resort's tradition of hospitality. They'll go out of their way, literally, to help you find a lost sweater or a stray tennis racket.

The spa and fitness center could do a brisk business just from guests who've overindulged at the resort's five restaurants. Pastries and breads are made at Ponte Vedra's own bakery. The restaurants take pride in providing interesting entrées and offering a wide range of choices, from Continental to Old Southern. Service is warm and gracious, in the southern tradition.

Sawgrass Marriott Resort

1000 PGA Tour Boulevard
Ponte Vedra Beach, FL 32082
800-457-4653
904-285-7777

A conference and sports resort with championship golf

Accommodations: 322 rooms, 24 suites, and 162 villas. **Rates:** Rooms $120–$315, suites $300–$500, villas $165–$285; packages available; lower rates on some weekends. **Minimum stay:** With some packages. **Added:** 9% tax. **Payment:** Major credit cards. **Children:** 17 and under free in room with parents. **Smoking:** Nonsmoking rooms available. **Open:** Year-round.

➤ **In addition to the hotel rooms, there are golf and beach villas. Like all Marriotts, Sawgrass offers some excellent packages.**

As they say at Sawgrass, you can play golf here for nearly a week and never play the same hole twice. The five descriptively named courses are Marsh Landing, Oak Bridge, Valley, Sawgrass Country Club, and the PGA Tournament Players Club Stadium course. The latter includes a 17th hole in the middle of a lagoon.

Golf is the focus, but tennis is also excellent. Four of the eight Har-Tru courts are lighted, and instruction is available for both adults and children. Swimming is at three beautiful pools. The resort's health club features a steam room and sauna, Universal weight equipment, and exercise classes. Off the property, there is horseback riding, deep-sea fishing, and swimming on Ponte Vedra Beach.

The view through floor-to-ceiling windows in the reception area is of a manmade lagoon with a huge outcropping of rocks from which water tumbles back into the lagoon. Beyond that is a free-form swimming pool and a green fairway. A curved stairway from the reception area leads down a level to the Cascade Lounge, which has little waterfalls and tropical beds that are planted with ferns, banana trees, and palms.

Accommodations are divided into "series." Several series 34 rooms overlook this lagoon and the swimming pool. These and the series 100 corner suites are worth requesting if you can afford them. All rooms are luxurious, with thick carpeting, designer fabrics, and large, tiled baths.

Casual but elegant dining is in the critically acclaimed Augustine Grille, a softly lit space with soothing pine green walls, scallop-backed leather banquettes, and golf prints on the walls. Cuisine is expensive but excellent.

More casual is the Café on the Green, overlooking the TPC Course and serving breakfast, lunch, and dinner. Four of the golf clubs have their own dining rooms for lunch and dinner. Cascades, just off the hotel lobby, is good for a sundowner. Champs is a larger, clubbier lounge with a spectacular view of the lagoon and waterfalls. Service is courteous and faster than in many hotels in Florida.

The high-rise architecture of the hotel is a bit institutional, with green-tinted windows and metal grills. But the staff at Sawgrass extends a warm welcome, and the rooms and the excellent recreation make up for the somewhat dull exterior.

St. Augustine

Carriage Way B&B

70 Cuna Street
St. Augustine, FL 32084
800-908-9832
904-829-2467
Fax: 904-826-1461

| A budget B&B in America's oldest city |

Innkeepers: Diane and Bill Johnson. **Accommodations:** 11 rooms, all with private bath. **Rates:** $69–$175; $10 extra adult or child; weekday discounts; senior citizen and travel club discounts. **Included:** Full breakfast; beverages and desserts; bicycles; newspapers. **Minimum stay:** 2 nights with Saturday stay. **Added:** 9% tax. **Payment:** Discover, MasterCard, Visa, personal checks. **Children:** 8 and older welcome. **Smoking:** On verandas only. **Open:** Year-round.

➤ **A fine old Spanish fort, Castillo de San Marcos is just a few minutes' walk from the Carriage Way. The Spanish Quarter has a number of other interesting structures, many of them presenting the crafts and small industries of earlier eras. On a typical day you might happen upon a blacksmith at work or a young woman selling candles or herbs.**

Carriage Way B&B is in Old St. Augustine, on a small corner lot at Cuna and Cordova Streets. The Victorian-style clapboard house is painted a smooth cream with country blue trim—it looks like somebody's grandmother's house, and right away you feel at home. Indeed, the Carriage Way is run by congenial grandparents Diane and Bill Johnson, who bought the inn in 1992, and they have a special way of doing things.

The verandas are among the most appealing features of the house. The narrow veranda on the ground floor is a nice place to watch the world — or at least one's fellow tourists — go by. The upstairs verandas, open to all guests, present a panoramic view of the Old City.

All the guest rooms have dark wood furniture from the turn of the century. Most pieces are simply old; some are real antiques. All give the place a homey, genuine feeling. Most rooms have carpeting in rose or deep green and small-print wallpapers. Some bathrooms have tubs; others have showers. There are telephones but no TVs or radios in the rooms. The house TV is in the parlor.

Just down the street are the newest accommodations, in a restored cottage originally built in 1885. One of the two rooms has a whirlpool tub. Both have the same unpretentious charm of the main house.

Guests can use the downstairs parlor and the dining room any time. There are homemade desserts, cold beverages, and hot tea and coffee in the dining room all day. The complimentary breakfast usually consists of fruit and orange juice, homemade white bread for toast, fruit bread or muffins, an entrée such as waffles, pancakes, or eggs with sausage or bacon, and tea or coffee. Although no lunches or dinners are served, there are sometimes sweet snacks on Saturday evenings, and guests can order special drinks or request a picnic basket for a small additional charge.

After breakfast, most guests go for a walk in the historic neighborhood. If you can do without 20th-century inventions like television in your room, you can probably get along without a car in St. Augustine, even for eating out. It's far more pleasant to walk through the narrow streets of this oldest of American cities than to struggle through in a car, trying to remember which streets run which way. Walking back and forth to this B&B, you'll pass the shops, taverns, and restaurants of the historic Spanish Quarter.

Many people take a horse-drawn carriage tour through the old city. These are all a bit different, with some drivers dressing the part in old-fashioned livery and others wearing simple pants and T-shirts. As the carriages thread through the old streets, the drivers give lively lectures on historic lore and points of interest. Many of the streets in the old section of town are brick, and the clip-clop sound of the horses' hooves is very pleasant. There are also sightseeing tours on small trolleys, and you can pick up a map for a self-guided walking tour from the Visitor Information Center, which has an orientation video.

Casa de la Paz

22 Avenida Menendez
St. Augustine, FL 32084
904-829-2915
800-929-2915

> **Views of the water and Old St. Augustine**

Innkeepers: Bob and Donna Marriott. **Accommodations:** 4 rooms, 2 suites. **Rates:** $120–$225. **Included:** Full breakfast. **Added:** 9% tax. **Payment:** Major credit cards. **Children:** 15 and older welcome. **Smoking:** On verandas and in courtyard only. **Open:** Year-round.

> ➤ **The location of this charming B&B is perfect for exploring the nation's oldest established city.**

Avenida Menendez, named after Admiral Don Pedro Menendez de Aviles, the Spanish founder of St. Augustine, is one of the main thoroughfares of the city's historic district. Many of the rooms in Casa de la Paz have beautiful views of lovely Matanzas Bay, directly across the street.

Walk out the arched door and turn left to explore the Castillo de San Marcos, the Spanish fortress constructed in the 1670s to protect the town from the British and other marauding enemies. The Spanish Quarter, starting on San Marco Avenue and winding through Charlotte, Cuna, and other narrow streets, is adjacent to the fort. The little streets are lined with Victorian and turn-of-the-century houses and interesting shops. This area is commercialized and even cute at times, but still historically interesting. La Parisienne, on Spanish Street, makes a fine lunch stop.

Or turn right and stroll down to another part of St. Augustine's old town. The oldest house in America is off Avenida Menendez on St. Francis Street. The house is built largely of coquina and has a patio where you can rest your feet after you've had your fill of history.

Though Casa de la Paz has a wonderful location for sightseeing, it is also a find in itself. Built in a Mediterranean Revival style, the house has white stucco, teal trim, and exposed timbers under a tile roof. The many windows offer lots of light and much architectural interest. Several are leaded and diamond-paned.

A courtyard in the back has a feeling of both openness and seclusion. The little courtyard patio has a small fountain, mature trees, and low-growing plants outlined by brick walkways.

All of the rooms in the back of the house look out over the yard, so if you can't get one of the water-view rooms in the front of the house, not to worry. Some rooms have a veranda. Each room is a little different—one has a little alcove, another a big well-stocked bookcase, and still another two odd little windows overlooking the water. All are decorated with antiques, such as English theatre seats, circa 1900.

The Captain's Quarters, with its third-floor dormer windows overlooking the bay and the old town, is often in demand. It has a bedroom and small sitting room and is popular with honeymoon and anniversary couples. The bath off the hallway between the rooms, like all the bathrooms, is bright and fresh looking.

Casa de la Paz is a traditional, homey B&B, so if you have no interest in sightseeing, you can simply stay here, reading and relaxing. The solarium in front of the house is furnished with small tables where guests gather for breakfast and at other times of the day. The living room of the house has big windows that look out over the avenue and the bay, and a fireplace flanked with bookshelves.

Throughout the house, elaborate moldings and chair rails accent period wallpapers and clean plaster walls. Most of the floors downstairs are pine—recently refinished, well polished, and graced with fine rugs.

The formal dining room is furnished with attractive Chippendale furniture. The breakfast served here is full: pancakes and baked apples or an egg dish, croissants, homemade muffins or bread, fresh fruit, juice, tea, and coffee. After breakfast, guests often enjoy the sunshine and water views from the solarium across the hall from the dining room.

Casa de Solana

21 Aviles Street
St. Augustine, FL 32084
904-824-3555

> One of the most distinctive historic inns in St. Augustine

Owners: Jim and Faye McMurry. **Accommodations:** 4 suites. **Rates:** $125–$175. **Included:** Breakfast; admission to Oldest House museum. **Minimum stay:** 2 nights on weekends, holidays. **Added:** 9% tax. **Payment:** Major credit cards, personal checks. **Children:** Discouraged because of the antiques. **Smoking:** By the fountain only. **Open:** Year-round.

➤ **The butter at breakfast isn't just a soft slab put on a plate; Faye and her assistant use butter molds to form flowers, swirls, pumpkins, or even Santas, depending on the season and their whim.**

The Casa was built in 1763 for Don Manuel Solana, a Spanish military official. At the time, St. Augustine had fewer than a thousand houses and was shortly taken over by the British. Today, Casa de Solana is the seventh-oldest house in the town. When horse-drawn carriages clip-clop down Aviles Street and pass the corner on which the Casa majestically stands, the drivers point out the house to tourists. So many history buffs and curiosity seekers want to see the house (without staying there as paying guests) that Faye and

Jim McMurry finally had to put up a polite sign on the door explaining that the house is not a museum and is not open except to inn guests. That should be reason enough to become one.

The main house stands squarely on the generous city lot, with an attached carriage house. At one time, there were also slave quarters on the side of the house. Although the McMurrys have obtained city approval to rebuild these for extra accommodations, they later decided against it, preferring to keep the Casa small. The house is made of blocks of coquina, a popular 18th-century building material of native shells that has proved enduring. At the Casa de Solana, the coquina surface has been covered with a thick coat of plaster and painted a sandstone-rose, an historically accurate color for the era. The veranda pillars and trim are painted a dark red-brown, which accentuates the Spanish feel of the house. There are lots of small-paned windows in the house and graceful fanlights above those in the first-floor entryway.

Surrounding the house and garden is a thick stucco wall, painted the same color as the house and covered with ivy, giving the garden a secluded, Mediterranean feel. The front of the house faces Charlotte Street, but house and garden encompass the entire narrow block from Charlotte to Aviles; you enter Casa de Solana through the back gate on Aviles Street. The garden and big lawn (well, big for an old St. Augustine lawn) are the first things you see. A Spanish fountain dominates the courtyard where the McMurrys have placed benches. A neat brick path leads to the entry door.

Inside are polished oak floors and one of the finest collections of antiques and Oriental rugs in St. Augustine. Casa de Solana was built as a grand house, and Faye and Jim have been sensitive stewards of the fine old place, adding some of their own southern elegance.

All the accommodations are suites. Though Casa de Solana might seem too Old St. Augustine to have TVs in the rooms, they all do. Most of the antiques in the sitting areas and bedrooms are valuables, not just old furniture. On the coffee table in each sitting room you'll find candy, a cut-glass decanter of sherry, and two glasses.

The British Suite, on the third floor, has a sitting area with a comfortable couch and two wing chairs. This bedroom has dormers and a brick chimney in the middle of the room. An antique Eastlake upholstered chair adds grace.

The Confederacy Room has a private first-floor entrance. Walls are of clean, white plaster, and interesting touches include decorations in a Confederate theme. There's an Oriental carpet in the bedroom, mahogany furniture, a queen-size bed, and an impressive fireplace.

The Colonial Suite on the second floor has a brass double bed, a sitting room with sofa and velvet chairs, and a little vine-shrouded balcony overlooking both lawn and garden.

The Minorcan Suite features a sitting room with a fireplace and Chippendale furnishings. The bedroom has a king-size bed in a beautiful mahogany frame. The bathtub is right in the middle of the bedroom, behind ruffled curtains; the sink and toilet are in a separate small bathroom. The windows overlook the garden and the brick courtyard.

The dining room of Casa de Solana is elegant, with a grand piano, a long, highly polished mahogany table, old chairs upholstered in fine needlepoint, and small crystal chandeliers. The room itself is large and airy, with deep windowsills filled with plants, elaborate blue swags above the windows, exposed rafters, and a handsome marble fireplace. A generous breakfast is served here at 8:30, usually something like egg and sausage casserole, muffins, and banana nut, pumpkin, or sweet potato bread, freshly squeezed orange juice, and coffee and tea. Faye serves whatever fruit is in season, often cantaloupe with strawberries. In keeping with southern tradition (St. Augustine is, after all, part of the South), Faye serves grits with all her egg dishes.

Though Faye is not the sort of innkeeper who sits and chats with guests for hours, she is very knowledgeable about St. Augustine history and heritage and is a wonderful source of information on museums, old buildings, and good places to eat.

Casa de Suenos B&B

20 Cordova Street
St. Augustine, FL 32084
800-824-0804
904-824-0887
Fax: 800-735-7534 or 904-825-0074
suenos@aug.com
www.casadesuenos.com

> This "House of Dreams" is
> a true retreat

Innkeepers: Sandy and Ray Tool. **Accommodations:** 4 rooms, 2 suites. **Rates:** Rooms $110–$170 per person double occupancy, suites $190; extra adult in room $15. **Included:** Full breakfast. **Added:** 9% tax. **Payment:** Discover, Diners Club, MasterCard, Visa, traveler's checks, personal checks. **Children:** 13 and over welcome. **Smoking:** Outside only. **Open:** Year-round.

➤ **It took more than a year to restore the Casa de Suenos, and it shows— in the handsome stucco exterior, the patterned oak floors, and in the original glass in the arched windows. This beautiful example of Mediterranean architecture was brought back with loving care and is now meticulously maintained.**

One of the many attributes of the Casa de Suenos is that it is the kind of place where you can't tell whether the person warmly greeting you on your arrival is the owner or a staff member who cleans rooms. Everyone connected to the Casa is personable and warm; everyone takes great pride in the house; and everyone cares about making each guest's stay here very pleasant. Thus, the atmosphere is just as lovely and comfortable as the surroundings.

If you're arriving at night, it's comforting to know that the Casa's special lighting system illuminates the doorbell, so that you know someone has heard you and is coming. Guests enter an imposing front hallway with a stairway curving up to the second story. On the first floor are two bedrooms, a small sitting room where the Tools host a social hour on weekend nights, and a dining room that is, no doubt, the prettiest in St. Augustine. Here, furnishings include fine antiques and an elegant chandelier above the polished wooden table. The arched windows with original wavy glass are exceptional.

A full breakfast is prepared by the innkeeper, Sandy Tool, who once worked as a gourmet chef. From the dining room, guests can hear the horse-drawn carriages outside before they even see them. On weekend mornings and holidays, soothing guitar music also accompanies breakfast. The guitarist comes back again in the late afternoon when complimentary wine and cheese are served in the sitting room. It is not unusual for the Tools' golden retriever to stretch out on the carpet.

Just off the sitting room is Nieves Room, which is accessible to the disabled; a ramp leads to the B&B's parking lot. This is a strikingly handsome room, decorated in dark green, with cream carpeting, a canopy bed, and a beautiful green and cream afghan strewn on the back of the sofa. To the right of the staircase is another first-floor room, the rose-themed Saragossa. The elegant fireplace is of light-colored stone and has a sunburst pattern carved in the pale wood above.

The upstairs rooms are richly decorated and appointed. The Cardova Suite is often requested by honeymooners and those returning to the Casa for an anniversary weekend. It has an ornate iron bedstead and filmy bed curtains. An Oriental rug covers the heart-pine floor. The bathroom has a big whirlpool tub and a chandelier, which somehow does not look out of place.

The Sevilla also has a whirlpool bath. It is the only room that has twin beds, although they are usually made up as a king. The Sevilla shares a second-floor veranda with the Valencia Suite and is therefore ideal for children or a couple traveling with those staying in the Valencia. The Valencia, also called the "Dream Suite," is the Casa's largest accommodation. It has a cherry four-poster queen-size bed, heart-pine floors, and another one of the Casa's big whirlpool baths.

All the rooms are named after a street in historic St. Augustine and have small touches such as a beribboned spray of eucalyptus above a mirror, a collection of frosted glass bottles, or a handmade quilt or afghan complementing the colors of the room. Baths are fresh looking and newly tiled. Four rooms have whirlpools, either in the bathroom or in the room itself. All rooms have cable TV and telephones with modem capability. A VCR, fax machine, and photocopier are also available upon request. The Casa has off-street parking, not a minor attribute in crowded St. Augustine.

For those who wish to explore the town by bike rather than walking, the Tools have complimentary bicycles. They and their staff are also happy to provide special services, such as arranging for a wedding, renewal of vows, or reception; a carriage ride through the historic district; or a business meeting or seminar (for groups of up to twelve). The Tools' most popular package includes dinner at the Old City House, a five-ticket events package, St. Augustine's Ghost Tour, and a carriage ride.

Cordova Street is in the heart of the historic district — close to cafés and restaurants downtown, the Spanish Quarter, and the waterfront. But with the clip-clop of horses on the pavement outside and the soft whir of paddle fans within, the Casa is also a wonderful retreat.

Casablanca Inn on the Bay

24 Avenida Menendez
St. Augustine, FL 32084
800-826-2626
904-829-0928
Fax: 904-826-1892
www.casablancainn.com

An indolent B&B on the Bay

Owners: Brenda and Tony Bushell. **Accommodations:** 2 rooms, 18 suites. **Rates:** $89–$159 rooms, $109–$225 suites. **Included:** Full breakfast. **Minimum stay:** 2 nights on weekends. **Added:** 9% tax; $15 extra adult in room. **Payment:** Major credit cards; traveler's checks. **Children:** 12 and over allowed. **Smoking:** In designated outdoor areas. **Open:** Year-round.

➤ **If Humphrey Bogart's most famous character had operated Rick's Place from St. Augustine instead of Casablanca and had had a mansion, this surely would have been it. Situated just across the street from Matanzas Bay, and diagonally across from the San Marco Spanish fort, this is an ideal location from which to explore historic St. Augustine. But the Casablanca is so relaxing, it's tempting just to sit on the front veranda and watch the boats and people go by.**

Architecturally an eclectic combination of stucco and clapboards, raised borders and dentil molding, stolid squareness and ornate columns, nothing else in St. Augustine looks quite like it. The main house was built in 1914, and the Casablanca is listed on the National Register of Historic Places. All that matters for the guest, though, is that the Inn lends itself to a Mediterranean languor. Breezy, colonnaded verandas wrap around the house on both the first and second floor. Guest rooms have access to the verandas or their own private decks. So, no matter where you wind up, there is always an area outside where you can sit and do absolutely nothing.

Guests can enjoy the two-course gourmet breakfast in the dining area inside or on the front veranda. A typical breakfast starts with a muffin or danish with juice and fresh fruit, followed by an entrée like egg casserole or cheese soufflé. Guests eat at two-person tables on the veranda or in the breakfast room, which doubles as a game room in the afternoon. This is a charming, whimsical room with old spool-legged tables, their tops painted with cards or a checkerboard or backgammon layout. The plaster walls are painted yellow, with a *trompe l'oeil* balustrade and flowers.

Throughout the day, the staff have homemade cookies and a variety of light alcoholic and non-alcoholic beverages for guests. Complimentary bicycles are available for those who can manage to pry themselves out of a rocking chair in order to sightsee in the nearby Spanish Quarter.

With 2 rooms and 18 suites at the Casablanca, there is more to choose from than at the average B&B. For those who wish to be in the main house and have a view of the Bay or neighboring historic houses fronting the Bay, the Casablanca has several rooms. One of the best of these is the first-floor Bayview, directly overlooking the water. It has a big picture window, a decorative fireplace, and queen-size sleigh bed. The room has a shower rather than a bathtub. For those who wish to be on the first floor but away from the excitement of the street and the waterfront, there's the Anastasia Suite tucked in the back of the Inn. This has a pleasant sitting area, queen-size bed, and Jacuzzi tub for two, as well as a shower.

The Anniversary Suite on the second floor has a private porch with a hammock for two, a queen-size four poster bed, and a double Jacuzzi and shower. The Celebration Suite is also ideal for those celebrating an anniversary or a wedding, with a cannonball four poster queen-size bed and double Jacuzzi. The Celebration has both a private sun deck and a porch with double hammock overlooking the Bay. The guest rooms in the back of the Inn are more secluded. They are reached by a landscaped walkway and have private sun decks. Perhaps because the Inn is painted a blazing white and walls reflect back sunshine, these sun decks are usually warm even in winter.

The Casablanca also has rooms in a newly restored coach house behind the main house. These have Jacuzzi tubs with showers and covered first-floor patios and second-floor porches overlooking the coach route.

All the rooms have 19th- and early-20th-century furniture, private baths with a shower or Jacuzzi, private entrances, and pillow-top mattresses to sink into at the end of the day. Of course, if you've spent the day on the porch watching sightseers walking to the nearby Spanish Quarter, you may not be very tired.

Castle Garden

15 Shenandoah Street
St. Augustine, FL 32084
904-829-3839
Fax 904-829-9049

A small, offbeat B&B with elegant rooms

Innkeeper: Kimmy and Bruce Kloeckner. **Accommodations:** 7 rooms. **Rates:** $75–$155; discounts for extended stays and senior citizens. **Included:** Full breakfast, bicycles, wine, private parking. **Minimum stay:** On weekends. **Added:** 9% tax. **Payment:** Major credit cards, personal checks if approved in advance. **Children:** 5 and up welcome. **Smoking:** Only on sun porch. **Open:** Year-round.

➤ **Castle Garden is a whimsical design constructed of blocks of shell stone and shaped like a medieval castle.**

The easiest way to find Castle Garden is to head for Ripley's Believe It or Not on the corner of A1A and Shenandoah Street. Although close to the center of activity, Shenandoah Street, which ends at the bay, is a quiet side street in an upscale neighborhood. Yet this B&B is within walking distance of the old Spanish part of town — an ideal location for anyone who wants to both rest and sightsee.

The Castle Garden was built as a carriage house for one of Henry Flagler's partners. He lived in the garish mansion that is now Ripley's Believe It or Not and had seventeen children. Behind the carriage house was a smithy, and the blacksmith's chimney is still visible in the back garden.

Admittedly, the building looks a bit odd from the outside, almost like a miniature Moorish castle that could be one of the local tourist attractions. But it has been restored and is a delight. The entrance is on the side of the house via a pleasant screened porch. The hallways are painted a soft peach, and the polished floors are original pine or new oak.

On the first floor is a front parlor with a breakfast room and the manager's kitchen behind it. One of the best guest rooms for honeymooners is also on the first floor and has a private entrance. It has a queen-size bed, a cathedral ceiling, a sitting area, and a large Jacuzzi gussied up with a swagged bath curtain. Castle Garden has one other lavishly decorated room and prides itself on its skill in pampering honeymoon couples. Several weddings have taken place in the back garden, where Spanish moss drapes the old trees.

All the rooms have queen-size beds except for one, which is furnished with a king-size bed or two twin beds, depending on the guests' preference. All guest rooms have private baths, but a couple of them are detached, with the bath being across the hallway or downstairs and through the kitchen. These rooms are good budget accommodations.

Breakfast is full and varied. The cereal is homemade granola, and there's always an egg dish and fresh fruit. All guests receive complimentary wine and chocolates on their pillow at night during their stay. Those staying in a bridal room receive a complimentary bottle of wine or champagne.

While the logical choice for entertainment might be Ripley's or the old section of St. Augustine, it's also pleasant just to stroll through Castle Garden's neighborhood. Head down to the quiet end of Water Street and enjoy the marshes and bay — it's a wonderful way to get a feel for the residential section of St. Augustine.

The Cedar House Inn Victorian B&B

79 Cedar Street
St. Augustine, FL 32084
800-233-2746
904-829-0079
russ@aug.com
www.CedarHouseInn.com

Victorian gingerbread and B&B warmth

Innkeepers: Russ and Nina Thomas. **Accommodations:** 5 rooms, 1 suite. **Rates:** $79–$185; rates usually lower during the week; corporate and weekly rates available. **Included:** Full breakfast, refreshments. **Minimum stay:** 2 nights on weekends and 3–4 nights on some holidays. **Added:** 9% tax. **Payment:** Major credit cards, traveler's checks. **Children:** Over the age of 10 welcome. **Smoking:** Outside only. **Open:** Year-round.

➤   **Staying at the Cedar House Inn is a little like staying at the house of a college friend, and the friend's parents are really, really nice.**

The Cedar House Inn provides a pleasant combination of privacy and togetherness. If you want, you can also feel like a kid again here — free of worries and well cared for. Innkeepers Nina and Russ have lived in various parts of Florida and around the country. Their enjoyment in being innkeepers and living in old St. Augustine is obvious to their guests.

The heart of this B&B is perhaps the library, where you can pull a book off the wooden bookshelves that Russ made, take a soda from the guest refrigerator, work on a jigsaw puzzle, play the guitar, or listen to an old Victrola record. A few framed pictures of Nina and Russ's kids and grandchildren add to the family feel. In the afternoon, there are always Nina's homemade cookies to snack on here. One thoughtful quirk is an old-fashioned telephone booth. "We thought it would be nice for guests to be able to call from here when they feel like telephoning someone, instead of having to go all the way up to their room."

Just outside the library's side porch is a hot tub sheltered in a gazebo — lots of fun in the evening. There are no restrictions on when to use it "as long as you're quiet and don't disturb other guests." The railed porch above the hot tub wraps around the front of the house, too. During Christmastime, the porch and house are beautifully lit and there are wreaths on every window.

Built in 1893, the Cedar House has traditional late-19th-century architecture: turned porch railings and posts, gingerbread brackets, and louvered wooden shutters at the windows. On the third floor are the original fishtail shingles. The white shingled siding on the rest of the house is asbestos rather than wood — probably a misguided 1950s renovation — but it's not very noticeable. Porch rail turnings are picked out in dusty rose and gray. Nina sweeps the wooden planks of the porch every day and, of course, there is white wicker to sit on. A suburban-size lawn fronts the property, and a cement and latticework wall near the street provides privacy. Lush vines cover the wall and there are flowerbeds in both the front and back yards.

Although staying here is like being at an old friend's, the Cedar House has its own measure of ornate Victoriana, and there is also plenty of privacy for honeymoon and anniversary couples. All of the rooms but one have a private entrance, usually from a porch, balcony, or deck. There is also entry from the stairway in the house.

The Cedar House has five bedrooms and one suite, each with a queen-size bed, private bath, TV, and telephone. Tom's Room has an old brick chimney and a stenciled wooden floor and is decorated with steamer trunks and antique cameras. Noni's Room has antique sewing machines and a dressed mannequin as unique touches. Walls and trim are in shades of violet and the bedstead is brass. Papa's Room has its own black iron stove but with electric logs instead of wood. The door to its second-floor balcony has a stained-glass window.

All of the rooms have a newly refurbished or completely new bathroom, with a clawfoot tub equipped with a shower head or a new whirlpool tub and shower. Most of the woodwork and the floors in the house are natural pine. Furnishings are period antiques: wing chairs, rockers, and stately armchairs. Light pours through the many windows, which are dressed with a combination of filmy lace curtains and decorative swags or valences above. The ceilings are all about 10 feet high, common in 19th-century houses before air conditioning. Both heat and air conditioning are individually controlled in each guest room.

The Cedar House Inn is within walking distance of many historic sites and Mantanzas Bay, but the Thomases also have bicycles for guests to use. Although there is parking on the premises, finding a parking place close to the fort or other tourist spots can be a problem, so it's very nice to have the bikes. The Thomases have only lived in St. Augustine for a few years and enjoy advising people on restaurants, local theater, and special events. With advance notice, they are happy to provide for a guest's own "special event," with honeymoon and anniversary packages, a birthday party for two, or a wicker picnic basket. They will also make dinner reservations for you and arrange for a horse-drawn carriage to take you there if you wish. Nina and Russ are attentive and helpful without being obtrusive, as they have their own busy lives to lead in America's oldest city.

Centennial House B&B

26 Cordova Street
St. Augustine, FL 32084
800-611-2880
904-810-2218
Fax: 904-810-1930
cenhouse@aug.com
www.centennialhouse.com

> **A luxurious, splendidly restored B&B on St. Augustine's carriage route**

Innkeeper: Steven Bruyn. **Accommodations:** 7 rooms. **Rates:** $100–$215; lowest rate is on weeknights. **Included:** Full breakfast, complimentary wine and cheese. **Minimum stay:** 2 days on weekends; holiday minimum varies. **Added:** 9% tax; $20 for extra adult in the room. **Payment:** Major credit cards, traveler's checks. **Children:** Over the age of 16 welcome. **Smoking:** Outside only. **Open:** Year-round.

➤ **Cordova Street is fast becoming the "B&B Boulevard" of St. Augustine. Centennial House is one of the newest houses to be restored to its turn-of-the-century charm. It is also one of the best.**

The exterior of Centennial House is rather plain-Jane: beige clapboards, single pane windows on the second-floor overhang, a brick stoop with simple wrought-iron railings, and cement steps to the front door. But inside, the Centennial House is hardly plain-Jane — it is beautiful, friendly, and warm. The owners and staff enjoy greeting guests at the little registration desk on the sun porch where guests first enter this B&B. The long, narrow sun porch has small-paned windows that run from the ceiling nearly to the floor and is furnished with small breakfast tables, each with two chairs slipcovered in cranberry red. Couples who want to eat alone can have breakfast here rather than at the large oblong table in the dining room. Everyone "orders" breakfast ahead of time on a little slip; it's somewhat like ordering hotel room service. Guests can choose either a full or Continental gourmet breakfast.

Through the sun porch door is the great room, a large sitting/dining area that has polished hardwood floors, Oriental rugs in deep ruby tones, comfortable chairs, and thickly cushioned sofas. One of the sofas backs onto the dining area. The big dining room table here has comfortable ladder-back chairs and is laid out with attractive place mats, perhaps to keep it from looking too formal.

At the top of the stairs is a common sitting room, which doubles as a game room. A small fridge has complimentary sodas. A glass-fronted chest is full of videos that guests can borrow; each guest room has its own VCR. There's also a game table for two here and a sofa. For some reason, the oak floor has no rug, which makes the room look a bit cold.

The guest rooms are mostly on the second floor, with one handicapped-accessible room on the first floor. The owners of Centennial House put a great deal into these rooms and their elegant private baths. A typical room has a wooden or Spanish-style iron bedstead with a king- or queen-size mattress covered with an ivory matelasse spread or a floral quilt. Windows usually have scalloped pull-down shades with a pretty valance above or ornate swags, festoons, and jabots. The new plaster walls are painted rather than papered and, except for the Centennial's first-floor room, the floors have solid-colored wall-to-wall carpeting, which keep the guest rooms from looking too fussy. As in most historic B&Bs, the decor and furniture are quite individual. One room might have a Victorian dressing table, another a marble-topped table or a mahogany desk.

The look is generally turn-of-the-century, although there is one interesting exception: the Safari Room. It is decorated in earth tones with accents of black in the iron bedstead and table lamps. Prints of African animals are on the walls, and the windows have long tie-back curtains and natural bamboo shades. There is a gas fireplace (one of several in the house) and a wonderful corner Jacuzzi in the bathroom.

All of the rooms have hair dryers and robes, Egyptian cotton towels, down blankets and pillows, paddle fans, and a TV and VCR concealed in an armoire. Most of the immaculate, tiled bathrooms have a whirlpool tub. Although people staying here are usually trying to get away from it all, there are copy, fax, and modem connection services.

In the morning there's a Continental or full breakfast, both with lots of fresh fruit. Complimentary wine and cheese are offered in the late afternoon. Most guests take off for the day to sightsee in the historic area that surrounds the Centennial House, but this is a great B&B on the occasional rainy day in St. Augustine. You can read a book before the fire, soak in a whirlpool tub, or play board games in the upstairs sitting room.

International Haus

32 Treasury Street
St. Augustine, FL 32084
877-GOOD-TO-GO
904-808-1999
info@internationalhaus.com
www.InternationalHaus.com

> **St. Augustine's friendly, do-it-yourself hostelry for travelers from around the world**

Innkeepers: Bob and Ellie Howell. **Accommodations:** 3 rooms with private bath; 2 rooms with shared bath; 2 dormitories with shared bath. **Rates:** $15 for a bed in male or female dorm; $35 for room with shared bath; $45 for room with private bath. **Included:** Kitchen privileges (pancake mix and syrup for do-it-yourself breakfast); towels provided if you don't have your own; patio grill; free Internet access. **Minimum stay:** 2 nights on weekends. **Added:** 9% tax; $10 extra person. **Payment:** Cash, major credit cards, traveler's checks. **Children:** Over age 6 welcome. **Smoking:** Outside only. **Open:** Year-round.

➤ **As in the hallways, every horizontal or vertical surface is painted in solid contrasting colors: blue, purple, bright red, yellow, green.**

This place is a little like a multinational, multigenerational summer camp, with a communal kitchen, common rooms, and very basic furnishings. The clientele here is mostly under thirty, as one would expect, but because International Haus includes some private accommodations, there is a mix of young couples and families, too. Innkeepers Ellie and Bob Howell have been managing hostels for many years — and doing it so well that they won a national manager's award for the international hostel they ran on Cape Cod.

International Haus is also in a prime location in St. Augustine's historic district. Treasury Street is one of the old city's most interesting streets. It is so narrow that past International Haus and heading toward Mantanzas Bay, Treasury becomes little more than a brick walkway about 5 feet wide, but it's still called a street. Old stucco buildings line the sidewalk. International Haus takes up the entire second floor of 32 Treasury.

As soon as you head up the stairs of the hostelry from the street, you know you've come upon something different: the plaster walls are painted yellow, the floorboards blue, the door trim purple, the doors green and red. It's a little like being in an Art Deco hotel on

Miami's South Beach — very colorful, very eclectic, very creative and fun.

In the hallway there's a registration desk set up, and the procedure for getting a room is pretty simple. You don't have to belong to Hostelling International to stay here, but you do have to respect other guests. Keys are given out for the front door and, if appropriate, your own room. Everything is locked up and secure at night, but there is 24-hour access to the building and a staff member is always present. Although a membership is not necessary to stay at International Haus, guests with a Hostelling International pass receive a discount here and at local shops and restaurants.

Many guests arrive on foot, but if you have a car, there is free parking on the side of the building. The communal kitchen is fully equipped and has a full-size refrigerator and stove and a large, deep sink. The countertops and terra cotta tile floor are new. The common room, or living room, is furnished with comfortable sofas, a table with a Chinese lamp, a low coffee table, the hostel computer, an organ, tropical plants, and, at the large windows, purple nylon curtains. A life-size pirate in the corner gives the room an offbeat, nautical look.

The dorm rooms at International Haus resemble those of a big European dormitory: bunk beds, bare wooden floors, lockers, and a communal bathroom. Windows have air conditioning units and the heat in the winter is by radiator.

Ellie and Bob are slowly upgrading all of the private rooms and putting ceramic tile in all of the bathrooms. As no-frills, family accommodations, these rooms are not bad at all, especially for the amazing price. A typical private room will have a double or queen-size bed with a blanket and no bedspread, plank-and-bolt bunk beds for the kids, faux bamboo shades and attractive tab curtains at the windows, a big walk-in closet, a locker, and a private bathroom with fresh ceramic tile around the old tub, a plaid shower curtain, a porcelain sink with a few rusty spots, and a toilet with a wooden seat. A couple of the rooms have a small refrigerator. Floors are usually painted and are pretty bare, except for an occasional scatter rug. The furniture varies — small tables, floor or table lamps, French provincial armchairs — everything looks as if it might have been retrieved from somebody's suburban attic.

The International Haus is the perfect place to stay if you are tired of high prices in a city where you plan to spend more time outdoors than indoors. It's a congenial, funky place full of (mostly) young people exploring the world. With its historic downtown location, it's also the perfect place from which to explore St. Augustine.

The Kenwood Inn

38 Marine Street
St. Augustine, FL 32084
904-824-2116
800-824-8151
Fax: 904-824-1689

> **One of St. Augustine's oldest B&Bs**

Innkeepers: Mark and Kerrianne Constant. **Accommodations:** 14 rooms and suites. **Rates:** Rooms $85–$110, suites $100–$185, $10 extra person; midweek discount on selected rooms. **Included:** Expanded Continental breakfast. **Added:** 9% tax. **Payment:** Discover, Visa, MasterCard. **Children:** 8 and older allowed. **Smoking:** Only on veranda. **Open:** Year-round.

➤ **Hallways to the guest rooms are carpeted and have handmade touches such as dried-flower arrangements or quilted wall hangings. Bathrooms are immaculate, with decor that coordinates well with the pretty bedrooms.**

The Kenwood Inn was already a wonderful B&B before Mark and Kerrianne Constant took over, and they have done much to improve this fine Victorian house. They've painted the clapboards pink with clean white trim and, according to Mark, "generally spruced up the place." But not so much that it's lost its Old World charm. The Constants are experts at caring for historic lodgings, having redone the Inn at Strawbery Banke in Portsmouth, New Hampshire, before moving to St. Augustine's historic district in 1988.

One of their loveliest achievements is the Country Shaker Suite. This has deep blue carpeting, whitewashed plaster walls, a pine bedstead with a handmade quilt, maple rockers, and old-fashioned ceiling fans. Running along the length of the sitting-room wall is a wooden Shaker peg board, from which hang antique dolls and household implements like iron rug beaters. The imaginative furniture includes a coffee table fashioned from a half-collapsed antique ironing board.

All of the guest rooms are fresh and comfortable. The three-room bridal suite on the third floor is particularly desirable, despite the climb, and has views of the water and most of St. Augustine's historic district. Since the Constants moved out of the inn into a house nearby, their former living quarters are available for guests. Their daughter's former bedroom is quite ruffly, with painted wood paneling, a rose and white bedspread, and an adjacent sitting room furnished in wicker. Both the bedroom and the sitting room have bathrooms.

The common rooms downstairs are elegant and warm, with well-polished floors of natural pine. Coffee and tea are available all day on the downstairs landing, as well as cookies and complimentary wine from 5 to 7 P.M. There's an honor fridge for those who wish to keep wine or their own snacks cold. A generous Continental breakfast of homemade coffee cakes and fruit is served in the sunny enclosed porch or at the handsome dining room table in the adjacent sitting room. This common room is light and comfortable, with deep-cushioned chairs, a white brick fireplace, and lace curtains at the large bay window that looks out over the front porch.

The other sitting room, near the front entrance, is more formal, with an ivory and gold brocade Chinese sofa, a Chinese rug, and some fine antiques. A door behind the sitting room leads to the courtyard and garden.

Unlike most St. Augustine B&Bs, the Kenwood Inn has a swimming pool. A thick stucco wall and heavy wooden gate on the street side make the oval, tiled pool and the patio area very private. The garden beyond has mature trees, including an old pecan, some bright annuals, and wisteria. There's also a little goldfish pond.

From the pool you can look up at the inn and get a sense of how it grew. The original house is a solid, squarish building, almost like a New England captain's home. The second-floor veranda, built between 1865 and 1885, has intricate gingerbread ornamentation. By 1886, the Kenwood was a boarding house. A wing added in 1911 lacks the gingerbread charm of the original but serves to screen the garden. Guests can explore the rest of the historic district on complimentary bicycles.

The porch on the Marine Street side of the house has been enclosed, so there isn't much room for rocking outside, but there's enough space near the front door for two cushioned wicker chairs and two rockers. An old-fashioned paneled door with two oval panes of etched glass and a brass pineapple knocker complete the Victorian picture. Sometimes you have to share the loveseat with the family cat.

Old City House Inn

115 Cordova Street
St. Augustine, FL 32084
800-653-4087
904-826-0113

> An inn and restaurant run
> by a person with exacting
> standards

Innkeeper: Linda Olsavsky. **Accommodations:** 7 rooms. **Rates:** $75–$145, 10% off Sunday through Thursday. **Included:** Full breakfast, parking. **Minimum stay:** 2 nights with Saturday stay. **Added:** 9% tax. **Payment:** Major credit cards. **Children:** Discouraged because of the furnishings. **Smoking:** Only on verandas. **Open:** Year-round.

➤   The Inn was built in 1873 as a stable for a mansion and was renovated as a rental cottage in the 1890s; it has also served as an antique store and a millinery.

In its first year of operation, the Old City House Restaurant won several four- and five-star ratings from Florida and national food critics. Lucky guests sample the wonderful fare for breakfast, which is included in the room rate. A typical breakfast might be quiche, strawberry pancakes, or a vegetable cheese crêpe, served with a breakfast meat or seafood, and a variety of fresh fruits, muffins, and juice. The kitchen will try to accommodate dietary restrictions. The dining room is airy and well lighted, with off-white plaster walls, tile-topped tables, and oak chairs. Service bustles, and the attractive presentations make meals even more appetizing. Dinner is served seven nights a week.

The inn itself is no less an achievement. Each room has a private entrance and is individual in decor and dimensions. The rooms are above the first-floor restaurant and, like many St. Augustine B&Bs, are less expensive on weekdays. Most have light plaster walls, new carpeting, and pretty floral or eyelet spreads on the queen-size beds. Bathrooms are spanking new but blend well with the old-fashioned rooms. Two have Jacuzzis for a bit of extra luxury. Each room or suite has something special: an alcove with a pretty love seat, lacy pillows on the bed, or a small private balcony.

The large deck on the second floor is for inn guests' use only. It's furnished with lawn chairs and tables with umbrellas and is perfect for reading and relaxing any time of the day. Below the deck, a patio for restaurant seating has an arched wood and plaster gateway to the street.

This is a city house — it's right in the middle of St. Augustine and opposite the old courthouse. The big deck overlooks the courthouse's parking lot, quite a busy place during the day. The downtown location is an ideal starting place for any tour of St. Augustine. The Lightner Museum, Henry Flagler's first hotel in town (now a college), the old Spanish fort, the brick streets, the park, and the craft shops are all within walking distance of the Old City House Inn.

The building was restored in 1990. Its first-floor facade is of coquina, and the other exterior walls are plaster, now painted a buttery yellow. Green and brick red paint accent the arched, small-paned windows. The red tile roof and railed balconies give the house a Spanish look. This is the type of inn guests like to come home to after a day of sightseeing.

The Old Powder House Inn

38 Cordova Street
St. Augustine, FL 32084
800-447-4149
904-824-4149

A Victorian built on the site of a gunpowder storehouse

Innkeepers: Katie and Kal Kalieta. **Accommodations:** 9 rooms. **Rates:** $105–$195 weekends; seasonally discounted rates Monday through Thursday. **Included:** Full breakfast, afternoon coffee or tea, evening wine or sparkling juice and hors d'oeuvres. **Minimum stay:** 2 nights on weekends. **Added:** 9% tax. **Payment:** American Express, Discover, MasterCard, Visa, personal checks. **Children:** Age 8 and older welcome. **Smoking:** Only on verandas. **Open:** Year-round.

➤ **The Old Powder House Inn is a real painted lady, a big clapboard house painted in shades of mauve, purple, raspberry, green, blue, and white, with gold leaf on some of the Victorian detailing.**

Cordova Street seems to be the place to open a B&B in St. Augustine; there are now several on this street. It's certainly an ideal spot. The old Spanish part of town, the busy bay, Flagler College, the park, the fort, and the courthouse are all are within easy walking distance. Yet this end of the street is quite peaceful at night.

The Old Powder House was one of the first B&Bs to open in St. Augustine in the 1980s. The original structure was built by Spanish settlers to store gunpowder, later burned down, and then this structure was built in 1899. Much of the original woodwork is still extant.

The hallways and common rooms are airy. Breezy verandas upstairs and down have Victorian fretwork and are furnished with wicker chairs and swings.

Each guest room has a theme: a cozy first-floor front room where a collection of antique clocks is displayed is called Splendid Time. Gauzy lace curtains hang at the windows.

Upstairs, Queen Anne's Lace is a good deal larger and has a more spacious bathroom. The high old-fashioned bedstead has a queen-size mattress and a lace canopy. Grandma's Attic, at the top of the stairs, has stenciled walls, old-time photos, and a puffy quilt on the king-size bed. It has a small but pretty bathroom. Serenity, in front on the second floor, has a king-size bed, mini-library, and wet bar.

All of the rooms at the Old Powder House Inn have private baths and are fresh and clean. The small-paned windows let in a lot of light and provide views of mature trees and other Victorian homes in the neighborhood. Exterior upkeep at the B&B has fallen a bit recently, though the back courtyard is still very pleasant.

The house was restored in 1989 by previous owners. The new owners, Katie and Kal Kalieta, who live on the premises, have done a good job of upgrading. They love to entertain and to tailor guests' visits to their own particular needs, essentially creating custom packages for honeymooners and others. At breakfast, tables are set with fine china and elegant stemware.

Guests can spend as much time as they want in the backyard, in the 10-person Jacuzzi, or on the screened porch at the front of the house, where they may help themselves to coffee and tea and fresh baked goods throughout the day. A full gourmet breakfast is served in courses in two quaint tea rooms on the other side of the sitting room. Each table is set for two, providing an intimate breakfast for a couple — and a little relief for parents traveling with children, who get their own table. (The Kalietas are happy to put two tables together if it's requested.) In the evening, Katie and Kal offer guests hors d'oeuvres and their choice of sparkling juice or a soothing glass of wine.

St. Francis Inn

279 St. George Street
St. Augustine, FL 32084
800-824-6062
904-824-6068
www.stfrancis.com

| A budget find in St. |
| Augustine's historic district |

Innkeeper: Joe Finnegan. **Accommodations:** 9 rooms and 4 suites, 1 2-bedroom cottage. **Rates:** Rooms $79–$189, suites $135–$189, cottage $159–219. **Included:** Full buffet breakfast, evening social, and admission to Oldest House, bicycles. **Minimum stay:** None. **Added:** 9% tax; $12 extra adult in room. **Payment:** Major credit cards, personal checks. **Children:** 10 and older allowed in suites and cottage. **Smoking:** On veranda and in garden only. **Open:** Year-round.

➤   The guest rooms have recently been updated with new carpeting and painted woodwork. Some of the old furniture is not quite antique, but it fits with the inn's unpretentious quality. The inn's staff regard its oddities with humor: "Ya gotta like old here!"

The St. Francis Inn is just down the street from "the Oldest House in America" as well as many of the other important sites of Old St. Augustine. Located across the street from a little park, it is a good place for both adults and their school-age children. A few of the suites have kitchenettes, and a cottage near the pool is appropriate for groups and families.

The St. Francis attracts mainly an adult clientele wishing to soak up the Old World ambience and spend quiet evenings in the antique-filled common rooms or courtyard.

The public rooms have white stucco walls and fine Spanish arches leading into the lobby area. There are several fine old fireplaces, all of which work, and plenty of well-worn Oriental rugs and antiques.

The suites with kitchenettes are convenient for those who want to fix some of their own meals. A couple of rooms open onto the second-floor veranda overlooking the brick street and St. Francis Park.

The five-room cottage, ideal for a group of friends or a family, was once slave quarters for the main house. It has a full kitchen, two bedrooms upstairs, and a sitting room that opens onto the small pool. Free parking is provided in a lighted parking lot across from the main house.

The pool seems spartan compared with the spectacular ones at some Florida hotels, but it is quite adequate. Even nicer is the brick courtyard that both the cottage and the back side of the inn overlook. Here there is a little goldfish pond surrounded with lush plants, a banana tree, and, closer to the street, a group of wrought-iron lawn chairs with a table. The trunk of a tree has grown over the old walkway, which gives an idea how long this little garden has been here.

The St. Francis Inn is the oldest established guest house in St. Augustine. The original home was built for Gaspar Garcia in 1791. The Spanish influence is obvious, with a stucco exterior over coquina, exposed timbers, and a second-floor veranda overhanging the street. Third-floor dormers and a mansard roof were added later. After trading hands several times — Spanish, British, and American — the house was converted to a boarding house in the mid-19th century and has remained a guest house since then.

The Secret Garden Inn

56½ Charlotte Street
St. Augustine, FL 32084
904-829-3678
www.secretgardeninn.com

Small, private suites in cottages overlooking a garden — perfect as a romantic hideaway

Innkeeper: Nancy Noloboff. **Accommodations:** 3 suites. **Rates:** $85–$135; rates lower on weeknights. **Included:** Continental breakfast. **Minimum stay:** 2 nights on weekends; 3 nights on some holidays. **Added:** 9% tax. **Payment:** Major credit cards, traveler's checks. **Children:** Over age 12 welcome. **Smoking:** Outside only. **Open:** Year-round.

➤   **This is a very private, romantic place where two people can just enjoy each other, read or sunbathe, and get lots and lots of rest.**

The Secret Garden B&B is easy to miss for the average passerby walking along Charlotte Street, a narrow thoroughfare in the historic district of St. Augustine. A little pathway leads from the street to a curved wooden gate with an arched arbor above that looks like something from the set of the movie *The Secret Garden*. Then a brick walkway curves across a postage-stamp lawn and modest but lovely garden, which includes wisteria, hibiscus, ginger plants, banana trees, and bright annuals. The pathway ends at two wooden bungalows painted deep orchid and tan.

Nancy Noloboff, the proprietor of this B&B, or her son, Nick, will show guests around. Guests are then pretty much on their own until the next morning, when Nancy, her long gray braid swinging across her back, delivers a gourmet Continental breakfast in their room or on its little deck or patio.

Two of the B&B's accommodations are second-story suites, each accessible by an exterior wooden stairway. Each has a small furnished deck under the trees. Moonflower is the highest of the two suites; you feel almost as if you're in a treehouse when you're inside. Its decor is indeed reminiscent of a moonflower, with light carpeting and plaster walls and a floral spread on the queen-size bed. Above a little round oak table and two chairs is a triangular paned window that lets in extra light and gives a glimpse of the trees. You walk right into the bedroom of this big room; the sitting area is not separate and there is no entryway or hallway. The kitchenette is small but serviceable, and the suite includes two closets. The tiled bathroom has a tub and shower. Best of all is the deck, with shade from the banana trees but just enough dappled sunshine, too.

Wisteria, the other second-story accommodation, has lilac walls and a slightly larger tiled bathroom than Moonflower, though there's no tub. A cut-out of a pretty floral wallpaper decorates the wall above the sink. The bedroom area has a wooden bedstead and antique armoire, and the sitting area has a floral print sofa. Curtaining above the small windows is minimal in order to let in as much sunshine as possible. The L-shaped kitchen here is especially nice and has a four-burner stove. The perchlike deck is furnished with a table and two chairs. On the first floor under Wisteria is

Nancy's small office, though this does not have any effect on privacy.

Across the brick walkway, tucked underneath the Moonflower suite, is Hibiscus. It has a brick patio and is the B&B's largest accommodation. Its kitchenette is small but includes a two-burner stovetop, microwave oven, and fridge. Guests first walk into a little sitting room with terra cotta tiles and then step up into the bedroom. The windows have roll-up shades in a fabric that complements the richly flowered quilted spread on the queen-size bed. There's an odd little wooden closet near the bed — almost like a cupboard, with a lace valence above and a sheer cotton curtain below.

There are quirks in each of the three suites that contribute to its charm and don't detract in any way from comfort. All of the suites have a tile or heart-pine floor, a table with fresh flowers that is set up for breakfast, a private entrance, and a view of the trees and garden. Breakfast is always a delicious combination of fruit, fresh baked pastries and sweet breads, fruit juice, tea, or coffee.

For all of its romance, this B&B is also down-to-earth and authentic. At one time, only the Spanish grandees and, later, American sea captains could afford to reside in the large houses of St. Augustine. Most people lived in boarding houses, small cottages, and bungalows. Houses were often built "cheek by jowl" with narrow lanes connecting them, and lawns and gardens were hidden behind stone walls.

Although the Secret Garden Inn is right in the middle of the historic district and easy walking distance to the Spanish Quarter and other St. Augustine sites, for most guests the memorable part of a stay here is the time spent on their patio or deck enjoying views of the garden and the butterflies and birds that come to this hidden, unhurried place.

Victorian House

11 Cadiz Street
St. Augustine, FL 32084
904-824-5214

A B&B with an easy informality

Innkeepers: Ken and Marcia Cerotzke. **Accommodations:** 4 rooms and 4 suites. **Rates:** Rooms $89–$125, suites $100–$125; 7th night free. **Included:** Full breakfast. **Minimum stay:** 2 nights on weekends. **Added:** 9% tax; $15 extra person. **Payment:** Major credit cards, personal checks, cash. **Smoking:** On verandas only. **Open:** Year-round.

➤ **The front porch is so old-fashioned and homey that you half expect to see your Grammy bring out cookies and a pitcher of lemonade.**

This cream-colored house with blue trim is true to its name, with several gingerbread dormers and a picket fence around the garden. Some of the rooms have small-patterned country wallpapers, and windows have light, ruffled curtains. Area rugs warm the wooden floors. All the guest rooms have handsome private baths. There are four rooms in the main house and four suites in an adjacent carriage house. Each is decorated in period antiques and charming prints and florals.

The generous breakfast includes a hot entrée, fresh fruit, juice, homemade breads and muffins, granola, herbal teas, and coffee. After the meal, guests can sit on the front porch and watch the scene on narrow Cadiz Street. The little garden and brick courtyard look neat and well cared for. The wicker chairs on the front porch are a bit worn, and the comfortable cushions a bit faded, but like everything at the Victorian House, they have a homey feel, as if life were too full to stop and make everything picture-perfect. The staff at the Victorian House are very friendly and accommodating.

At the Victorian House, you're right in the middle of the historic district. Aviles Street is narrow as an alley, with tightly packed houses, some only a few feet from the pavement. Walk east toward the waterfront and you're on the Avenida Menendez, a main thoroughfare, and Matanzas Bay. Walk north, south, or west and you'll pass some of St. Augustine's most famous attractions. On St. Francis Street is the Oldest House in America; the museum, bookstore, and old brick courtyard are well worth a visit. As a fan of historic St. Augustine and one of the first people to restore an old house here, Ken and Marcia can tell you some of the best sights to see.

From the Victorian House you're within walking distance of the Oldest Store (free to Victorian House guests), the Lightner Museum in the Flagler-built Alcazar Hotel, and Plaza de la Constitucion, a parklike gathering spot off King Street. A bit farther are the Castillo de San Marcos and the Spanish Quarter, which is almost like an open-air museum. After you've taken it all in, you can rest your tired feet on the porch of the Victorian House.

Westcott House

146 Avenida Menendez
St. Augustine, FL 32084
904-824-4301

> **A lovingly restored
> Victorian overlooking the
> bay**

Owners: Robert and Janice Graubard. **Accommodations:** 9 rooms. **Rates:** $95–$195. **Included:** Continental breakfast. **Minimum stay:** 2 days on weekends. **Added:** 9% tax. **Payment:** American Express, MasterCard, Visa, Discover. **Children:** 8 and older. **Smoking:** On verandas only. **Open:** Year-round.

➤ **The Victorian parlor is graced with a blue and gold carved fireplace, polished wooden floors, a beautifully upholstered settee, and ornate swags at the bright windows. The Victorian furniture is dark and heavy. Everywhere, a vivid imagination, concern for authenticity, and a bit of whimsy are apparent.**

Westcott House is one of the prettiest Victorian B&Bs in all of Florida. This is partly due to the house itself. the three verandas and Italianate gingerbread details on the exterior and the fireplaces, fine banisters, and old pine floors inside. But it is due also to the painstaking year-round maintenance bestowed on both the house and grounds. Westcott House is a home that is well loved.

This has not always been the case. The house was built in the late 19th century by Dr. John Westcott, a prominent St. Augustine citizen. Among his many achievements was the development of the part of the Intracoastal Waterway that links the St. Johns River to Miami. After his death, the house fell into disrepair. The place was in such a state of decay that it was questionable whether it could ever be brought back.

The eight guest rooms are all beautifully decorated and appointed. The Menendez Room, at the front of the house on the first floor, is decorated in rich blues. Rosalinda is decorated in shades of pink and rose, with ponderous Victorian furniture. Anastasia has an incredible mahogany vanity with triptych mirrors. Esmeralda is white and green. Other guest rooms have lace curtains or elaborate swags, and queen- or king-size beds. The private baths off the rooms are immaculate, and a few have clawfoot tubs. Bathrobes are complimentary during your stay.

Outside, the same attention to detail is obvious. The clapboards are painted a delicate salmon, and the long, louvered shutters are pale blue. On the front porch are wicker furniture and hanging ferns. The porch overlooks a small lawn and a flower bed at the foot of a low coquina wall.

At the side of the house is another first-floor veranda. There's a smooth lawn and more flowers and greenery in the side garden, as well as a small fountain. The pretty back garden overlooks the quiet, well-to-do residential neighborhood of Marine Street. The backyard has a brick courtyard with groupings of white iron lawn tables and chairs. Many guests take breakfast here, or you can have breakfast on the side veranda, in the parlor, on the front porch, or in the privacy of your room. The innkeeper serves fresh fruit, cereal, bagels, juice, and coffee.

Guests are treated to complimentary wine on arrival, and most feel quite pampered here. Turndown service includes a snifter of brandy and fine chocolates waiting by the bed. At any time, you can count on the staff to assist you.

But it's the sunny location on Matanzas Bay — part of the Intracoastal that Dr. Westcott helped develop — that makes this restored Victorian so special. From the lawn and garden, you look directly across Avenida Menendez to the water. You can hear seagulls overhead, halyards rattling against masts, people laughing and joking from their boats, and the clopping of hooves as horse-drawn carriages pass.

Westcott House is close to everything that people come to St. Augustine for. The city's yacht pier is a half-block down the avenue. There are restaurants, boutiques, carriage and trolley tours, museums, and historical sites within walking distance. The beach is a short drive across the beautiful Bridge of Lions. If the weather's fine, you can go sightseeing or spend the day at the beach. If not, there's always the pleasure of staying inside.

Stuart

HarborFront Inn B&B

310 Atlanta Avenue
Stuart, FL 34994
561-288-7289
Fax: 561-221-0474

**An eclectic riverfront B&B
near Stuart's Old Town**

Hosts: John, JoAyne, and Amy Elbert. **Accommodations:** 2 rooms, 3 suites, 1 cottage, 1 apartment. **Rates:** Rooms $85–$115, suites $140–$165, cottage $140, *Silver Lady* yacht $185; off-season discounts midweek; $10 for extra adults; Romance Packages available. **Included:** Full breakfast for those in rooms and suites; free dockage on a first-come, first-served basis with advance notice. **Minimum stay:** 3 nights in cottage and apartment. **Added:** 7% tax; breakfast $5 per person for cottage and apartment. **Payment:** American Express, Discover, MasterCard, Visa, personal checks, cash. **Children:** 12 and older welcome. **Smoking:** Outside only. **Open:** Year-round.

➤ **A breezy porch stretches the width of the back of the house. Guests eat breakfast out here and often linger to talk with other guests or read.**

This hideaway B&B is located on a narrow back road bordering the St. Lucie River, just off Route 1 near the historic section of Stuart. Built in 1908, it was once accessible only by water. The house looks almost like a vacation cottage, with an exterior of natural shingles and lots of porch and deck space overlooking the water. The deep blue trim and crimped tin roof are typical of houses built at this time in Florida. The additions to the main house, as well as the guest house suites that are a part of the B&B, all have been built in keeping with this style.

The inside of the HarborFront is an interesting mix of summer-camp informality, 1920s interior decor, and custom-made contemporary cabinetry. A few years ago, an expert woodcarver redid the dining room and bar, carving fantastic shapes and creating unusual curved handles on the bar cupboards. The dining area extends into the living room where there is a large fireplace and a comfortable sofa. The furniture is a mix of modern, traditional, and funky.

The longer one explores the house and grounds, the more quiet surprises one finds. Decks sprout everywhere on the sides and back of the house and cottages, providing lots of space for sitting and gazing out at the river. In the center of the house is a small atrium where the Elberts' pet parrot judiciously looks over guests from his large cage.

A large tree growing near the suite cottage at first seems like just a pleasant shade tree until one realizes that the shiny green orbs hanging from the branches are real avocados — and the next day, there are avocados on the menu. A hammock is strung between two banyan trees, and wonderful little sitting areas have been created here and there in the large backyard. Recently, the Elberts added a spa to the garden that overlooks the river.

Although HarborFront is small and informal, there are several accommodation options. The largest is the Cottage. This has a small bedroom with a queen-size bed, cable TV, sitting room, oak cathedral ceilings, well-equipped kitchen, and bathroom with shower and tub. The furniture style is a mix of 1950s Formica and nautical. Most people staying in the Cottage cook for themselves, but breakfast is available for an extra charge.

The Guest House has two suites, both of which have private entrances and sliders to decks. The Garden Suite has a king-size bed, wicker sofa, and a modern bath with shower. The Riverfront Suite is larger, with a living room with an impressive water view, a separate bedroom with a king-size bed, and a bath with two sinks and an oversize shower. With its pleasant deck, this suite is especially nice for a honeymoon couple.

In the main house, all the guest rooms are on the first floor. The nicest of these is the Sun Room Junior Suite, which has a full riverfront view, a private deck, queen-size four-poster bed, sitting room, and bathroom with a shower. As the name suggests, it is very sunny and furnished mostly in white. The Nantucket Room is also attractive and includes a queen-size four-poster bed, sleep sofa, and full bath. The Nantucket Room can be joined with the Guest Room, which has a double bed, a sofa that converts to a twin bed, and a large bath with a tub and shower.

Still another option is an overnight stay on the *Silver Lady*, the HarborFront's yacht. It is moored at the B&B's backyard dock and is also available for half-day or full-day cruises.

Breakfast is generous, and different every day. One morning it might be waffles, another time an egg dish. Fresh fruits from the garden are used as much as possible. Guests usually eat on the porch overlooking the river or in the atrium.

Just a few blocks away are the boutiques and craft shops of Stuart's historic district as well as quite respectable live theater. (You do have to cross a busy street to get there, so it's easier to drive the short distance.) Sailing and fishing are available at nearby marinas. Good places for dinner are Luna's for Italian food and Flagler's Grill in the historic district.

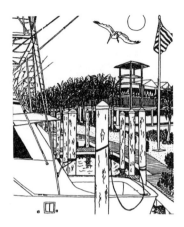

Pirates Cove Resort and Marina

4307 S.E. Bayview Street
Stuart, FL 34991
800-332-1414
561-287-2500

An Intracoastal marina
resort that's as comfortable
as your favorite blue jeans

Accommodations: 48 rooms and two suites. **Rates:** Rooms $90–$175, suites $130–$175. **Added:** 6% tax. **Included:** Covered parking. **Payment:** American Express, Discover, MasterCard, Visa, traveler's checks, cash. **Children:** Under age 18 free in room with parent. **Smoking:** Allowed; nonsmoking rooms available. **Open:** Year-round.

➤ **The Pirates Loft is one of the few lively night spots on the water for several miles around, with entertainment five nights a week and dancing in the bar and lounge area.**

Although the marina and restaurant here have been known among boating Floridians for years, the resort is not well-known to out-of-state tourists, so those who make it here get a feeling of having made a discovery, a real find. Port Salerno was originally a fishing village. This is the kind of small, nautical town where kids leave their bikes unattended while they fish off the local docks.

Pirates Cove Resort is quiet during the day but active at night because of the Pirates Loft Restaurant and Lounge, a favorite watering hole on the coast that serves three meals a day. The place draws a good crowd of locals as well as boaters and resort guests at night. Port Salerno is 40 miles north of Palm Beach and only five miles south of Stuart, another old town (by Florida standards) on the waterfront. Stuart has a riverwalk along the banks of the St. Lucie River and outdoor concerts at an old-fashioned gazebo as well as a historic district with some interesting pottery and gift shops.

All the rooms at Pirates Cove have waterfront views with small balconies, cable TV, and spacious vanity/bath areas. Some wheelchair-accessible rooms are available, a little unusual for a marina resort. A few rooms that overlook the pool are close to the restaurant, so if you're a light sleeper you might want to be at the end of the building or in another building near the marina's dry rack storage facility. Rooms and mini-suites have rattan furniture and are decorated in the colors of tropical orchids.

There's plenty to do at the resort for those who love the water and fishing. Pirates Cove is the home port for the *Safari I*, a deep-sea fishing boat that sails twice a day. The marina also has an excellent charter fleet. For those who arrive on their own boat, facilities include showers, laundry rooms, a fully stocked marine store, and full repair services. There's also a bait and tackle shop. Game fish in the waters off the coast include kingfish, wahoo, blue marlin, sailfish, and mahi-mahi. The marina has full and half-day charters in backcountry waters for fly and light tackle fishing. The resort is an official information center for "Islands of the Bahamas," providing information on various island resorts. It also has fishing permit applications and customs and immigration forms available.

For landlubbers (or fishing folk who want to see the area's nightlife), there is theater nearby in Jupiter and a number of good restaurants in Stuart and Jupiter. Only an hour away is Palm Beach and the Kravis Center for the Arts. Most people staying at Pirates Cove, however, are quite happy to spend most of their time here, where the atmosphere is laid-back and you don't have to impress anybody.

Pirates Loft, the resort's restaurant and lounge, is rustic and informal, wood-paneled and decorated with old jugs and nautical flags. With paddle fans above and lots of windows overlooking the marina and pool patio, it's an open, breezy place.

Although the focus is on the water here, the grounds are very attractive, landscaped in a natural, subtropical scheme with covered wooden walkways and arching wooden bridges over grassy areas — well maintained without being overly manicured. The resort's amenities include a heated swimming pool and a patio paved with octagonal stones and furnished with lawn chairs and chaises. Bicycles are available for rent, and there are golf and tennis privileges for resort guests within easy driving distance. Conference facilities overlooking the pool can accommodate up to 100 people. Another nice amenity here is poolside bar and food service.

Vero Beach

The Driftwood Resort

3150 Ocean Drive
Vero Beach, FL 32963
561-231-0550
Fax: 561-234-1981

A whimsical, funky place with excellent accommodations

Accommodations: Number of accommodations varies, depending on rental pool. **Rates:** Hotel rooms $55–$90, oceanfront rooms $110–$170, 2-bedroom villas $140–$230. **Minimum stay:** None. **Added:** 10% tax. **Payment:** Major credit cards; cash; checks. **Children:** Welcome in all accommodations. **Smoking:** Permitted. **Open:** Year-round.

➤ **The Driftwood prides itself on being a place where guests can get a suite for what they would pay for a room anywhere else. This is a good place for families and the budget-conscious.**

The Driftwood Resort has a long history in pretty Vero Beach. In fact, at one time, it *was* Vero Beach, here before anyone thought of this small settlement as a vacation resort. Its first owner, Waldo Sexton, one of the few settlers here in the early part of this century, was a man of few financial resources and much imagination. He built his beachside home out of driftwood that washed up on the beach and began taking in overnight visitors simply because there was no other place for them to stay in the area. As the years went by, he decorated the place with whimsical finds, most of them also swept in by the ocean: old bricks, brass odds and ends, ornate wrought-iron bedsteads, decorative pieces from shipwrecks, broken ceramic tiles, and later, artifacts from his travels around the world.

Today's visitors take Ocean Drive along the beach and turn into the driveway flanked by stone columns topped with whimsical iron birds that look as if they may have been constructed out of an old automobile heater. The small reception center is furnished with antiques and photos of the Driftwood and Vero Beach in the old days. Extending from the reception center is a row of units that have brightly colored carved wooden doors and an odd assortment of decorations out front: ornate iron railings that may have once been bedsteads, terra cotta Italianate friezes, worm-eaten wooden mastheads, and iron bells.

Inside, these units are very attractive, with Italian ceramic tiles on the floor and comfortable cushioned furniture in bamboo or bleached hardwood. The suites typically have an open layout with a sitting area and well-equipped kitchen, a small bedroom with a king- or a queen-size bed, and one or two bathrooms. Parking for both the resort and the restaurant, which is open to the public, are practically on the front steps of these accommodations, so they can get a little noisy.

On the other side of the parking lot are slightly newer accommodations with brick and driftwood exteriors and marvelous Italian ceramic tiles embedded in the walls. Inside are nicely furnished suites that seem a bit quieter than their counterparts across the parking lot.

The newest accommodations at the Driftwood are four-story villas approached by winding brick pathways that give a secluded feeling. These villas have interesting details such as brick archways in the kitchen area, Italian tiles, or stained glass windows. There are large terra cotta tiles on the floor and carpeting in the bedrooms. Some of these villas, such as 123A and 124A, can be combined to make two-bedroom, two-bathroom suites, ideal for couples traveling together or families with older children.

Still other units at the resort have a 1950s beachy feel, with wood floors and compact kitchen appliances, and long plank kitchen tables. All have a separate bedroom and at least one tiled bathroom. The accommodations are packed pretty tightly on this oceanfront lot, so no matter where guests stay, they are close to the pool and the wooden stairs down to the beach. Kitchens and kitchenettes in all the accommodations allow guests to cook for themselves, but there is also a lively restaurant. Waldo Sexton really let himself go here, with stained glass windows, pecky cypress walls, and crazy artifacts from all over the world.

There are those who believe that the quirky ambience of the Driftwood has been "ruined forever" now that it's become a time-share resort, mostly occupied by time-sharers who bought a perennial week in the sun in addition to weekenders. It is true that the feeling is not as homey as it once was. The people behind the desk are certainly not as cordial as they could be — welcoming guests to the Driftwood is just another job to them. But for those who have no past experience with the Driftwood and minimal expectations, the caliber of the welcome is insignificant. The breezy location on the beach, the comfortable accommodations, the exuberant atmosphere of the resort's bar and restaurant, and the crazy collection of art and shipwrecked treasures make this place a treat.

The Panhandle

Apalachicola
Gibson Inn, 143
Destin
Sandestin Golf & Beach Resort, 145
Mexico Beach
Driftwood Inn, 148
Niceville
Bluewater Bay, 149
Panama City Beach
Marriott Bay Point Resort Village, 151
Pensacola
New World Inn, 154
Pensacola Grand Hotel, 155
Seaside
Seaside, 157
Tallahassee
Cabot Lodge, 161
Governors Inn, 162
Wakulla Springs
Wakulla Springs Lodge, 165

Best Beachside Accommodations

Mexico Beach
   Driftwood Inn, 148
Seaside
   Seaside, 157

Best City Stops

Pensacola
   Pensacola Grand Hotel, 155
Tallahassee
   Cabot Lodge, 161
   Governors Inn, 162

Best Eclectic Find

Wakulla Springs
   Wakulla Springs Lodge, 165

Best Resorts and Spas

Destin
   Sandestin Golf & Beach Resort, 145
Niceville
   Bluewater Bay, 149
Panama City Beach
   Marriott Bay Point Resort Village, 151

Best Small Hotels, Inns, and Motels

Apalachicola
   Gibson Inn, 143
Pensacola
   New World Inn, 154

"The farther north you go in Florida," an old saying goes, "the more southern the state becomes." The soil begins to look like the coppery earth of Georgia and the vegetation is similar to that of other southern states, with magnolias, camellias, azaleas, and loblolly and other pines growing in abundance. Spanish moss hangs from big live oaks and old, twisted myrtle trees.

Food is also different. In north Florida you can get hush puppies — cornbread deep-fried like a doughnut, sometimes with herbs or green peppers chopped in. You can also find biscuits and grits, sometimes with red gravy, fresh okra, and black-eyed peas. Iced tea is served in the restaurants year-round; you need to specify hot tea when you want that instead. Fried chicken is done the right way here — deep-fried and flaky.

Culturally, too, northern Florida is more southern. You can spend a week or more in Key West without ever hearing a southern accent, but not in **Tallahassee** or **Pensacola.** People are friendly and take time for conversation. There are many fundamentalist churches, and country music is popular. Lots of Georgians, Louisianans, and Alabamans come to the northeast or Panhandle coast to vacation or retire, as the breezes are cooler than back home. All the major cities have airports and offer basic accommodations in chain hotels or motels, but some charming inns and cottages have opened in recent years, particularly in the harbor section of Pensacola and along the Gulf of Mexico, also known as the Emerald Coast. The waters of the gulf have a dozen shades of blue and green and the white sand has a fine, powdery consistency. In some areas, it is possible to hire a boatman for a ride through the bayous and other backwaters near the gulf.

The Panhandle is warm and pleasant in the fall, but it's at its best in spring, when the flowering trees and shrubs are in bloom. No garden-lover visiting Tallahassee should miss the Maclay State Gardens — broad pathways of bricks salvaged from Tampa streets lead to formal, informal, and woodland gardens. The azaleas and dogwoods of March give the gardens their most spectacular color, but the tree-high camellias are also showy in late winter. Other attractions in the Tallahassee region are the Museum of History and Natural Science and Bradley's Country Store. There are few distinctive accommodations here, though inns are beginning to catch on.

Most hotels and B&Bs in northern Florida offer the same rate year-round, but when making reservations, it's best to check on rates for the precise period you'll be staying. On the Gulf Coast of the Panhandle, the high season and the highest prices are in summer. The lowest rates are in winter, when the area is apt to be damp and chilly. Spring and fall are considered "shoulder" seasons by some resorts. In Tallahassee, rates at some hotels change according to whether the legislature is in session.

Partly because of the rather run-down nature of some of the towns bordering the gulf, the Emerald Coast has been called the "Redneck Riviera." Because it is a summer destination, not a winter one, the coast has not been extensively developed, and it is less prosperous than other areas of Florida. The towns tend to be nondescript places with more convenience stores and bait shops than anything else. But lack of development has become a plus in Florida, and the area is becoming increasingly popular, particularly with Midwesterners. Both out-of-staters and Floridians consider the Panhandle curve of the gulf a "find" in all but the coldest months.

The dip in the Panhandle into the Gulf of Mexico is marked by the historic town of **Apalachicola.** Apalach, as local residents refer to it, is a fascinating place. Before the Civil War, steamships traveled the Apalachicola River carrying cotton from Georgia to be shipped to Europe and New England mills. Later, Apalach became a major lumber port. In the early 1800s, a strategically positioned fort on the river's banks was fought over by the Spanish, Americans, British, runaway slaves, and Choctaw Indians.

In the 20th century, the area fell on hard times, and its beautiful coastline was ignored by developers who were essentially ravaging the natural beauty of the southeast coast. This neglect has been something to be grateful for; and now, ironically, there is an effort to attract tourist dollars by advertising the area as "Florida's Forgotten Coast." St. George Island, a barrier island a few miles from Apalachicola, was recently named one of the top 10 beaches in the United States, partly because there are no hordes of people lying on the sand. In Florida, especially on the southeast coast, an uncrowded beach is an exciting thing.

West of Apalachicola is Panama City, a somewhat depressed town that is beginning to make a comeback. South of the city is **Panama City Beach,** characterized by motels and high-rises along the pretty beach and some tacky commercial attractions that probably wouldn't survive as secondary attractions in the Disney World region. But there are some wonderful surprises too. In some areas, you can drive along the two-lane beach road with the water on the west side of the highway and piney woods or grassy land on the east — something you don't see on the southeast coast. Unbelievably, some of the Panhandle Coast is actually *rural.* One lovely area here that should never be missed is Shell Beach and St. Andrews State Park near Marriott's Bay Point Resort.

There is great fishing along the coast, both in rivers and in the Gulf of Mexico. Hundreds of years ago, the Indians of the gulf lived peacefully along these shores, largely because the plentiful fish and game made conflict unnecessary. Basically nomadic, the Indians roamed up and down the coast. They swam and partied a lot, and during celebrations would roast the catches of the day over hickory campfires along the beach.

Between Panama City Beach and Pensacola, there are a number of impressive beaches, Fort Walton being one of the most beautiful. The most notable resort town along this stretch is **Seaside,** a planned community patterned after New England and Old South beach towns. At the entrance to Seaside, signs are posted for motorists to slow down for the pedestrians. But there's little need for a sign. People driving by for the first time are so amazed at the 19th-century buildings and the absence of cars on the brick-paved streets that they automatically slow down and rubberneck during the whole four minutes it takes to drive past the town.

North of Seaside is DeFuniak Springs, a planned community of the 1880s, created as a winter home for intellectuals and visionaries from Chatauqua, New York. Turn-of-the-century brick buildings line up opposite the town depot and railroad tracks, looking almost like a movie set. But the prettiest part of DeFuniak Springs is around the lake, a few hundred yards from the depot where Victorian houses, Old South mansions, and small bungalows encircle the water. Also sited on the lake is a small library in a white clapboard building, reputedly the state's oldest public library.

The principal city near the border with Alabama is **Pensacola,** an old harbor town that has experienced quite a revival in recent years. The most interesting area here for out-of-town visitors is the historic waterfront area, which looks almost like the French Quarter in New Orleans. Many of the buildings are brick and have wrought-iron balustrades on their second-floor verandas. The community is proud of its revitalization and has some sidewalk and seafood fairs during the year, which they stage as much for their own enjoyment as for the tourists'. Pensacola is sited on a large bay so there are water views from many parts of the city.

Apalachicola

Gibson Inn

U.S. Highway 98 and Avenue C
P.O. Box 221
Apalachicola, FL 32320
850-653-2191

> One of Florida's oldest inns

Owner and general manager: Michael J. Koun. **Accommodations:** 29 rooms, 1 suite. **Rates:** Rooms $75–$90, suite $95–$125; $5 discount on weekdays; packages available. **Minimum stay:** With some packages. **Added:** 6% tax; $5 extra person. **Payment:** Major credit cards. **Children:** Free in room with parents. **Smoking:** Nonsmoking rooms; smoking lounge. **Open:** Year-round.

➤ **Narrow hallways lead to lots of nooks and crannies and to second-floor and third-floor guest rooms, all decorated in a 19th-century Old Florida style, with paddle fans and wood slat blinds.**

Apalachicola is a hard word to pronounce, but the town itself is an easy place to get used to, particularly with the Gibson Inn as a base. It's a slow-paced town, but anyone who asks, "What's there to do here?" is not looking hard enough.

In 1907, at the height of Apalachicola's prosperity, a South Carolinian named James Fulton Buck built the Franklin, the town's first inn. In the late 1920s, when the lumbering of cypress trees had died out and the town had become a center for oystering, the Gibson sisters — Sunshine and Annie — bought the place and changed its name.

Shortly after the Second World War, when army officers were billeted in the Gibson, it began to deteriorate, and by the time the present owners bought it in 1983, it was a refuge for derelicts. Fortunately, though, no one had ever "modernized" the interior. Beneath layers of paint and filth were the original black cypress and heart-pine banisters, railings, wainscoting, and paneling, all remarkably well preserved. The inn is squarish and solid-looking, with a tin roof, a widow's walk, and wraparound verandas on the first and second floors. Painted deep blue, the inn has white latticework, windows, and veranda railings.

The Gibson's restaurant has a wide following. Fashioned after a steamboat dining room (steamships once plied the Apalachicola River), it has solid post and beam construction. Matchstick paneling runs halfway up the walls, with cream-colored plaster and old photographs above. Globe lanterns of brass and green glass hang from the ceiling. The seafood here is excellent, though service can be a bit slow.

The guest rooms at the Gibson Inn have white iron or mahogany four-poster beds, woven rugs on the polished pine floors, camelback sofas, antique armoires and side tables, ceiling fans, and pedestal washbasins with porcelain or brass fixtures. At the same time, there are all the modern amenities: air conditioning, cable TV, and private telephones.

Room 208, on the second floor, is one of the inn's best. The kingsize bed has a crocheted canopy top and a dhurrie rug is on the pine floor. Although other rooms have access to the veranda from the hallway, this is the only guest room with direct access to this breezy spot — through French doors in both the bedroom and sitting room.

Although the Gibson Inn is the sort of place where you could spend half the day reading in your room or rocking on the veranda, there are some interesting things to do on the water and in the town. Just off the coast of Apalach are four pretty barrier islands that provide miles of beaches and excellent fishing. These islands were the source of Apalachicola's fame as an oystering center during an earlier era. Many guests set out on a walking tour that stops at the John Gorrie Museum and two historic Greek Revival structures, the Trinity Episcopal Church and the Raney House. These are on the National Register of Historic Places — as is the Gibson Inn.

Destin

Sandestin Golf & Beach Resort

Emerald Coast Highway (Route 98)
Destin, FL 32541
850-267-8000
Reservations:
800-277-0800
850-267-8150
Reservations for Sandestin Beach
Hilton Golf & Tennis Resort:
800-HILTONS
www.sandestin.com

> **A huge resort on one of Florida's lesser-known beaches**

Accommodations: More than 740 rooms, suites, and villas. **Rates:** Vary according to the type of accommodation and location, with bayside inn rooms least expensive and oceanside suites and 4-bedroom villas most expensive. Sandestin Golf & Beach Resort suites: $75–$560. At both locations, discounts, packages, and weekly rates are available. **Added:** 10% tax. **Minimum stay:** 3 nights on major holidays and with some packages. **Payment:** Major credit cards. **Children:** Free in room with parents. **Smoking:** Nonsmoking rooms available. **Open:** Year-round.

➤ **It is enough simply to enjoy the beach and water at Sandestin, but there is more to do. In addition to several swimming pools, golf, and tennis, there are catamaran sailing lessons, sailboat and motorboat rentals, bicycle rentals, fishing, Jet Skis, volleyball on the beach, a fitness center, a children's activities program, and a number of water sports. There's also a marina and a yacht club.**

Sandestin sits on more than 2,400 acres of land off the Emerald Coast Highway. There are several miles of beach on the property, pretty lagoons, and acres and acres of white sand dunes. Sandestin offers a great deal of recreation and, in some cases, accommodations directly on the ocean. In an area of mediocre motels and fast food restaurants, Sandestin offers a sense of insularity and, because of the activities offered here, a little excitement.

The resort is split by the highway, with some villas, a new Hilton hotel, tennis courts, and a golf course on one side; and another golf course, the inn, the conference center, and more villas on the other side. This poses fewer problems than one would think; trams pick up guests at stops scattered about the property. The high-rise beachside suites are in two buildings a few steps (and an elevator ride) from the gulf. These have small terraces on the parking lot side of the building and generous ones on the ocean side. The views from the top floors are breathtaking and, because the architects incorporated so much glass into the building, you almost feel as if you're still outdoors. The towers have spacious executive suites on the low end of the price range, and four-bedroom apartments on the high end. There are also one- and two-bedroom suites.

The clustered Bayside Villas, more spacious and more expensive, are a better choice for those who don't like high-rise buildings. Also desirable are two- and three-bedroom villas near the beach, the rustic Fairways units overlooking the golf course, and the Linkside villas, which back up to a canal or golf course. The Villas at Vantage Point are rather gaudy, with a pink stucco exterior, a too-blue barrel tile roof, and a two-level floor plan that's a little impractical for families with small children.

Although the villas and other accommodations are privately owned, many are in a rental pool and available by the day, week, or longer. All suites and villas have fully equipped kitchens and are well cared for. Owners compete to provide the most attractive furnishings and decor on the rationale that the more elegant the surroundings, the more likely the accommodation will find a steady stream of renters. All property owners in the rental pool must abide by high decorating and maintenance standards set by management.

Most convention-goers and budget-minded couples stay at the resort's inn, on the bay side of Emerald Coast Highway, next to the conference center. These also have kitchenettes, with a small refrigerator, stovetop, coffeemaker, and toaster. A small balcony looks out over the resort or the bay, though by Gulf Coast standards the water is a bit disappointing — a dull green that gets brown close to shore, with none of the little islands and sandbars that dot other parts of the coast. However, the inn is a center of activity: grass and clay tennis courts, a swimming pool and golf course, the brightly tiled Cafe, and the conference center are all here.

A hotel on the gulf side of the resort has 400 additional suites. Their standard suites have bunk beds in an entryway, a king-size bed, sofa, dining area, and refreshment center with a fridge and stovetop. The bathroom has a tub shower, toilet, mini-television, hair dryer, and telephone, and there's another sink and vanity in the dressing area, easing the bathroom bottleneck in the morning. Decor is fresh and pretty.

The lobby and meeting rooms downstairs are open and airy, with comfortable new furnishings. The Hilton has its own restaurant and lounge and a snack grill by the pool. Across the dunes is Sandestin's Elephant Walk restaurant. Its three interconnecting buildings have Old Florida-style green metal roofs with conical towers and cupolas, barn red wooden clapboards, and lots of walkways overlooking the water for after-dinner strolls.

Because this is a residential community with many year-rounders, there are also some special pleasures not available at impersonal hotels — like an informal group that meets every morning to jog. Guests can keep abreast of special events on the Sandestin Information Station, channel 10.

Within the complex are tennis and golf shops. There is also excellent shopping at the Market just outside the security gate. Though relatively new, the Market is architecturally "Old Florida," with a stucco exterior and conical towers on the gray metal roofs. Covered walkways join 31 specialty shops and an informal restaurant. The tropical landscaping includes lagoons, fountains, and small islands frequented by watchful blue herons.

Mexico Beach

Driftwood Inn

2105 Highway 98
P.O. Box 13447
Mexico Beach, FL 32410
850-648-5126
Fax: 850-648-850

A budget find on the Emerald Coast

Owner: Peggy Wood. **Accommodations:** 20 rooms and 4 houses. **Rates:** Rooms $75–$95, 2-bedroom/2-bath Victorian houses $95–$130; weekly and monthly rates available in winter only. **Included:** Continental breakfast. **Minimum stay:** 2 days on weekends; 3 days on holiday weekends. 2-month minimum on winter rentals. **Added:** 10% tax; $10 for extra adult. **Payment:** American Express, Discover, MasterCard, Visa; cash; checks. **Children:** Welcome. **Smoking:** Allowed. **Open:** Year-round.

➤ **In the back of the inn are gardens with Greek statuary, a tiny waterfall, and other whimsical decorations. Lawn chairs under a thatched pavilion give shelter from the noonday sun. A wooden walkway leads to sand dunes and the pristine beach.**

The Driftwood looks small and unassuming, but it has a good deal of variety in its accommodations, with rooms in the inn that sleep from two to six, two-room units, and two-bedroom Victorian houses located just across the street. The architecture of the original inn is Old Florida: red tin roof, gray clapboards, white latticework and trim, and gingerbread detailing on the broad, overhanging eaves. It's basically an expanded motel, but a motel with much charm. The office and gift shop at the front of the inn look almost like an old-time depot. The entrance is flanked by subtropical gardens and small fountains.

Most of the inn units are located on two floors of the main building, which had a major refurbishment in 1995. They are extremely compact, with an efficient little kitchen and a bed/sitting room. A porch is furnished with a table and chairs. Furnishings are traditional and include antiques.

The two conical beach cottages next to the main inn have attractive, balustraded verandas overlooking the gulf. With two units in one building and four in another, these are more spacious and have a bit more privacy than the inn. Just across the street are four two-bedroom Victorian houses, clustered around a small courtyard with a gazebo and a rose garden. The houses also have the Old Florida architecture of tin roofs, verandas, and pastel clapboards. The houses have an open, airy feeling and are furnished with 1920s- and 1930s-style furniture. Recent additions to the complex are a tea room and a charming wedding chapel.

With advance notice, pets are allowed at the Driftwood — unusual for Florida. All accommodations have cable TV and a telephone. In the morning, the staff sets out coffee and sweet rolls. The staff also caters gatherings.

Mexico Beach is little known even in Florida. Clapboard and stucco cottages line the main road and spread out onto little side streets. There are a few eateries and stores, but for the most part, this is not a highly populated — or commercial — area. The inn is located directly on Highway 98, but 98 has only two lanes and no rush-hour traffic.

Niceville

Bluewater Bay

1950 Bluewater Boulevard
Niceville, FL 32578-9981
800-874-2128
850-897-3613
www.bwbresort.com

A resort and golf club overlooking a bay

C.E.O.: Richard Tucker. **Accommodations:** 85 rooms, suites, villas. **Rates:** Studios and efficiencies $75–$125, 1-bedroom villas $75–$159, 2-bedroom villas

$124–$215, 3-bedroom villas $155–$217; weekly and monthly rates; discounts; packages. **Minimum stay:** 2 nights with packages. **Added:** 6% tax. **Payment:** Major credit cards. **Children:** Free in room with parents. **Smoking:** Nonsmoking rooms available. **Open:** Year-round.

➤   **The water of the bay is a deep cobalt blue that invites swimming and boating as well as gazing from a chaise longue.**

Bluewater Bay sits on 2,000 acres north of Destin, just outside Niceville, a quiet Panhandle town. Much of the land overlooks the Choctawhatchee Bay. The various accommodations are well sited in the pine forests, and within the complex is a large residential development. There are jogging and bicycle trails along the roads and lots of kids playing basketball in their driveways.

At the resort, the feeling is either nautical or golf-oriented. Hotel-style accommodations consisting of one-bedroom studios and efficiencies are at the marina. The two-bedroom suites overlook the bay, and many three-bedroom units overlook the golf course.

There are some outstanding villas in the pine and deciduous woods around the beautiful golf courses. Gleneagles Green's two- and three-bedroom accommodations are stucco with shake roofs. The handsome Villas of St. Andrews are stone and stucco with one or two levels. Attractively decorated and ideal for a small family or two vacationing couples, these are the first choice of many guests. On the bay are the Bay Villa Condominiums, with efficiencies, one- and two-bedroom units, and two- and three-bedroom multilevel townhouses. All two- and three-bedroom accommodations have washers and dryers. There is also a laundromat at the marina.

The restaurant, located at the resort's golf club, is open for breakfast, lunch, and dinner. There is also a snack bar at the tennis shop and a lounge. Many guests cook for themselves, and there are supermarkets close by. If you are staying at a daily rate or have a tennis or golf package, daily maid service is provided, which includes light kitchen cleaning.

There are 19 tennis courts, 10 clay and 9 hard. Twelve are lighted. The pro shop has stringing service, ball machine rental, and video analysis equipment available. Tennis is free on the hard surfaces, and the charge for night play is minimal. Golf is on four 9-hole courses where guests can play a short game or combine two for an 18-hole game. The courses, designed by Tom Fazio and Jerry Pate, are ranked among the best in the state.

In the summer, the recreation center has activities for kids: field trips, arts and crafts, and tennis and golf instruction. The center has bike rentals and mini-golf. Babysitting service is available. The resort publishes *Out of the Blue,* a newsletter that lists current activities for both kids and adults.

Panama City Beach

Marriott Bay Point Resort Village

4200 Marriott Drive
Bay Point
Panama City Beach, FL 32408
800-874-7105
850-234-3307

A beautiful resort on a picturesque bay

General Manager: David Bartek. **Accommodations:** 355 rooms and garden suites. **Rates:** Rooms $89–$189, garden suites $109–$199; packages available. **Minimum stay:** On holidays and special weekends. **Added:** 9.5% tax. **Payment:** Major credit cards. **Children:** Under 18 free in room with parents. **Smoking:** Nonsmoking rooms available. **Open:** Year-round.

➤ **A short ride on the resort's pontoon boat takes you to Shell Beach, one of the most beautiful in Florida, with seven miles of fine, pale sand and gentle surf.**

Bay Point rests on a mainland lagoon and a quiet bay, but it feels like an island resort. Once you arrive at Bay Point, you won't want or need to leave. It has everything in the way of sports, recreation, dining, even shopping. Service is marked by the informality you would expect at a resort and the courtesy and graciousness you would find at a fine southern hotel.

The resort is near Panama City. The ride from the regional airport past miles of shopping malls and fast-food restaurants is unappealing, but as you drive through the security gates of Bay Point you leave it all behind.

Guest accommodations are in Bay Point's pink and gray Old Florida-style hotel. Built in 1986, it is five stories tall, with a gray tile roof and recessed balconies overlooking the water and the golf courses. The grounds are beautifully landscaped, with large beds of annuals, thousands of azaleas, tall loblolly pines and native magnolias, and a few palm trees and tropical ferns.

Guest rooms at Bay Point are roomy, with a choice of a king-size bed or two doubles, good traditional furniture, and reading lamps on the bedside wall. The rooms are equipped with refrigerators and coffeemakers and have good closet space. Upstairs rooms have small balconies, while first-floor lanai rooms have patios with a table and lawn chairs. Bathrooms have timed heat lights and a retractable drying line. Ironing boards, irons, and hair dryers are standard in every room.

Those who wish larger accommodations can rent the garden suites overlooking the golf fairways. Bay Point Resort, like all Marriotts, has some great packages. There are additional reductions for small groups and conventions, and much can be said for staying at Bay Point during the off-season; October and November are especially beautiful.

The back of the hotel faces a natural lagoon fronting on St. Andrews Bay and the St. Andrews State Park. Still farther out are the beach and the Gulf of Mexico. At Bay Point's marina, you can rent sailboats, Windsurfers, or snorkeling equipment, and charter boats for excellent deep-water fishing. With 200 slips, this is the largest private marina on the Gulf Coast.

Bay Point is famous for golf. Its Lagoon Legend course is said to be one of the toughest in the South. On this 7,080-yard, par 72 course ("the Monster"), 16 of the 18 holes have water hazards, and there are lots of berms and sand traps. But golfers play it with humor and compare games over a drink at the Lagoon Legend Clubhouse afterwards. Club Willard Meadows, designed by Willard Byrd, is a flatter, easier course with fewer water hazards. It still offers a challenging game on its open fairways, with some difficult sand and water hazards.

Tennis is also outstanding at Bay Point. There are 10 Har-Tru courts, four of which are lit at night. The pro shop rents and restrings rackets. Tennis instruction is available, and the pros can match you with other players. The resort hosts a number of competitions during the year.

There are several swimming pools, including a heated indoor pool and indoor and outdoor whirlpools, and a small but well-equipped fitness room. Bicycles are available for rent and, with 10 miles of paved roads and paths, Bay Point Resort is an ideal place for walking as well as bicycling. Its 1,100 acres are beautifully landscaped and maintained, and security is excellent. In March, 5,000 azaleas bloom in a spectacular display. One favorite stroll is the boardwalk across the Grand Lagoon to Teddy Tucker's, a weathered boathouse that serves drinks and casual meals.

The resort has a variety of restaurants, and the food and libations are excellent. One of the most popular restaurants, particularly with conventioneers, is Bayview. A buffet area serves large groups. Typical selections include broiled steaks and seafood specialties with delicate sauces. Service is courteous and a good deal speedier than in most Florida restaurants. Windows overlook the flowers and plants of the terrace outside and the Grand Lagoon and bay beyond.

Another popular restaurant is Stormy's Grill, adjacent to the Lagoon Legend Golf Course, serving sandwiches for lunch and steak and seafood for dinner. Stormy's includes a martini bar.

Two thirds of Bay Point's business is with convention groups. There are two conference areas to choose from — in the country club's conference center, which is across the parking lot, and in the hotel proper — with a total of 40,000 square feet of meeting space, including two ballrooms. Conference banquets are lavish.

Convention participants and their families can enjoy all the facilities of the resort. In the summer months, this includes an excellent kids' camp. The program is a bit like summer camp and includes a wide range of activities. Full- and half-day programs are available.

The Panhandle was once the home of Indian tribes who fished and crabbed. Their feasts are reenacted at Marriott's Indian fish roast every Friday and Saturday on the veranda of Fiddler's Green. Part of the resort was at one time an Indian "junkyard," where native women would toss cracked or broken pots.

Contributing to the self-contained island atmosphere is Bay Town, the small shopping center with an upscale women's clothing boutique, a post office, a bank, a dry cleaner and laundry, a hair salon, a gift shop, a deli, and a restaurant overlooking the marina. Bay Town is one more reason you won't want to leave this gracious "island" until you have to.

Pensacola

New World Inn

600 S. Palafox Street
Pensacola, FL 32501
850-432-4111

> **Once a harborfront
> warehouse, now a
> Pensacola landmark**

Manager: Janice Sheehan. **Accommodations:** 14 rooms and 2 suites. **Rates:** Rooms $70, suites $100; various discounts available; $10 for extra person. **Included:** Continental breakfast. **Minimum stay:** None. **Added:** 10% tax. **Payment:** Major credit cards. **Children:** Welcome; 18 and under free in room with parent. **Smoking:** Allowed. **Open:** Year-round.

➤ **The waterfront district and South Palafox are great for poking around in, with charming boutiques and antique shops selling silver, brass, Belgian lace, furniture, and art work. A few blocks away is a park and Pensacola's Museum of Art.**

New World Landing was originally a box factory. Today it's a popular inn, restaurant, and convention center. Restored and previously owned by Pensacola preservationists Kay and Arden Anderson, New World Landing was renovated with an eye toward luxury as well as history. Throughout the inn, the look of a 19th-century factory blends with Victorian opulence. Outside, a bow of windows dresses up the exterior of the restaurant, and a scalloped awning embellishes the brick-paved inn entrance. Beside the inn is a small city garden.

The oak floor of the entryway and check-in area is a dark parquet — not the original factory floor, but elegant and fitting for this hotel. The red brick ceiling supports have been left standing and give character to the lobby. The wooden check-in counter looks as if it were salvaged from an old hotel or a 19th-century dry goods store. A small sitting area opposite check-in has wing chairs and a camelback sofa. Here and throughout the hotel, the walls are decorated with 19th-century etchings and photographs.

A wide oak staircase takes guests to the second floor, where fourteen guest rooms, two suites, another sitting room, and a spacious hallway have been created out of the original huge open space. All the accommodations have been furnished with ceiling fans, four-poster beds, and deep carpets. The furniture is a mix of good reproductions, mostly in Queen Anne and Chippendale styles, and genuine antiques. The bathrooms have old brass fixtures, oak toilet seats, and Corian sinks. There are telephones in both the bedroom and bath.

The restaurant at New World Landing is made up of three separate and individually decorated dining rooms. The main dining room is the Barcelona Room, with Spanish decor, overlooking the garden at the entrance. Most often used for banquets is the Marseilles Room, with mirrored walls, fine wall paneling, brass and crystal chandeliers, and ornate window treatments. The Pensacola Room, another banquet facility, is more down-to-earth, with large photographs of waterfront and city activity in the 19th century. The food here is quite good and leans toward the Continental. Also popular is the inn's Liverpool Pub, an old-style bar with lots of brass and wood.

Though both the inn and the restaurant are intimate in scale, full-size gatherings are easily handled in New World Hall. The convention center can accommodate up to 1,000 for meetings, 800 for dining, and 600 for dancing. The hall can also be partitioned for smaller meetings.

New World Inn is a good jumping-off place from which to explore Pensacola's history. You can ride one of the inn's bikes or walk to a number of interesting buildings in the historic district overlooking the bay. Because the town escaped urban renewal in the 1950s and 1960s, many distinctively southern buildings remain. The Quayside Market, across the back parking lot, is a brick shopping complex with New Orleans-style wrought-iron balconies.

Pensacola Grand Hotel

200 E. Gregory Street
Pensacola, FL 32501
850-433-3336
Fax: 850-432-7572
Reservations: 800-348-3336

A grandly restored train depot

General Manager: Nancy Halford. **Accommodations:** 212 rooms and suites. **Rates:** Rooms $80–$105, suites $125–$250; $5 less on weeknights; honeymoon package available. **Minimum stay:** None. **Added:** 10% tax. **Payment:** Major credit cards. **Children:** Free in room with parents. **Smoking:** Nonsmoking rooms available. **Open:** Year-round.

➤ **Guests can wander through the elegantly refurbished waiting room of the old train station or relax with a drink in the club bar, then enjoy the comfort of a modern hotel room.**

Pensacola's recent revitalization is reflected in the Grand Hotel's blend of old and new. The historic Louisville and Nashville Depot has been painstakingly restored. The "old" — the stained and leaded glass, mosaic floors, and golden oak of the old station — is here; the "new" is the glass and steel high-rise addition behind it.

The two-story 1912 depot is a boxy structure of light brick. A wing that once stretched out along the railroad tracks has been cleverly converted into retail shops, an old-fashioned barber shop, and meeting space. There's also a restaurant, The 1912, which has excellent seafood.

Throughout the old depot, the original details and furnishings have been preserved and restored. In the waiting room lobby, an elaborate stained-glass lamp hangs above an exquisite green marble table. The adjacent picturesque bar has an equally captivating atmosphere.

The new building begins in the back of the reception area. The transition is marked by a change from mosaic floor to carpet, where the train tracks once ran. Here the walls are of modern black and green marble, and the new elevators have elegant brass doors. Curving up from the middle of this lobby and reception area is a brass and Plexiglas spiral staircase that leads up to the second-floor meeting space.

The old depot is a lot of fun, and the guest rooms in the modern glass tower rising behind it are quite comfortable. Some of the nicest are the two-level suites with Jacuzzi. Other suites are luxurious one- or two-bedroom accommodations. Some rooms look out at the highway, so ask about the view when making reservations.

Seaside

Seaside

County Road 30-A
P.O. Box 4730
Seaside, FL 32459
850-231-4224
800-277-8696
Fax: 850-231-2373

> **A beachside town of cottages encircling a town center**

Founder: Robert Davis. **Accommodations:** 200 suites, cottages, penthouses, and town homes. **Rates:** Dreamland Heights Suites from $241, Honeymoon Cottages from $367, Motor Courts from $145, Ruskin Place Townhouses from $467, (rates unavailable at press time for Josephine's French Country Inn rooms), vacation cottages $252–$1,214/night, $1,080–$7,220/week; off-season, midweek packages available. **Minimum stay:** 4 nights in vacation cottages during summer and holidays. **Added:** 10% tax; $25 reservation processing fee; 1% arts and entertainment fee. **Payment:** Major credit cards, traveler's checks, personal checks, cash. **Children:** Welcome. **Smoking:** Most accommodations are nonsmoking. **Open:** Year-round.

➤ **Although Seaside was initially a summer destination for Floridians and other southerners, it is becoming popular for fall and spring vacationers and it has become famous throughout the country for its town planning. A few people live here year-round. The beach pavilions on the dunes have become a symbol of Seaside and the relaxed style of life it promotes. Each brick street at Seaside has its own pavilion, and recent additions have**

**been extremely imaginative. They're particularly pleasant for drinks in the
late afternoon when the sun is going down over the Gulf of Mexico.**

Located on 80 acres of the Panhandle's Emerald Coast between
Panama City and Pensacola, Seaside is a planned community patterned after a 19th-century beach town. The developers took the
best from American beachside towns, threw in a little Disney fantasy, and added their own caprice.

Seaside was originally a parcel of beachfront property, covered
with palmetto and other scrub vegetation, that developer Robert
Davis inherited from his grandfather. With sandy soil, bordered by
wet marshes and dense woods of myrtle and oak, the land was un-
fit for agriculture. But several acres were right on the water, and
the rest had access to the water by the narrow secondary highway
that bisected the property. Davis built Seaside, a remarkable collection of Victorian- and early-20th-century-style beach cottages with
a town center and resort amenities.

Guests stay in the privately owned cottages in the resort's rental
pool, which are available at nightly, weekend, weekly, and seasonal
rates. The Dreamland Heights suites, the Motor Court, and the
French Country Inn appeal to those staying for a short period. Admittedly, staying here is expensive and there are costly and annoy-
ing add-ons, but Seaside is truly an experience.

Architectural styles in the cottages for rent remind one of seaside
towns like Key West, Nantucket, Cape May, Savannah, Charleston.
The cottages have crimped tin roofs and clapboards painted in
blues, grays, and ice cream colors like raspberry and lemon. Although all houses have heating and cooling systems, simple cross-
ventilation through open doors and windows works well at Seaside. The cottages have porches in a variety of styles: front porches,
back porches, side porches, widow's walks, screened towers, and
cupolas. Latticework and gingerbread are everywhere.

The interiors are well planned, with efficient, fully equipped
kitchens, antique furnishings (or good reproductions), comfortable
beds, washers and dryers, and homey touches like rocking chairs
and handmade quilts. Guests are welcomed with a basket of bottled water, gourmet coffee, a bottle of wine, and fresh flowers.

Groceries are available at the community's excellent but expensive produce and meat market. Both Destin and Panama City have
large supermarkets, and most families buy supplies on their way to
Seaside. Visitors can also find a variety of restaurants in Seaside
and nearby towns.

There is a wide range of accommodations: in addition to dozens
of cottages, there are suites on the third and fourth floors of the

Dreamland Heights building, an award-winning contemporary building (too contemporary for some tastes) by the architect Steven Holl. These suites have two floors, high ceilings, dramatic decor, roof terraces, and great views of the gulf. Children under the age of 12 are not permitted in these accommodations.

The Motor Court accommodations, just behind Central Square, are the most modest and the least expensive at Seaside. What they lack in water views they make up for in price and in their accessibility to Seaside activities. These accommodations are not for the claustrophobic, but they are cleverly designed and compact, with many built-ins. In only a few hundred square feet, there is a bedroom with queen-size bed, kitchenette, and sitting room with TV and VCR. Furnishings and decorative touches are circa 1950: Formica tables and Naugahyde chairs, movie posters, and art deco memorabilia.

The Honeymoon Cottages, right on the beach facing the gulf, are ideal for couples. Tall and narrow, they have a bedroom and bath on the first floor and a kitchen and sitting room on the second. They are small but well designed, with Scandinavian-style fireplaces in the sitting rooms, efficient kitchens, and ceramic tile baths. Offering special honeymoon packages, these accommodations are operated like a small luxury hotel, with bathrobes, nightly turndown service and refreshments, and room service. Each morning a breakfast basket is delivered to the cottage. Both floors of the honeymoon cottages have back porches that look out over the gulf and the sand dunes. The downstairs porch behind the bedroom has a deck and a Jacuzzi for two. Canvas curtains can be drawn across the screens for privacy. When it's breezy on the beach, the curtains billow out like sails.

Ruskin Place, Seaside's arts center, keeps some townhouses above the galleries and boutiques. Most of these are for rent by the day or week. The buildings look like row houses in an Old South or New England city and overlook the promenade and gardens of the artists' colony.

The oldest looking accommodations in Seaside are actually the newest: Josephine's French Country Inn. The inn was built in the style of a plantation home, with imposing white pillars, a crimped tin roof with chimneys at either end, a widow's walk on the third floor, verandas on the first and second floors, and a rose garden and white picket fence out front.

The floor plan is that of a traditional plantation house: a formal foyer (with grandfather clock), a front parlor on one side of the house and a dining room on the other, kitchen in the back, and a long hallway leading to a couple of back bedrooms. The dining room is an intimate restaurant; a fire crackles in the green marble fireplace on all but the warmest months.

The rooms all have antique and reproduction furnishings, brass light fixtures, pine floors, and fireplaces, where most guests enjoy the brunch delivered to them each day. Each room has a kitchen alcove with a microwave, small sink, coffeemaker, half-size fridge, and small-screen television.

Other accommodations under the wing of Josephine's include a guest house behind the main house with two one-bedroom suites. These are often used as honeymoon suites and are like a young couple's "first apartment."

Seaside's wide sweep of beach is surely one of the most beautiful in Florida. The sand is white and fine; the dunes have gentle contours and are covered with palmetto, catbrier vine, and sea oats. At times the water turns a dark indigo near the horizon and, because the sand beneath the water is so white, a pale aquamarine on the sandbars near the shore.

Although many people at Seaside cook in their cottages, there are a number of restaurants. Cafe Bouzouki serves fine Greek cuisine. Bud and Alley's is a Gulfside bistro with coastal cuisine and a rooftop deck. Shades, on Central Square, has a popular bar and a dinner menu that includes barbecued ribs and shrimp, crab cakes, and hamburgers. Josephine's Dining Room, at the Inn, serves roast duck and lamb, grilled steaks, and chicken dishes complemented by good wines. Cafe Spiazzia is an Italian café featuring pizza by the slice, gelato, and espresso. Pickles, Dawson's Yogurt, and the Modica Market have takeout for sandwiches, pretzels, hot dogs, ice cream and yogurt, homemade desserts, and drinks. Catering is available through Seaside Group Services.

Days at Seaside can be lazy or packed with activity. It's easy to start a game of volleyball on the beach behind Bud and Alley's restaurant. You can rent sailboats, catamarans, boogie boards, and "aqua trikes," and arrange for lessons in sailing and windsurfing at the Cabana Man. Large sailboats and deep-sea fishing craft can be chartered in nearby Destin. Kite flying is very popular at Seaside because of the steady breezes. The resort has three swimming pools, six tennis courts, shuffleboard, and world-class croquet. Bicycling is a favorite pastime at Seaside, and bikes can be rented at Seaside's swim and tennis area. Everybody at Seaside is a great walker — the best kind of exercise, because you can stop and chat with your neighbors.

Those who planned Seaside have done everything possible to promote neighborliness. For example, every house at Seaside must have a white picket fence, but rather than have the fences meet one another at property lines, town planners left a few feet of space between them for walking paths. The very layout of the town promotes friendliness: clustered around a town center, Seaside has its own post office, bank, shopping area, and town hall, as well as the recreational area. Cars are discouraged on the brick thoroughfares; most people bicycle or walk on the streets and oyster-shell paths. There is a sense of community here that is unusual and precious.

Tallahassee

Cabot Lodge

2735 N. Monroe Street
Tallahassee, FL 32303
800-223-1964 in U.S.
850-386-8880
Fax: 850-386-4254

A chain with exceptional hospitality

General Manager: Mickey Brady. **Accommodations:** 160 rooms. **Rates:** $69–$75 single; $6 extra person. **Included:** Continental breakfast and afternoon cocktails. **Minimum stay:** 2 nights on football weekends. **Added:** 10% tax. **Payment:** Major credit cards, personal checks with Diners or American Express credit card. **Children:** Under 18 free in room with parent. **Smoking:** Non-smoking rooms available. **Open:** Year-round.

➤ **Several separate buildings house the guest rooms, but there are only two floors to each, so the place seems small and innlike.**

Tallahassee has dozens of modern chain motels, but very few go beyond the ordinary and the boring. Cabot Lodge stands out as a rare property. It's not authentic Old Florida; construction is fairly recent, and the widow's walks on the roofs are just for show. But Cabot Lodge is very clean and neat, with chain-hotel efficiency, and the Old South hospitality is genuine.

The accommodations are standard motel rooms but are attractively decorated. Rooms have either one king-size bed or two doubles. Although there are no suites, families and couples traveling together can take connecting double rooms.

The main building, like all the guest room units, is a plantation-style structure of yellow clapboards with green trim and white-railed balconies. Its common room sets the Cabot Lodge apart from the other places on Route 27 — this spacious room looks and feels like a living room, with comfortable wing chairs and sofas. Guests can come anytime to sit and talk with friends, enjoy the tea and coffee that are always available, or borrow a book from the library.

Every evening from 5:30 to 7:30, complimentary cocktails are served at the small bar in the living room. Kids get free soda, and there's popcorn for everyone, popped on an old-fashioned popper. Guests really enjoy this, and, says one member of the staff, "If people linger past 7:30, it's O.K. This is the South."

Continental breakfast is laid out here, too, with fresh orange juice, croissants, and tea and coffee. Guests can eat in the living room or on the back porch, which runs the width of the building. The old green and white rockers and white tables and chairs give Cabot Lodge a homey feeling. The porch overlooks an oblong pool and a sunning area with lawn chairs and chaise lounges.

The young staff members — often college students — are polite and accommodating. They'll turn the porch into a reception area for a wedding or family reunion, or help you find the lodge's jogging trail by walking you all the way there. This is real southern hospitality, proffered without pretension.

Cabot Lodge is near the intersection of Route 27 and I-10, a short drive from the airport and downtown. Most people staying at Cabot Lodge are in Florida's capital city on professional or government business. The lodge caters to these busy people, but it is also appropriate for vacationing couples and families. Since 1993, there has been a second Cabot Lodge just off I-10 on Thomasville Road. Though it is a high-rise and lacks the charm of the original, it has the same high standards.

Governors Inn

209 S. Adams Street
Tallahassee, FL 32301
850-681-6855
800-342-7717 in Florida

A city hotel with southern ambience and service

Accommodations: 40 rooms and suites. **Rates:** Rooms $129, suites $149–$229; corporate, weekly, and monthly rates and packages available. **Included:** Continental breakfast and cocktails. **Minimum stay:** 2 nights on some football weekends. **Added:** 10% tax; $10 for extra adult. **Payment:** Major credit cards.

Children: Under 12 free in room with parents. **Smoking:** Nonsmoking rooms available. **Open:** Year-round.

➤ **There are several rooms for business meetings, conferences, and parties, including the Tallahassee Room, popular for small gatherings. Because the Governors Inn is close to state government buildings, conference rooms are in demand. Reserve well ahead of time, especially if the legislature is in session.**

The Governors Inn is outstanding for service, imaginative guest rooms, sensitively restored architecture, and a location convenient to the capitol district. The inn is the achievement of Bud Chiles, the son of Florida's late governor, Lawton Chiles, Bud's wife, Kitty, and some fellow visionaries. The group bought abandoned downtown property a few hundred feet from state government buildings on the lower end of Adams Street. Now referred to as Adams Street Commons, this area has since been rehabilitated as part of Tallahassee's historic district. It has cobblestone streets and charming brick and stucco buildings. The Chileses' work in opening the Governors Inn in 1984 was instrumental in the revitalization of the area.

A stucco building with awnings, the inn stands at the corner of Adams and College Avenue. It occupies two narrow buildings that were 19th-century hardware stores. The interior of Governors Inn is elegant, but nonetheless retains hints of its humble warehouse origins. At the top of a winding stairway is a second-floor corridor that links the two storefronts. The original stores had very high ceilings on both the first and second floors. The architect has made three floors of this space, creating some very interesting loft guest rooms.

No two rooms are alike. They differ not only in their decor but also in shape, height, the use of skylights, and the odd angles of their ceilings. All of the rooms are named after a governor and have a framed drawing of him, with a biographical sketch hanging on the wall. The furnishings are either antique or good reproductions in cherry, mahogany, or oak.

Many of the guest rooms are duplexes. The most popular for businesspeople, legislators, and lobbyists are the loft suites, with at least one couch, upholstered chairs, and a desk or table or both. The bedroom is in a loft accessible by a spiral staircase. The junior suites have a small work area with a desk or table and a double bed. Even these smaller, lower-priced rooms are elegantly decorated.

The largest suite, and one of the most luxurious, is the Governor Holland. It has an armoire hiding the TV and a large sitting area. The couch opens into a bed, as do all couches in the suites. The bath is extra large, with a whirlpool tub. The Governor Holland has one of the best views, overlooking Adams Street Commons. Other views at this urban inn overlook brick buildings or a College Park street scene.

Many businesspeople like to spend time in the Florida Room, the lounge off the lobby that manages to have the atmosphere of both a British club and a southern parlor. Inn guests meet here for complimentary cocktails from 5:00 till about 6:30. In the morning, a Continental breakfast of fruit, croissants, freshly squeezed orange juice, and coffee and tea is served here on fine china and silver.

The staff at the Governors Inn try to ensure a restful and gracious atmosphere. Many amenities make life easier for busy people: free valet parking, shoeshine service, complimentary morning newspaper, room service, several phone jacks in the rooms, copiers, a small library, and a message center. Weekend rates that are significantly lower than the weekly rates make the Governors Inn a great getaway for couples.

Wakulla Springs

Wakulla Springs Lodge

Wakulla Springs State Park & Lodge
550 Wakulla Park Drive
Wakulla Springs, FL 32305
850-224-5950
Fax: 850-561-7251

A 1930s-era lodge and nature preserve in the woods

Accommodations: 27 rooms. **Rates:** Rooms $69–$90, suite $250. **Minimum stay:** None. **Added:** 9% tax; $5 crib; $5 rollaway. **Payment:** Discover, MasterCard, Visa. **Children:** 12 and under free in room with parents. **Smoking:** Nonsmoking rooms available. **Open:** Year-round.

➤ **Swimming is popular at Wakulla Springs, with locals who come for the day as well as lodge guests. The deep river basin is clear and cold, and serves as one big swimming hole — but mainly for the ducks and alligators.**

Less than 15 miles south of Tallahassee, in the midst of pine forest and marshland, Wakulla Springs is one of the world's largest and deepest freshwater springs, with water so clear you can look down and see the bottom over a hundred feet below. The water from the spring — thousands of gallons gushing forth each second — forms the Wakulla River. The state park operates wildlife observation and glass-bottom boat tours on the river so that visitors can observe the spectacular wildlife that has found a haven here.

Since the 1940s, public access to the springs has been controlled. No private boating or fishing is allowed, and only one area is designated for swimming. As a result, the wildlife here is allowed to thrive in its "primal density," as the state's brochure says. Primal is right: vultures brood on cypress trees, dozens of baby alligators sun themselves on the bank next to their mothers, brown snakes slither up branches overhanging the river, long-legged egrets stand stock-still waiting to catch fish, and anhingas plunge underwater, then stand drying their wings on a stump in the river.

This is just during the summer, when the bird population is relatively low for the park and some of the other animals are too hot to be out. In fall and winter, the numbers of waterfowl swell, with the arrival of thousands of migratory birds, which rarely fly away when the tour boats come by.

The numbers and variety of deer, turkeys, snakes, alligators, rare snails, and jumping fish are breathtaking. They thrive in river, riverbank, and marsh, and in forests of wild magnolia, hickory, oak, and pine. Eerie cypress trees, always draped with Spanish moss, stand above the swamps and river. Nurturing it all is the spring — deep, ancient, amazingly clear.

Although Wakulla Springs has been a wildlife refuge for years, the state acquired the park in 1986, renaming it the Edward Ball Wakulla Springs State Park. Ball was a financier related by marriage to the DuPonts, who initially owned the land. In the late 1930s he developed it — or sensitively underdeveloped it — as a vacation refuge for his wealthy friends. From the beginning, it was not a sybaritic resort but a place for those who wanted a simple place to observe wildlife in a natural state.

Edward Ball built the two-story lodge in 1937. The architecture is Spanish Mission, with a red tile roof, a stucco exterior, generous archways, and in some cases, ornate grilles over the windows. It looks the way a lodge ought to, with a great stone fireplace, comfortable sofas and chairs, and high, beamed ceilings. These beams are intricately painted with Aztec and Toltec symbols, as well as river scenes, wildflowers, Spanish galleons, and geometric designs, painted by a German immigrant who left his work unsigned.

Guests entering the lodge from the back garden come into a glass-enclosed porch that is part of an arched loggia. The ceiling here is of pecky cypress and the walls are of adobe. Small bamboo tables and chairs make the porch a good place for playing cards or talking with friends, and the porch can be set up for conference groups and wedding parties. The terrace overlooks the back lawn and the wide paths that slope down to the springs and swimming area.

Marble is used extensively inside. Some of it is from France and Italy, but most is from Tennessee, brought here by train in the 1930s. The beautiful stone — gray and white or pink-veined — is used everywhere on the stairs and floors, and runs halfway up the high walls.

The dining room, just off the lobby, is lent a warmer ambience by many arched windows overlooking the yard and a large bird feeder. The food served is one of the best-kept secrets of Florida: hearty, healthful, cheap, and, in some cases, very southern. Breakfast can be as large or small as you wish, with a la carte offerings and a "real southern breakfast" of ham or fried chicken, grits, biscuits, and coffee.

For lunch, guests can fill up on the excellent navy bean soup or oyster stew. There are a variety of salads, fresh Apalachicola oysters, country ham, pork chops, native fish, and a good, reasonably priced steak. The waitresses are mostly local and friendly; the service is leisurely but good. A few fancier entrées are added at dinner, like quail and a seafood platter. There is also a children's menu. Desserts are rich and tempting: pecan pie, Key lime pie, strawberry shortcake. Prices are as low as you'd expect in a state park.

In the off season, Wakulla Springs is particularly popular with ornithologists and conservationists, though the conference center hosts a variety of business, church, and professional groups. There are small conference rooms in the lodge itself and a larger, separate conference area near the boat dock. Another popular room for groups is part of Edward Ball's original private quarters. With a large conference table as well as a comfortable sofa and easy chairs, it's suitable not only as a small conference room but as a parlor suite for reunions and vacationing groups.

Adjoining the parlor are the two best guest rooms in the lodge. These rooms, which can be rented separately or together, have marble floors with Oriental rugs, huge walk-in closets, and beautiful Spanish grilles over the windows.

The other guest rooms are less spectacular but have recently been spruced up with new bedspreads and drapes. The furniture is well worn, and some of the old Oriental rugs on the marble floors are a little thin. Though the rooms are a bit austere, they're high-ceilinged and spacious. The closets are all walk-in, and the furnishings include some antiques. All of the rooms have heating and air conditioning.

The fact that most of the rooms are spare will hardly cramp your visit. Nobody comes to Wakulla Lodge to sit in a room all day. The lobby is a favorite gathering place for visitors in cool weather. The one TV in the lodge is here, and there are magazines, games, and checkers tables. During balmy weather in the spring and fall, everyone is outside. A charming stone path winds across the wide lawn and back garden to the spring. In winter, the big camellia bushes that line the path are in bloom. It's easy to spend an hour or two here on one of the Victorian-style white iron and wood benches, watching the birds swoop, mullets leap from the water, and hyperactive gray squirrels strew nutshells all over the path.

Miles of nature trails in the state park wind through fields and vine-entangled forests of beech, pine, hickory, live oak, maple, and wild magnolia. The soil here is not sandy like most of Florida's; it's a pale coppery red. Apply insect repellent liberally when walking on the nature trails or anywhere at Wakulla Springs: the birds are not the only flying creatures who thrive here.

If possible, visit Wakulla Springs in the off season or on a summer weekday. On summer weekends, the place can be mobbed with day visitors, and the boat rides lose some of their charm when there are two more boats behind you with guides broadcasting their tour spiel. Still, glass-bottom boat trips, a bargain at $4.50 for adults and $2.25 for children, are the highlight of most people's visit — but don't feed the alligators!

Wakulla Springs has a long, legend-filled history. Native Americans called it the "mysteries of strange water" and often visited the springs for their healing powers. Ponce de Leon sailed up the St. Marks River to reach Wakulla in 1513, apparently certain that this was the true Fountain of Youth. On a later visit in 1521, he was attacked by Indians defending their territory and died in Cuba of his wounds, deliriously begging to return to the springs. Wakulla Springs has always had an aura of mystery and grandeur for those who came here, no matter what they were seeking. Perhaps the most striking thought for visitors skimming over the clean, crystal waters in a boat today, past vultures and long-necked herons, is that this is what the subtropical world was like before it was so drastically civilized.

Central Florida and Disney World

Best B&Bs

Gainesville
Magnolia Plantation, 176
Sweetwater Branch Inn B&B and the McKenzie Home, 179
Lake Buena Vista
Perri House Bed & Breakfast Inn, 187
Lake Helen
Clauser's Bed and Breakfast, 202
Maitland
Thurston House, 208
Micanopy
The Herlong Mansion, 210
Mount Dora
Darst Victorian Manor B&B, 213
Dora Way B&B, 215
Lakeside Inn, 217
Magnolia Inn, 176
Ocala
Seven Sisters Inn, 221
Orlando
Courtyard at Lake Lucerne, 224
Sanford
The Higgins House, 235
Winter Park
The Fortnightly Inn, 237
Park Plaza, 239

Best Budget Finds

Kissimmee
Wynfield Inn — Main Gate, 186
Orlando
Wynfield Inn — Westwood, 186

Best City Stop

Orlando
Orlando Marriott Downtown, 229

Best Eclectic Find

Lake Wales
Chalet Suzanne, 205

Best Resorts and Spas

Grenelefe
Grenelefe Golf & Tennis Resort, 182
Howey-in-the-Hills
Mission Inn Golf and Tennis Resort, 184
Lake Buena Vista
The Walt Disney World Resorts, 191
Walt Disney World Swan and Dolphin, 200
Orlando
Hyatt Regency Grand Cypress Resort, 227
The Peabody Orlando, 230
Westgate Lakes Family Resort, 232

Central Florida was at one time the least developed part of Florida — a fact not lost on Walt Disney when he sent his minions out to buy land for Disney World in the 1970s. In the center of the state, the geological origins of the Florida peninsula are at their most obvious. Much of the soil is a grayish white mix of sand and limestone, excellent for citrus. Of course, many of the citrus groves in this agricultural region have been cut down to make way for housing developments, mobile home parks, restaurants, Disney World, and various secondary attractions. Nonetheless, it is still possible to go for a Sunday ride in the citrus-growing regions south of **Orlando** and **Lake Buena Vista** and smell the orange blossoms.

Palmettos grow in profusion in the sandy soil, with tall pine trees above. Some parts of central Florida along highways that run east and west, like Route 60, are almost desertlike, with only low plant growth. But when you add topsoil to the sand and plant flowers and trees and give them plenty of water, even these areas become lush. Orlando and all of the areas developed just south of the city have a profusion of flowering and green plants, both native and imported. The landscaping at Disney World and Sea World is particularly beautiful.

In culinary offerings, central Florida is given over to fast food, though there are fine restaurants north of Orlando in **Winter Park** and to the south at Chalet Suzanne in **Lake Wales,** as well as in

Orlando proper. The Walt Disney World hotels, the Hyatt Grand Cypress Hotel, and other major hostelries near Disney World have good, sometimes outstanding, dining.

Northeast of Orlando is the city of **Gainesville,** site of the University of Florida. Farther south is Florida's beautiful horse country and the historic town of **Ocala.** These two towns, as well as **Sanford** to the northeast of Orlando, have historic districts that are worth exploring. But the city most often visited in Central Florida is, of course, Orlando, site of a number of corporate headquarters, and Lake Buena Vista, the town just south of the city that is synonymous with Disney.

Disney World is made up of the Magic Kingdom, EPCOT, Animal Kingdom, and the Disney-MGM Studios. The Magic Kingdom itself has several separate "kingdoms": Fantasyland, Adventureland, Frontierland, Toontown, and Tomorrowland. Fantasyland is usually the favorite of young children, while older children love the other four. However, it's not easy to predict who will like what at what age, so it's best to try to see a bit of each "land" the first day and then decide on where to go on succeeding days. Although many people who haven't visited Disney World assume that the Magic Kingdom is the place for families with small children, the Magic Kingdom is fun for all ages, including grandparents and honeymooners.

EPCOT has two entities: futuristic technology and international culture. EPCOT had become a disappointment in past years; some of the buildings at the front of the park were looking shabby and a bit absurd in their futuristic pretensions — essentially like tired Star Trek sets. Recently, however, the buildings have been spruced up and new exhibits added, so that EPCOT is more attractive and topically educational.

The Disney-MGM Studios Theme Park is fun and flashy. It is similar to the traditional California and Florida movie studio parks, but with rides, performances, and shops and restaurants, many of them decorated in a glitzy, art deco style. Disney-MGM Studios is especially fun at night, so many tourists enter the gates in the late afternoon and stay till midnight.

Disney's newest theme park is Animal Kingdom, featuring Lion King characters, safari rides, and fantasy adventures such as a dinosaur dig. The park also has hundreds of free-roaming animals.

There is a running debate over whether it's better to stay at a hotel on Disney property or somewhere off the grounds. This comes down to a matter of budget and taste. If you're going to Florida to relax or play tennis and plan to make Disney World a one-day side trip, it's probably better to stay in one of the excellent resorts or B&Bs nearby. If you have small children and are traveling to Florida exclusively to see Disney World, consider staying at one of the Disney hotels or resorts on the monorail, which goes directly to the Magic Kingdom. Most of the hotels on the monorail are quite expensive, but being able to get on this futuristic conveyance with little kids every morning and back again at the end of a long day is worth the money for many families.

Disney accommodations need to be reserved as much as a year in advance if you're arriving during the summer or a holiday, and four to six months ahead if you're coming at a less popular time of year. This is particularly true of the three hotels on the monorail. However, cancellations do occur. If the Disney people at Central Reservations tell you there are no vacancies at the hotel of your choice, get directions anyway and stop by at 3 P.M. on the day you want a room. You might luck out.

A few tips for enjoying Disney World: start early, bring sunscreen, and wear your most comfortable shoes. If you aren't burdened with a lot of baby bottles and paraphernalia, bring a second light pair of shoes to change into after lunch. Be certain to make dinner reservations at least 24 hours ahead, especially at EPCOT's ethnic restaurants in the World Showcase.

Consider visiting the parks from mid-September to mid-December. Many locals visit during the weeks between Thanksgiving and Christmas, a good sign that this is a quiet time. If you don't have this much flexibility, try planning your vacation so that you are visiting the parks on Thursday, Friday (the lightest day of the week), or on Sunday morning. For more information, call 407-934-7639 or write to the Walt Disney World Central Reservations Office, P.O. Box 10000, Lake Buena Vista, FL 32830, and read and plan as much as you can before going.

Another tip: when you go through the gates at the Magic Kingdom, head left — not right, like everybody else; it makes for less crowding. At EPCOT, walk to the international exhibits in World Showcase at the back of the park first, eat lunch at one of the ethnic restaurants there, and then visit Future World at the front of the park in the afternoon when everybody else is at the international exhibits. If you're going to be visiting Disney World for an entire week, it's wise to invest in one of the paperbacks on Disney World; Birnbaum's guidebook is the most comprehensive.

Gainesville

Magnolia Plantation

309 S.E. Seventh Street
Gainesville, FL 32601
800-201-2379
352-375-6653
www.magnoliabnb.com

> A step back in time to a
> quieter, more gracious era

Proprietors: Cindy and Joe Montalto. **Accommodations:** 6 rooms. **Rates:** Rooms $90–$160; special rates for corporate and weekday guests; wedding packages; special rates for extended stays and reunions. **Included:** Full breakfast, beverages and home-baked snacks during the day. **Minimum stay:** 2 nights for cottages; 2 nights for rooms during football weekends and some special events. **Added:** 9% tax. **Payment:** Major credit cards, traveler's checks. **Children:** Discouraged because of antique furnishings. **Smoking:** On verandas only. **Open:** Year-round.

➤ **Views from the large, double-hung windows are of magnolia trees and flowers on the sides and front of the house, and in the back, of a brick-paved patio and a pond. This wonderful retreat also has two waterfalls of native limestone. A tiny arched bridge leads to a natural wood gazebo.**

Innkeepers Cindy and Joe Montalto met and fell in love as students at Gainesville's University of Florida. After leaving the university and pursuing their careers, they dreamed of returning to Gaines-ville and opening a B&B. The realization of their dream was a true labor of love — and a nearly backbreaking one — as they shoveled out debris, refinished floors, and painted the walls of the faded Victorian mansion they bought in Gainesville's historic district.

The architecture of the house, usually called French Second Empire, looks more like New Orleans than Old Florida. The mansard roof is of red and green slate tiles in the variety of shapes popular during the Victorian era: rectangular, hexagonal, square, and fish scale. On one side of the house is a four-story tower, and on the front and back are old-fashioned verandas with Italianate brackets. Cindy and Joe had the Victorian details of the clapboard structure painted in several different historic colors.

Downstairs is a ladies' parlor and a gentlemen's parlor, each with a fireplace (there are 10 fireplaces altogether). These were left intact, with the original faux marble design painted on the slate and a beautiful tile hearth. The parlors are furnished with an old piano and a pedal organ, wing chairs, and other period antiques.

At the large oval table in the dining room, Cindy and Joe serve imaginative breakfasts of what they call "funk food": chocolate chip pancakes, French toast stuffed with orange marmalade, honey, and cream cheese, macadamia nut French toast, piña colada muffins, waffles with whipped cream and apples, soufflés and quiches. There is always fresh fruit, juice, coffee, and tea. A complimentary glass of wine is served upon each guest's arrival.

Cindy and Joe offer several special packages, which they call "romantic notions." Their Mini Wedding and Reception for 10 or fewer people includes two bottles of champagne, bride and groom toasting glasses, and the services of a notary public to perform the ceremony. Dinner for Two is at a local restaurant and includes theater tickets, a horse and carriage ride to and from the theater, and candlelight, champagne, and soft music in the room upon the couple's return to the B&B. Cindy and Joe are forever thinking up new ideas and also invite guests to create their own romantic notions.

Guest rooms further the theme of romance. In the back of the house is the Magnolia Plantation's only first-floor bedroom, Jasmine. It features a queen-size sleigh bed, a marbleized slate and tile fireplace, an old-fashioned paddle fan, and an ensemble of family pictures on the mantel. Windows are tall and the ceiling high, as was common in Florida before the advent of air conditioning. Although there certainly is air conditioning at the Magnolia Plantation today, Cindy and Joe have worked hard "to give people an idea of what life was like" a century ago. Thus they have not installed separate modern showers but have opted for brass shower attachments above the old-fashioned tubs.

On the second floor is Heather, a small back room with pink walls and a white iron queen-size bed. Azalea features a mahogany four-poster queen-size bed and a clawfoot tub right in the room; the toilet and corner sink are in the little bathroom, a converted closet. The walls are rose and the large windows are framed by green and rose stenciling.

Gardenia is Magnolia Plantation's bridal chamber. On the pale yellow walls are wedding photographs of Montalto family members and other memorabilia. The antique Eastlake double bed has a regular mattress topped by a thick feather bed and a white lace spread. Two wing chairs stand before the lace-curtained windows. A clawfoot tub, its underside painted deep cobalt blue, is right in the room, draped in white netting, while a porcelain sink and toilet are in a little bathroom.

Magnolia, the former master bedroom, has its original clawfoot tub, push-button toilet, and old sink. This room has an antique bedstead that accommodates a queen-size mattress. The walls are a light teal, and ruffled balloon curtains in deep rose are at the windows. The fireplace is of heart pine, intricately carved and incised with gold. All fireplaces are equipped with gas logs.

Brick walkways on each side of the Magnolia Plantation lead to cottages that Cindy and Joe bought and restored, with long-term stays and couples in mind. Miss Huey's Cottage was built in the 1800s and then moved to its present site in the 1940s. Homey and unpretentious, this cracker-style house has two bedrooms and a bath, a living room, and a small, efficient kitchen. The living room has a sofa and easy chair, a TV/VCR, and a gas fireplace. The front and back porches have rocking chairs and views overlooking flowerbeds, flowering shrubs, and shade trees. This cottage (and some of the Plantation's other accommodations) has its own telephone and answering machine. Cindy's new cookbook is in the kitchen.

The Secret Garden and Jessica's Courtyard, both in the second cottage, are more elegant. A brick walkway curves around a fountain and beautiful tiered flowerbeds. French doors lead into a glassed-in sun porch furnished in wicker. Each unit has two bedrooms, a full kitchen, a living room/dining room, its own private garden and shared bathrooms, which have large Jacuzzi tubs plus a shower. One bedroom has a queen-size bed; the other has twin beds, which Cindy and Joe can easily and comfortably convert into a king. Cindy and Joe have done lots of special things in the rooms. In one of the Secret Garden bedrooms, they converted the closet into a built-in Jeffersonian bed with storage underneath. Decor is Shaker or traditional.

Magnolia Plantation has been a family effort in many ways. Joe's father, a landscape architect, helped Joe build the pond and waterfalls, and his mother hunted down antique furnishings for the house. His aunt and uncle donated their German lace curtains, and Cindy's aunt gave them heirlooms that had belonged to her grandparents. Cindy's mother, who lives in a small carriage house behind the inn, takes care of the gardens and manages the inn when the couple are away. Magnolia Plantation is truly a family home, and Cindy and Joe love sharing it with guests.

Sweetwater Branch Inn B&B and the McKenzie Home

625 E. University Avenue
Gainesvil|| e, FL 32601
800-595-7760
352-373-6760
www.sweetwaterinn.com

> An ideal place for a business retreat, parents' weekend, anniversary celebration, honeymoon — or for the wedding itself

Innkeeper: Cornelia Holbrook. **Accommodations:** 13 rooms, 1 carriage house, 1 honeymoon cottage. **Rates:** $72–$150; corporate and extended-stay rates. **Included:** Full breakfast, evening wine. **Minimum stay:** Some on football weekends, graduation, etc. **Added:** 9% tax. **Payment:** Cash, credit cards, traveler's checks. **Children:** Welcome in the Carriage House. **Smoking:** Allowed on the verandas and in the garden. **Open:** Year-round.

➤ **Here you can sit and read under the shade of a vine-covered arbor, soak in an old clawfoot tub or modern whirlpool bath, fall asleep under a lace canopy, and awaken to the fragrance of a gourmet breakfast.**

The Sweetwater Branch Inn is just a stone's throw from the University of Florida and is one of Gainesville's best B&Bs. It is also an acre-plus complex that includes the Cushman-Colson (or Main) House, the McKenzie Home, McKenzie Hall, the Honeymoon Cottage, and the Carriage House. Brick walkways, arched bridges, and lovely gardens tie it all together.

There are dozens of picture-perfect scenarios for wedding photos, and weddings are a major part of business here. Make no mistake about it, Sweetwater *is* a business enterprise; above the star-shaped, wrought-iron gate to the property is a sign: "Event Parking — private lot between 1st and 2nd Avenue." But whatever brings you to Gainesville and the Sweetwater Branch Inn, you can have a wonderful time here.

Innkeeper Cornelia Holbrook grew up in the McKenzie Home and has lovingly restored it and the Cushman-Colson House, both Queen Anne Victorians. When Cornelia began her business, she started out with seven rooms at the Cushman-Colson House and called it the Sweetwater Branch Inn, after the little stream that runs through the back of the property. She then bought the McKenzie, built the McKenzie Hall in the back of the property for business meetings and seminars, and opened the Carriage House and the Honeymoon Cottage. The office, for guest registration and event planning, is located behind the Cushman-Colson House and includes the Carriage House accommodation, an apartment that sleeps five and can be rented by the night, week, or month. The garden courtyard in front of the Carriage House leads to a pathway that winds past a small landscaped pond and over a bridge to the brick patio and the flowerbeds, trellised arbors, fountains, and gazebo of McKenzie Gardens.

Most guests stay in either the Cushman-Colson House or the McKenzie Home. The clapboards of the Cushman-Colson House are painted in soft pastels. Geometrical gingerbread railings and brackets accent the broad porch. A typical bedroom in the Cushman-Colson House has 19th-century oak furniture, pine floor and Oriental rugs, and a private bath with a clawfoot tub with shower head. Many guest rooms have a little alcove, a sun room, or a sitting area, so that rooms often feel more like suites. A nice extra on the second floor is the surprisingly spacious landing, which has three light-filled windows and is furnished with an old-fashioned fainting couch. Downstairs are formal parlors furnished with period furniture set up primarily as dining rooms for guests. There's also a little breakfast room, its walls painted with bright sunflowers.

Next door, the McKenzie Home is even more impressive, with gables and dormers, scrolled porch brackets, balconies, bay windows, chimneys, and a turret. Painted in shades of blue, cream, and yellow, with the turnings of the veranda railings picked out in chocolate brown and Williamsburg blue, the McKenzie is surely one of the most exquisite examples of Queen Anne architecture in the United States. The first-floor veranda, which sweeps around the house and even includes a gazebo in one corner, is worth the price of an overnight stay. From this porch you can see along the vine-covered arbor to University Avenue. The street is busy, but the lawn and landscaping serve as a buffer between the traffic and this other world, which is, visually, out of another century.

Inside is a small oval anteroom and parlor on one side and, on the other side, two parlor/dining areas used for wedding receptions and other events. The fireplaces in both the anteroom and the parlors have gargoyle-like iron fire screens, imported from Italy, in the shape of a roaring lion's face. The wide trim around all of the doors and floorboards are of carved wood in an intricate floral pattern, a very unusual feature. A carved spiral staircase leads to the upstairs bedrooms. Although the downstairs of the house is usually reserved for wedding receptions, the rooms upstairs are available for a stay as short as one night.

The rooms are furnished with old writing desks and chairs and queen-size four-poster and sleigh beds. Elaborate window treatments frame the long, southern-style windows. The private baths have varied decor and amenities, including a step-down 1930s bathroom tiled in pink, with glass brick accents and a two-person shower. Views are usually of the gardens and, occasionally, the street. Giovanna's room has a working gas fireplace that can be lit in the winter. Luisa's Room, in the attic, has the best whirlpool tub at the inn and a stained-glass window.

The Honeymoon Cottage was built in 1885 and has a living room with a fireplace and a Jacuzzi. The bedroom also has a fireplace, as well as a full bath and a small kitchen. The price of the cottage is lowered on weekday nights as are the other accommodations at the B&B. All accommodations have TVs and phones, with a complimentary morning newspaper as well as terry-cloth robes for use during your stay. A fax machine is also available.

Breakfast is gourmet: quiche, crepes, croissants — something new each day — and always an assortment of fresh fruits and juice. The Sweetwater is very proud of its own blend of Costa Rican coffee. You can eat at one of the formal dining room tables with other guests or at one of the small tables in the Cushman-Colson breakfast room. By prior arrangement, you can also have breakfast brought to your room. In the evening, a complimentary glass of wine is provided.

Grenelefe

Grenelefe Golf & Tennis Resort

3200 State Road 546
Grenelefe, FL 33844
800-237-9549
941-422-7511
www.grenelefe.com

A sophisticated Florida resort in citrus country

Managing Director: Dominique Audran. **Accommodations:** 850 villa suites. **Rates:** Villas $119–$305. **Added:** 10% tax. **Payment:** Major credit cards, personal checks. **Children:** Under 18 free in room with parents. **Smoking:** Non-smoking rooms available. **Open:** Year-round.

➤ **Even if you aren't an avid fisher, the experience of fishing here should not be missed. The locals who take guests out in their boats are an independent lot and have many colorful stories to tell.**

Grenelefe is only 30 minutes from Disney World, but there is a country feel to this citrus-growing region, reflected in the split-rail fences and broad velvety lawns of the resort. This is a place where you can get away to play tennis or golf (and, if you're here for a convention, to work a little), but it's close enough to EPCOT and the Magic Kingdom for a day or two of Disney fun.

A large percentage of Grenelefe's business is in conventions and executive retreats. The reception center and conference center are on a rise overlooking a championship golf course. The conference center, which can accommodate up to 2,000 people, provides high-tech equipment and professional staging and lighting. Facilities include an outdoor pavilion overlooking the pool that can seat up to 600 and is often used for barbecues. The conference center is well away from the villa accommodations. This is appreciated by families and couples on vacation as well as by businesspeople who wish to have a self-contained environment without children underfoot during the day.

This is one of the best resorts in Florida for golf and tennis; it is also a great place to fish. Spring-fed Lake Marion has 6,400 square acres of fresh water, and there is a rustic tackle shop and dock, where guests can sign up for excursions with local fishermen. A large blue heron lives near the dock and strides deliberately up and down the weathered pier. Dense native forests skirt the lake, and hundreds of alligators make their home here, the babies sunning themselves on lily pads while big gators dive underneath when boats pass. Needless to say, swimming is forbidden in the lake.

For exciting landlubber activity, there is always tennis and golf. Grenelefe has 20 well-tended courts, two of grass and 11 lighted. The complex includes a 1,700-seat tennis stadium. Every year, the resort hosts adult and junior tournaments. This is a good place to watch, learn, and play the game.

Golf is just as impressive. There are three beautiful courses: the East Course, with level greens and traps to the sides; the South Course, a British design with numerous sand traps and water hazards; and the challenging West Course, which has been ranked best in Florida for several years by *Golfweek* magazine. All three courses have been sculpted out of the forests, marshlands, and fields of Grenelefe.

The clustered low-rise villas overlook the fairways. Grenelefe has 850 accommodations, with spacious kitchens, pullout couches in the living/dining rooms, double beds in all bedrooms, and decks overlooking the fairways. Each kitchen comes with an icemaker, full refrigerator, and coffeemaker, and the living room has cable TV with movie channels. All the villas are privately owned and individually decorated, and many have been recently refurbished.

The groups of villas form small communities, with shared swimming pools and recreation areas tucked into the woods. Although there is a large pool behind the conference center, most vacationers use the private ones. The property also has miniature golf, a basketball court, bicycle trails (with rental bikes available), and nature walks.

The abundance of herons in the resort's marshes inspired the name of the resort's premier restaurant, the Grene Heron. Apart from Chalet Suzanne in nearby Lake Wales, this is the best restaurant in the area. The menu features both Continental and traditional American dishes.

Also on the property is Camelot, a large, airy restaurant serving three meals a day, with excellent service and an imaginative menu. This casual eatery has an open feel, with lots of windows overlooking the South Golf Course and a patio. The seafood buffet is especially good. Lancelot's, a lounge, serves some food during the day and has a soup and sandwich buffet from 11:30 A.M. to 2 P.M. for busy conventioneers and golfers in a rush to get back on the links. It's open to the public in the evening.

Grenelefe is named after a character in Robin Hood and has borrowed many names from English myths and storybooks. The roads running through the woods to the villas have names like Canterbury Drive and Robyn Lane. But apart from the names, there is nothing cutesy about Grenelefe, and nothing glitzy either. This is a down-to-earth place for tennis, golf, and fishing, wildlife watching, fine food, and sound sleep.

Howey-in-the-Hills

Mission Inn Golf and Tennis Resort

Highways 19 & 48
10400 County Road 48
Howey-in-the-Hills, FL 34737
800-874-9053
352-324-3101
Fax: 352-324-2636

> **A Spanish-style golf and tennis resort in hill country**

Manager: Trey Purser. **Accommodations:** 189 rooms. **Rates:** Rooms $125–$215, suites $145–$435, villas $230–$460; packages available. **Minimum stay:** 2 nights with packages. **Added:** 9% tax; $7 rollaway. **Payment:** Major credit cards, personal checks. **Children:** Under 12 free in room with parents. **Smoking:** Nonsmoking rooms available. **Open:** Year-round.

➤ **The resort is meticulously maintained, with lots of flowerbeds and clay pots of colorful annuals on the patios. The buildings have buff-colored stucco walls and terra cotta tile roofs. Arched walkways lead through lovely courtyards with copper and wood benches. Spanish tiles are everywhere: on the floors, in the fountains and pool, and even embedded in some of the walls.**

Howey-in-the-Hills is in the low, rolling hills of this citrus-growing region. To those used to the Appalachians or Rocky Mountain foothills, these "hills" will look like little rises in the landscape, but you have to remember that most of the rest of Florida is as flat as a pancake. Another stretch of the imagination is in the resort's name: there never was a mission here. The family who bought the land and adjacent 1920s-era golf course with the idea of creating a resort simply wanted to design it on a Spanish mission theme. They did a wonderful job.

The Mission Inn feels like a secluded estate, though its only 35 minutes northwest of Walt Disney World, EPCOT, and Sea World, and about 15 minutes from the charming town of Mount Dora. But Mission Hills is very much a destination resort, with plenty to fill every day on the property itself. Mission Inn's 18-hole championship golf course is consistently rated among the top 25 in a state with over 1,000 of them. Recently, a second golf course was added, making a total of 36 holes. There are also tennis, shuffleboard, and volleyball courts, jogging trails, and bicycles for rent. For children there is a playhouse with a Spanish tile roof. The inn is surrounded by lakes and ponds, affording plenty of opportunity for sailing, motorboating, and fishing.

El Conquistador, the inn's elegant dining room, serves both American and Continental cuisine. Many dishes have delicious cream sauces, and the desserts are rich. The informal alfresco eating area that overlooks the golf course features buffet tables that are almost spilling over with food throughout the morning and afternoon. The casual Nicker's Restaurant, in the resort's clubhouse, overlooks another part of the course.

The guest rooms, all of which overlook either the golf course or the tennis courts, are luxurious and beautifully appointed. Deluxe hotel rooms, one- and two-bedroom suites, and club suites are available in the center of the resort. The most secluded accommodations are the Mission Santa Cruz villas, small, luxurious homes with two bedrooms, a living room, kitchen, dining area, wet bar, patio, private courtyard, and garage. No two are exactly alike.

No accommodation is inexpensive at Mission Inn, but the amenities justify the price. In the villas, you can cut down on expenses by cooking some of your own meals. Holiday packages are available for all accommodations; inquire about them when calling for information.

The Mission Inn has excellent conference facilities, with some meeting rooms off the charming arched walkways. The main conference center is near the Plaza de la Fontana, a romantic spot with a tiled fountain and mission bell.

Kissimmee

Wynfield Inn — Main Gate

5335 U.S. Highway 192 East
Kissimmee, FL 32741-9401
800-346-1551
407-396-2121
Fax: 407-396-1142
wynfieldfl@aol.com
www.orlando.com/wynfield

| **A budget motel a few minutes from Disney** |

Accommodations: 216 rooms. **Rates:** $49–$99. **Included:** Coffee and tea in lobby. **Minimum stay:** None. **Added:** 12% tax; $10 rollaway; cribs free. **Payment:** Major credit cards. **Children:** Under 17 free in room with parents. **Smoking:** Nonsmoking rooms available. **Open:** Year-round.

➤ **The Wynfield is about 10 minutes from the main entrance to the Magic Kingdom and 15 minutes from EPCOT and Sea World. The inn provides bus transportation to these attractions for a small fee.**

For anyone looking for reasonably priced accommodations close to Walt Disney World, this is the place to be. The Wynfield Inn is a family motel with a well-designed outdoor recreational area and a friendly staff.

This is an immaculate clapboard motel, New England style. The lounge feels like a friend's living room, with comfortable sofas. Free coffee, tea, and fruit are always available in the lobby, 24 hours a day. Near the lobby but sequestered from it is an electronic game room that is used night and day by teens and their younger brothers and sisters. Also well away from the lobby and living room are vending machines and laundry facilities.

The Wynfield has a large landscaped patio with a pool for adults and an adjacent wading pool for little ones. Adjacent to the Wynfield is a small restaurant. There are also plenty of restaurants at Disney World and other area attractions.

The rooms are identical, with serviceable motel furniture and wall-to-wall carpeting. Hair dryers, irons, and ironing boards are available at the front desk. The rooms are in three-story units built around the pool, so most have views of the swimming pool and grounds. Unlike many places in the Orlando/Disney World region, the Wynfield Inn has a meeting place but no convention space, making for a quiet family retreat as well as substantial savings.

Lake Buena Vista

Perri House Bed & Breakfast

P.O. Box 22005
Lake Buena Vista, FL 32830
800-780-4830
407-876-4830
Fax: 407-876-0241
birds@perrihouse.com
www.perrihouse.com

A contemporary country B&B that's a 3-minute drive from Disney

Innkeepers: Nick and Angi Perretti. **Accommodations:** 8 rooms. **Rates:** $79–$159. **Included:** Continental breakfast. **Minimum stay:** 2 nights. **Added:** 11% tax. **Payment:** Major credit cards, traveler's checks, personal checks. **Children:** Allowed. **Smoking:** Not allowed except on patio or porch. **Open:** Year-round.

➤ **The Perri House is one of the best accommodation values available in the Lake Buena Vista and Orlando area. It's so close to Disney that if you bring a bike, you can bicycle from State Road 535 to the Disney Village Marketplace.**

Angi and Nick Perretti like to refer to their place as a B&B&B — bed and breakfast and birds. They are quite proud of their participation in the Backyard Wildlife Habitat Program of the National Wildlife Federation and have planted dozens of trees and plants on their 20 acres to attract winged wildlife — to say nothing of all the birdhouses that their B&B guests have given them.

Entering the property, guests drive past shrubs and a green lawn punctuated by birdhouses, swan statuary, and fragrant trees. The drive splits just before you reach the house, winding around to the parking area and private guest room entrances in back. The B&B, which is also Angi and Nick's home, is built of pale pinkish brick in a contemporary ranch-style with art nouveau gingerbread accenting the front entrance. Nick and the Perrettis' almost-grown children constructed the house themselves — quite a feat. They also built the wooden deck and gazebo. Obviously, these are talented, high-energy folks. They are also warm hosts, interested in everyone who comes to stay with them.

The newness of the Perri House means that there are all sorts of conveniences that an old place wouldn't have. Each guest room has a private door accessible from the outside and a designated parking space. Nick and Angie have had plenty of space and time to do everything right.

Each bedroom is decorated around a bird or flower theme. Five have king-size beds, one has two queen-size beds, and two have a queen-size bed and twin daybeds. Angi has cribs up in the attic for families traveling with infants. There is a good deal of flexibility, so the Perrettis typically have a variety of guests: families with young children visiting Disney World, honeymooners, birdwatchers, and businesspeople who've had their fill of impersonal Orlando hotels. Because the filling breakfast buffet is included in the rate, this is an ideal budget accommodation.

Each morning at 7, coffee is ready. Between 8 and 11 A.M., a complimentary breakfast of juice, fruit, cereals, baked goods, and coffee and tea is spread out on the kitchen's pink countertop. Guests share breakfast talk at a large oak table with pressback chairs. This part of the house has an open floor plan, with sitting room, dining area, and kitchen all basically one big room. Angi's taste in decor is frilly or contemporary or exotic, depending on the mood she is expressing. Here the mood is ruffled and country, with yards and yards of pink and blue Waverly fabric and coordinating wallpaper. Angi is a gifted seamstress and won an honorable mention in a magazine contest for "imaginative use" of fabric in these rooms. She even made stuffed swans of matching fabric to decorate the sofa.

Just outside the sitting room is the pink cement patio, with a serpentine-shaped swimming pool and a hot tub. A gazebo and attractive wooden deck are elevated a step or two above the pool. The patio is surrounded by several acres of rambling yard, which the Perrettis are constantly augmenting with everything from birdbaths to a wishing well to more birdhouses sent to them by former guests.

A wide hallway joins the eating and sitting area to the living room and guest rooms beyond. The Perrettis call this their Hall of History. They have pictures of their children here, framed thank-you notes from guests, and a large map with pins designating the home town of every guest who has ever stayed at Perri House. The Perrettis have hosted people from all over the world.

The hallway leads into a softly lit library, where Angi has used her talents to create an exotic space furnished with contemporary leather sofas.

Perri House is an unusual B&B where contemporary decor is juxtaposed with Victorian frothiness and solid oak. Nick and Angi are a busy, energetic couple who obviously enjoy people, but they also understand the need for tranquillity. There's a pleasant feeling of isolation and quiet here, and the hosts' love of birds and other wildlife is evident. There are only a few other houses nearby, so often the predominant sound outside is the chirping of birds. Occasionally, however, the sound of an airplane punctuates the stillness, reminding guests that Perri House is only 20 minutes from Orlando International Airport. The city of Orlando is also about 20 minutes away, and Disney World is only several minutes away. So guests are in the "thick of things," yet it never feels that way because of the seclusion of Angi and Nick's 16 acres.

Vistana Resort — Lake Buena Vista

State Road 535
P.O. Box 22051
Lake Buena Vista, FL 32830
800-877-8787
407-239-3100

A large resort with a feeling of community

Accommodations: Several hundred villas. **Rates:** 1- and 2-bedroom/2-bath villas $155–$315. **Minimum stay:** 3 nights. **Added:** 12% tax. **Payment:** American Express, Discover, MasterCard, and Visa. **Children:** Free in room with parents. **Smoking:** Allowed. **Open:** Year-round.

➤ **Although Vistana caters to families, the resort is romantic enough for an anniversary celebration or a honeymoon.**

Vistana is an extremely pretty resort and a good value. Manmade streams, waterfalls, and fountains accent the rolling lawns and flower beds. Each cluster of villas has a theme based on one of the resort's landscaping features, such as the Palms, the Springs, or the Falls. Most of the villas are of stucco and stained wood. The Fountains has Old Florida architecture: a blue and buff exterior with lattice trim and a tin roof. The newest is pretty Cascades.

Most two-bedroom, two-bath villas have a whirlpool in the master bathroom, ceiling fans, TV/VCR, screened porch, and a washer and dryer. The well-equipped kitchens have a microwave and a dishwasher — maid service includes loading and unloading it. An iron and ironing board is another little extra. Most villas have a barbecue grill outside. With a queen-size sleeper sofa in the living room, a typical villa can sleep six to eight people comfortably.

The resort has a general store for supplies (though the prices are lower at the local supermarket). If you wish, your refrigerator will be stocked before your arrival with items you request. The area has many restaurants, and Vistana competes respectably with its Flamingo Café and Zimmie's Casual Eatery and Bar.

For those who come to the resort for R&R, there are flower-bordered walkways and bridges, a massage therapist, and a sauna and steam room. Vistana's six swimming pools have bubbling hot Jacuzzis, some secluded in grotto outcroppings. The Super Pool holds 250,000 gallons of water. For those who want electronic entertainment, there's a video game room at one of the resort's recreation centers.

In addition to the spectacular swimming pools, there are 14 championship tennis courts, a tennis pro shop and pros to give lessons, shuffleboard, basketball, a fitness center, and a 12-station fitness course. The staff at the recreation centers organize activities for kids, and bicycles and pool floats can be rented. For younger kids, there's a climbing structure. Kiddie pools are next to the adult pools, and children as young as four can play tennis.

Meanwhile, all of Disney World awaits just a few miles outside the security gates. Vistana has a number of packages that include admission to the Disney parks and other attractions, such as King Henry's Feast and Mardi Gras. Without a doubt, Vistana is a perfect resort for active families.

The Walt Disney World Resorts

Central Reservations
P.O. Box 10000
Lake Buena Vista, FL 32830
407-WDISNEY (407-934-7639)
www.disney.com

An excellent array of accommodations

Accommodations: More than 10,000 rooms, suites, villas, and campsites. **Rates:** All-Star Resorts $80–$89; Beach Club Resort & Yacht Club Resort $260–$1085; Boardwalk Villas $260–$1,300, Boardwalk Inn $260–$1,200; Caribbean Beach Resort $130–$160; Contemporary Resort $225–$1,150; Coronado Springs Resort $130–$665; Dixie Landings Resort & Port Orleans Resort $130–$160; Fort Wilderness: Campsites $45–$75, Homes $179–$214, Cabins $199–$234; Grand Floridian Beach Resort $294–$1,580; Old Key West Resort $224–$885; Polynesian Resort $269–$1,200; Villas at the Disney Institute $220–$1,300; Wilderness Lodge $200–$700; packages available. **Included:** Transportation to and from Disney attractions via monorail, bus, or boat. **Minimum stay:** With some packages. **Added:** 11% tax; $10–$25 extra adult in hotels. **Payment:** Major credit cards, personal checks for deposit. **Children:** Under 18 free in room with parents. **Smoking:** Nonsmoking rooms available. **Open:** Year-round.

The Walt Disney World Resort corporation operates this mind-boggling array of accommodations. All the hotels and resorts are well planned, lavishly landscaped, very comfortable, and superlatively maintained. Smoking, nonsmoking, and handicapped-accessible rooms are available. Some hotels have concierge service, others do not. All offer free transportation to Disney attractions, some by boat or the monorail, others by bus.

The Contemporary Resort, the Polynesian Village Resort, and the Grand Floridian Beach Resort are on the monorail to the Magic Kingdom. These are good for those with small children who are in Orlando principally to see the Magic Kingdom. The ability to get on the monorail in the morning without having to drive or wait for a bus or tram can save time and anguish. These three resorts are expensive, particularly the Grand Floridian.

The Fort Wilderness Campground, the All-Star Resorts, the Caribbean Beach Resort, Coronado Springs, Port Orleans, and Dixie Landings are the least expensive accommodations. However, you do have to wait for a bus to get back to these resorts and sometimes the wait can seem awfully long — another good reason to consider coming to Disney during the "value season."

All of the Disney resorts have an astounding list of amenities: children's playgrounds and electronic game rooms, fitness centers, jogging tracks, shopping malls, laundry rooms, swimming pools, boat and water sports rentals, marinas, manmade beaches, movies and a stage theater, restaurants, snack bars, lounges, and lots of organized activities for both the day and evening. When planning a vacation, call or write to Walt Disney World Central Reservations several months ahead and request their *Vacation Information* booklet, which lists individual amenities, prices during high season and "value season," and special packages. It includes complete descriptions of properties and a map of Walt Disney World that allows you to see precisely where each hotel and resort is located with respect to Disney attractions. At the most popular Disney resorts, reservations should be made four months in advance, and for stays in winter and during school vacations, as much as twelve months in advance.

All-Star Resorts

Currently, these are Disney's most reasonably priced accommodations. Disney "imagineers" devised these after extensive market research indicated many visitors to the theme parks did not stay at Disney resorts because they were too expensive. The complex is divided into three separate areas; the name *All-Star* referring to sports, movies (mostly cartoons), and music.

The cleverness of the imagineers and Miami's Arquitectonica designers is everywhere — sometimes a little more than you might like. For example, the gift shops aren't named that, they're called "Sport Goofy Gifts" or "Maestro Mickey's." A pool at the music resort is in the shape of a piano and the pool bar at the sports resort is called "Team Spirits." In the basketball section, the Hoops Hotel has orange vinyl basketballs sticking out of the building's facade and a huge megaphone and whistle. The landscaping includes a "team" of five Sabal Palms playing five Washingtonia Palms and the background music is a stirring orchestration of "A League of Our Own." Still, it's fun for little kids to walk under an enormous Buzz Lightyear or football helmet, and parents don't have to worry about kids getting lost. If they're staying at the Country and Western resort, the kids will know it from the huge cowboy boots outside and the country and western music that is playing everywhere.

Each of the three complexes has a themed center for guest registration and luggage delivery. Each center has a large food court, an electronic game arcade, swimming pools with life guards on duty from 10 A.M. till 10 P.M., kiddie pool and playground, a gift shop, and extras like fax, notary public, and photocopying services.

After registering here, guests go to their individual hotels, which have names like Fantasia, Mighty Duck, Surf's Up, Touchdown!, Country Fair, Broadway, or Jazz Inn. The hotels have vending machines and ice machines on every floor and laundry facilities. Rooms have two double beds or a king-size bed (50 percent can be connected) and are cleverly designed, with colorful bedspreads, theme-related fixtures, remote-control TV, telephone, clock radio, and a bathroom with a toilet and shower and separate vanity area adjacent to the closet. Rooms don't have a lot of closet space, so the beds are raised for easy souvenir and luggage storage. You can request ahead of time the hotel you prefer, and if it's low season, you'll have a good chance of getting it.

The Beach Club Resort and the Yacht Club Resort

The Beach Club and the Yacht Club are known as Disney's EPCOT resorts, although plenty of people staying at these accommodations go to all of the Disney attractions. A galleon-style bridge spans the lagoonlike waterway near these resorts and a festive launch travels between them and EPCOT, as well as to the Swan and Dolphin resorts. Trolleys also run every few minutes between the Beach Club and Yacht Club resorts and EPCOT.

The Beach Club and the Yacht Club are similar architecturally and are sometimes thought of as one resort: the clapboards simply change width and color as you move from one to the other. They are more subdued than some of the other Disney fantasy resorts — they look like New England waterfront hotels. Both have turrets and other Victorian touches. The outdoor areas are planted extensively with hundreds of azaleas, begonias, and other annuals and perennials. The two resorts share a meandering grotto swimming pool with some shallow parts that are perfect for children under six. Here and there are waterfalls and tropical plantings. The fantasy pool includes a windmill and a large shipwreck, where kids can climb up to a water slide. Adults can retire to a little "island" for a soak in a Jacuzzi. The atmosphere is active here but not frenetic.

The Beach Club's atmosphere and decor are similar to the Yacht Club's, but without the nautical theme. Generally, the Beach Club is a little more understated. Outside are pretty flower beds and a Queen Anne–style porte cochere. Inside, the lobby invites sitting, with lots of wicker and tassled Victorian sofas and polished floors. Lobby windows overlook the gardens and water, and large urns of fresh flowers accent the marble floors. The male staff are dressed in striped blazers and bow ties; female staff wear blue sailor outfits or long dresses with leg-o'-mutton sleeves. Everyone — waiters, housekeepers, lobby clerks — makes a point of saying hello and seems genuinely welcoming.

At the Yacht Club, wrought iron and brass street lamps grace the brick and wooden walkways. White wooden rockers on the porch await guests who want to rest and rock a spell. First-floor hallways open out onto interior brick courtyards with white garden benches cushioned in blue gingham. Guest rooms are decorated in fresh colors and have roomy baths. At the very least, rooms look out over the beautifully planted gardens; some have both garden and water views. A few have red and white awnings over the windows. The lobby has several sitting areas furnished with cherry or mahogany reproduction pieces and leather chairs. The staff work in period costumes, with band marches or classical music playing in the background.

The Boardwalk

Designed to be a replica of a 1940s Atlantic City resort, the Boardwalk is one of Disney's smaller resorts. It's a luxury resort with two-story garden suites, smaller luxury suites, and rooms with concierge extras. Guests have a choice of staying at the Waterfront Villas directly on the boardwalk or at the New England–style inn. Located on the southern shore of Disney's Crescent Lake across from the Yacht and Beach Clubs, boat rides leave every few minutes for Disney-MGM Studios and a walkway to EPCOT. But the real action is on the broad wooden boardwalk, which reminds one of a spiffed-up, very clean Coney Island. There is lots of old-fashioned carny fun for kids: wavy mirrors, shoot-the-loop, water pistols, face painting, hand waxing, a sports club with an interactive video arcade, and plenty of hand-held food for sale by boardwalk vendors. For teenagers and adults there are beer halls and sidewalk cafés, a dance ballroom with live music from the 1940s to the 1990s, and Jellyrolls, a singalong club with twin pianos.

The Caribbean Beach Resort

With 2,112 guest rooms, the Caribbean Beach Resort is one of the largest hotel complexes in the United States. Located on 200 acres not far from EPCOT Center and the Disney-MGM Studios, the resort surrounds a 42-acre lake and is made up of five "villages," each named after a Caribbean island. This is indeed a fantasy resort and includes a large pool patio with Disney rocks and the "ruins" of a fort rising above the lagoonlike swimming pool. The Caribbean-style rooms are extremely comfortable, and the prices are fair.

The Contemporary Resort

The Contemporary Resort is like something out of Tomorrowland. The monorail comes right into the middle of this A-shaped hotel, making it the most accessible to the Magic Kingdom. It is an enormous place, crammed with more kids than a Y camp in August. There are 1,050 rooms in the tower, along with two garden wings, four restaurants, two snack bars, two lounges, six shops, a marina, a manmade beach, a health club, two swimming pools, and convention space. Some people find the Contemporary overwhelmingly large, but the accessibility to the monorail, which comes through the hotel every few minutes, makes this hotel very desirable for families with young children.

Coronado Springs Resort

Located on a fifteen-acre lake, the Coronado Springs Resort is a Southwestern-theme hotel that is moderately priced and has 81 rooms that are accessible to the disabled. Designed primarily as a convention hotel, it provides trade show and exhibit space as well as extensive meeting space. The emphasis on the conventioneer clientele does not, however, mean that families are forgotten here. Amenities include a Mayan pyramid and waterslide at the resort's main swimming pool.

Fort Wilderness Campground

Fort Wilderness Campground is the least expensive of Disney lodgings. Located between the Magic Kingdom and EPCOT on 740 acres of woodlands, the campground has laundries, showers, and a full schedule of activities that are fun for children and adults. There are three options here: fully equipped campsites, Fleetwood mobile homes (now called Wilderness Homes), and Disney's new Wilderness Cabins. Each of the 817 campsites has a 110-volt electric outlet, a picnic table, and a barbecue a short distance from the portable bathrooms. The mobile homes have fully equipped galley kitchens, attractive bathrooms, color TVs, linens, and housekeeping service — you're not exactly roughing it here. The cabins are cozy log houses with exposed beams and vaulted ceilings.

The Grand Floridian

The Disney people have outdone themselves at the Grand Floridian. This is a replica of a turn-of-the-century grand hotel, with white clapboards, stained glass, latticework, lacy railings on the verandas, and dormers, turrets, and towers rising from the red shingled roof. The grounds have brick terraces and are planted with masses of flowers. Bellhops at the front portico wear knickers and white golf sweaters.

Inside are huge planters of flowers, furniture custom-made in Spain, original artwork, intricately crafted moldings, and an Oriental birdcage with peach-colored parakeets especially bred for the Grand Floridian. The lobby is five stories high, with stained glass domes and massive chandeliers. The guest rooms are just as impressive. Despite the high rates, the Grand Floridian usually has a 100 percent occupancy rate. This is partly due, no doubt, to the articulate and courteous staff. All personnel at the reservation desks have bachelor's or master's degrees and are multilingual. The resort has two lounges and five excellent restaurants, with food well complemented by decor. High tea is served every afternoon in the Edwardian-style Garden View Lounge.

Old Key West Resort

These accommodations are expensive, but they're quite charming. The units are like spacious apartments with full kitchens or kitchenettes, so families can save a little by cooking some meals. The Key West-style buildings have tin roofs, fishtail shingle and clapboard siding in pastels and tropical colors, gingerbread detailing on the verandas, and louvered shutters at the windows. Views are often of the golf course or water. Amenities include a sauna, video library, tennis, four pools, an exercise room, children's playground, and boat rentals at the small marina. The buildings are in clusters, and there seems to be an effort to create a sense of community.

Polynesian Village

For those who want a fantasy South Seas experience, there's the Polynesian Village. Its jungle motif is carried out spectacularly in the lobby, where an atrium planted with ferns, banana trees, orchids, gardenias, and other tropical plants rises three stories high; waterfalls splash in the midst of it all. Service is friendly and courteous, and the atmosphere is low-key. The clean, attractive accommodations are in 11 low-rise lodges, each named for a Pacific island. There are 855 rooms, but because they're spread out, guests don't feel crowded. Many rooms have a balcony or patio and views of the Seven Seas Lagoons or the swimming pools and gardens. With two queen-size beds and a daybed, the rooms can easily accommodate five. The jungle theme extends throughout the complex, in the decor of the rooms and in the lagoons, rustic bridges, and tiki figures that accent the grounds. As at all the Disney resorts, there are lots of activities for adults and children.

Port Orleans and Dixie Landings Resorts

Port Orleans and its sister resort, Dixie Landings, are located between EPCOT and Disney Village. They are both quite large but designed so well they are not overwhelming. Port Orleans has a New Orleans and Mardi Gras theme, with buildings that have French Quarter–style grillwork, verandas, and mansard roofs. A landscaped promenade leads to a fantasy lagoon pool and play area. The arched tail of a blue and pink plastic serpent forms a bridge over the pool, which has a couple of shallow areas for small children.

Accommodations are in three-story stucco "townhouses." Black iron gates and ivy-covered brick posts at the entrance to the townhouse groupings create a feeling of authenticity — it's not all plastic. The entire resort is landscaped beautifully with many willow trees, magnolias, and curly-bark birches growing along the banks of a manmade lagoon. Guests can take a launch along the waterway to neighboring Dixie Landings, or stroll along the curving path beside the water.

The guest accommodations at Dixie Landings are straight out of a Southern movie set: large, white mansions with pillars, verandas, and green louvered shutters. The imposing brick entryways that lead to the mansions include fountains, gazebos, black wrought-iron archways, lanterns, and formal flower beds. Inside are the standard features of Disney resorts: a choice of rooms with king-size beds or two doubles; fresh, clean bathrooms; and small touches that extend the fantasy theme.

At the reception center and play area, the theme is a combination of Tom Sawyer and King Cotton. Guests check in at a brass-and marble-appointed "bank," have a drink at the "cotton coop," dine at the "Colonel's cotton mill," and then stroll outside along a manmade riverfront to rustic-timbered Dixie Landing. Recreation is out on "Ol' Man Island" and includes the Muddy Rivers Bar, a "fishin' hole," a playground, and a swimming pool that meanders around a big oak tree and worn-looking wooden steps that lead to a water slide. It's a combination of Frontierland and Adventureland — very appealing for school-age kids who might find the pink-plastic fantasy of the Port Orleans pool a little childish. Guests can use the facilities of both resorts and can also take a free riverboat ride to Pleasure Island entertainments and the Disney Marketplace shops that are just across Buena Vista Lagoon.

Villas at the Disney Institute

The Villas comprise a far-flung group of accommodations that provide visitors with a number of choices. Most have kitchens, or at least refrigerators and sinks, and are good for large or extended families. Though the Villas are more expensive than most Disney hotel rooms, they can be more economical in the long run if you plan on preparing most of your own meals. You don't have to take a course at the Institute to stay here.

There are five kinds of villas: one- and two-bedrooms near the village clubhouse; club suites with either a bed/sitting area or a larger duplex floor plan with a living room with foldout couch downstairs and two queen-size beds upstairs; spacious two-bedroom "fairway" villas with some handicapped-accessible units and views of the Lake Buena Vista Golf Course; conical, three-bedroom "treehouse" villas on concrete supports with decks overlooking the pines or the golf course; and "grand vista" suites, super-deluxe homes with well-stocked refrigerators. Bicycles and a golf cart are included in grand vista suite rates.

These accommodations may seem off the beaten path, but after a couple of days at Fantasyland with ten zillion kids, the seclusion is nice. Walt Disney World shuttle buses make frequent stops throughout the grounds, taking guests to the Disney attractions and the village clubhouse.

Some villas have been set aside specifically for the Disney Institute. Patterned after the Chautauqua, New York, summer program, the concept behind the Institute is that there are people who want to learn while on vacation. Disney offers dozens of classes on animation, cooking, home design, storytelling, family genealogy, and video-making, sometimes taught by celebrities. The minimum stay at these villas is three nights.

The Disney Institute classes take place in a replica of a lakeside town that includes an outdoor amphitheater on the town green, 28 program studios, and a broadcast-quality performance center.

Wilderness Lodge

For several years, the Victorian-style Grand Floridian has been Disney's showcase resort hotel, but now the Wilderness Lodge vies for the honor. This is a wonderful place that truly inspires awe in even the most jaded traveler. Although there are the standard cement-form rocks in the pool area, Disney has also made use of a great many natural materials, some strikingly beautiful. The six floors of the lodge have natural wood railings overlooking the dramatic lobby, with corridors that lead off to seating areas, the restaurants, the library, and guest rooms. The best rooms are on the top floors overlooking Bay Lake and the pools. Decor reflects the western theme, with patchwork quilts on the two double beds or king-size bed and finely crafted, natural wood furniture.

The atrium lobby is the heart of the resort. Six-story high "columns" of fat pine trunks support the atrium, dominated by a hand-carved totem pole. Colors are sandstone, turquoise, melon, black, and tan. The massive fireplace in the corner is made of striated sections of soft-hued stone, said to mirror the colors of the Grand Canyon. The patterned floors in the 60-foot atrium lobby are composed of multicolored hardwoods in the design of a Navajo rug, accented with stone flooring and recreations of Native American rugs. Disney and their Denver architects have succeeded in creating the feel of a western lodge and show genuine respect for Native American artwork.

The feeling of authenticity changes a bit when one goes outside to the water recreation area, however, where it's back to those cement-form rocks again. But it's best to suspend belief and just enjoy the theme park scene. The lodge, with various appendages, is constructed in the shape of a U; the recreational area is in the middle of the U. This area is a small re-creation of Yellowstone National Park, with a bubbling hot spring that begins in the lobby and then flows outside, becoming a small creek that gradually widens and intensifies until it becomes a waterfall. The water cascades about 15 feet into a swimming area, which includes hot and cold spas, a water slide, and a kiddie pool. The terraced landscaping includes a variety of evergreens, birches, cypress, ornamental grasses, and juniper. There's also a geyser that erupts at set intervals and a manmade, white-sand beach that borders pretty Bay Lake. Here guests can take a boat to the Magic Kingdom — an especially fun thing to do in the evening.

Walt Disney World Swan and Dolphin

1500 Epcot Resorts Boulevard
Lake Buena Vista, FL 32830-2786
800-227-1500
407-934-1829
www.swandolphin.com

| **Fun on a massive scale** |

Accommodations: 2,267 rooms and suites. **Rates:** Rooms $295–$465, suites $410–$3,100; packages available. **Included:** Free shuttle to Disney parks. **Added:** 11% tax. **Payment:** Major credit cards. **Children:** Under 18 free in room with parents. **Smoking:** Nonsmoking rooms available. **Open:** Year-round.

➤ **Massive swans and dolphins are set at the pinnacle of the hotels. Visible for miles, they create instant recognition.**

The Walt Disney World Swan and Dolphin are located in the EPCOT resort area between EPCOT and the Disney-MGM Studios. The Swan and the Dolphin are owned and managed not by Walt Disney World Resorts but by Sheraton and Westin, respectively. Designed by the eccentric architect Michael Graves, they are unique hotels.

The Swan exhibits a flamboyance reminiscent of Florida's art deco era. Aqua waves are painted on the stucco exterior, and two massive swan statues on top of the hotel ride the waves. The swan motif is carried out everywhere inside the hotel, with swan mosaics, swan benches, swan statues, and swan fountains.

At the Dolphin hotel, huge dolphin fabrications surmount the building. Outside there is beautiful landscaping with front walkways leading around the hotels to a separate convention entrance.

The Swan and the Dolphin have a total of 17 restaurants and lounges, 4 pools, a tennis center, 2 health clubs, and a children's activity program. Like Disney's official resorts, guests enjoy early entry at the theme parks on selected days and advance tee times on five Disney World golf courses. Kids can see Disney characters padding around the dining rooms, and occasionally one will sit down at the table.

Meeting space is excellent, and a hard-working staff can facilitate just about any type of gathering. From these meeting rooms, convention-goers have easy access to the hospitality suites on the second floor.

In the hallways, wallpaper and carpets create a beach scene; the carpet pattern looks like a boardwalk with beach towels laid out on the sand. Guest rooms have the same Caribbean ambiance as those at the Dolphin, with tropical decor and spacious baths. There are, of course, lots of activities for businesspeople who come here with their families.

The resort shares a recreational area with the Dolphin. The two hotels are linked by a waterway spanned by a bridge that looks like a Spanish galleon.

Everything about the Walt Disney World Dolphin is oversize and fantastical. The exterior is sandstone-colored stucco, with tropical leaves painted on the side in aqua and enormous dolphins surmounting each end of the building. The fountain behind the resort is fun: water surges over a series of aqua shells several stories high and then tumbles into a large dolphin fountain. The fountain is a good example of why the Dolphin's design is sometimes referred to as "entertainment architecture" — it backs up to the causeway leading across the water to the Swan, so people at that hotel can also enjoy the fountain's whimsy.

Public rooms at the Dolphin are built on a massive scale. The rotunda lobby is several floors high; its canopied ceiling is draped in aqua, red, and ivory striped fabric. Tendrils of fake wisteria (with silk "blossoms" in several unlikely colors) climb up the green lattice columns — it's a little tacky, but fun.

Outside, a crescent stretch of manmade beach joins the Swan and Dolphin, forming a wonderful playground for both kids and adults. It's landscaped with palm trees, grasses, and beds of bright annuals and subtropical plants. There are three whirlpools, a lap pool, a grotto pool with a waterfall, beach and water sports activities, four tennis courts, and a play structure for kids. The resort offers Camp Dolphin for children and a Body by Jake Health Studio. The Swan and Dolphin share 17 restaurants, including a 1950s-style ice cream parlor at the Dolphin that has an old jukebox and a high, canopied ceiling. At these two resorts, it's all one big fantasy.

Lake Helen

Clauser's Bed and Breakfast

201 E. Kicklighter Road
Lake Helen, FL 32744
904-228-0310
800-220-0310
Fax 904-228-2337
www.clauserinn.com

> One of the few real country B&Bs in Florida

Innkeepers: Tom and Marge Clauser. **Accommodations:** 8 rooms. **Rates:** $95–$140; $25 for third adult in room. **Included:** Full breakfast. **Minimum stay:** 2 nights during special events. **Added:** 11% tax. **Payment:** American Express, Discover, MasterCard, Visa, personal checks. **Smoking:** Prohibited inside. **Children:** No children under 16. **Open:** Year-round.

➤   Many people staying at Clauser's Bed and Breakfast take off for a state park or go antiquing in the area for the afternoon. But it's just as pleasurable to stick around "home." Guests can play croquet, horseshoes, badminton, or volleyball in the yard, or relax on the porch swing and rockers on the front veranda.

Lake Helen and the surrounding towns are so small they are little more than attractive crossroads set in the midst of woods and thickets. Yet the area has easy access to I-4; the Atlantic is less than a half-hour away; and Disney World is only about an hour from here. This is country, with easy access to civilization — if you really want it. You might not, once you get to Clauser's Bed and Breakfast and put in some rocking time on the front porch.

The Clausers are interesting, well-read people; "homebody" is written all over them. Though in his professional life Tom is involved in finance, he is a clever workman, and Marge is a great cook and craftswoman. Together they have created a restful country retreat. Built in the 1880s and listed in the Register of Historic Places, this farmhouse is a fine example of Old Florida architecture, with tin roof, white clapboards, slate blue shutters, and a gingerbread-trimmed porch that wraps around three sides of the house. The Clausers have added flower beds and flowering shrubs to the rich growth of pines, live oaks, and magnolias already on the property.

The big kitchen and screened back porch overlook a screened Victorian gazebo with a cupola and a tin roof to match the house. Inside is a hot tub with scented water.

Behind the house are new accommodations in what is called the Carriage House. It's a new building designed for guests, not a converted carriage house, but Tom and Marge worked very hard to create something that would fit the country ambiance. Like the Main House, this has a tin roof. Sheathed in gray vinyl siding with a broad stone chimney, the Carriage House has a big porch in front furnished with oak and metal benches and rockers. In addition, there are screened porches at either end of the building and screened porches behind every guest room. So there's plenty of opportunity to enjoy the out-of-doors and rock and rest when the mood strikes.

Through the Victorian front door with its oval, leaded-glass window is a tiled front hallway and a pub called Sherlock's, which is a lot like anybody's neighborhood bar, homey and down-to-earth. Guests enjoy relaxing here in the evening, especially on a cool night when a fire is crackling in the stone fireplace. Marge and Tom also have complimentary decanters of port and sherry available in the Main House parlor and on a sideboard on the second floor of the carriage house. Beyond Sherlock's is a small gift shop where Marge sells collectibles and various handcrafts she and others make.

There are two guest rooms on the first floor. The Windsor is very English, with green and floral chintz, a hardwood floor, and antiques. It has a queen-size bed and a day bed. The Cross Creek is homey, with Old Florida memorabilia and quilts on the queen-size and day beds.

The upstairs rooms are the Lancaster, decorated in a Pennsylvania Dutch theme, the Lexington, festooned in lots of red, white, and blue and featuring a modern Jacuzzi in the bathroom, the Charlevoix, with Battenburg lace on the king-size bed and French provincial furniture; and the Laredo, probably the Clausers' most creatively decorated room. Two walls are of real split cedar logs, and interesting touches include a wall wreath made of barbed wire, a mirror framed by a horse collar, an old trunk used as a table, a king-size log bed, and in the bathroom, a galvanized bathtub from an old ranch house that Marge found at a feed store.

On the second floor in the main house are two more guest rooms with private baths. Lilac and Lace has a queen-size bed, lilac walls, and many touches of white lace. Just off the room is a veranda, a wonderful place to sit when the tall magnolia tree in the front yard is in bloom. The private bathroom has a clawfoot tub and a shower. Peaches and Cream, decorated in soft peach shades, has a king-size bed covered with an heirloom bedspread and a small dressing room. The private bath has both a shower and a clawfoot tub. All rooms have two terry robes hanging in the closet.

Downstairs are the kitchen, parlor, and a dining room that is used as a breakfast room when there are too many guests to fit around the table in the big country kitchen. Breakfast is everything one would expect from a great country cook: homemade apple muffins or coffee cake, homemade jams and jellies, French toast or pancakes, sausage or bacon, bananas and cream or strawberries, and fresh-ground coffee. Country-style dinners are served Friday and Saturday evenings by reservation. On the back of the house, the screened wraparound porch overlooks the Carriage House, tall trees, and the pleasant yard. For a true country B&B experience, Clauser's is hard to beat.

Lake Wales

Chalet Suzanne

3800 Chalet Suzanne Drive
(U.S. Highway 27 and
Chalet Suzanne Road)
Lake Wales, FL 33853
863-676-6011
Fax: 863-676-1814

> **A famous gourmet getaway and fantasyland**

Owners: The Hinshaw Family. **Accommodations:** 30 rooms. **Rates:** $159–$229; packages available. **Included:** Full breakfast. **Minimum stay:** None. **Added:** 10% tax; $12 extra person; $10 for crib. **Payment:** Major credit cards, personal checks. **Children:** Welcome. **Smoking:** Allowed. **Open:** Year-round.

➤ **Anyone who wants to can design and make a commemorative tile. The autographed tiles are added to the border of the rose garden wall. Some have been made by celebrities, but most were done by honeymooning couples.**

Chalet Suzanne was Fantasyland before Walt Disney ever thought of it: Tyrolean towers and terraces and turrets, rambling in all directions and painted in ice cream and sherbet colors. You might wonder if the people who've recommended it in guidebooks have lost their minds. This crazy place? With masonry cracks on half the buildings and an occasional broken brick in the walkway? Well, yes, especially if you love good food and Old Florida quirkiness.

Chalet Suzanne has been owned and run as a country inn and restaurant by the same family since its creation more than 65 years ago. Its founder was a brilliant eccentric named Bertha Hinshaw. She and her husband were both from wealthy families, and Bertha spent a good deal of her early married life collecting antiques, artwork, and fine china and silver in Europe. The Hinshaws lost most of their money in the 1929 crash, and took to raising chickens and rabbits on the central Florida land that is now the Chalet Suzanne.

Then Mr. Hinshaw died, leaving Bertha with two children and no apparent means of support. However, Bertha had two assets on which to capitalize: the land she was living on and an imaginative genius in the kitchen. She opened a restaurant that soon became famous and a "Tyrolean village" to house her overnight guests. After a fire in the 1940s, she rebuilt part of the village out of chicken coops, stables, and rabbit hutches. She often slept on a narrow bed in her tiny office.

Over the years, Bertha added more guest rooms to her storybook inn and more dining rooms to the restaurant. As she became more prosperous, she began collecting in Europe again, and Chalet Suzanne became a mix of Austrian, Italian, French, Spanish, and Oriental architecture and decor.

Bertha's son Carl and his wife Vita now run the inn and oversee the restaurant with their grown children. Carl is in charge of the kitchen and the cannery that cans and sells the famous Chalet soups and sauces, while Vita runs the dining room and oversees the wait staff.

Each dining room is a different size and shape, and all are distinctively decorated. The Swiss dining room has stained glass windows along one wall, a paneled ceiling, and a tiled mantel. The English dining room has wooden beams and an intricately stenciled ceiling. The main dining room is octagonal, with a mix of interesting hanging lamps over the tables and a view of Lake Suzanne. All the restaurant rooms have eclectic combinations of antique chairs and wood or tile-topped tables, which are set with lace tablecloths, fine silver, and unmatched china. The place settings include unusual soup bowls that were made by a European couple who have a studio on the chalet property.

Meals at Chalet Suzanne are outstanding and expensive. Most visitors opt for a room-and-meal package to soften the blow. Dinner begins with a chalet specialty, a cinnamon-broiled half grapefruit with a succulent chicken liver in its center followed by long-simmered soup. Entrées include lump crab with herb butter, filet mignon, shrimp curry, lamb chop grill, lobster Newburg, and Chicken Suzanne, probably the most famous of the chalet specialties. Every part of the meal is slowly, carefully prepared.

For breakfast, popular selections are the chalet's egg dishes and Swedish silver dollar pancakes with a warm lingonberry sauce. Lighter fare, such as salads and ham, as well as lobster thermidor and Chicken Suzanne, are served at lunch. Children's menus are available at all three meals. Off-season packages include breakfast and dinner.

The first-floor Lakeview Room is one of the nicest of the distinctive guest rooms, decorated in shades of blue. The Banana Room, of course, is decorated in yellow. The Balcony Suite, often requested by honeymooners, has a big round bed surrounded by a gauzy drape suspended from the ceiling. The room includes a balcony dining nook overlooking one of the dining rooms. The pistachio green Tower Room has a balcony overlooking the lake. All rooms have private baths. Bedrooms and bathrooms have been upgraded with new tile and carpets and drapes. Several rooms now have Jacuzzis. The Chalet's new wheelchair-accessible room, the Brick Road Suite, is especially nice.

The exterior and the grounds are lovingly cared for. Bertha Hinshaw's creative use of the tile she collected from all over the world is one of the most impressive things about Chalet Suzanne. On the exteriors of some of the buildings, she had brightly colored Spanish and Italian tiles embedded in the stucco. In the bathrooms, she used a variety of European and domestic tiles. Those used in the deep Roman tub might be dark green, while the rest of the bathroom might be tiled in yellow and blue, with broken pieces used along with whole pieces.

This is a place for people who like to stroll. The accommodations, the gift shop, the cannery, and the ceramic studio are connected by charming brick paths, many of which were laid by Carl Hinshaw as a boy. The cracks and unevenness that have occurred over the years add to the charm. One pathway leads to the chalet's lovely rose garden, a favorite of honeymooners.

The garden is near the Chalet's 2,450-foot lighted airstrip (both Carl and his son are pilots), so if you happen to have a private plane, just call ahead for clearance. The airstrip is about the only thing on the property that brings you back to the 20th century. There is a storybook feeling everywhere at Chalet Suzanne. To stay here is to eat like a king and sleep like a princess.

Maitland

Thurston House

851 Lake Avenue
Maitland, FL 32751
800-843-2721
407-539-1911
Fax: 407-539-0365
thurstonbb@aol.com
www.thurstonhouse.com

> **A carefully restored
> Victorian overlooking a lake**

Innkeeper: Carole Ballard. **Accommodations:** 4 rooms. **Rates:** $120–$140. **Included:** Full breakfast on weekends, Continental breakfast on weekdays; wine and snacks. **Minimum stay:** On some weekends and special events. **Added:** 11% tax. **Payment:** American Express, Visa, MasterCard, personal checks. **Children:** 12 and older welcome. **Smoking:** Outside only. **Open:** Year-round.

➤ **The yard and gardens at Thurston House have tall old palms, 20-foot-high camellias, and a hundred-year-plus camphor tree that is so broad Carole has planted flowers in its flat center.**

Carole Ballard moved with her husband from Massachusetts to central Florida with the hope of finding a historic house that she could make into a B&B. This wasn't an easy task, as many old houses had been demolished many decades ago. But she found a beautiful example of Queen Anne Victorian architecture in the Thurston House and did an exemplary job of bringing it back to its original beauty.

The building had been standing empty for some time and, fortunately, no disfiguring modernizations had been made. There was, however, a good deal of paint on every surface in the house. It took Carole six months to strip the accumulation from the cypress and pine woodwork. She also stripped and polished the brass drawer pulls and fixtures in the house that, amazingly, were intact. The result of Carole's hard work is extremely gratifying for anyone who loves the grace and detail of fine old houses.

The risers and treads of the heart pine staircase have an unusual swirled grain. Carole points out the plainer grain of the risers past the landing, out of sight of visitors in the parlor. A stained and leaded glass window casts muted shadows of green and gold on the staircase.

The four bedrooms are named after the families who lived in the house. Thurston, the smallest, is in the back of the house. It has a whitewashed wicker queen-size bed and sponge-painted yellow walls. The other three bedrooms are named after the families who lived here in the present century. Furnishings are good reproductions or antiques.

The Hirsch Room has a four-poster queen-size bed with curtains draped around it. The walls are sponge-painted blue. The bathroom has the original clawfoot tub with a showerhead above. Like all of the rooms at Thurston House, the Hirsch has a desk and telephone. This room also has a many-drawered highboy, which makes up for its small closet. The O'Heirs were the most recent family to live in the house. Their namesake room is decorated in shades of maroon, with a queen-size verdigris bedstead. The bathrooms in all of these rooms are very nice.

Carole decorates with restraint, holding off from the fussy country knickknacks that clutter some Victorian B&Bs. She does incorporate special touches, however, such as her practice of leaving bath towels on the bed, tied into a little package with ribbon.

Downstairs are more wood floors and comfortable furnishings. In the back parlor, guests can enjoy a glass of wine around the tiled fireplace, read or chat, or watch television.

The dining room is dominated by a built-in cabinet of pine, where a generous Continental breakfast is served weekdays. A typical weekend breakfast might be French toast or an omelette, fresh fruit and juices, carrot muffins, and cold cereal. Guests may finish the meal with tea or coffee in the sitting room, on one of the screened porches, or outside on the old-fashioned bench sheltered by a trellis of bougainvillea.

The grounds overlook a peaceful lake, with wild grasses and reeds growing along its edges. You can fish (but not swim) here, and play horseshoes or croquet on the lawn. There is boating nearby. Carole and Joe have an herb and vegetable garden out back, and they have lovingly brought back mature plants and trees that were languishing before their arrival. Although Thurston House is only 10 miles north of Orlando and about 30 minutes from Disney World, there is a country feeling to the place. Joe and Carole have a little more than five acres of land, and the property backs onto a wooded area, creating still more privacy.

Micanopy

The Herlong Mansion

Cholokka Boulevard
Micanopy, FL 32667
352-466-3322

A white-columned mansion in a quiet antebellum town

Owner: Sonny Howard. **Accommodations:** 6 rooms, 4 suites, 2 cottages. **Rates:** Rooms $70–$129, suites $169–$179; cottages $135–$150; rates reduced on weeknights; group discounts. **Included:** Full breakfast. **Minimum stay:** None. **Added:** 9% tax; $5 rollaway; $20 extra person in room. **Payment:** MasterCard, Visa, personal checks. **Children:** Welcome. **Smoking:** Only on veranda. **Open:** Year-round.

➤   **The Herlong Mansion hosts many weddings and receptions. The wide veranda lends itself to bands playing and garlands draped over the white balustrades. The brides must feel like Scarlett O'Hara at Tara.**

Anyone visiting Gainesville or Ocala should make a point of driving to nearby Micanopy. It's the clichéd "little town that time forgot." Micanopy is reputed in these parts to be the oldest town in

Florida after St. Augustine. It feels even older, perhaps because it's never been a large center of commerce.

The peace and unchanged feel about this town are extraordinary. Spanish moss drapes the big old oak and pecan trees that canopy the main street, Cholokka Boulevard, on which there are an ancient cemetery and a park with a gazebo. Picturesque brick and wood frame stores line the street. No doubt these were once groceries and feed and grain stores; they are now mostly antique and craft shops. Dominating the boulevard — and the town — is the Herlong Mansion.

It is truly a southern mansion. The original house was a simple two-story farmhouse with a detached kitchen, built in 1845. Between 1909 and 1913, the Herlongs, who made their fortune in timber and citrus, built a brick Greek Revival structure around the farmhouse with Corinthian columns and first- and second-story verandas. The house has 10 fireplaces and leaded glass windows that reach nearly to the ceilings. The finest lumber went into paneled wainscoting and hardwood floors.

The Pink Room has white wicker furniture, a pastel dhurrie rug, and a bathroom with an old sink, clawfoot tub, and a new tile floor. The Pine Room has cypress woodwork and a maple floor. Its modern bath has a deep red Oriental rug. The pleasant Blue Room still has the original wavy glass windowpanes. It's furnished with old rockers and a small Chinese rug.

The Herlong Suite has a canopied mahogany bed, and a big brick and oak fireplace lends the room an imposing air. The sitting room has diamond-paned leaded windows and a sofa. In this suite, its original tile floor intact, is the first indoor bathroom in Micanopy.

At the end of the wide upstairs hallway is a door leading to the second-floor veranda, which Mrs. Herlong used as a sleeping porch. Now it is a lovely spot to sit and sip a glass of wine or iced tea while surveying the quiet street below.

On the third floor are six large rooms built in 1993, all beautifully furnished. The Governor's Suite has its original leaded glass windows and a queen-size antique faux-grained bedstead. Inez's Suite, with a brass queen-size bed, is even more impressive. Elaborate sconces flanking the leaded glass windows can be dimmed during a soak in the Jacuzzi.

Amber's Suite, on the first floor, is no larger than the other original bedrooms but is impressive because of the adjoining bathroom. Originally Mr. Herlong's office, it has a large whirlpool tub and a gas-log fireplace with an old wood mantel. A dark wood Victorian dressing table, heavy drapes, a chair upholstered in needlepoint, and an old-fashioned porcelain sink complete the picture. The bedstead is carved with tropical leaves and flowers.

In the back yard is the Pump House, owner Sonny's latest restoration and newest accommodation. The little white building, constructed in 1920 for the water system of the old mansion, now has a queen-size bed with a beautiful oak mantel mounted above to create a headboard. The full bath has both a modern shower and a Jacuzzi. The Pump House is wheelchair-accessible.

To the left of the driveway under some fine old trees is the Carriage House, a building that was essentially a utility shed until Sonny renovated it. It's now a small apartment that is quite popular with those who want a quiet retreat. Just inside the door is a little kitchen, then the bedroom and a new tile bathroom. The cottage has been freshly wallpapered with a plaid paper and duck border. The ornate bedstead is quite handsome, and the old floors have been replaced with a parquet wooden floor. The cottage is an obvious choice for honeymooners or those celebrating an anniversary; a gazebo just a few steps from the cottage door makes it even more romantic. The oval gazebo is furnished with two wicker rockers and a table. In spring and summer, the fragrant star jasmine on the white latticework blooms.

Mount Dora

Darst Victorian Manor B&B

495 Old Highway 441
Mount Dora, FL 32757
888-53-DARST
352-383-4050

A reproduction Victorian inn overlooking Lake Dora

Innkeepers: Jim and Nanci Darst. **Accommodations:** 4 rooms, 2 suites. **Rates:** $125–$175 rooms (per person double occupancy); $180–$220 suites. **Included:** full breakfast. **Minimum stay:** 2 nights on holidays and high season weekends. **Added:** 9% tax; extra person in room $25. **Payment:** American Express, Discover, MasterCard, Visa, traveler's checks, personal checks for deposit only. **Children:** 12 and over welcome. **Smoking:** In designated outdoor area only. **Open:** Year-round.

The Darst Victorian Manor looks like a Queen Anne mansion lifted from the coast of Maine. Instead, it's a cleverly built rendition built only a few years ago. Rather than being sheathed in weatherbeaten clapboards or shingles, it's covered with practical blue-gray vinyl siding. However, this isn't to say that the Manor is without the requisite Victorian touches, such as turrets, gables, small-paned windows, a gingerbread white-railed porch, and tall chimneys.

Nanci and Jim Darst are from Oklahoma — the "heartland," as Nanci says. They built the Manor specifically as a B&B and slowly collected the various antiques and artifacts that decorate the house. They've come across some great finds, such as the ornate mantel from the Pullman railroad estate that surrounds the parlor's tile fireplace. The Darsts are quite fond of these and other possessions and request that guests and their visitors respect the furnishings. Only older children are welcome at this B&B.

Nanci has decorated all the downstairs common rooms in an ornate Victorian style. Chair-rail moldings, flowered wallpaper borders, crown moldings, and tulip-shaped light fixtures complete the turn-of-the-century look. Guests are invited to read and visit with one another in the parlor and other downstairs common rooms, or sit out on the wicker-furnished porch. Tea is offered to guests every afternoon.

A gourmet breakfast is served on fine china and silver in the fireplaced dining room. This is quite definitely a full breakfast — no bagels and quick coffee here. A typical breakfast includes fruit cup followed by an egg dish or stuffed French toast, and bacon or sausage. Coffee and tea are hot and fresh. After breakfast, guests relax in the parlor or on the porch, take off for Disney World, shop in the downtown boutiques, or take a drive along old Highway 441, which meanders around Lake Dora and through citrus country. Because the Manor overlooks the lake, the porch is a wonderful place to watch the sun melting into the water at the end of the day.

The guest rooms afford a pleasant place to sleep and to relax. All are decorated in a frothy Victorian style with rich wall colors and fabrics and antique and reproduction furniture. The guest rooms have modern private baths with Victorian touches complimentary to the decor of the individual rooms. Thick velour robes encourage guests to lounge around or soak in a hot tub.

The Manor's turreted three-room suite on the third floor, called Queen Victoria, has a king-size mahogany bed and a remote-control fireplace. A smaller, two-room suite on the third story, Queen Anne, is furnished with a queen-size canopy bed and has a bird's eye view of Lake Dora. Judi's Room, on the second floor, is decorated in 1920s French deco style and has a bay window. Oak Splendor is indeed splendid, with turn-of-the-century oak furniture, a queen-size bed, and a view of the lake. This is another room with a fireplace controlled by a wonderfully indolent remote.

Darin's Room, named after the Darsts' son and decorated in blues and white, has twin beds and a bay window sitting area. The Priscilla is the only room with a double bed. It is on the ground floor and is wheelchair accessible. Rooms are a bit expensive here, and there are certainly less costly accommodations nearby, but the Victorian Manor offers good value for the price.

Dora Way B&B

1123 Dora Way
Mount Dora, FL 32757
352-735-5994
www.dorawaybb.com

> **A whimsical B&B in a
> 1940s-style ranch house
> overlooking Lake Dora**

Innkeepers: Sandy and Gary Holstein. **Accommodations:** 3 rooms. **Rates:** $125; extended rates upon request. **Included:** Continental breakfast and evening wine. **Minimum stay:** 2 nights on weekends. **Added:** 9% tax. **Payment:** Major credit cards; traveler's checks. **Children:** Under 18 not allowed. **Smoking:** In outdoor areas only. **Open:** Year-round.

➤ **There are summer and winter arts festivals here, an October crafts fair, a popular Christmas Walk, and some excellent community theater year round.**

The Dora Way B&B is less than a mile from downtown Mount Dora, the kind of town that is rare in Florida, with a real town square, small parks, community shuffleboard courts, antiques shops, and big old shade trees. The terrain is also rare. There are hills here — real hills — and wooded gullies and grassy valleys and streets that curve around hillsides. In spite of some malls and a little suburban sprawl outside the downtown area, there is still a remarkably peaceful pace to life here.

Dora Way is on the outskirts of town in a residential neighborhood overlooking Lake Dora. The house itself, built in 1947, has been beautifully maintained. Large picture windows overlook the raintree in the front yard, the railroad tracks that lead to the town depot, and the lake, where there are day and evening cruises. The house is quite large, so that owners Gary and Sandy Holstein have their own apartment on the right side of the house and guests stay on the other side of the house and share the space in between with the Holsteins. Before moving to Mount Dora, Gary and Sandy had a farm near the White Mountains and before that a 17-room inn in Maine.

Sandy is a great collector of art deco furniture, vintage hats, old purses, cosmetics from the 1950s, and Bakelite jewelry, and her collections decorate the guest rooms. Each is named after a color and has an old hat on the door in that color. The Pink Room surely wins the prize for whimsy and charm, though all three rooms have great personality. Sandy's grandmother's brass bed is against one wall, but that is about all that is traditional or predictable here. The walls are adorned with a Howdy Doody puppet, baby shoes, a "Red, Red Robin" hat with a little beak from Sandy's tap dance days, and her pink and blue autograph book from the 1950s. An old pink and black clock radio plays "Kukla, Fran and Ollie." The original blue and pink tiled bathroom has both a bathtub and a large stall shower.

The Orange Room at end of the hallway is furnished with a French art deco bedstead with built-in mirrored night tables on each side. An armoire and dressing table complete the bedroom set — all are of the same unusual Amboera wood. The blanket chest in the room was found by Sandy's grandfather under a cottage in Connecticut in 1926. An orange chenille spread is on the queen-size bed and hand-hooked rugs are on the oak floors. The bathroom has a large tiled shower stall and a sink with a French provincial vanity. An ivory fringed shawl serves as a swag above the bathroom window.

The Orange Room is large enough to hold two rocking chairs as well as a Morris chair, the oak arms of which are carved with lion's heads. The front corner window overlooks Lake Dora and the rain-tree in the front yard, a tree that blooms with yellow flowers in the spring. A collection of ladies' hats is on the hat stand in the corner: "little-old-lady" hats, beaded black cocktail hats, hats with feathers, hats with flowers. At one time, Sandy had 600 hats in her collection, but she's cut way back.

In the Green Room, old green shoes dangle from an oak suit press and wide, flamboyant neckties from the 1940s hang on an oak drying rack. A Lucite art deco floor lamp lights up the room in the evening. But there are traditional touches here in the Shaker-style cherry bedstead and the crewel embroidery of violets by Gary's grandmother. There are also braided rugs on the oak floors and grandma's rocker. A big picture window frames the lake and the raintree. The bathroom is brand new and has a tile floor, large tile shower, and pale tan pedestal sink.

All of the rooms have comfortable queen-size beds and terrycloth robes in the closets. Amenities in the bathrooms include glycerin soap and complimentary shampoo. Sandy's kitschy collections are even in the bathrooms: lipsticks with rhinestone tops, framed Gibson Girl postcards, embroidered South of the Border guest towels, plastic lipstick holders, and so on.

By delightful contrast, the large living room, in the center of the house, is decorated with the very Victorian furniture of Gary's grandfather. Large windows look out over the lake and the front yard. The adjacent screened porch is paved with flagstones and has a porch glider, a wicker sofa and chairs, and a nice view of the shaded backyard. Sandy and Gary's cat and greyhound dog are often in attendance here, too. Up a few steps from the enclosed porch is a large Jacuzzi.

A breakfast of fresh fruit, fruit Kringles or fresh croissants from the local bakery, juice, and coffee and tea is served each morning on the porch or in the sitting room/dining area. Sandy and Gary both have jobs outside their B&B business, so this is not a B&B where the innkeepers are overly talkative or intrusive. At the same time, the Holsteins love the Mount Dora area and are a good source of information about local sights and events. Mount Dora is close enough to Orlando to attract people from that part of the state for dinner or shopping, and, conversely, Orlando and Disney World are an easy day trip from Mount Dora. There are also beautiful rivers and springs in Silver Spring and the horse country of Ocala nearby.

Lakeside Inn

100 N. Alexander Street
Mount Dora, FL 32757
800-556-5016
352-383-4101

> An old charmer located
> near the town depot

Accommodations: 88 rooms and suites. **Rates:** $90–$180 rooms, $110–$200 suites. **Included:** Continental breakfast. **Minimum stay:** With some packages. **Added:** 9% tax; $10 for extra adult. **Payment:** Major credit cards. **Children:** Under 12 free in room with parents. **Smoking:** Allowed; nonsmoking rooms available. **Open:** Year-round.

➤ **When a local train roars into Mount Dora, it passes the Atlantic Coast Line Depot (now the chamber of commerce), and you could swear that you've gone back in time at least forty years, maybe a hundred.**

Built in 1893 as a country manor, the Lakeside Inn is listed on the National Register of Historic Places. In the 1920s and 1930s, it became a winter mecca for northerners, including President Calvin Coolidge. Like so many old resorts in Florida, it has had its ups and downs, and service is sometimes slow in the inn's dining room. Still, the present restored inn is a pleasure.

The buildings that make up the Lakeside Inn share a similar architectural style, with high-peaked dormers, green asphalt roofs, double-hung windows, and white-railed porches. The original manor houses several guest rooms, the restaurant, lounge, and meeting rooms. The interior of the entire structure is Old Florida: polished pine floors, coffered ceilings, floor-to-ceiling windows. The pillared porch out front is a treasure, with rocking chairs, paddle fans above, and green canvas awnings.

Accommodations, in various buildings of stucco or clapboard, are slowly being redecorated. When making reservations, you may wish to request a room that has been newly carpeted and renovated. Ideal for families are the parlor suites, which have a sitting room, some with a pullout sofa. The modernized bathrooms have new tile and attractive pedestal sinks. All rooms have peaceful views of the lawns, the lake, the grounds, or the old manor house. Amenities include cable TV, telephones, and complimentary bathrobes. A few ground-floor rooms are accessible to the disabled.

The gardens are planted with hundreds of azaleas that are gorgeous in the spring; subtropical and southern native trees and shrubs take over in the winter. The manicured lawns hark back to 1920s croquet and lawn bowling courses.

Recreation includes a swimming pool overlooking the lake and tennis on lighted courts. Limited docking facilities are also available for those who wish to bring a boat. The Lakeside Inn lends itself to leisurely walking, whether at night or by day. Particularly pretty for an evening stroll is the walkway opposite the manor house that slopes down a wide lawn to the lake and pool. Adjacent to the property on the banks of the lake is a municipal park, with enormous oak trees dripping with Spanish moss.

Mount Dora itself, with its many antiques shops and boutiques, is fun to explore. Some of the buildings on Donnelly Street and Fifth Avenue have New Orleans-style grillwork on the second-floor balconies. Ivy grows on lampposts and on porches. The Masonic Temple, a yellow and white 1893 gingerbread house on Donnelly Street, is part of the historic district tour that many people take. Though some old-timers complain that Mount Dora is becoming too boutiquey and too busy, it retains a pace that many Lakeside Inn guests enjoy getting used to.

Magnolia Inn

347 East Third Avenue
Mount Dora, FL 32757
800-776-2112
352-735-3800
Fax: 352-735-0258
magnolia@cde.com
http://magnolia.cde.com

> **A 1920s guest house just a few blocks from downtown Mount Dora**

Innkeepers: Dave and Betty Cook. **Accommodations:** 4 rooms, 1 suite. **Rates:** $125–$185. **Included:** Full breakfast, afternoon refreshments. **Minimum stay:** 2 nights on weekends. **Added:** 9% tax. **Payment:** Major credit cards, traveler's checks. **Children:** Adults only. **Smoking:** Outside only. **Open:** Year-round.

➤ **This B&B has become a nice place to stay for couples who want to get away and be by themselves and for those who want to have the "traditional B&B experience" of getting to know other guests.**

Betty and Dave Cook have done a wonderful job of bringing back a house that is a beautiful example of 1920s residential Florida architecture: a stucco exterior now painted ocher to blend with yellow-orange brick pillars, large windows with awnings, a tile roof with a wide third-floor dormer, a porte cochere on one side of the house, and an enclosed porch with a railed balcony above on the other side. This place was converted into a B&B a few years ago and painted a chalk white, but not enough was done cosmetically to make it look first-rate. The Cooks seem to have had a clear vision of how such a house should look and also a very clear understanding of how to be good B&B hosts. They exert every effort to make a stay comfortable and pleasant but do not impose themselves on guests.

In their brochure, the Cooks refer to Magnolia Inn as an "estate," perhaps because it is set back on a rather large lot, but their B&B is definitely not out of the way or out of town. The Magnolia is within easy walking distance to Mount Dora's downtown area, with its charming historic buildings, pleasant parks, horse-drawn carriage rides, and boutiques and antiques shops. It's worthwhile visiting the chamber of commerce, in the town's old train depot, and taking a walking tour to see the gingerbread Victorians in the historic district. Some of the buildings on Donnelly Street and Fifth Avenue have New Orleans-style grillwork on the balconies and ivy growing on porches and nearby lampposts. There is some great shopping here for everything from designer clothing to reasonably priced handmade quilts. The town's art galleries and annual craft show draw people from central Florida and beyond. Should you run out of things to do during a long stay, Orlando is only 25 miles away and Disney World is about 50 minutes away.

The Cooks make staying "close to home" quite attractive, however, largely because of the small pool house in the back yard. Although Betty and Dave refer to this as a "gazebo," it really hearkens back to the pleasant small pavilions built in the early part of this century beside a swimming pool. Shaded by trees and overlooking the pretty back garden, the pool house has a big hot tub inside, comfortable chairs, a table with checkers set out, and a dart board. Guests can easily spend most of the day here.

Also in this back area, just a few steps from the main house, is the Magnolia's one cottage accommodation, the Carriage House Suite. It has a king-size bed in the bedroom area and a sitting room with a lounger and a love seat covered with many pillows. The large bathroom includes a dressing area.

In the main house are the other guest rooms, which all have a wooden floor and oriental carpet, ceiling fan, and a private bath that complement the decor of the rooms. Each room has a theme, such as "Hats and Hearts," "Magnolia," or "Garden." Each is ornately decorated to reflect that theme, with hearts, hats, flowers, or cherubic accents. The large bedsteads for the king- and queen-size beds are imposing Victorian creations of walnut or mahogany. Other furnishings are in solid wood or white wicker. All of the rooms have both a tub and shower in the bathroom, a CD player and FM stereo, and stereo TV.

On the back of the house itself, overlooking the back garden and pool house, is a pleasant sun porch. Vividly colored cushions brighten the chairs here. In the front of the house is the parlor, ornately decorated but comfortable. The full breakfast each morning is homemade, and the room rate also includes afternoon refreshments.

The Cooks have created a B&B for relaxing. In the side yard is a nice swing bench and by the garden wall is a hammock. All of the gardens surrounding the house are colorful and well kempt, inviting rest in the out-of-doors.

Ocala

Seven Sisters Inn

820 S.E. Fort King Street
Ocala, FL 34471
800-250-3496
352-867-1170

**The B&B standard for
graciousness and beauty**

Owners: Bonnie Morehardt Oden and Ken Oden. **Accommodations:** 14 rooms. **Rates:** $95–$185; rates reduced on weekends, packages and special discounts available. **Included:** Full breakfast. **Minimum stay:** With some packages. **Added:** 6% tax. **Payment:** American Express, Discover, MasterCard, Visa, personal checks. **Children:** Under 12 not allowed. **Smoking:** Permitted on the porch only. **Open:** Year-round.

➤ **Ocala is known as an unspoiled Florida town; it is out of the way yet bustling with a life of its own. The town is in the center of Florida horse country, and there are plenty of horse farms to visit. This is beautiful, peaceful country, with sweeping, grassy hillsides and acres of thick woods.**

Built in 1888 and opened as a B&B in 1985 after an extensive renovation, this Queen Anne Victorian is considered by many critics to be Florida's finest historic B&B. The wooden clapboards and Victorian trim are painted several shades of blue and pink, like a San Francisco "painted lady." On one side of the house is a turret; in the center on the second floor is a small railed porch tucked between two windows. A broad walkway leads to the front steps and wraparound porch. Surrounding the house are beds of impatiens and other flowers, and baskets and pots of flowers adorn the balustraded porch. Next door is a recently restored Victorian house, which is now part of the inn.

Ken and Bonnie Oden and their staff host those who canoe in the nearby Ocala National Forest, set up murder mystery weekends for groups, and organize office Christmas parties, business retreats, special candlelit dinners, and wedding parties. Despite the range of activities, the Odens are also considerate of their B&B guests, limiting most special events to weeknights.

The first owner of this B&B did indeed have seven sisters. Each guest room was named after a sister and decorated according to that sister's taste. The result has been impressive, with awards from magazines and organizations across the country, including a Best Restoration Project in Florida award given by the state Historic Preservation Society.

Perhaps the most frequently photographed of the seven rooms is Sylvia's, also the largest, which is usually referred to now as the Honeymoon Suite. Four big windows form a lacy backdrop for the elaborately dressed king-size bed. The light walls contrast with the dark wood of the fireplace and the fluted woodwork around the windows.

Another special room is called Lottie's Loft, a large attic room with sloped ceilings and dormer windows that bring in lots of sunshine. The big space is divided into sleeping, sitting, and bathing areas tied together with a beach theme. Just climbing up the stairs to the room is an experience: one stairway wall is painted an improbable raspberry, the other, blue, with floorboards and molding painted shades of blue and lavender. At the top of the stairs is a balustrade with turned posts painted ivory, green, pink, and periwinkle. A beach towel is draped over the railing, a 1910-style street lamp is overhead, and a beach umbrella and plastic beach ball are on the pine floor opposite the stair landing. Around the corner is a swirl of aqua ceramic tile, bubbled glass bricks, colorful variegated tile and — *voilà!* — an aqua Jacuzzi right in the middle of a little sitting room. Just beyond is a traditional bathroom with a shower under the eaves.

Bed choices in this large open space include a king-size bed or, at the other end of the attic, twin beds. Tying these two sleeping areas together are complementary cotton fabrics picturing underwater and beach scenes in bright primary colors and muted blues. Striped curtains hang down above the twins, creating a cabana-like effect. All of the beds have down comforters and beach ball pillows. You have to duck a bit to get around the king-size bed because of the sloping eaves. Everywhere there are playful accouterments: a purple plastic fan, a rag rug in the shape of a fish, beach balls, a green plastic, see-through telephone, a twirly paper fish lamp, a bug-eyed fish spoon holder, a pair of pink and gold flamingo statuettes. There's no rhyme or reason — the tchotchke sometimes serves a purpose and sometimes is just part of the fantasy.

The best word to describe Ken's Room on the first floor is *sumptuous.* Colors are red, gold, black, and teal. The metal bed is canopied and draped, and spread with brocade. A tile and oak fireplace and an Oriental rug on the pine floor give the room a masculine flavor. The sleek bathroom is set off by elegant columns. The focal point here is a deep red whirlpool bath, and the two pedestal sinks and the toilet are striking ebony. Art nouveau and Greek accents lend a tone of sybaritic luxury. French doors, heavily draped for privacy, lead into the hallway.

The furnishings in all the rooms are period antiques, wicker, or reproduction French country pieces that have been painted to match the room. The armoires are particularly beautiful, some hand-painted and some with inlaid and burled woods and oval mirrors. There are plenty of special touches: Dresden plates, lacy pillows, grapevine wreaths, a wood goose atop an armoire, rose-papered hatboxes, or a quilt thrown over a banister.

On the first floor is the breakfast room/dining room. Decorated by Bonnie, it has a French country feeling. Walls are painted a soft yellow, with designer fabric draping the nearly floor-to-ceiling windows. The view from the tables is of the Victorian house next door and a large oak tree.

The full breakfast can be described only as exquisitely gourmet. It usually begins with a crystal glass of fruit juice, followed by a sweet roll, hot tea or coffee, fruit with yogurt, and then the entree of breakfast meat with a baked egg dish or stuffed French toast. The Seven Sisters version of scrambled eggs is especially good: encased in puff pastry with a pesto sauce of chopped olives, feta cheese, and shallots. Breakfast and special dinners are served on china and silver. Ken and Bonnie will also fix a picnic dinner basket for your room; it can include anything from peanut butter and jelly sandwiches to a fine feast.

After breakfast, guests can see the sights in Ocala or nearby Silver Springs. Some guests simply go back to their rooms, which are almost too pretty to leave. The only jarring note is the modern apartment building directly across the street.

Orlando

Courtyard at Lake Lucerne

211 N. Lucerne Circle East
Orlando, FL 32801
800-444-5289
407-648-5188
Fax: 407-246-1368

An oasis in downtown Orlando

Owners: Charles Meiner, Eleanor and Sam Meiner, and Paula Bowers. **Accommodations:** 30 rooms and suites. **Rates:** Rooms $89–$225, apartments $115–$150. **Included:** Continental breakfast and complimentary wine. **Minimum stay:** On holiday weekends. **Added:** 11% tax. **Payment:** Major credit cards. **Children:** Over 12 welcome. **Smoking:** Nonsmoking rooms in the Norment-Parry and I. W. Phillips; a few nonsmoking rooms in the Wellborn. **Open:** Year-round.

➤ **By purchasing the Norment-Parry's neighbor, the Wellborn, and then moving the Phillips House behind the Norment-Parry, Meiner created a space of several hundred square feet that he could transform into a peaceful garden.**

Orlando was once a sleepy southern town of turn-of-the-century mansions, wood-frame family homes, and low-slung bungalows. Ladies and gentlemen sat in wicker rockers on their grand porticoes or modest porches, fanning themselves and gazing out at the lakes and ponds that fringed their quiet neighborhoods. Today, the casual visitor to this overdeveloped metropolis might see this as a "once upon a time" story, but that's not quite the case. At the Courtyard at Lake Lucerne, the southern grace and hospitality of old Orlando survive.

The Courtyard comprises four inns: the Norment-Parry Inn, the I.W. Phillips House, the Wellborn, and the Dr. Phillips House. The front veranda of the Norment-Parry, the first B&B of the three to open, sets the mood. With gingerbread details on the pillars and white wicker furniture, it overlooks Lake Lucerne and the Orlando skyline.

The Norment-Parry is the oldest house in the city and looks the part, with an exterior of buff-colored clapboard siding, white trim, and slate blue shutters. In its history, which stretches over a hundred years, this inn has been the home of a judge (Norment) and a tax collector (Parry), a rooming house, a Salvation Army dormitory, and a halfway house. Several years ago it was bought by a local attorney, Charles Meiner, who gathered antiques for it on trips to England. Unfortunately, an exit ramp from the expressway obstructs some of the Norment-Parry's lake view. Still, the lake is beautiful, and so are the rooms at the inn.

The first-floor Crawford has a blue and white bedroom and a large sitting room with two daybeds. The Honeymoon Suite has a bathroom big enough to accommodate a couple of curved-back antique chairs, as well as an old clawfoot tub and a modern shower. The small Gena Ellis Suite is perhaps the cleverest in the house. Since it had no bathroom and no space nearby to build one, the decorator simply created one right in the bedroom, separating it with a change from bedroom carpeting to white ceramic tile.

All of the rooms are furnished with Meiner's antiques and have deep-pile carpeting and TVs. The colors, furnishings, and fabrics in the rooms are baroque and sensual. Guests revel in the Victorian plushness.

The I.W. Phillips was an old beach house that Meiner had moved a few hundred feet behind the Norment-Parry several years ago. He set about transforming it into an elegant hostelry, adding French doors leading out to verandas on both the first and second floors and sparing no expense in materials, fixtures, or craftsmanship. He installed stained-glass windows that he had saved for years and refinished the oak floors, staircases, and woodwork. As with the Norment-Parry Inn, Meiner furnished the house with his own English and American antiques.

The Honeymoon Suite at the I.W. Phillips House is spacious and elegant, with pink and ivory curtains at the large windows, a settee upholstered in rose satin, a large Victorian wardrobe, and a king-size bed. Two sets of French doors open onto a porch overlooking the brick courtyard. All of the bathrooms in the Phillips House are posh, and the Honeymoon Suite's is *la prima:* it has a deep Jacuzzi tub with a stained-glass window above, a steam shower, a modern toilet and bidet, a sink and vanity in the dressing room, and another sink in the bathroom proper.

The other rooms are lushly decorated with rich satins and brocades on the sofas and easy chairs, marble-topped tables, wardrobes of burled wood, and solid bedsteads. Suites have generous sitting areas and access to the 12-foot-wide verandas. The mood is turn-of-the-century ease and elegance.

The newest addition to the property is the Dr. Phillips House, with guest rooms on the second and third floors that mirror the elegance of those of the I.W. Phillips House — and then some! Downstairs is a restaurant, so Courtyard guests no longer must go downtown for dinner.

At the Wellborn, Meiner and the decorators let their imaginations go wild. Originally a small, genteel apartment building, it is one of Orlando's best examples of art deco architecture: it has both sharp and curved lines, a metal balustrade, and corner windows. Inside, there are 15 one-bedroom suites, each with a bedroom and bathroom, a sitting room, and a small kitchen. The decor is classic 1950s, with a zebra-striped couch in one suite, black polka-dot chairs in another, and whimsical treasures from Thailand in yet another. The room colors are red and black, black and white, banana, or off-white. A few pieces of furniture are originals.

The best room at the Wellborn is the elegant and eclectic Honeymoon Suite. It has a bathroom big enough to live in, with a wall of glass bricks above the double whirlpool bath and mirrors on all four walls. Among the suite's treasures is a 1930s Japanese safe inlaid with mother-of-pearl that serves as a night table.

The bathrooms and kitchens in all the Wellborn suites are freshly tiled and painted. Artwork is generally along the lines of posters of Fred Astaire and Ginger Rogers. The rooms are airy and sunny, most with corner windows in the living rooms that have narrow blinds. There is a variety of bed sizes to choose from, mostly queens and some kings. Many of the suites have pullout sofas in the living rooms; the largest suites can hold a family comfortably. Front rooms overlook the Orlando skyline, Lake Lucerne, and occasionally the highway. Back rooms face the courtyard fountain and gardens, and most first-floor suites have paths to the courtyard.

The courtyard itself is one of the best reasons for staying here. There are curving brick pathways, beds of azaleas and impatiens, magnolias, palm and banana trees, plaster urns of subtropical flowers, and English park benches. Water splashes soothingly in the fountain. It is no wonder that dozens of weddings and receptions are held here.

The Courtyard at Lake Lucerne was recently named one of the top 10 inns in Florida, and the Meiners and their staff do all they can to maintain their enviable reputation. Upon arrival, all guests are offered a carafe of wine. Also complimentary is the generous Continental breakfast, served in the large drawing room of the I. W. Phillips House. Breakfast includes bagels or English muffins and cream cheese, yogurt, cereals, a fresh fruit compote, orange juice, and coffee or tea. Guests may eat breakfast leisurely in the drawing room, out on the porch, or on one of the garden benches by the fountain.

The Norment-Parry does not have a swimming pool or recreational activities for guests, but all of Orlando, including Church Street Station and the Historic District, is right at the doorstep. There are also some lovely residential brick streets near Lucerne Circle that are ideal for a stroll. A number of side streets off Delaney end at quiet Lake Avenue, which curves around a small lake that is home to ducks and other wildlife. These streets, with their gracious homes and huge oak trees dripping with Spanish moss, offer lovely reminders of old Orlando.

Hyatt Regency Grand Cypress Resort

One Grand Cypress Boulevard
Orlando, FL 32836
800-233-1234
407-239-1234

**A grand destination resort
close to Disney World**

General Manager: Jack Hardy. **Accommodations:** 750 rooms, 72 suites. **Rates:** Rooms $205–$540, suites $695–$2,640; packages available. **Minimum stay:** Depending on season. **Added:** 11% tax; cribs free. **Payment:** Major credit cards. **Children:** Under 18 free in room with parents. **Smoking:** Not permitted. **Open:** Year-round.

➤   **At one end of the lobby is an exquisitely carved Chinese jade ship in a museum case — a great draw for wide-eyed children. Elsewhere are other works of Oriental art and mammoth vases of birds-of-paradise and orchids.**

The Grand Cypress is not only close to Disney World, it's also one of the most exciting resorts in Florida. Outdoors, the recreation area is the centerpiece. Huge swimming pools with grottoes, waterfalls, and lush greenery are all the rage now in Florida, and the Grand Cypress's vies with the best of them. Guests walk out the back door to landscaped grounds and a rope and wood slatted bridge across part of the pool. The area is a little overdone with statuary, but kids and adults love this aquatic playground. The pool twists around outcroppings of volcanic rock and palms, several waterfalls, and an 80-foot water slide.

Just beyond the pool is 21-acre Lake Windsong. On the walkway that runs along the lake are bicycles for rent, some with child seats, which reflects the family atmosphere here. The lake has a pretty beach and a small marina with sailboats, canoes, and paddleboats for guests. Adjacent are the tennis courts and racquetball and shuffleboard courts. There's also a fitness center and several miles of jogging trails. Golf is at the Grand Cypress Golf Club, with a 45-hole course designed by Jack Nicklaus. There's a pitch-and-putt course to practice on as well. The Grand Cypress Equestrian Center offers expert instruction in both western and English riding. There's also a day-care center and a children's program.

Accommodations are comfortable, with pretty decor and Hyatt's standard amenities. The best rooms, particularly for convention-eers, are the executive-style Regency Club suites and deluxe rooms. Services include a concierge, a club lounge stocked with magazines, Continental breakfast and evening cocktails in the club, daily newspaper delivery, secretarial services, and an extra dollop of luxury in the room itself.

Each of the resort's five restaurants appeals to a different palate and pocketbook. Hemingway's, at the end of a covered walkway on the grotto of the huge pool, has a Key West decor and specializes in seafood. Cascade, the Grand Cypress's main dining room, serves Continental cuisine. It is quite dramatic, with a floor-to-ceiling mermaid wall fountain and views of the lush grounds. The Palm Café is casual, serving pizza, salads, and sandwiches as well as a traditional menu for breakfast, lunch, and dinner. The country and western White Horse Saloon specializes in free-range beef, chicken, and ribs, with live music every night.

More formal is the elegant La Coquina, serving New World cuisine in a small dining room overlooking Lake Windsong. The Sunday champagne brunch is one of the best in Florida: a huge buffet is spread out in the spotless kitchen. The first time through, guests choose from dozens of different salads, breads, cheeses, and whipped butter spreads; the second time they choose from a variety of delicious entrées; finally they create their own grand finale with a tart, Key lime pie, fresh fruit, cheesecake, or a torte.

The Grand Cypress is a great place to stroll and sit and people-watch. The lobby is impressive, if perhaps a little overdone. Guests walk into a tropical garden, with large palm trees growing in beds set in the tile floor and a profusion of philodendrons cascading from atrium planters several floors above. Here and there are large pieces of driftwood planted with exotic tropical greenery and small pieces of statuary. Orchids sprout from the trunks of the palm trees, colorful parrots jabber from their cages, and an improbable little brook runs through it all.

Orlando Marriott Downtown

400 W. Livingston Street
Orlando, FL 32801
407-843-6664
Fax: 407-839-4982
Reservations: 800-574-3160
Marriott Reservations: 800-228-9290

> **A high-style hotel with
> high-tech business services**

Accommodations: 290 rooms and suites. **Rates:** Rooms $120–$180; VIP rooms and packages available. **Minimum stay:** With some packages. **Added:** 10% tax. **Payment:** Major credit cards. **Children:** Under 18 free in room with parents. **Smoking:** Nonsmoking rooms available. **Open:** Year-round.

➤   **If you're planning a convention or meeting in Orlando and want to be right in the city, this is the place.**

Orlando Marriott Downtown is a modern city hotel in every way. Just off I-4, it has over 14,000 square feet of meeting space, including a large ballroom on the mezzanine floor and seven meeting rooms. Business services include access to a professional audiovisual service and the assistance of a well-trained convention staff. The Marriott adjoins Orlando's Expo Centre, which has more meeting and exhibit space totaling 75,000 square feet. In addition to banquet facilities, the hotel has a full-service restaurant and a new sports café, as well as room service. In downtown Orlando, there are a number of restaurants and casual cafés in the Church Street Exchange, a shopping, dining, and entertainment complex near the old Church Street depot.

Although the Marriott is primarily a hotel for businesspeople, many conventioneers bring their families, who enjoy day trips to Walt Disney World, EPCOT, and Sea World — all only about 30 minutes away. Across the street from the hotel are the Orlando Sports Arena and Bob Carr Performing Arts Center. Next door is Orlando's Centroplex, a sports complex that offers a range of facilities including lighted tennis courts. The hotel also has a deck with a swimming pool and large whirlpool.

Guest rooms at the Omni are both businesslike and luxurious, with desks and chairs of dark polished wood and modern tile baths. The views are cityscapes. The top floors have the advantage of concierge services and various perks. All guest rooms are equipped with new telephones and can be hooked up to a computer modem.

After work or sightseeing, the nicest place to unwind in the hotel is the Lobby Lounge, where tea, cocktails, and snacks are served. Above, an atrium lets the sun shine in brilliantly. Decor is art nouveau, with lots of dark wood furnishings that are influenced in style by Japanese restraint and fluidity. The sunken lounge has a number of small groups of chairs and sofas, and plants and flowers spill out of built-in planters. Soft music from the highly polished grand piano accompanies evening cocktails.

The Peabody Orlando

9801 International Drive
Orlando, FL 32819
800-732-2639 or 800-PEABODY
407-352-4000

A luxury hotel that offers easy access to the convention center

General Manager: Alan C. Villaverde. **Accommodations:** 891 rooms and suites. **Rates:** Rooms $330–$410, suites $520–$1,500; packages available. **Minimum stay:** With some packages. **Added:** 11% tax. **Payment:** Major credit cards. **Children:** Under 18 free in room with parents. **Smoking:** Nonsmoking rooms available. **Open:** Year-round.

➤ **In the Atrium Lobby, ducks spend their days paddling in the fountain. At 11:00 every morning, yards of red carpet are laid out for the mallards to walk across to their lounge domain for a day of quacking, preening, and**

swimming. At 5:00 in the evening, they waddle back across the lobby to return to their nighttime home.

In an area full of hotels and motels, The Peabody Orlando, with its stucco and glass exterior, looks like nothing special at first glance. But the spectacular entrance, with tropical plantings and the sound of rushing water from a pair of massive stone and tile fountains, will change your mind.

Inside is more rushing water from fountains in the lobby and lounge areas. The hotel is quite elegant as well as fun. There is a feeling of tropical richness throughout the public rooms. Everywhere there are lovely arrangements of orchids and other exotic flowers, interesting art and pottery, marble floors and deep-pile carpeting, beautifully furnished sitting areas, and enormous stucco baskets of flowers and palms.

The Peabody Orlando has 57,000 square feet of meeting and banquet space. If that's not enough, across the street is the 1.5 million-square-foot Orlando/Orange County Convention Center, the largest meeting facility in central Florida. The Peabody offers good deals for conventions and other functions, particularly during the off-season.

The food at Peabody's several restaurants is uniformly good. Capriccio serves northern Italian cuisine in an elegant atmosphere, while Dux, Orlando's only Mobil four-star restaurant, provides nouvelle American in an intimate one. The B-Line Diner, a 1950s-style diner and deli, is open 24 hours. The atrium Lobby Bar and the Mallard Lounge serve drinks, coffee, and pastries.

There's plenty of recreation available to work off culinary indulgence. The Peabody Orlando has four tennis courts lit for night play, an outdoor whirlpool, a heated pool, and a large children's pool. All of these are found on a rooftop recreational floor, with the street noise four stories below — lush plantings all around add to the sense of isolation. The athletic club inside has 17 Nautilus stations, as well as a sauna, a steam room, a whirlpool, and rooms for facials and massages. Golf can be arranged by the staff at a number of area courses.

Sooner or later, even conventioneers spend time at EPCOT, MGM-Disney, or Disney World, and The Peabody Orlando has transportation to and from all of them. After several hours of walking through the theme parks, it's pleasant to come back to the guest rooms here. The duplex presidential suites are the best accommodations, but the standard accommodations are far from shabby: thick carpeting, comfortable easy chairs, remote control TV, 3D-O (an in-room video game system), and the morning paper delivered to your door. The modern baths have a hair dryer and mini-TV, which kids love.

Westgate Lakes Family Resort

10000 Turkey Lake Road
Orlando, FL 32819
800-424-0708
407-345-0000

A lakeside villa resort with plenty of water sports

Accommodations: 295 villas. **Rates:** 1-bedroom villa $115–$160, 2-bedroom $225–$250; packages available. **Minimum stay:** With some packages. **Added:** 11% tax. **Payment:** Major credit cards, personal checks. **Children:** Free in room with parents. **Smoking:** Nonsmoking rooms available upon request. **Open:** Year-round.

➤ **There's a high level of service here, with a personal service manager on duty to help you rent tennis equipment or a car, hire a babysitter, or give you information on how to get to the many nearby attractions. Sea World is just five minutes away, and Disney World is about 15 minutes down the road.**

The Westgate Lakes Family Resort is one of the nicest places to stay in the Orlando area for families tired of the crowded motels closer to Walt Disney World. It's also an excellent convention and conference hotel. The complex has one- and two-bedroom villas with fully equipped kitchenettes, living/dining rooms, separate bedrooms, and daily maid service. There are patios on the first floors and balconies on the upper floors. The villas are clustered so guests don't feel overwhelmed, with each cluster grouped around a whirlpool spa. There's almost a clubby feel to the villa groupings.

The older villas have recently been redecorated with cushiony carpets and new sofas. The two-bedroom villas are spacious, ideal for those who will be in the area for a week and want some room to spread out. One bedroom is on the first floor along with a kitchen and dining and living room area, and the other is on the second floor.

The two-level one-bedroom villas also have a second-floor bedroom and are just as beautifully decorated. With the pullout couch in the sitting area, these accommodations are spacious enough for a family of four. Here you can save money and still feel you are living a life of luxury. When you telephone for reservations, ask the clerk where to buy groceries on your way in so you can save by making breakfast, sandwiches, and snacks.

The best value at the resort is the single-level one-bedroom villa. These villas have all the amenities of the higher-priced accommodations, but no stairs to deal with.

When you're ready to treat yourself to dinner out, try the resort's main restaurant, which also serves breakfast and lunch. The informal Terrace Café, overlooking the pool and grounds, serves great sandwiches and fresh fruits. Both children and parents enjoy the Pelican's Landing Bar and Grill, where barbecued hamburgers and hot dogs and cool drinks are available all day. In the evening, there's the Cove Lounge for exotic cocktails, snacks, and live entertainment.

A tremendous range of activities is available on the resort's 300 acres overlooking Sand Lake. There's a small beach at the lake and a pier running out to a dock where you can rent Jet Skis and various boats. Water skiing and Jet Skiing lessons are also available — the staff will help you with whatever water sport you're interested in. Several types of waterfowl can be seen fishing and preening here; it's fun to watch.

Westgate Lakes also has a free-form swimming pool, a jogging path, health club, sauna, game room, and shuffleboard, as well as lighted tennis courts, a volleyball court, and bicycle rentals. For young children, there's a wooden jungle gym and a play area in an attractively planted setting. Throughout the property, the landscaping is beautiful and well maintained.

The resort is ideal for those mixing business with pleasure. The crush of conventioneers that is common at some Orlando hotels is not a worry here: plenty of corporate conferences are held at the resort, but they are carried out quietly. The hotel uses the impressive Oleander Ballroom for large groups and has seven smaller function rooms overlooking Sand Lake. Businesspeople can get plenty of work done while their families enjoy the pool and the lake.

Wynfield Inn — Westwood

6263 Westwood Boulevard
Orlando, FL 32821
407-345-8000
800-346-1551
Fax: 407-345-1508
www.wynfieldinn.com

| A well-managed family motel with easy access to Disney World |

Accommodations: 299 rooms. **Rates:** $49–$99. **Minimum stay:** None. **Added:** 12% tax; $10 rollaway; cribs free. **Payment:** Major credit cards. **Children:** Under 17 free in room with parents. **Smoking:** Nonsmoking rooms available. **Open:** Year-round.

The Wynfield Inn — Westwood is near Wet 'n' Wild on International Drive, Walt Disney World, and several other attractions in the region, so there's lots to see within easy driving distance. It is much like the Wynfield Inn — Main Gate East (see listing under Kissimmee): the same pleasant lobby with 24-hour snacks, the same decor and furnishings, and the same friendly service. The only difference is that the Wynfield Inn — Westwood has more rooms and a bigger pool. This Wynfield is farther from Disney's Magic Kingdom but closer to Sea World and Universal Studios. Free shuttle to these attractions is available to all guests.

Sanford

The Higgins House

420 South Oak Avenue
Sanford, FL 32771
407-324-9238

> A Victorian B&B in a
> historic town 20 minutes
> from Orlando

Innkeepers: Walter and Roberta Padgett. **Accommodations:** 3 rooms and 1 cottage. **Rates:** Rooms $80–$95, cottage $120–$150; weekly rates available. **Included:** Continental breakfast; afternoon wine and cheese. **Minimum stay:** None. **Added:** 10% tax. **Payment:** Major credit cards, personal checks. **Children:** Welcome in cottage; under 12 not allowed in main house. **Smoking:** Permitted outside only. **Open:** Year-round.

➤ **The Padgetts make their own beer, called Cochran after James Cochran Higgins, and enjoy sharing it with guests in the bar.**

The Higgins House was built in 1894 by James Cochran Higgins, a superintendent for the railroad in Sanford who raised thirteen children here. At the time, Sanford was probably more important than sleepy little Orlando. Incorporated in 1877, the town was named after a pioneer citrus farmer who grew citrus and various tropical fruits from Africa and South America. Sanford is still the seat of Seminole County and, in recent years, there has been an effort to promote it as a historic place. Old brick and embossed concrete buildings line lakeside streets and walkways, some of which are paved in brick. The town has 3 museums, 25 antique shops, a museum school with experimental gardens, and a 1920s theater. Lake Monroe feeds the St. Johns River, which wends its way east to the city of Jacksonville.

Oak Avenue runs from downtown up to the Cultural Arts Center and Centennial Park, a large square of lawn and trees with a gazebo where several weddings have taken place. Across from the park is the Higgins House, a beautifully preserved example of Queen Anne architecture — a rarity in central Florida. The house is painted a rich blue. White planters of ferns and flowers hang from the porch. On the second floor above the porch is a tiny gabled veranda, with more hanging planters and a window box of bright flowers.

Inside are heart pine floors, paddle fans, natural woodwork, spacious common rooms, and Victorian-era bedrooms. All the rooms have queen-size beds. The Queen Anne, on the first floor, is decorated in rose and blue. The private bath has a clawfoot tub with an underside of deep rose.

Upstairs are the pink and white Wicker Room and the Victorian Country Room, each with a private bathroom, lace curtains, and Victorian touches. Also upstairs is a small gift shop and the little veranda perched above the front door. Innkeepers Walter and Bertie lived in each of the rooms as they finished them so that they could see for themselves what the noise level was and what little things needed fixing.

The three guest rooms are not really appropriate for small children, so Bertie and Walter bought a cottage next door for families and those who wish to rent by the week or month. This two-bedroom, two-bath accommodation is one of a small group of privately owned clapboard cottages. The Padgetts' is painted a pale yellow and has a master bedroom with private bath and a smaller bedroom with a bathroom off the living room. The house has a small porch and a well-equipped galley kitchen. With the rollaway bed, the cottage accommodates a family of five.

The health-conscious breakfast includes fruit, granola, yogurt, juice, fresh-baked muffins, homemade jams and jellies, tea, and coffee. The formal dining room is rather unusual, the walls covered with gathered rose fabric. In the back of the house is an informal sitting room and bar with a comfortable sofa and big TV.

Throughout Higgins House, large windows provide views of the lawn and flower beds and mature trees outside. Behind the house is the Padgetts' prize garden. Steps lead from the back porch to a two-level deck and hot tub. Beyond is a landscaped area and raised beds of beautifully tended herbs, vegetables, and flowers. Mandavia vines, with trumpet-shaped, deep pink flowers, climb along the wooden fence and lattice trellises. On the side of the house is another smaller, crescent-shaped deck and a curving brick path that leads to more flower beds.

The front porch, with its swings and hanging planters, is another favorite spot for guests. Historic Sanford, the lake, and the marina are a short walk away. Nearby are fishing, sailing, and canoeing. The Higgins House is 20 minutes from New Smyrna Beach and 40 minutes from Disney. Sanford is known as a cultural and recreational area, and the Padgetts are planning future events that will contribute, such as a wine-tasting party in November, Christmas festivities, and cultural activities in conjunction with the Arts Center.

Winter Park

Fortnightly Inn

377 E. Fairbanks Avenue
Winter Park, FL 32789-4422
407-645-4440
Fax: 407-909-0082

A well-restored house near Rollins College

Innkeepers: Frank and Judi Daley. **Accommodations:** 3 rooms and 2 suites. **Rates:** Rooms $85–$105. **Included:** Full breakfast; sherry; bicycles. **Minimum stay:** During special events. **Added:** 11% tax. **Payment:** Major credit cards, personal checks. **Children:** Not encouraged. **Smoking:** Permitted only on exterior porches. **Open:** Year-round.

➤ **Downstairs are the common rooms, a large sitting room and adjoining dining room. Here folks may sit and talk in the evening, play the piano, or have a good read.**

With Rollins College and a mixed population of older people and young professionals, Winter Park has long needed a good B&B for those visiting friends or relatives. Now it finally has one. The Fortnightly Inn is on the residential end of Fairbanks Avenue, which leads to Winter Park's gracious downtown area, Rollins College, and the park. The Fortnightly Inn is an easy walk from town, past large, well-kept homes and small businesses.

Set back a bit from the street, the inn is painted a soft, rosy beige. Nicely landscaped with large old trees, pretty flower beds, and pots of flowers on the porch, the house looks like the kind of comfortable place Scott and Zelda Fitzgerald might have lived in.

Built in 1922, the house has some lovely features, which the Daleys have accentuated. There are a great many windows in the house, some with the original wavy glass, kept sparkling clean. The Daleys have made the most of the sunshine that filters into the downstairs windows by hanging pretty lace curtains on the bottom half while keeping the paned windows above free of any treatment.

The Daleys have three rooms and two suites, all straightforwardly numbered rather than named. They're of different sizes and shapes, and each is decorated distinctively. Except for a few good reproductions, all the furnishings are antiques. The rooms feature a carved walnut bed, a mahogany sleigh bed, two antique iron beds, and a four-poster mahogany rice bed. The rice bed is queen-size, and the others are full-size. Soft paint and provincial wallpaper complement the antiques. Handmade quilts and lacy white pillows add homey touches.

Many of the private baths adjoining the rooms, though remodeled, have clawfoot bathtubs with hand-held showers. All rooms come equipped with alarm clocks and flashlights, and guests can request a television. Most of the rooms are spacious and have sitting areas with settees or wicker chairs. The two suites have sunny enclosed porches, and Number 2 has a large deck.

A fridge on the back porch is stocked with soft drinks, bottled water, juices, and plenty of ice. There's complimentary sherry in all the guest rooms. The Daleys do not live in the house, but a staff member is on hand from 7 A.M. to 7 P.M. Guests can sit in the common rooms as late as they wish. The Daleys have a piano, violin, and guitar available for musical guests. However, quiet is appreciated after 10 P.M.

Guests staying in suites may have breakfast on their sun porch, but most eat in the formal dining room. Breakfast varies but is always a feast, with dishes like quiche tarts, shirred or coddled eggs, French toast, country ham biscuits, muffins, hot apple oatmeal, fruit, juices, and coffee and tea. The morning repast is served on antique china and silver, with fresh flowers in the center of the polished dining room table. A cordial, professional staff prepares and serves the meal and will answer any questions that guests may have about how to spend their day.

Park Plaza

307 Park Avenue
Winter Park, FL 32789
800-228-7220
305-647-1072
Fax: 407-647-4081

**An Old Florida oasis
overlooking the town park**

Accommodations: 16 rooms, 11 suites. **Rates:** Rooms $85–$200, suites $175–$200; weekly and monthly rates available; special discounts. **Included:** Continental breakfast. **Minimum stay:** None. **Added:** 11% tax. **Payment:** Major credit cards. **Children:** Under 5 not permitted. **Smoking:** On balcony only. **Open:** Year-round.

➤ **Orlando has expanded so much that Winter Park almost seems like a section of it, making the Park Plaza an even better location for people who are doing business in the city. However, Winter Park and the Park Plaza are really worlds apart from the hectic pace of Orlando.**

The sophisticated enclave of Winter Park, northeast of Orlando, is a haven from the crowds and traffic of Orlando and Disney World, overlooking the wonderful park from which the town derives its name. The Park Plaza is a small place, with old-fashioned polished mahogany paneling. It feels like the Florida of the 1920s.

The guest rooms can be reached by elevator or a flight of stairs. Rooms all have natural or painted wicker furniture, brass beds, Oriental rugs, plants, and ceiling fans. Some are fairly small; others have a sitting area and a large alcove for the bed. The clean and refurbished private baths are as homey and individual as the rooms. Travelers used to pastels and lots of windows may find the rooms a bit dark, but it's authentic Old Florida. One of the best suites is 212, which has a king-size bed and a sitting room furnished in white wicker. Suite 214, with a queen-size and a twin bed, is good for those traveling with a child.

Most of the guest rooms have French doors onto a balcony reminiscent of New Orleans' French Quarter, with a wrought-iron railing and an awning above. Dozens of flowers and ferns are in pots on the wood floor of the balcony; tendrils of flowers and vines spill through the railings to the streets below.

The best balcony views are from rooms on New England Avenue, overlooking the park. Rooms on the other side of the hallway make up for a slightly less desirable location by being a bit larger.

The balcony is not deep, but there is plenty of room for white wicker chairs and small round tables, each of which holds a flowerpot. Continental breakfast is included in the room rate and can be served in your room or on your little wedge of balcony. Breakfast alfresco is always a high point of a stay at the Plaza Hotel. Only leafy plants screen the individual sections of the balcony outside guest rooms, allowing guests to get to know their neighbors if they wish.

The Park Plaza is a good choice for travelers who don't want to drive. The Amtrak station is a walk away, and the Orlando airport is a 20-minute cab ride. Winter Park is a real town, a rarity in Florida. Park Avenue itself is an upscale shopping area. There are many restaurants here, among the best of which is the Park Plaza Gardens, next to the hotel. While this restaurant is no longer run by the owners of the hotel, hotel guests still have many meals here, and the Park Plaza Gardens continues to provide room service for the hotel. It has a garden feeling, with a brick floor, green pillars, lots of potted plants and trees, and a glass roof. Tables are set with pink and white linens and white china. The ice cream parlor chairs fit right in. There is a European sophistication to this well-managed restaurant, and the Continental cuisine has won many awards. The Sunday brunch is particularly good.

The Southeast Coast

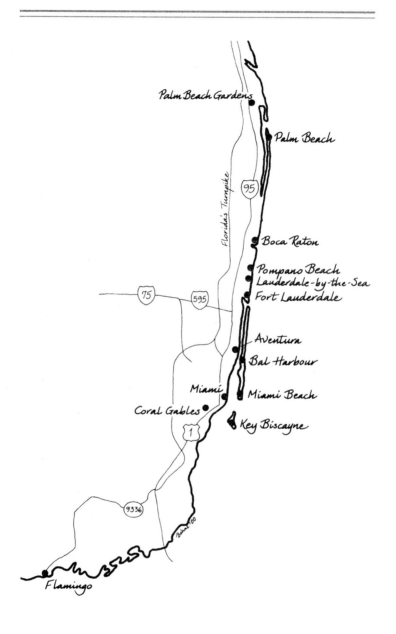

Best B&Bs

Best Beachside Accommodations

Best City Stops

Best Eclectic Finds

Miami Beach
Colony Hotel, 292
Island Outpost Art Deco Hotels, 301

Best Island Getaways

Key Biscayne
Sonesta Beach Resort Key Biscayne, 274
Miami
Fisher Island, 281

Best Resorts and Spas

Aventura (North Miami)
Turnberry Isle Resort & Club, 249
Boca Raton
Boca Raton Resort & Club, 253
Coral Gables
The Biltmore Hotel, 256
Fort Lauderdale
Fort Lauderdale Marina Marriott, 266
The Registry Resort and Spa, 273
Miami
Doral Golf Resort & Spa, 278
Palm Beach Gardens
PGA National Resort & Spa, 320
Pompano Beach
Palm-Aire Resort & Spa, 321

Best Small Hotels, Inns, and Motels

Coral Gables
Hotel Place St. Michel, 258
Flamingo
Flamingo Lodge, Marina & Outpost Resort, 262
Fort Lauderdale
Riverside Hotel, 271

The Atlantic coast of Florida is so thickly settled that it's sometimes difficult to see its topographical features. At first the only thing obvious about the coast is a string of famous beach towns and fabled cities stretching from north to south: Palm Beach, Boca Raton, Fort Lauderdale, Miami Beach, Miami, and the thin green ribbon of the Keys stretching south and west into the Gulf of Mexico. But to look at a map with no cities printed on it is to see that many of these beautiful beaches are on barrier islands and peninsulas. The narrow rivers, inlets, and elongated lakes between these islands and peninsulas form channels for Florida's Intracoastal Waterway. Some of the most famous vacation spots on the east coast are on islands that are little more than sandbars, with the Atlantic on one side and the Intracoastal on the other, making for breezes and a perfect environment for water sports.

The Southeast Coast is often called the "Gold Coast." Though there is some discussion about where, exactly, the Gold Coast begins, **Palm Beach** is as good a guess as any. The name refers to a town, an island, and a county. The county, striving to overcome its pampered image, includes **Palm Beach Gardens** and West Palm Beach, which are actually on the mainland. Originally built by Flagler for his railroad workers and the servants at Palm Beach mansions, West Palm Beach is now a vibrant center with a much larger population than the town of Palm Beach. Palm Beach Gardens was developed by John MacArthur and is home to the PGA National Resort as well as a smashing shopping mall, the Gardens.

To the west of West Palm Beach and Palm Beach Gardens is Lake Okeechobee, the huge body of water that appears as a big blue spot on aerial photographs of the United States. The lake is a mecca for people who love to fish. A good side trip from Palm Beach is a drive along the southern end of Okeechobee to Clewiston, a small agricultural city in the middle of cane country. When Florida was first settled, the area south of Lake Okeechobee was part of the Everglades. Much of the marsh was drained, starting in 1881, to create land for sugar cane production.

The town of Palm Beach is beautifully situated, overlooking Lake Worth on the west and the Atlantic on the east. The municipality of Palm Beach is an enclave of the privileged, with plenty of antique shops, galleries, and boutiques.

Half an hour south of Palm Beach is **Boca Raton,** a wealthy coastal city with a colorful history of pirates and Spanish explorers. The name in Spanish means "mouth of the rat," referring to the sharp rocks lining the mouth of the harbor that brought many a Spanish bark aground. Like Palm Beach, Boca Raton has many Addison Mizner mansions built in an elegant Spanish Renaissance style.

The best-known towns south of Boca Raton are **Pompano Beach, Lauderdale-by-the-Sea,** and **Fort Lauderdale.** Fort Lauderdale has long had a reputation as a wild beach town, particularly when college students descended in hordes during spring break. However, it is shedding its notoriety and is now also appreciated as a city of canals and beautiful residential areas. The town has some European-style restaurants and upscale shopping on Las Olas and a museum of art. Those who wish to avoid the spring-break crowds can simply pick a lodging in a quiet part of town or come at another time of year.

South of Fort Lauderdale are beach towns and then the northern outskirts of **Miami.** An international city of commerce, finance, and culture, Miami is sophisticated and cosmopolitan. Along Brickell Avenue and Biscayne Bay, it is also one of the most beautiful cities in the United States. At the same time, certain areas of Miami are among the most troubled and economically depressed of any city in the world. So one needs to take care and stay away from run-down neighborhoods. Visit the Miami Center and the Coconut Grove section, as well as nearby **Coral Gables** and Key Biscayne.

Although Miami has certainly been overdeveloped, there is a new sensitivity to preserving what is extant. The Fairchild Tropical Garden on Old Cutter Road has 83 acres of flowering trees, orchids, and ferns and one of the world's largest collections of palms and cycads. Some of the most interesting diversions acknowledge Miami's Spanish and Cuban heritage, like the Vizcaya Museum and Gardens and Little Havana. Dining in the Miami area is an adventure in itself, with the restaurants often reflecting the international flavor of the city. Little Havana, on the Tamiami Trail (Highway 41), also known as Calle Oche, has many Cuban restaurants. There is also good Vietnamese food in the city. Across the bay, several Miami Beach hotels have fine menus.

Miami Beach is sometimes mistakenly thought of as part of the city of Miami. In fact, Miami Beach is an island running north and south along Biscayne Bay and the eastern edge of Miami — a little like Manhattan, but thinner. The areas first developed in Miami Beach, mostly for elderly and wealthy New Yorkers, were South Collins Avenue, Ocean Drive, and neighborhoods west to the bay. Some of the most exciting and innovative development occurred during the 1930s and 1940s, resulting in the art deco neighborhoods that have recently had a resurgence in popularity.

The art deco style was so popular and the South Beach neighborhood of Ocean Drive and South Collins Avenue so fashionable that the building boom here lasted for years. But to many, the style began to look silly and dated after its heyday. The neighborhood declined in the 1960s as development moved north along Collins Avenue, and eventually the area became economically depressed and socially fragmented.

An interest in art deco led to the restoration of individual buildings and some revitalization of the neighborhood in the 1970s and 1980s. But even today, the art deco district of South Beach is not consistently thriving on Collins Avenue and some side streets between beachside Ocean Drive and Collins. Although the hotels are popular again, particularly among Europeans and budget-minded Americans, rooms may be small, service minimal, and a good night's rest difficult because of the Ocean Drive street noise and loud bands.

South of Miami and Miami Beach are a number of keys that dot the waters of Biscayne Bay. The most famous is **Key Biscayne,** with the town and a number of accommodations in the center of the island and a good deal of open land and public beach beyond. Crandon Park, with ample parking and a long stretch of beach, is at the northern end of the island, and Cape Florida State Park, with a fine old lighthouse, is at the southern end. There are also many inlets and coves along the shores of Key Biscayne, and a marina. Though some residents of Key Biscayne grumble that the place is becoming too commercial, it is peaceful compared with most of the Miami area.

The Everglades, the largest subtropical wilderness in the United States, are so vast they stretch nearly to the outskirts of Miami. It is still possible to get a taste of this wilderness by driving on Highway 41, the Tamiami Trail, from Miami to Tampa. The populations of waterfowl, alligators, and other animals here have been greatly reduced in recent years, and there are few wild flamingos.

But kingfishers still sit on telephone wires and dive for fish, and herons and egrets stalk the swampy gullies beside the road. The wild vines and native trees of Florida, as well as plants imported decades ago, grow luxuriantly.

An alternate route through the Everglades is Highway 84 (also known as Alligator Alley), which runs through the Big Cypress Seminole Indian Reservation. If you have an interest in the Everglades and its "River of Grass," you'll want to explore Everglades National Park, where you can get a closer look at the wildlife on boardwalks built over the swamps and inlets. Except for houseboats and lodge rooms at **Flamingo,** there are no accommodations in this vast park, but there are many well-maintained campgrounds. (See camping guides in the Recommended Guidebooks chapter at the end of this book, or contact: Superintendent, Campsites, Everglades National Park, P.O. Box 279, Homestead, FL 33030, 800-600-3813.)

Aventura

Turnberry Isle Resort & Club

19999 West Country Club Drive
North Miami, Aventura, FL
33180-2401
800-327-7028
305-936-2929
Fax: 305-933-6560
www.turnberryisle.com

A hotel with a spectacular new spa

Accommodations: 395 rooms and suites. **Rates:** $175–$465, suites $355–$3,500, 2-4-night spa packages $909–$1,299 per person double occupancy. **Included:** Exercise classes, tennis, spa and beauty treatments, club privileges. Tax, service charges for spa packages. Airport transfer and spa wardrobe included in some packages. **Minimum stay:** With spa packages. **Added:** 12.5% tax; $30 for extra person in rooms and suites; $50 charge for non-spa occupant in spa room. **Payment:** Major credit cards. **Children:** 12 and under free in room with parents; no children under 16 for spa packages. **Smoking:** Restricted at spa; nonsmoking rooms available. **Open:** Year-round.

➤ **Turnberry Isle is beautiful, with curving flower beds and greenery everywhere, all meticulously cared for. One of the highlights of the day is taking a morning walk through the grounds and along the bay. Afterward, guests can enjoy a gourmet breakfast in the dining room overlooking the country club pool.**

Turnberry Isle truly is an isle — a lush, subtropical sliver of land in Biscayne Bay between Miami Beach and Fort Lauderdale. Turnberry's European Spa and Fitness Center was created by spa designer Tag Galyean. The three floors are connected by a spiral staircase that overlooks a dramatic waterfall and fountain. There are 26 treatment rooms and a 3,650-square-foot fitness center, which includes an aerobics studio, cardio room, and weight room. There's also a beach club on the Atlantic.

The Turnberry Isle complex is devoted to enabling club members and guests to indulge themselves and live the good life. Some come here in order to see and be seen, and the resort and country club are reputed to be rather cliquey. But this need not impinge on a guest's experience at the spa itself. Spa guests are mostly interested in getting healthy, losing weight if they need to, and indulging in a well-earned rest.

The spa allows only a minimum of guests, and those few are given a great deal of attention. Spa personnel will discuss your tailor-made program with you before the regimen begins.

Spa guests have the use of two golf courses, two swimming pools, 19 tennis courts, a jogging track, a Swedish sauna, massage rooms, and a Turkish bath. Spa clothing, except for footwear, is provided.

Skin and body treatments include herbal wraps, aromatherapy baths, facials, Saltglo-loofah treatments, Swiss shower treatments, massages, pedicures, and manicures. The entire Turnberry Spa experience is one of being quietly cared for and guided into better physical health and self-confidence.

When it comes to food, don't think a stay at the spa will mean dry toast and mineral water. Meals are delicious, with enormous variety. Diets for participants here to lose weight are generally designed to provide plenty of energy for daily exercise.

Most spa guests stay at the resort's country club, which are closest to the spa building. Rooms are understatedly opulent, with a Mediterranean ambience. The club is a spectacular place, with polished marble floors and Oriental appointments in the lounges and public rooms. Guest rooms are in three hotel buildings named after exotic flowers that face a large pool and patio. Turnberry will accommodate as far as possible guests' choice of rooms and how serious a spa regime they carry out. When making reservations, be sure to ask about all the spa packages and what treatments they include, as well as the various accommodations available.

Bal Harbour

Sheraton Bal Harbour Beach Resort

9701 Collins Avenue
Bal Harbour, FL 33154
800-999-9898
305-865-7511
Fax: 305-864-2601

An activity-oriented resort and a quiet retreat

Accommodations: 642 rooms and suites. **Rates:** Rooms $129–$449, suites $550–$1,500, Garden Villa suites $650; extra person in room $25. **Included:** Breakfast with some packages. **Minimum stay:** During holiday seasons. **Added:** 11.5% tax; valet parking fee. **Payment:** Major credit cards. **Children:** Welcome; under 17 free in room with parent. **Smoking:** Allowed. **Open:** Year-round.

➤ **Several of the Sheraton's 10 acres overlook the ocean, where the color of the water is a Caribbean turquoise.**

Although the address says Bal Harbour and this is, indeed, a separate municipality located between Fort Lauderdale and Miami, many first-time visitors think of the area as the northern end of Miami Beach. Both Bal Harbour Village and Miami Beach are part of a series of small islands that are just off the coast, connected by a number of bridges and causeways. Because the Sheraton is just north of Miami Beach, guests here can enjoy the night life of South Beach but return to the quiet of the hotel for a good sleep — something not always assured in the trendy hotels further south on Collins Avenue and on Ocean Drive. During the day, they can also enjoy the peaceful pleasures of Bal Harbour Village and visit its exclusive shops, directly across the street from the hotel. Because it's relatively quiet and because this is a full-service resort, the Sheraton is also a good convention hotel.

The Sheraton is located on more than 10 acres, so there is plenty to do on the property. There's volleyball on the beach, water sports rentals, elevated tennis courts, and a large swimming pool, as well as golf nearby. Cabanas are available for rent, and there is a nice outdoor restaurant for drinks and snacks as you relax in the sun. Between the beach and the hotel is a tropical garden with large irregular paving stones that meander around the recreational area, leading to the pro shop, fitness center, and, finally, to the informal Edible Express on the ground floor of the hotel.

A recent $60 million renovation yielded two new restaurants: the art deco Al Carbón Restaurant in the lobby next to Waves Bar and the poolside Beach House, which serves up fresh seafood and Continental cuisine.

Both in the hotel and outside, where speakers are hidden behind the tropical foliage, music, mostly Muzak, seems to play nonstop. The only other jarring note here is that the lobby lounge is a little kitschy. There's a sunken garden in the center of the lobby, "planted" with what appear to be real palm tree trunks, dry palm fronds sticking out from their tops. However, the easy chairs are comfortable, the marble floors are attractive, and a "wave" of etched glass in an art deco design is interesting. Glass bricks add to the lobby's 1930s retro look.

Standard guest rooms at the Sheraton are outfitted with a king-size, queen-size, or two double beds, combination wood and Formica furniture, and a small desk and easy chair. The bathrooms have a tub shower. All rooms have two telephones, a clock radio, a safe, a well-stocked minibar, remote TV, a hair dryer, and coffee-maker.

The Sheraton's Garden Villa one-and-a-half-bathroom accommodations are even nicer. These two-story units overlooking the swimming pool and ocean are like small apartments without a kitchen. They have a living/dining area with a sofa and easy chair, a TV, minibar, and a dinner table with four chairs. Double doors with frosted glass lead to a spacious bedroom with double beds. There's a big closet here and a television atop the chest of drawers. An iron and ironing board are in the big walk-in closet.

The one disadvantage for those traveling with a family is that the bathroom here is a little small for four people — especially if two of them are teenagers. Downstairs units have a porch and up-stairs units a railed balcony, both with chaise longues and a table. If you're going to be staying for a while and can afford these accommodations, they're worth it.

When making reservations for either the Garden Villas or the regular suites and rooms, be certain to ask about the view. Some rooms have a slice of the ocean, others a full view, and some a view of Bal Harbour, Miami Beach, and Miami ("City View"), the latter being the least expensive but still certainly not a view of parking lots.

Whatever the view, there's always greenery visible. The luxuriant landscaping makes the Sheraton very appealing. In the evening, the tropical garden behind the hotel is softly lighted. Just outside the Garden Café is a little grotto waterfall. The cement and stone pathways that lead to the swimming pool and breezy beachfront beyond are adorned with large pots of brightly colored tropical flowers — all very lush and romantic.

Boca Raton

Boca Raton Resort & Club

501 E. Camino Real
Boca Raton, FL 33431-0825
800-327-0101
561-395-3000

One of Florida's grand old resorts

Accommodations: 963 rooms, 39 suites, 60 1-bedroom villas. **Rates:** Rooms $150–$495, suites $240–$475, golf villas $165–$450; packages available. **Minimum stay:** 2 nights with packages. **Added:** 10% tax. **Payment:** Major credit cards. **Children:** Under 16 free in room with parents. **Smoking:** Nonsmoking rooms available. **Open:** Year-round.

➤ **Although there are people dressed to the nines, attire is mostly casual, except at dinner. This is, after all, a resort, and many guests come primarily to play tennis, swim in the pool overlooking the water, or golf on the excellent courses.**

Addison Mizner, the self-taught architect and Florida promoter, built the Boca Raton in 1926 as the Cloister Inn. Mizner spared no expense in building, furnishing, and landscaping his grand "inn." The picturesque building is a mix of Mediterranean styles, with arched colonnades, Venetian detailing around windows, and decorative rooftop spires reminiscent of a fancy wedding cake. Renamed the Boca Raton Hotel and Club after Mizner went bankrupt and left town, it eventually became a premier resort of the wealthy.

Although the Boca Raton now comprises the Boca Raton Beach Club, the Tower, golf villas, and the Boca Country Club, the old

Cloisters lobby and the original accommodations are still the heart of the resort.

From the arched courtyard, guests enter the spectacular lobby through a row of mahogany and beveled glass French doors. Furnished with dark, intricately carved antiques upholstered in fine leather and vibrant fabrics, the lobby has the feel of a Mediterranean colonnade. Beams of heavy cypress arch over the Venetian-style room, and hand-tied Oriental rugs cover the polished terra cotta floors. Oil paintings hang on the pale stucco walls, many of them found by Mizner in old churches and universities in Spain and Central America.

The Country Club provides a great choice of recreation, including 36 tennis courts. A well-organized children's program is tailored to four age groups, from toddlers to teenagers. Activities are both educational and recreational and include kids' art shows, scavenger hunts, kite flying, sports, banana boat rides, dance parties, and teens-only cruises.

The resort's Beach Club is just across the Intracoastal Waterway from the Cloisters, accessible by ferry and shuttle bus. The Club rents sailboats and motor boats, Windsurfers, and scuba and snorkeling equipment. Staff members offer windsurfing lessons and will arrange for scuba diving, fishing, and snorkeling charters through the marina. The excellent fitness center has a weight room and an aerobics studio, as well as steam, massage, and sauna rooms. Rounding out the choices are two pools and a heated whirlpool. The Beach Club's guest rooms have views of either the Intracoastal or the Atlantic from private balconies. The restaurants here are quite good.

History buffs and aficionados of grand hotels may feel that the Beach Club is too modern in architecture and lacks the Cloisters' character. But the beach alone makes a trip across the Intracoastal Waterway worthwhile. The covered open-air launch, *Mizner's Dream*, while not as fast as the resort's shuttle bus, offers twice the fun and romance.

Guests board the launch at a landing next to the Tower, a Boca addition of many years ago that, like the Club, has its detractors and its adherents. Perhaps someday, this 27-story, free-standing high-rise will be thought of as funky and interesting, like the art deco hotels in Miami Beach. Right now, painted to match the Cloisters, it looks too big, too pink, and too towering. It does, however, provide great views of the Intracoastal from guest rooms, a good deal of conference space, and an excellent rooftop restaurant.

The resort also has pleasant golf villas, perfect for golfing foursomes because of their proximity to the course and their views of the greens.

Wherever resort guests are staying or dining, sooner or later they come back to the Cloisters. Here there are Spanish-tiled fountains in little hideaway gardens, small shops and an art gallery off the lobby, charming guest rooms, and some wonderful restaurants and lounges.

The Cathedral Dining Room, with its adjoining Patio Royale, mixes Mediterranean and Moorish decor. On the terra cotta floors of its anteroom are ornate wrought-iron Moorish candlesticks standing about six feet tall. These set the mood for the dining room with its soaring pillars, rich carpets, and elegant napery and china. This is a place where you can feast with your eyes as well as your mouth.

The breakfast buffet offers a cornucopia overflowing with fresh fruits and berries, silver serving dishes of eggs and breakfast meats, a variety of fresh pastries, and omelets made to order. Occasionally, the sheer numbers of guests in the dining room can cause glitches, and making oneself understood with a non-English-speaking waiter can be frustrating. Still, this is the most romantic place to eat at the Boca Raton.

Standard rooms at the Cloisters are smaller than those at the Beach Club, but their charm cannot be denied. Large windows have a heavy, room-darkening drape to draw when guests wish to sleep late or take an afternoon siesta. The traditional furnishings are reproductions in walnut and mahogany. Even the standard rooms come with a mirrored desk, an "in-room butler" stocked with snacks and beverages, and closet safes.

The bathrooms are marble, with polished brass 1920s-style fixtures. The separate dressing rooms have vanities holding china jars stocked with things like cotton balls and emery boards, and a porcelain basket holds more amenities, including a sewing kit, a shoeshine kit, and potpourri sachets. Each guest at the Boca Raton receives a complimentary bottle of iced champagne.

Recently, service at the resort has slipped a bit, especially during special event weekends, when the staff seems overwhelmed. Whether this problem stems from the resort becoming too large, management errors, or difficulty in finding good help is hard to say.

Coral Gables

The Biltmore Hotel

1200 Anastasia Avenue
Coral Gables, FL 33134
800-727-1926
305-445-1926
Fax: 305-913-3152

Here is the world's largest hotel pool, where Esther Williams swam

General Manager: Dennis Doucette. **Accommodations:** 280 rooms and suites. **Rates:** Rooms $215–$299, suites $365–$2,250; packages available. **Added:** 12.5% tax. **Payment:** Major credit cards. **Children:** Welcome; children 19 and under free in room with parent. **Smoking:** Nonsmoking rooms available. **Open:** Year-round.

➤ **Most guests eventually end up in the courtyard, with its colonnade and vividly tiled fountain. This is a restful place for reading or sitting in the sunshine.**

The Biltmore has a long and colorful history, which the present owners and managers are proud to share with visitors who know little of this Florida legend. The hotel looks like a Spanish palace rising above Miami and the small city of Coral Gables — itself a 1920s version of a Spanish town. After years of neglect, this fine old hotel has been restored with the help of $55 million from its owners, Seaway Hotels Corporation, the expert sales and marketing efforts of Westin, and the devotion of its staff.

The crescent-shaped hotel overlooks the Biltmore Golf Club and the swimming pool where Esther Williams performed in 1940s aquatic extravaganzas. The newly refurbished stucco is painted salmon with light trim. A red tile roof, arched colonnade, 300-foot bell tower, and an eclectic mix of Moorish and Mediterranean styles make the hotel a local treasure.

The Biltmore was built in 1926 by George Merrick, who also designed the limestone archways and streets of Coral Gables in this country's first venture into city planning. Less than two years after the Biltmore opened, the land boom in Florida collapsed (along with Merricks finances), and the hotel languished. Like the Don CeSar on St. Petersburg Beach and the Casa Marina in Key

West, the Biltmore was eventually converted into an army installation. After the service moved out, it sat empty for several years.

Now the hotel attracts people from Europe, Asia, and Latin America as well as Floridians and other Americans. The beautiful lobby has massive Corinthian columns soaring from a pink and gray marble floor to a vaulted gothic ceiling painted blue with gold stars. The plaster walls are buff, faintly mottled for a slight patina. Furniture is dark, carved, and ornate. The three grand ballrooms and the formal dining room have painted and coffered ceilings. Drapes and upholstery fabrics are heavy brocades, damasks, velvets, and tapestries. Rugs on the marble floors are intricately patterned Orientals.

The Biltmore has 48,000 square feet of function space, with three ballrooms and a number of smaller meeting rooms including the clubby Biltmore Lounge. A private cigar salon and wine bar called the Cellar Club Library features a selection of fine cigars, wines, and cordials. Tennis is played on 10 lighted courts, and golf is on a Donald Ross–designed course that begins its smooth meanderings just beyond the huge swimming pool. The hotel's health club has more than 80 pieces of fitness equipment, sauna and steam rooms, and services that include some excellent spa treatments.

The courtyard is very pleasant for lunch or for dinner on balmy nights. The casual café also provides service indoors in a Spanish-style restaurant decorated with beautiful Mediterranean tiles. The Café serves three meals a day, including a delicious lunchtime buffet and a popular Sunday brunch. Formal dining is in La Palme d'Or, with artistic presentations of authentic French cuisine.

Coral Gables is a lushly beautiful city, and there are some spectacular views of it from the Biltmore's elegant rooms. A typical room has ornately painted Mediterranean bedsteads, new firm beds with goose-down bedding, armoires, and new tile baths. The deluxe king rooms, with a king-size bed and a velvet sleep sofa, are good for a family.

If you want to splurge, you might try the Everglades suite. Al Capone once hid out here, stationing his bodyguards at the floor-to-ceiling windows where they could see out over Coral Gables in four directions. The oak doors and timbers of this Spanish-style suite look as if they've been salvaged from the Armada. The floors of stone are covered with fine carpets. In addition to bedrooms, there is a large central living/dining room with a carved coral fireplace, and an oversize marble bath with a Jacuzzi and a shower with three massaging showerheads.

There are rumors of ghosts at the Biltmore — men in 1920s dinner jackets and women in nurses' uniforms from the 1940s. Surprisingly, there are no reports of Spanish courtiers.

Hotel Place St. Michel

162 Alcazar Avenue
Coral Gables, FL 33134
305-444-1666
800-848-4683 (hotel)
www.HotelPlaceStMichel.com

A European-style hotel in
fashionable Coral Gables

Owners: Stuart Bornstein and Alan Potamkin. **Accommodations:** 24 rooms and 3 suites. **Rates:** Rooms $125–$165, suites $160–$200. **Included:** Continental breakfast, fruit upon arrival, and morning newspaper. **Minimum stay:** During some major events. **Added:** 12.5% tax; $10 extra person. **Payment:** Major credit cards except Discover. No checks. **Children:** Under 12 free in room with parents. **Smoking:** Allowed. **Open:** Year-round.

➤ **The Hotel St. Michel was built in 1926 as the Hotel Sevilla and, from the outside, looks somewhat like a small European palazzo — the sort of place where a lesser relative of the Medicis might reside.**

The name recalls Paris, and well it should, for the Hotel Place St. Michel is reminiscent of a good Parisian hotel. And the name Alcazar, the elegant Coral Gables boulevard on which the hotel is located, brings to mind a Spanish palace with Moorish archways and Spanish tiles. The hotel has that kind of palatial beauty — just on a smaller scale.

The entrance sets the mood: a red canvas awning above an arched doorway with a coat of arms above. Inside, cool terrazzo tile floors, buff-colored stucco walls, archways of rich ceramic tiles, and French windows open into a bistro-style restaurant on one side of the hallway and the hotel lobby on the other. A concierge presides at the ornately carved registry desk, with an Eastlake mirror and pigeonhole postal cases mounted on the wall behind. French doors lead into a sitting/breakfast room of velvet settees. The Hotel St. Michel had a fire in 1996 and the owners worked very hard to replace their furniture and decor. The hotel is better than ever.

A brass elevator goes to rooms on the second and third floors. Hallways are furnished with breakfronts and other period pieces. Above each room are stained glass transoms in art nouveau designs of green, mustard yellow, and cream. Rooms have two double beds, or a queen- or king-size bed.

Each room is different in shape, size, and decor. The parquet floors are covered with fine old rugs, and the furnishings are Victorian antiques. Rather than building closets, the owners furnished the rooms with large antique armoires. Televisions sit on old Singer sewing machine tables. The modern tile bathrooms have pedestal sinks and stenciling on the walls. The bathrooms have beautifully veined marble and new brass fixtures giving a Victorian feeling of luxury. Some rooms are smaller than others, so be certain to inquire about space when making reservations.

Two especially nice rooms are 306, with two corner windows, and 302, with its own Victorian-style sitting room. There are special touches in all the guest rooms: vases of flowers, gold and white French telephones, carved antique bedsteads, bentwood armchairs upholstered in fine fabrics, and lovely paintings.

Guests enjoy a Continental breakfast in their rooms with the newspaper, or they may take their morning meal downstairs in the sitting room. Breakfast features fresh croissants with jam and marmalade, fruit juice, and tea or coffee. Other complimentary offerings are fruit on arrival and chocolates on the pillow with nightly turndown.

For lunch and dinner, there are a number of charming cafés and restaurants on Ponce de Leon Boulevard and elsewhere in Coral Gables, one of the most beautiful cities in Florida. The Cuban section of Miami, on the Tamiami Trail, offers many dining options. Closer to home is the Restaurant St. Michel, just across the tiled lobby entryway. This is a favorite dining spot for Miamians as well as hotel guests. The mood is European, and the menu is even more so, with escargot, grilled swordfish with Mediterranean pepper relish, lobster sautéed in mushrooms and scallions, and crepes for dessert.

Like many old Florida hotels, the Hotel St. Michel has had its ups and downs, and it's heartening that the management is preserving the beauty and dignity of such a worthy place.

Omni Colonnade Hotel

180 Aragon Avenue
Coral Gables, FL 33134
800-THE OMNI
305-441-2600
Fax: 305-445-3929

**An elegant hotel built
around Greek Revival–style
offices**

Accommodations: 140 rooms, 15 two-level suites, 2 presidential suites. **Rates:** Rooms $160–$339, suites $215–$450; discount weekend rates available. **Minimum stay:** 2 nights during special events and holidays. **Added:** 12.5% tax. **Payment:** Major credit cards. **Children:** Under 16 free in room with parent. **Smoking:** Nonsmoking floor. **Open:** Year-round.

➤   **On the first floor of the hotel are two good restaurants, Doc Dammers Bar and Grill and the more formal Aragon Café; both have established excellent reputations in a short time. There are also some boutiques and the rotunda, where bar mitzvahs, luncheons, and receptions are held. The ballroom is on the second floor.**

Coral Gables was developed by a longtime Florida resident, George Merrick, during the Miami land boom of the early 1920s. Unlike many other developers, George Merrick did not simply pave over cleared jungle and build houses. Next to the Coconut Grove section of Miami, he designed a Mediterranean-style town with broad boulevards, fountained rotaries, and well-built houses tucked behind thick vegetation.

When the 1926 hurricane hit the city of Miami and the surrounding area twice in 24 hours, the only houses that remained in one piece were those built by Merrick. Among them was the Colonnade, Merrick's office building, from which Merrick sold $150 million worth of Coral Gables real estate. Merrick lost all his money in the Florida real estate crash of 1926, but luckily, both the Colonnade and Coral Gables survived.

The original Colonnade building is a Greek Revival rotunda in pale pink stucco. Inside are fine coral and deep green marble floors, elaborate moldings, and white columns that reach up to a Greek Revival atrium. The hotel was built behind the original Colonnade in 1988. The shift from one to the other is nearly seamless from the inside, largely because the designers used the same marble columns and archways that Merrick favored. They were even able to closely match the marble.

The public rooms and guest rooms display attention to detail and excellence. Even the hallways are attractive, with plaster friezes and brass and etched crystal light fixtures that hark back to the 1920s. The marble and tile bathrooms have polished brass and ceramic fixtures and a vase of fresh flowers. The hotel has 17 suites, including two-level suites with spiral staircases, which are tempting if a guest wants to really live in opulence. But this is an expensive hotel even for Coral Gables, and most people find the superior and deluxe rooms more than adequate. The superior rooms, with two double beds, have plenty of space for a family and include a small sitting area with a sofa. Mahogany furnishings include handtooled armoires that hide a television. There are two telephones and a minibar in every room.

Since early 1994, the hotel has been managed by Omni Hotels, which completed a $2 million upgrading in 1996. Business services include fax machines in every guest room with a direct incoming dial feature and a phone system with multilingual voice messaging. Other services include champagne on arrival, nightly turndown, hair dryers, irons, and ironing boards in every room, and tea or coffee with a wakeup call. The staff is friendly and professional.

The Aragon Café is an elegant private dining room and meeting facility on the first floor near the marble rotunda. The adjacent Doc Dammer's Bar and Grill has a complete dinner menu and specializes in Miami Nueva cuisine — a mix of Latin American, Caribbean, and Floridian flavors. For recreation on the property, there's a rooftop sun deck with a new pool and Jacuzzi and a fitness club with sauna. Nearby are boating and fishing, tennis and golf, museums, theater, and shopping in the boutiques of Coral Gables.

Flamingo

Flamingo Lodge, Marina & Outpost Resort

Everglades National Park
1 Flamingo Lodge Highway
Flamingo, FL 33034-6798
800-600-3813 (reservations)
941-695-3101
Fax: 941-695-3921
evergladesinfo@amfacpnr.com
www.flamingolodge.com

> **Modest digs in a wildlife refuge in the Everglades**

General Manager: Peter Hulse. **Accommodations:** 102 rooms, 1 suite, 24 cottages, 4 Pontoon houseboats, 4 Gibson houseboats. **Rates:** Rooms $65–$95, suites $99–$145, cottages (up to 4 adults) $89–$135; extra person in room $10. **Included:** Continental breakfast May 1–October 31. **Added:** 11.5% tax. **Payment:** Credit cards, traveler's checks. **Children:** Under 18 free in room with parent. **Smoking:** Nonsmoking rooms available. **Open:** Year-round.

> ➤ **The great thing about the houseboats is that you don't have to be an experienced boater to rent one these floating observation platforms. There is an orientation program to teach you how to navigate the boats, where to go for the best scenery, and where not to go.**

The Everglades are finally receiving the respect and affection they have long deserved. After decades of either neglect or near-destruction instigated by farmers and developers who wanted to dry up this beautiful "river of grass" in the early part of the century, the Everglades are now a national park. They are also accessible to nature lovers who are not fazed by the hour or more that it takes to get here from Miami. Many residents and visitors to Florida become acquainted with the wildlife of this unusual area by staying for a weekend or longer at Flamingo Lodge, Marina and Outpost Resort.

There is still some grumbling among environmental extremists who wish to reclaim all the land that was once part of the Everglades (now constituting much of modern southeast Florida in the form of farms and businesses and homes) and return it to its pre-1920s pristine state — which would also mean no visitors to enjoy its beauty. The Florida state government has managed to strike a reasonable balance between the needs of nature lovers, farmers, and businesses so that nobody fully wins their point, but nobody loses out completely.

The National Park Service has a staff of rangers who are equipped with a great deal of knowledge and are a low-key, soft-spoken group, very pleasant to talk to. The park has five visitor centers, although Flamingo is the only one with motel and cottage accommodations. The centers offer a number of tours and cruises, some on land, some by water.

Most first-time visitors drive from Miami to Flamingo and explore the other centers on subsequent visits. The Florida Turnpike south of Miami connects to Route 9336 in Florida City. This rural road meanders west and then south and seems to go on and on. After several minutes many people think they must have taken the wrong road because they *still* haven't reached the Flamingo Outpost. When they do reach the "Lodge," they are apt to be surprised that it is essentially a budget motel. So what is the attraction? Why do people come back here after year? Because it is beautiful: the marshes, the jungly woods, the water, the wildlife, the sunsets — very, *very* beautiful.

Admittedly, the accommodations at Flamingo Lodge are more modest than beautiful. The Lodge is just a zigzag line of one- and two-story motel units with a few dry-looking palm trees sticking up from the slightly scruffy lawn out front. The best time to come to the park is in the winter dry season, because it's cooler and there are far fewer mosquitoes then, but everything is quite dry. So don't look for frothy green plants or golf-course manicured lawns. The impressive landscaping is nature's own, and it's not at the motel.

There are, however, great views of Florida Bay, especially from the second floor of the Lodge accommodations. In general, rooms closest to the Lodge office have the best views, because those at the end have trees blocking the view. Many people also prefer second-story rooms, again because of the view. Ask for the best room available at the time you are making reservations, since the price is the same for all of them except the suite.

Rooms are basic but attractive: wood-paneled, with two double beds, two chairs, TV, and telephone. The Lodge has one suite, with the advantages of a microwave and a great view of Florida Bay.

The cottages are about one mile down the road from the motel, near the campgrounds. Located on a cul-de-sac, these have views of the woods rather than the bay and are a little newer and more attractive. Each unit has a living room with a pull-down double sofa bed and a dining table. There's a telephone but no TV. The separate bedroom has two double beds. Two units, with only one bed, are designed for the handicapped. All the kitchens have a full-size refrigerator and stove, coffeemaker, and flatware and dishes. The bath has a shower.

The houseboats at the marina are also straightforward, and have been described as "floating mobile homes." They are lots of fun, with two pullout double beds, a twin-size bunk and a double-size bunk, a small head with shower, and a galley kitchen. The houseboats have a covered "back porch" that is a great place to sit and watch wildlife, have a cookout, sunbathe, or fish. The houseboats sleep six to eight and are equipped with cookware, dishes, propane for cooking, linens, navigational charts, and safety equipment. The longer Pontoon houseboats are not air conditioned, so they are unsuitable for all but the hardiest souls during the summer and even late spring and early fall.

Except for the houseboats, all accommodations are serviced by the cleaning staff every day and are as well maintained as the park budget allows. Staff in the office are very friendly and do their best to make visitors' stays pleasant. They do a lot with what little they've got in the budget. All buildings are owned by the Department of the Interior, and anyone who thinks national parks are a boondoggle will soon be set straight here.

The term *resort* has to be used loosely. Behind the Lodge office is a screen-enclosed swimming pool and patio area, with the Florida Bay beyond. (No swimming is allowed in Florida Bay or the ponds in the park.) Gas grills for everyone's use are in the breezeway near the pool. The patio is attractive, with lots of potted plants.

A short walk from the motel and pool is the restaurant and lounge, a gift shop, and a visitor center overlooking the bay. Next to this complex is the marina where there's a supply store, boat slips and the dock, and even a fish-cleaning shed. Arrangements for boat rentals and cruises are made here. An amphitheater at the other end of the resort, near the cottages and campground, is the site of various programs given by the rangers. Also near the campground is Eco Pond, a refuge for waterbirds, which has a lookout platform and a park ranger on hand who points out features of the pond's ecosystem. This is a good place for first-time visitors to start exploring the beauty of the park. However, the plethora of flying, biting insects at the park means that those who do not bring bug spray as well as sunscreen (even in winter) will regret it.

All visitors are encouraged to see as much as possible of Everglades wildlife, some of which is endangered in other areas of the nation. During peak season, rangers conduct "Early Bird" strolls to see birds at 7:30 A.M. and give daytime and evening talks at the Visitor Center and the campground amphitheater. Bicycles, skiffs, kayaks, and canoes are available for rent at the marina for those who wish to venture out on their own. Some of the tours are available in the winter only, while others are offered every day throughout the year. Because some of the most interesting areas in the Everglades can only be seen by boat, it is really worthwhile to take one of the cruises.

In spite of the modest accommodations, most people who stay here count their visit to Flamingo Lodge as one of the most memorable experiences of their lives. Thinking back to that experience, they may scratch their heads and wonder why, especially if they have memories of a toddler or teenager banging on the door of the tiny bathroom in the morning. But the wildlife and landscape are so beautiful here, they really do take one's breath away. The fishing can't be beat, the atmosphere is relaxed, and the rangers and office staff really care about the place and the animals — including people-animals. Only the river wildlife at the Panhandle's Wakulla Lodge can come close to the Everglades. This is also a place where visitors can learn a little about how to live better, because the exquisite birds and other wildlife are more likely to reveal themselves to those who watch quietly, wait patiently, and are willing to listen rather than talk.

Fort Lauderdale

Fort Lauderdale Marina Marriott

1881 S.E. 17th Street
Fort Lauderdale, FL 33316
800-433-2254
800-228-9290
954-463-4000

> **A relaxing marina resort with beach privileges**

Accommodations: 580 rooms and 17 suites. **Rates:** Rooms $105–$230, suites $350–$625; packages and discounts available. **Minimum stay:** None. **Added:** 11% tax. **Payment:** Major credit cards, personal checks. **Children:** Free in room with parents. **Smoking:** Not permitted. **Open:** Year-round.

➤ **You don't have to have a yacht to enjoy yourself here. There are sailboat rentals (and lessons), windsurfing, paddle boards, boogie boards, and floats for rent by the hour or day. There's also tennis, a fitness room, a sauna, and a pool.**

This Marriott has a fresh nautical feel; even when there isn't a breeze off the marina, you feel as if there is. The marina location is accentuated by the generous windows in each guest room, 20-foot windows in the lobby, and more windows overlooking the marina on guest room floors near elevators and at the end of hallways. If the mere sight of water helps you unwind, you'll be in a state of profound relaxation in no time.

The pool and marina have a laid-back atmosphere and Tahitian and Old Florida motifs. The snack bar and marina buildings have thatch or wooden shake roofs. You can spend the whole day in your swimsuit. Start the day with a swim, then relax by the pool; you don't have to move very far to get a drink or a snack. If you get too warm, take a stroll along the boardwalk at the breezy marina under shady tropical trees.

The Marriott has four tennis courts and can arrange for scuba diving, fishing, and sailing from the marina. There's a game room for the nimble-fingered and a health club. Nearby are golf, Jet Skiing, parasailing, and some good restaurants. But you don't have to go far to eat well. There's plenty of variety at the Marriott's two indoor restaurants and outdoor mesquite grill.

Other services at the hotel and marina include valet or self-parking, safety deposit boxes, auto rentals, a tour desk for area attractions, a gift shop, room service, and — especially nice for mariners — a guest laundry facility. The marina has 55 slips and, as at any busy marina, it's important to call ahead for space. Visitors should be forewarned that this is a working marina. Across the waterway from the hotel is a rusting corrugated steel marina building. It's all part of the scene for a seasoned mariner but might be a surprise for someone expecting only pretty yachts.

Accommodations in this high-rise overlooking the water are varied. Altogether, there are 580 guest rooms and 17 large suites, each with color TV with HBO, radio, minibar and refrigerator, iron and ironing board, large closet, and tile bath. (Bathrooms in the standard rooms might be a little snug for some people.) The West Villa rooms are the least desirable, with views of the parking lot, so it's wise to discuss view when making reservations. Weekend and Marriott Getaway rates are the best throughout the year. All the rooms have balconies, and the higher up you go, the more fantastic the views of the marina, Port Everglades, and the Intracoastal Waterway.

Lago Mar Resort

1700 S. Ocean Lane
Fort Lauderdale, FL 33316
800-255-5246
954-523-6511

A beachside resort that people return to year after year

Accommodations: 52 rooms and 160 suites. **Rates:** Rooms $115–$235, suites $145–$335, 2-bedroom suites $195–$675; $10 for extra person; packages available. **Minimum stay:** None. **Added:** 11% tax. **Payment:** Major credit cards. **Children:** 17 and under free in room with parents. **Smoking:** Allowed. **Open:** Year-round.

➤ **Over the years, sedimentation has broadened the Fort Lauderdale coastline; the beach is now wider than ever.**

Lago Mar is friendly and quiet (but not too quiet) — an ideal family resort that is, in fact, family-run. The resort has undergone a number of changes in the past several years, including a new three-story main building, expanded ground-floor lobby and conference center, new suites, refurbished bathrooms and kitchens, a large swimming lagoon, and a new garden dining area, all of which make for greater service and elegance.

The new stucco and brick-paved portico has a large tiled fountain. The elegant lobby and reception area are perhaps three times their previous size, and large groups can be accommodated with ease. On the walls are rather haunting paintings of the tropics, the kind of thing the artist René Magritte might have done if he'd sojourned in Florida.

The accommodations give guests a good deal of choice, with one- and two-bedroom suites, efficiencies, and a few smaller guest rooms. Views are of the ocean or the landscaped garden and pool. In the newest building, even the hallways have coffered ceilings and graceful moldings. The new guest rooms have a kitchen that includes a microwave and coffeemaker. The dining area in the ocean-front suites is a little small for a family of four or five, with an iron table and chairs that might be more appropriate on the balcony. Other than that, the appointments are handsome.

Bathrooms in the oceanfront suites include an oval tub large enough to wash the salt and sand off several little kids or provide a romantic soak for two when the kids have gone to bed. Everywhere in the rooms and suites, the effort to provide lasting beauty and comfort is obvious.

Although it is oriented toward families, Lago Mar is also popular for corporate meetings and retreats. The Executive Conference Center is self-contained and has a guest elevator to the luxurious one- and two-bedroom suites on the upper floors. The living/dining areas double as hospitality or small meeting rooms. The center has its own lobby, a private reception patio, and four meeting rooms, which can handle up to 200 people. High-tech support is available, of course, but this is the sort of place where corporate decisions can be thoughtfully made while gazing out at the dappled greenery of the garden. Seventy-five percent of Lago Mar's conference clients are returnees.

The resort is wonderful during holidays. Thanksgiving is a week-long feast, with brunches and parties in the dining room overlooking the pool or in the new Lakeview Room overlooking pretty Lake Mayan and the dock. Many families book the week of Christmas and enjoy a holiday barbecue, caroling around the tree on Christmas Eve, and the arrival of Santa Claus — by water taxi. At Easter, there's a massive egg hunt on the lawn.

Activities include nine-hole golf, an exercise room, shuffleboard, tennis, beach volleyball, fishing off the dock, two swimming pools and a kiddie pool, Jacuzzis, an electronic game room, and a playground. Shop Row has a health club, clothing stores, liquor store, gift shop, and tennis shop.

A step away from Shop Row is Lago Mar's private beach, with the blue Atlantic surging beyond. Property to the north and south of Lago Mar is owned by Marriott and residential condo communities, so the beach is secluded and private. Amenities include chaise longues and hooded cabanas.

The dining room and lounge have been redecorated, with a New Orleans–style overhang extending from the dining room for alfresco dining overlooking the lagoon pool and sea grape trees. There's also the Soda Shop for snacks (with a mini-grocery) and a grill and bar. The weekend brunch at Lago Mar includes omelets made to order and fresh tropical fruits. Some families also cook their own meals. The always-cordial staff at the front desk also advise guests on the many excellent restaurants in the Fort Lauderdale area.

Lago Mar Resort is only 10 minutes from the airport and a few city blocks from the overdeveloped Fort Lauderdale "strip" on Route A1A. The area between Mayan Lake and the ocean is residential and secluded; there are private homes and small condominium developments, as well as Marriott's Harbor Beach Resort and Lago Mar. Picturesque canals join the lake to the back gardens of homes and the Lago Mar's docks.

Marriott's Harbor Beach Hotel

3030 Holiday Drive
Fort Lauderdale, FL 33316
800-222-6543
Reservations: 800-228-9290 or
800-233-1234
954-525-4000

An informal but sophisticated resort on 16 acres of beachfront

Accommodations: 624 rooms; 35 suites. **Rates:** Rooms $150–$365, suites $500–$1,400; packages available. **Minimum stay:** None. **Added:** 11% tax. **Payment:** Major credit cards. **Children:** Free in room with parent. **Smoking:** Nonsmoking rooms available. **Open:** Year-round.

➤　**Windsurfing lessons are offered by the hour. For those who want a less rigorous water activity, floats are rented by the day.**

Located on prime beachfront land, the 15-story Harbor Beach Marriott is in the quiet Harbor Beach section of Fort Lauderdale — not far from the Fort Lauderdale "strip," but worlds away in spirit. The service is friendly and the atmosphere informal.

A weathered boardwalk leads to the beach, a wide swath of pale sand with warm Atlantic waters that have just enough wave action. The beach is dotted with hooded cabanas for rent, along with water sports equipment. Also on property are tennis courts and, nearby, championship golf. The fitness center has a sauna, exercise and massage rooms, StairMaster machines, and a state-of-the-art conditioning circuit consisting of 10 individual CYBEX stations.

The beach is nice for lazy strolling as well as sunbathing. Walk south past the residential condos and Lago Mar Resort to Port Everglades, where hundreds of ships dock every year. Or go past the front of the resort through the pretty residential neighborhood of Harbor Beach to Lake Mayan and the canals.

For those who prefer freshwater swimming and a chaise longue by the patio, the Harbor Beach Hotel has an enormous free-form pool with a waterfall surrounded by palm trees. You can easily spend all day sunning and relaxing here. When you get hungry, you need move only a few feet to get a grilled sandwich or salad at Cascades.

For a change of pace in the evening, try the Kinoko, a Japanese restaurant and steakhouse, or Sheffield's, an English-style restaurant that has earned a four-star rating. Both restaurants require jackets for men. The Sea Breeze Grille is less formal, with offerings such as duck breast salad, smoked chicken, and salmon and tuna sashimi. OceanView, with the atmosphere of an island plantation house, has more standard fare. The Lobby Bar, the Oyster Bar, and the poolside Cascades Bar all serve drinks. Service in the restaurants and bars is friendly but not as swift in some as it could be.

The airy lobby has large windows with spectacular views of the sea and sky. The lighting and artwork of the lobby area enhance its Florida atmosphere and give the Marriott a sophisticated feel that is unusual in a beach resort.

Most of the resort's rooms could be called "standard luxury." All are attractively furnished, with whitewashed wicker and wood furnishings, comfortably upholstered rattan chairs, painted metal lamps with linen shades, and tropical floral prints. Baths are tiled and modern. All accommodations at Harbor Beach Hotel have balconies from which you can see the port, the ocean, and the canals of the city. If you can afford it, ask for an ocean-view room. The oceanfront rooms have an even more impressive view, but they are more expensive, and the sliding glass doors to the balcony sometimes whistle unnervingly when the wind off the ocean is strong. When making reservations, ask about the views and try to get up as high as possible. If you cannot afford an ocean-view room, you might be able to get something with a view of Fort Lauderdale's canals.

Riverside Hotel

620 E. Las Olas Boulevard
Fort Lauderdale, FL 33301
800-325-3280
954-467-0671
Fax: 954-462-2148
RiversideHotel@worldnet.att.net
www.riversidehotel.com

A small hotel with Continental and Floridian charm

Accommodations: 90 rooms and 7 suites. **Rates:** Rooms $124–$209, suites $199–$369; packages, weekend, and corporate rates available. **Included:** "Beach Express" trolley service. **Minimum stay:** With some packages. **Added:** 11% tax. **Payment:** Major credit cards. **Children:** Under 16 free in room with parents. **Smoking:** Nonsmoking rooms available. **Open:** Year-round.

➤ **Having "real wood" furniture in a hotel room may seem insignificant to a New Englander or Midwesterner accustomed to old country inns, but in Fort Lauderdale, any hotel room not furnished with plastic is worth noting.**

Facing fashionable Las Olas Boulevard and with its back on the New River, the Riverside is one of the finest small hotels on the Gold Coast. A vibrant mural is painted on the streetside facade of the hotel's restaurant — it's a whimsical eyecatcher. Built in 1936, the Riverside is owned by one of Fort Lauderdale's first families, with the second generation now running the hotel.

Its best rooms are tower rooms, which overlook the alfresco eating area and pool and the resort's private docks on the river (write ahead to reserve mooring space if you want to bring your boat). Each room is a bit different, but all have stucco walls and either two double beds or a king-size bed. The bureaus and bedsteads in the guest rooms are carved Jacobean oak. The owners even had TV stands made by a local woodworker to match the Jacobean pieces. French doors lead out to balconies.

The canopy king river-view rooms are especially nice for a honeymoon or anniversary couple. Even the standard rooms have a small fridge and cable TV. Rooms are air-conditioned, though the hallways are not. The immaculate bathrooms are a bit small in some rooms but are attractive, with generous use of Italian tile. Several rooms were recently combined to form spacious suites, and two wheelchair-accessible rooms have been added.

For fine dining in the evening (as well as for breakfast and lunch), try Inndigo, with southeast Asian cuisine served indoors or out. The Golden Lyon Lounge overlooks Las Olas Boulevard and serves some food as well as cocktails with fine music. The Grill Room is like an officers' club and features Florida specialties on fine china and silver. Lunch and dinner are served in the Wine Room, where racks of wine — 400 different kinds — provide an impressive selection to complement the excellent food. The food in these restaurants is popular with residents and visitors to the city as well as hotel guests.

The lobby of the Riverside looks both Continental and Old Florida, with terra-cotta-tile floors, cushioned wicker chairs in several sitting groups, and two wonderful old fireplaces of carved coral tabby. The hotel has room for business functions and banquets in the Champ Carr Room, Sagamore Room, and Board Room.

The Wyndham Resort & Spa

250 Racquet Club Road
Fort Lauderdale, FL 33326
800-247-9810
954-389-3300
Fax: 954-384-6878

A resort and spa dedicated to refreshing body, mind, and spirit

Accommodations: 500 rooms and suites. **Rates:** Rooms $135–$210, suites $205–$255. **Minimum stay:** None. **Added:** 11% tax; spa treatments. **Payment:** Major credit cards. **Children:** Under 17 free in room with parents. **Smoking:** Nonsmoking rooms available. **Open:** Year-round.

➤ **Many people coming to Fort Lauderdale's Wyndham combine spa treatments with games of golf or tennis. The golf course meanders around and behind the spa and hotel buildings. The tennis courts are a few blocks from the spa — a nice walk in the morning, or you can take the free van.**

Although the address of The Wyndham is Fort Lauderdale, the spa and resort are quite far out of town, part of a complex that includes a residential section. Guests can feel quite removed from the world, yet the resort is full of active, interesting people, here for any number of reasons.

The resort is a friendly place with an element of tropical elegance. The lobby, of wood and coral stone, is lushly planted. The conference center at the other end of the main building has its own lobby and reception area with a sunken living room and a waterfall of coral stone. Between the two reception areas is the spa dining room, with excellent cuisine. Facilities include generous meeting space and two amphitheaters.

Behind the main building is a patio and lagoon pool, complete with manmade rocks and a waterfall. Nearby is the spa and fitness center, which, like the dining room, was recently refurbished.

The resort offers guests a good variety in rooms and suites with different combinations of bed sizes. Rooms with a king-size bed have a bathroom with a bidet and a double sink. All the accommodations have pretty views of the pool, golf course, or garden.

Recreation options include squash and racquetball courts as well as tennis and championship golf. The resort also has a lot for kids to do in their Discover Program. Spa guests can feel part of the action at the resort but also enjoy the peace and privacy of the spa and special dining room. The spa has a full complement of treatments and a supportive staff. The spa has a number of different treatment options: the Sampler, the Retreat, and the Experience. These include both soothing and bracing treatments such as massages, aromatherapy, facials, reflexology, sea kelp wraps, shiatsu, kur treatments, and loofah treatments. Nutrition profiles, manicures and pedicures, shampoos and haircuts, and personal training are also available. The two-night package is particularly good for working people who are stressed out and want some R&R. Even a short stay can be surprisingly recuperative.

Key Biscayne

Sonesta Beach Resort Key Biscayne

350 Ocean Drive
Key Biscayne, FL 33149
305-361-2021
Reservations: 800-766-3782
(European toll-free numbers also
available at this number)
Fax: 305-361-3096

A favorite resort of both Americans and Europeans

Accommodations: 292 rooms, 12 suites, 4 vacation homes. **Rates:** Rooms $190–$465, suites $625–$1,700, vacation homes $630–$1,295; packages available; MAP $60 per adult, $25 per child, FAP $82 per adult, $40 per child; 8.5% food tax, 15% gratuity with MAP and FAP plans. **Minimum stay:** With some packages. **Added:** 12.5% tax. **Payment:** Major credit cards. **Children:** 17 and under free in room with parents. **Smoking:** Nonsmoking rooms available. **Open:** Year-round.

➤ **The resort's 9 Laykold tennis courts (three of them lighted for night play) are in a parklike setting opposite the Sonesta entrance. The tennis program, operated by two full-time pros, includes lessons, tournaments, and clinics with video playback.**

In a quiet residential section of Key Biscayne, with Biscayne Bay to the west and the Atlantic to the east, the Sonesta Beach Resort looks like an expansive ziggurat. It's big, but because the architects spurned the original skyscraper design, it doesn't look it from the exterior. Service is friendly for a chain hotel, and the location and amenities cannot be beat. Guests are only 20 minutes from the excitement and nightlife of Miami. They can also walk out the Sonesta's back door to an impressive view of the Atlantic Ocean. This isn't just a plain strip of beach; tropical plants and palms dot the sand, here and there small huts give shelter from the sun, and right on the sand is an interesting Tahitian-style bar with a sea grape tree growing through its thatch roof. Chaise longues and hooded cabanas are available for rent, along with sunfloats, kayaks, aqua bikes, catamarans, daysailers, waverunners, sailboards, and parasailing. Scuba diving and snorkeling can be arranged through the hotel.

The Sonesta's free children's program, Just Us Kids, transports children to area attractions like the Parrot Jungle, the Museum of Science, the Miami Seaquarium, and Metrozoo. At the resort, there's swimming and castle building on the beach, arts and crafts, including jewelry making on the oceanside patio, tennis clinics, and movies.

The Sonesta's fitness center has the finest in workout equipment and offers exercise classes, skin treatments, indoor tanning, steam room, sauna, and whirlpool. There's also an Olympic-size heated pool with two Jacuzzis. Bicycles can be rented for $10 a day, and the residential neighborhood surrounding the Sonesta Beach Resort is good for leisurely cycling. There is no golf on the property, but the Key Biscayne Golf Course, considered the best public course in the state, is just a few minutes away.

In the evening, there is all of Miami and Miami Beach to enjoy. But the hotel can keep those who want to stay closer to home entertained and well fed. You can dance to the oldies spun by the disc jockey in Desires, a lounge and bar off the lobby with a pool table. Desires has a big-screen TV and is a popular gathering spot for local Miami Dolphins fans during big games.

The Purple Dolphin serves three meals a day, with a menu influenced by Caribbean, American, Floridian, and South American flavors. The Friday night buffet should not be missed. The Jasmine Café serves American cuisine. The Two Dragons Restaurant is like eating in a miniature "teahouse of the August Moon." In addition to regular tables, some spaces are divided into small eating areas sheltered by peaked wicker canopies. On the beach, the Seagrape Bar and the Snackerie serve beverages as well as sandwiches and light meals.

Every accommodation at the Sonesta has views of the Atlantic or Key Biscayne. All rooms and suites have balconies or patios. Which of the two water views is the more beautiful is difficult to say, but the best views are from the corner rooms, which overlook both the bay and the ocean as well as the impressive Miami skyline. These have walk-in closets, tile bathrooms, and large bedrooms.

Those who can spend a bit more or who wish to eat in will like the Sonesta's villas. These have fully equipped kitchens, daily maid service, a private heated swimming pool, spacious bedrooms, and at least two baths. All accommodations have carpeting, wicker and wood furniture, and sliding glass doors to the furnished balcony or patio.

The Sonesta has a healthy convention business. Facilities include a 7,000-square-foot ballroom overlooking the ocean and 12 meeting rooms. The resort's Business Center is open Monday through Friday during business hours and provides fax transmission, desktop publishing, photocopying, secretarial services, office supplies, and rental of a personal computer and printer. Banquets are held inside or, even better, by the pool overlooking the beach. A convention manager and banquet staff oversee meetings and meals.

Lauderdale-by-the-Sea

A Little Inn by the Sea

4546 El Mar Drive
Lauderdale-by-the-Sea, FL 33308
800-492-0311
954-772-2450
Fax: 954-938-9354
alinn@icanect.net
www.alittleinn.com

An unpretentious place on the beach where families often make their winter reservations a year in advance

Owner: Uli Brandt. **Accommodations:** 30 rooms and suites. **Rates:** Rooms $79–$119, studios: $99–$159, 1-bedroom apartments $129–$189, 2-bedroom apartments $218–$298; weekly specials in summer; rates may be higher during holidays and some weekends. **Included:** Continental breakfast. **Minimum stay:** During holidays and some weekends. **Add:** 11% tax; $10 extra person in room. **Payment:** Major credit cards, traveler's checks. **Children:** Under 12 free in room with parent (up to 2 children). **Smoking:** Allowed. **Open:** Year-round.

➤ A Little Inn by the Sea is just north of downtown Fort Lauderdale on a strip of beach that has many motels and condos. The Little Inn is a low-rise

structure of two to three stories (depending on which end of the inn you are staying in) with a freshwater pool and patio in between. Accommodations all have large windows overlooking the pool or the ocean and, usually, a balcony or a first-floor patio.

Right on the beach, this friendly motel has a furnished patio for all guests to enjoy. Nobody feels at all self-conscious about spending a great deal of time sitting out here, gazing at the ocean, talking with family and friends, or just watching the Lauderdale-by-the-Sea beach scene. In fact, there's no need to feel self-conscious about anything at Little Inn by the Sea. It's a very comfortable place to spend a weekend or a week.

Little Inn by the Sea is basically a nice motel, not an inn serving full-course meals nor a B&B with all guests sitting down to breakfast together in a big Victorian dining room. But it has the feeling of an inn because of its informality and graciousness. Decor is "Florida Informal": cool tile floors, cushioned rattan and bamboo furniture, shell lamps, colorful prints on the walls, and paddle fans whirling softly above.

A child's wagon sits in the lobby, filled with children's books. The inn definitely caters to young families, although it's also a great place for a couple's getaway weekend.

Accommodations include efficiency/studios that have a fully equipped kitchen, sofa bed, and a king-size bed, two double beds, or two twin beds. These units are perhaps the motel's best buy. The one-bedroom apartments have a living/dining area, kitchen, king-size bed or two doubles, and a sleeper sofa. The two-bedroom suite sleeps six and is similar to the one-bedroom unit in furnishings but also has a second bathroom. The motel's standard room has a king-size bed or two double beds, and for a few extra dollars you can get a private balcony. Little Inn by the Sea is a good place for a week's or longer stay; even the standard rooms have a small fridge. In the morning, there's a newspaper at your door and a generous breakfast buffet waits downstairs in the Mediterranean-style lobby.

The pool patio is the heart of this resortlike motel. Between the inn grounds and the pool, there's a low wall with an iron railing above, and beyond that, the palm-studded beach and the Atlantic. A Little Inn by the Sea has chaise longues on the sand for the use of all guests. There's also free tennis and bicycles, a barbecue grill near the pool, and a rooftop sun porch for adults only. Within walking distance are shopping and nice restaurants. Nearby via automobile are opportunities for golf and deep-sea fishing, which the friendly staff can arrange.

Miami

Doral Golf Resort & Spa

4400 N.W. 87th Avenue
Miami, FL 33178-2401
800-331-7768
305-592-2000
Fax: 305-594-4682

**One of the best spas in
Florida — and in the world**

Accommodations: 48 rooms (plus rooms at the Doral Golf Resort). **Rates:** 3 night/2 day spa package begins at $950 per person double occupancy; other packages available at various seasonal rates. **Included:** All meals, facilities, classes, several treatments and services depending on package. **Minimum stay:** Varies, depending on package. **Added:** 12.5% tax; current service charge. **Payment:** Major credit cards, personal checks. **Children:** Under 16 not permitted. **Smoking:** Discouraged; allowed outside only. **Open:** Year-round.

➤ **The spa was founded by Howard Doral (of the Doral Hotel and Country Club family), who teamed up with Leandro Gaultieri, the owner of the Saturnia spa in Italy. What they have achieved is superlative in terms of program, design, and the overall spa experience.**

The Doral Golf Resort & Spa is fashioned after the Terme di Saturnia, a famous Italian spa that uses volcanic mineral water and fango, a volcanic mud, for spa treatments. The Spa in Miami imports the purple-tinted fango for mud treatments said to tone the skin and soothe the body. This may sound like a lot of hocus-pocus to the uninitiated, but this is a well-run and beautifully designed spa that pampers and shapes up its clients. Skeptics leave as enthusiasts.

The Spa is part of the adjacent Doral Golf Resort, a landmark hotel in Miami. The spa and the hotel have separate entrances, but spa guests have access to the tennis courts, championship golf courses, nightlife, and other amenities of the hotel.

The marble reception area of the spa leads to fitness and aerobics rooms. Off the hallways are rooms for massages, mud treatments, and herbal wraps. These are small and softly lit. All personnel are quiet and respectful of clients' privacy when passing by, so guests can totally unwind during treatments. The amazing array of treatments includes massages (including shiatsu and reiki), facials, hydrotherapy, auto-bronzing, aromatherapy, passion fruit body glow, and fango mud treatments — some sound a little crazy, but they all feel great. The anti-cellulite program includes a lymphatic massage, a toning wrap, and hydromassage. The Spa also has a stress reduction program presented by the resort's behavioral counselor.

The Spa has long been sensitive to the benefits of herbs, especially the therapeutic value of inhaling their strong aromas or having them applied to the body. Two of the most relaxing herbal treatments are the herbal wrap and aromatherapy massage. The herbal wrap is a treatment that dates back thousands of years to the Egyptians. At the Doral Spa, it begins with several sips of hot herbal tea and a few minutes spent in the steam room, which is perfumed with eucalyptus. Next, the client lies on a padded bed in a dimly lit room. Muslin sheets have been soaking for hours in a large tub of hot water in which float bags of sage, rosemary, juniper, comfrey, calendula, chamomile, rosebuds, and ginger, herbs chosen for properties that stimulate, cleanse, or soothe the body. A technician wrings out a few sheets, places them on and around the guest's body, and then puts a thick, rubberized sheet on top. A large blanket goes over it all, and cold compresses are placed on the client's forehead to avoid dehydration and to moderate body temperature. The lights are dimmed in the treatment room and classical music is played softly while the guest rests for 25 minutes. The various herbs are supposed to rid the body of toxins. One thing is certain: this is *extremely* relaxing and wonderful for smoothing skin.

Aromatherapy massage is even more relaxing, if that's possible. Spicy aromatic oils are smoothed onto the face and body and then gently, deeply rubbed in by an expert masseuse. The combination of deep massage and the aroma of the fragrant oils results in an experience that is almost ethereal. If all world leaders had one of these each morning, there would be no war.

A wide range of activities balances all this relaxation: power walks, Boxaerobics, yoga, aqua-aerobics, tap dancing, tai chi, and high-energy workouts. The Spa has steam baths, sauna, Swiss showers, whirlpools, indoor and outdoor swimming pools, a large aerobics room, and a dance studio.

The resort hosts lectures and talks on subjects like cuisine education and home exercise, but it isn't all serious. The dance studio offers tap dancing just for the fun of it. This spa also features a library and a theater. The theater shows movies in the evenings, with popcorn for everybody (no salt or butter). The indoor pool is quite beautiful, with floor-to-ceiling etched-glass panels. The influence of Italian design is evident here and throughout the interior.

The outdoor spaces behind the spa are just as elegant. Oblong blocks of coral stone pave the colonnade just outside the back doors. A long balustrade stretches along the terrace. Several steps below is an arching fountain and a reflecting pool with more fountains and candleflame cypress trees. Surrounding this symmetrical perfection are formal Italian gardens — it's like stepping into a Roman palazzo. In the pool in the garden, hundreds of gallons of hot mineral water gush out of spouts and cascade into the pool, pummeling the tired back muscles of guests.

In the Villa Montepaldi, a summer house–style dining room, guests can be serious about dieting and still enjoy the food. In this airy, sun-washed room, spa participants are given small, medium, or large portions, depending on their needs as determined during an earlier consultation with a nutritionist. Menu selections are made with an eye toward "fat points" as well as calories and nutritional benefits. All food items are listed with a calorie count, and menus come with a calculator so that guests can keep track when ordering. The chef makes eating right painless by preparing food that is appetizing and beautifully presented. A meal might include a leafy salad, roast chicken with lemon, and a baked potato with yogurt and chives, followed by fresh fruit.

No one lives a spartan life at bedtime, either. The 48 rooms and suites, some designed by Piero Pinto, are nothing short of palatial. Some of the suites were designed to be shared by two friends, or by a mother and daughter or father and son. They have two double beds on raised platforms at opposite ends of the room. Bed hangings of striped raw silk can be pulled around the bed to give privacy. Each side of the room has its own television and opulently appointed bathroom with Jacuzzi. The sitting area has a stereo and a television set with a VCR (movies can be borrowed from the library).

Suites designed for couples are just as luxurious, with a formal foyer, a king-size bed, and an attractive sitting area. The furniture in the accommodations is mostly bleached oak in an art nouveau style. Floors are of white ceramic tile or marble or contemporary carpets.

All accommodations include safes and padded satin hangers in the spacious closets. Room doors have doorbells so that guests need not be disturbed by loud rapping from a friend or the maid. Rooms also come with Do Not Disturb lights in the hallway that guests can turn on by pushing a button inside the room. At the Doral Golf Resort & Spa, everything has been thought of to ensure invigorating exercise, rest, and sybaritic luxury. If guests lose a few pounds as well, that's wonderful.

Fisher Island

One Fisher Island Drive
Fisher Island, FL 33109-0001
800-537-3708
305-535-6020
Fax: 305-535-6003

**A private, plush community
a few minutes from Miami**

Accommodations: Number of accommodations in rental pool varies. **Rates:** Suites $315–$640, villas $525–$765, 2-bedroom condos $690–$1,215, cottages $655–$1,530; $25 membership fee per day per couple for nonmembers; spa packages available. **Included:** Golf cart with some units. **Minimum stay:** 3–7 nights over some holidays. **Added:** 12.5% tax. **Payment:** Major credit cards. **Children:** Under 12 free in room with parents. **Smoking:** Allowed. **Open:** Year-round.

➤ **If you want a sybaritic, secluded island getaway in Florida, this is it: tennis, golf, swimming, and an outstanding new spa that is among the best in Florida. Gardens and lawns are luxuriant, and the club even maintains a plant nursery where the island's tropical and subtropical plants and flowers are grown. The beach is glorious.**

This secluded 216-acre island in Biscayne Bay is named after Carl Fisher, who developed Miami Beach in the 1920s. Covetous of the 254-foot yacht of his friend William Vanderbilt, great-grandson of the famous Commodore, Fisher exchanged his island paradise for it. Fisher was pleased, and Vanderbilt was too, creating a hideaway vacation estate for himself and his family.

The estate has recently been converted into an exclusive country club and condominium community. Exclusive is an understatement: the security on the island is so tight, Secret Service agents have complained that it's harder to get onto Fisher Island than into the White House. Though most of those who stay here belong to the Fisher Island Club or own a condominium, a limited number of cottages, condos, and club villas can be rented by the public.

Although the island feels away from it all, it's 15 minutes or less from Miami, depending on whether you arrive by ferry, motor launch, seaplane, helicopter, or your own boat. As quickly as you can get on the island, you can also get off, to enjoy the cultural offerings and nightlife of Miami. But it's unlikely that you'll get bored on Fisher Island. There are 17 tennis courts, three of them grass, four courts for paddle tennis, a jogging trail, and a 9-hole golf course. There is one marina for club members and residents and another for guests. Swimming is at the island's beautifully tiled pools, including the one installed by Vanderbilt. Landscaping is lush, and everywhere there are lovely places to walk.

New to Fisher Island is the European-style spa, complete with private treatment rooms, a lap pool, sauna, aerobics rooms, and a bougainvillea-draped Roman whirlpool and waterfall. Treatments include hydromassage, herbal wraps, and facials. The spa has its own salon and a good café with outdoor seating.

The accommodations are as splendid as everything else at Fisher Island. The most costly is Rosemary's Cottage, beside William Vanderbilt's mansion and named for his daughter. Built on the same Mediterranean lines as Vanderbilt's house, the cottage is white stucco with a tile roof and decorative wrought-iron grilles over the windows. The floors are gray marble, and the full kitchen has counters of decorative Italian tile. The enclosed back porch has terra cotta tile and a hot tub. Rosemary's Cottage is furnished with fine antiques and has old-fashioned cushioned window seats under most of the windows. The cottage has two bedrooms, a sitting room, and a dining room that can be made into a third bedroom. The high-season $900 per night rate is easier to manage if three couples rent the place; off-season rates are considerably less.

Across the broad lawn are the original servants' quarters. These are rented by the night or longer for a rate about half that of Rosemary's Cottage. They are charming, with country pine furniture, dhurrie rugs on the marble floors, king-size beds, distinctively decorated bathrooms with whirlpool tubs, and spacious patios.

Some part-time residents rent their seaside villas for a few weeks or months of the year. Like all the accommodations, these are decorated with beautiful furnishings and a generous display of marble and ceramic tile. All have an outdoor hot tub and patios or balconies. Views of the water and pristine beach are nothing short of spectacular.

Fisher Island has a bank, dry cleaner, grocery store, and a pizza parlor that delivers to your door. Restaurants include the friendly Beach Club; Café Porto Cervo, serving pasta dishes under Mediterranean-style archways and exposed juniper beams; the Grill, with its spacious patio overlooking the marina; the Racquet Club snack bar; the Golf Grill; and the formal dining rooms of the Club. The Club is in the original Vanderbilt mansion, and if you dine nowhere else on the island, you should dine here. It is worth it just to see the lovely rooms of the mansion, which have been beautifully restored by expert craftspeople, some from Europe and Cuba.

The main dining room, the Vanderbilt Room, blends beautifully with the rest of the old home. It has paneled walls painted a delicate green, with hand-painted flowers and fine moldings. A pianist plays sonatas on a grand piano. Both the cuisine and the service are excellent.

Just outside the Vanderbilt Room are a coral-paved patio and the swimming pool that Vanderbilt installed in the '20s, complete with ornate fountain, Mediterranean-style stone railings, and statues of lions standing guard. Brown Jordan lawn furniture and tables with umbrellas encircle the pool. The view is of the ocean and palm trees.

Next to the main dining room and also overlooking the pool and the sea is the Vanderbilt library. Now used as a lounge or dining room for small groups, it has a clubby ambience, with mahogany paneling, floor-to-ceiling arched windows, and a large marble fireplace. Upstairs are three bedrooms that have been converted into small dining rooms. All rooms in the original mansion have fireplaces and are beautifully appointed with antique furniture, silver candelabra, and fine art collections.

Many corporate meetings take place on the second floor of the mansion, as well as in the separate conference center. Fisher Island is popular for corporate retreats because it is so quiet and free of distractions.

The Club rooms, both the original mansion living quarters and recent construction, were built with the finest materials and the truest craftsmanship. Window frames are bronze; wall and ceiling paneling is of teak, oak, or mahogany; Spanish-style grilles are of heavy black wrought iron; marble and ceramic tiles are imported from Europe; and carving on the moldings and pillars is expert. Nothing is out of plumb, nothing mismatched.

The Club is the focal point of the island community, and the condominium villas and other new construction on the property are influenced by its Mediterranean architecture. But there is also a strong feeling of Old Florida here. The stucco of the mansion's exterior is embellished around doors and windows with bleached coral stone from southern Florida. The circular courtyard is paved with large blocks of the same beautiful coral. Dominating the courtyard is a huge old banyan tree whose limbs spread over the old stones. The gardens are lush with oleander, bougainvillea, palms, and ferns. Aviaries house cockatoos and colorful macaws, and peacocks strut before their hens.

Grand Bay Hotel

2669 South Bayshore Drive
Coconut Grove
Miami, FL 33133
800-327-2788
305-858-9600

> **Miami's premier business hotel**

Accommodations: 181 rooms and suites. **Rates:** Rooms $200–$325, suites $325–$750, penthouse $1,100; corporate rates and packages available. **Minimum stay:** With packages. **Added:** 12.5% tax. **Payment:** Major credit cards. **Children:** 18 and under free in room with parents. **Smoking:** Nonsmoking rooms available. **Open:** Year-round.

➤ **The pool has a whirlpool at each end and a gentle waterfall in a recessed grotto a few steps away. Above loom the other eleven floors of this Mayan palace, with their balconies and massive planters of cascading bougainvillea.**

The Grand Bay, much sought after for corporate retreats and small conventions, is also a popular sophisticated weekend destination, with good reason. The prices are high, but so are the standards.

The hotel is on Bayshore Drive in Coconut Grove, just opposite the grove's marina. The Grand Bay looms like a Mayan temple, with brilliant purple bougainvillea spilling from concrete planters along the sloping side of the building. European influence is evident everywhere. Registration is as it would be at a fine Continental hotel: at inlaid Louis XIV desks in a quiet anteroom off the entrance. As you sign in, you are served a cool glass of orange juice.

You can finish your juice in the elegant lounge, which has floor-to-ceiling windows and Moroccan leather sofas. Philodendron plants cascade halfway to the floor from planters on the mezzanine. Tea is served here each afternoon, with apéritifs, canapés, and scones.

The Grand Bay has the feel of a small European hotel, but it offers 181 rooms, 49 of them suites. The standard rooms come with a king-size bed or two doubles. The junior suites are a bit larger, with a desk and plenty of work space. The penthouse and deluxe suites are spectacular. Two are bilevel, with spiral staircases to the second-floor bedroom and bath. Standard rooms and small junior suites have balconies, while the more costly suites and penthouses have large private terraces.

All of the rooms and suites are a cut above an average hotel's best and have recently been redecorated. Bathrooms are luxurious, with amenities from a hair dryer and telephone to heat lamps and a bidet. Some suites have Jacuzzis in the baths, large living rooms, and fine wood floors. Even rooms in the lowest price range have a spacious sitting area. Other amenities include minibars, television, clock radios, fax machines, padded hangers, terry robes, and maid service twice a day, including evening turndown with mineral water.

Business services available include excellent telecommunications and secretarial services. The large Continental Ballroom can be divided into three smaller rooms, and there are three other 450-square-foot meeting rooms. The entire space is beautifully appointed.

The Bar at Bice is a popular meeting place for Miami executives and overnight business guests. This softly lit lounge is reminiscent of a men's club. The Bice Restaurant, overlooking an austere Italian garden, is an airy bilevel dining room decorated in art nouveau style. Food is regional Italian, with crisp vegetables and beautiful presentations.

Service everywhere at the Grand Bay is reminiscent of the best small hotels in New York and London. The staff is cordial, intelligent, and dignified. In a city where hoteliers have great difficulty hiring courteous workers, the Grand Bay maintains high standards.

On the mezzanine is a swimming pool and patio screened by a tropical garden, as well as a small but well-equipped health club. Poolside services include a beverage and snack bar and a masseur. After a long day, this is a wonderful place to unwind.

Hotel Inter-Continental Miami

100 Chopin Plaza
Miami, FL 33131
800-327-0200
305-577-1000
Fax: 305-577-0384

A big-city hotel with a cosmopolitan clientele and Latin ambience

Accommodations: 639 rooms. **Rates:** Rooms $149–$289, suites $410. **Minimum stay:** None. **Added:** 12.5% tax. **Payment:** Major credit cards. **Children:** Under 14 free in room with parents. **Smoking:** Nonsmoking rooms available. **Open:** Year-round.

➤ **The view from the rooftop pool is nothing short of astounding — the city spreads below, and Biscayne Bay and the Miami River stretch out to bay islands and the Atlantic beyond. Cruise ships are docked nearby at the Port of Miami. Many guests stay here the night before embarking on one of them.**

The Hotel Inter-Continental Miami, a tower of Italian marble, stands on the shores of Biscayne Bay and the Miami River. Accessible by elevator to its architectural twin, the Miami Center office building, the Inter-Continental is one of the best business hotels in Florida. Nearby is the financial and business district and, just a few miles beyond, the upscale shops and residences of Coconut Grove.

The 30 deluxe suites have an interesting mix of Oriental and art deco decor, including mahogany armoires, red lacquered chairs, and chrome and black granite tables. Every suite has two luxurious baths, one with a Roman shower bath.

Altogether, there are 639 rooms and suites in the 31 stories of this marble and glass tower. A standard room has a king-size bed or two doubles, a refrigerator with minibar, a clock radio, and a large marble bath.

Convention space and services at the Inter-Continental are outstanding. A total of over 60,000 square feet of meeting space includes the hotel's Grand Ballroom, which can accommodate up to 2,700 people for receptions and 1,350 for banquets. There are more than 20 smaller rooms for informal meetings, private dinner parties and receptions, and conferences. Facilities include a well-equipped business center with photocopying, fax, and telex machines.

A favorite lounge for guests attending conventions or conferences is the Oak Room, which has the air of a private club and is frequented by Miami executives as well as hotel guests. This is a popular place at happy hour and during sports events. The room is paneled with dark oak, and the low bar has armchairs of rich leather. The four-star restaurant at the Inter-Continental has won a number of awards for its American and fine regional cuisine.

The Royal Palm Court, just off the lobby, serves breakfast, lunch, and dinner and resembles a large gazebo. Its green lattice panels are trimmed with pink molding, and overhead is a charming ceiling mural of tropical birds and foliage. Food is good, and while the service can be a bit slow, waiters are friendly and polite.

The hotel is sited on several acres of land, and there is room for a rooftop recreational wing with a swimming pool and a jogging trail landscaped with subtropical foliage.

The high-ceilinged lobby on the first floor is a meeting place for a cosmopolitan clientele. Thirty-foot-tall palm trees reach to an atrium ceiling paneled with tiger maple. Dominating the center of the big room is a 70-ton marble sculpture by Henry Moore surrounded by a fountain with dozens of water jets. The sculpture is representative of the hotel itself: modern and distinctive, but sometimes lacking warmth.

Hyatt Regency Miami

400 S.E. Second Avenue
Miami, FL 33131-2197
800-233-1234
305-358-1234
Fax: 305-358-0529

> **A first-rate hotel in a busy, active part of town**

Accommodations: 612 rooms and suites. **Rates:** Rooms $135–$220, suites $185–$420; rates may be lower on weekends, some unannounced specials. **Minimum stay:** None. **Added:** 12.5% tax. **Payment:** Major credit cards. **Children:** Under 15 free in room with parents. **Smoking:** Nonsmoking rooms available. **Open:** Year-round.

➤ **The lobby's centerpiece is an atrium sitting area dominated by a contemporary sculpture rising three floors high. Throughout the day, guests gather here on sofas and easy chairs to read or talk with the soothing sound of the coral fountains in the background.**

Although the Regency is surrounded by a number of hotels, it stands out as a result of its excellence as a convention hotel, its service, and its restful ambience. Approximately 60 percent of this Hyatt's business is from meetings and conventions. The hotel is adjacent to the Miami Convention Center and has three floors of meeting space, including an impressive ballroom, a concert hall, a 28,000-square-foot exhibit center, an auditorium that seats 444 and has multilingual facilities, and more than two dozen smaller function rooms. Much of the meeting space has been recently redecorated.

Miami is the "cruise ship capital of the world": the nearby Port of Miami welcomes millions of cruise ship passengers every year. Many of these passengers stay at the Hyatt before embarking on their trips, including some teenage school groups who can be a little boisterous. But the international staff takes it in stride; the staff members are friendly and professional. In a city where service is sometimes a problem, the Hyatt Regency's staff seems genuinely happy to be working here, and the hotel has one of the lowest turnover rates among service personnel in the city.

Against the far walls of the lobby are small shops, the informal Riverwalk Café, and Currents lounge. One draw for the hotel's restaurants and lounge is the view of the Miami River, which more accurately could be called a canal but is still interesting as a working waterfront. For a closer look at this vibrant, busy waterway, sit outside on the coral-paved patio or stroll along the palm-lined Riverwalk. Sightseeing boats pull up at the dock.

The Hyatt's recreation area includes a heated swimming pool accented by white planters of bougainvillea, white chaise longues, and tables with umbrellas. Large planters of tropical plants rimming this recreational area create a buffer between the noise of the city and the pool. A poolside bar is open on weekends and holidays.

Even the standard rooms at the Hyatt are large and have many extras, including a comfortable sitting area and a small, furnished balcony. All the rooms have a clock radio and TV with pay movies and have recently been redecorated. The bathrooms are large and have a separate dressing area. Rooms reserved on the business plan or regency plan are even better, with larger sitting areas and some complimentary foods offered. A variety of bed sizes is available in all three room types, and a standard room can be made into a parlor suite. If you can afford it, request a room with a view. The higher you go in this skyscraper, the better the view of the Miami River, Biscayne Bay, and the busy city.

Mayfair House Hotel

3000 Florida Avenue
Coconut Grove
Miami, FL 33133
800-433-4555
800-341-0809 in Florida
305-441-0000

**An all-suite art nouveau
hotel in trendy Coconut
Grove**

Accommodations: 179 suites. **Rates:** 1-room suite $159–$239, 1-bedroom suite $189–$269, 2-bedroom suite $450–$500. **Minimum stay:** No. **Added:** 12.5% tax; $35 extra person. **Payment:** Major credit cards, personal checks with major credit card. **Children:** Under 12 free in room with parents. **Smoking:** Non-smoking rooms available. **Open:** Year-round.

➤ **Guests need never fear boredom at Mayfair House. Besides the diversions of World of Mayfair, where there are restaurants, sidewalk cafés, bakeries, and a number of shops and boutiques, visitors also enjoy the Coconut Grove nightlife at CocoWalk, which accommodates everyone from latter-day hippies to yuppies.**

The Mayfair House is part of the Streets of Mayfair, an imaginative shopping complex in Coconut Grove, on the southern edge of Miami. Though it's fallen on hard times, with more vacancies than the owners would like, this shopping complex is one of the most beautiful on the east coast of Florida. There's greenery everywhere, waterfalls and fountains, and imported tile cleverly worked into the design of fountains, benches, walkways, and murals.

Yet the Mayfair House is self-contained; guests don't feel as if they're in the middle of a shopping mall. There is a hushed gentility to the place that seems stuffy to some visitors, upscale to others. The plaster walls of the public rooms and hallways are sculpted curves, with unexpected angles in the corners of the ceiling. Appointments in the lobby include art nouveau brass floor lamps in the shape of a snarling serpent and modern oil paintings. Many of the mahogany doors are hand-carved in intricate Oriental or art nouveau patterns.

Each of the 179 suites is different in shape, decor, and size. Some have room dividers of art nouveau etched glass or wooden slates that have an Oriental look. Most of the artwork and appointments are new, but the designers preserved some original panels of Tiffany stained glass. Furniture includes hand-carved bedsteads and, in 39 of the suites, antique English pianos.

The suites share some wonderful characteristics. Each has a Jacuzzi, in the bedroom, the living room, or on a trellised balcony. All bedrooms have a sofa, table, and chairs, and there are TVs and telephones in the bathrooms as well as in the bedrooms. The closets have heavy mahogany doors and built-in drawers and cabinets. The marble baths have extras such as a clothes hamper, hair dryer, and makeup mirror. Kimonos are left on the bed at turndown.

Other services include limousine transportation within a limited area and 24-hour room service, which includes in-suite catering for private dining. The hotel also has a rooftop pool and spacious sun deck.

The Mayfair Grill, the hotel's restaurant, is now under new management and is very good. The 27 suites have separate dining rooms for board meetings and business entertaining; a separate executive conference center has various meeting rooms and a wide range of audiovisual equipment. The Mayfair Ballroom, with striking use of copper and marble, can accommodate up to 400 people theater-style or be divided into three separate rooms.

Miami Beach

Blue Moon

944 Collins Avenue
Miami Beach, FL 33139
800-724-1623
305-673-2262
Fax: 305-534-5399
blmoon@bellsouth.net
www.merv.com/bluemoon

**A Mediterranean-style hotel
a block from the beach**

Owner: Merv Griffin. **Number of accommodations:** 75 rooms and suites. **Rates:** Rooms $145–$215, suites $325–$425. **Minimum stay:** During some special events and holidays. **Added:** 12.5 % tax; valet parking fee. **Payment:** Major credit cards, traveler's checks. **Children:** Allowed; infants free in room with parent, cribs available. **Smoking:** Allowed in patio garden; nonsmoking rooms available. **Open:** Year-round.

➤   **The Blue Moon draws a cosmopolitan clientele from throughout the U.S., Latin America, the British Isles, and Europe, many of whom return year after year. The restoration of this 1930s-era hotel won a BBC award for excellence in historic preservation. Previously known as the Lafayette, the Blue Moon is also listed on the National Register of Historic Places.**

Though the hotel is located in the middle of the art deco district, the architectural style is more Italianate than art deco or modern, with arched doorways, bell towers, balustrades, and dentil molding embellishing the stucco facade. Steps lead up from the street to a wide, terra-cotta-tiled terrace. French doors open into a cool, peaceful lobby that is elegantly furnished with upholstered and slip-covered chairs, mosaic tables, interesting art work on the plastered walls, even a small fountain. Classical music plays softly, setting the mood of gentile quiet and European service that the hotel has become famous for in fast-paced South Beach.

At the far end of the multi-leveled lobby is a small balustraded staircase that ascends to the dining and bar area. Here one finds more cool tile and soft lighting as well as lovely stained glass windows. A gourmet Continental breakfast is served here and on the patio each morning for those who wish it. The new Italian bistro restaurant here has already won an excellent reputation for itself.

At the back of this attractive area are French doors that lead out to the patio garden and the pool beyond. The sometimes-harsh South Beach sun is shaded by blue canvas umbrellas above the round tables. Guests often linger here to read and doze throughout the day. Brightly colored bougainvillea, palms, and fig trees create a screen of green and pink and yellow so that the place feels very private. Even though this is the middle of Collins Avenue and only one block from the high life of Ocean Drive, there is only the dimmest roar of traffic. The prevailing sound is of splashing water in the fountains and classical music. If the excitement of South Beach were not so close at hand, this would be the place to sit all day. Then again, maybe it is . . . even with the excitement of South Beach.

The guest rooms are on the top floors of the Blue Moon, some affording ocean views. All the rooms at the hotel have been upgraded as part of a $2 million renovation that began shortly after Merv Griffin bought the hotel. Rather than acting as a silent investor, Griffin personally selected the handsome fabrics and furnishings. Understated and elegant, the guest rooms are decorated in blue, yellow, and neutral tones, with thick comforters and striking bedskirts and pillows. Original artwork and ceramic pieces are in each room. Fresh flowers and mineral water are standard amenities, along with an upscale line of English toiletries in the tiled baths.

All rooms and suites have a telephone with two lines and private voice mail, a safe, a clock radio with CD player, a television with VCR, and an armoire with a coffeemaker and minibar. The hotel's blue moon logo is embroidered on the waffle-weave bathrobes. Turndown service includes moon-shaped chocolates and a different celestial poem each evening.

Colony Hotel

736 Ocean Drive
Miami Beach, FL 33139
1-800-2-COLONY
305-673-0088
Fax: 305-532-0762
www.colonyhotel.sobe.com

A well-run hotel and restaurant in the heart of South Beach

Accommodations: 50 rooms. **Rates:** Rooms $129–$159; group and package rates available. **Included:** Continental breakfast. **Minimum stay:** None. **Added:** 12.5% tax; $10 additional person; group and package rates available. **Payment:** Major credit cards except Discover. **Children:** Age 16 and under free in room with parent. **Smoking:** Allowed. **Open:** Year-round.

➤ **A good housekeeping staff keeps the sheets clean and the furniture dusted — something that cannot be said for every hotel in the art deco district. Colony management runs a tight ship.**

In the few years it's been open, the Colony Hotel has established a very good reputation. Its bar, which has both indoor and outdoor seating, is one of the most popular on Ocean Drive. While the facade of the hotel has few sculpted embellishments, its restoration has been faithful to its art deco heritage — the hotel features a smooth stucco exterior with 1930s-style "streamline" detailing, recessed windows outlined in chrome, narrow overhangs bordered with a horizontal aqua stripe, white cloth awnings on the first-floor windows, and its name in neon on a wraparound marquee.

The small lobby is furnished in a mid-20th-century style, with zebra and leather chairs, a zebra rug, and brass pots of palms and banana trees. The wraparound registration desk has pigeonhole key boxes behind. All that's missing is a Humphrey Bogart character to ask mysteriously for his key.

The oceanfront rooms are the best in the house. All rooms are furnished in keeping with the mood of the era: venetian blinds hang at the windows, ceiling fans twirl slowly overhead, and art deco appointments complete the look. Rooms have double or queen-size beds, modern baths, and cable TV. Compared with new hotel rooms, the Colony's seem small, but they are typical of the era. Decor is attractive and appropriate for the period, rather than outlandish or arty. Amenities include concierge service, in-room safes, beach towels, cable TV and in-room movies, and valet parking. Be forewarned: this is an old hotel, though nicely refurbished, and the elevator is creaky, the bathroom faucets old — or, as they say in the business, "original."

The Colony's room rate includes Continental breakfast for all guests: muffins, croissants, orange juice, coffee and tea. The Colony is centrally located, so you are never far from "home" at mealtime, whether you're at the beach or the local art museum.

South Beach is one of the best places in the world to people-watch, and an oceanside room is a good vantage point. Guests also enjoy sitting at the sidewalk tables of the Colony's bar, which is open to the public and busy day and night. If you want to get closer to the action, there's the beach across the street and the street itself. The eclectic group here includes teenagers on in-line skates and skateboards, young women in bikinis, retired couples, would-be models, actors, and singers, art students, and photographers. A sidewalk table at the Colony is a good place to take it all in, day or night.

Delano

1685 Collins Avenue
Miami Beach, FL 33139
800-555-5001
305-672-2000
Fax: 305-532-0099

A visit to the Delano is like being on the set of a surreal movie

Accommodations: 184 rooms, 24 suites plus cottages/condos. **Rates:** Rooms $335–$375, suites $695–$1,175. Extra adult in room $25. **Minimum stay:** 2 nights on weekends. **Added:** 12.5% tax. **Payment:** Major credit cards. **Children:** Allowed, under the age of 17 free in room with parent using existing bedding. **Smoking:** Allowed with no restrictions. **Open:** Year-round.

➤ **The Delano is not just a hotel — it's an experience. It looms above the street like a great white giant, with ivy cascading from its second-floor balcony and an improbable wooden carving of bears greeting guests at the summit of its terraced entry steps.**

The Delano opened in 1995 with a great deal of hype; media were invited from major cities and the hotel was hailed for its daring innovation in design. The creativity — even whimsy — of this place is still its greatest delight. Inside one walks across a wooden floor of wide pegged planks to the first of a series of creamy, diaphanous curtains hanging across the entire width of the large lobby. At any moment, it seems, the swanlike neck and dark eyes of an Italian film actress should peer from behind the sweep of filmy drapings. But this doesn't happen because this is, after all, a hotel. Still, there's always the chance . . .

The Delano is also a comfortable, homey place to stay. Often a shawl or fringed blanket will be casually draped over the back of a chair or sofa as part of the decor. The groupings of furniture that encourage lobby socializing are often disparate: upholstered, leather, and slip-covered chairs of various vintages will be together just as they would be in a less-than-perfect suburban living room. Juxtaposed to such groupings are African tables and chairs lacquered in glossy primary colors, the back of the chairs looking like a man's head. Exotic artwork is everywhere, as if the Delano design team bought the wide-ranging art collection of an eccentric world traveler.

Outside are more exotica and tchotchke: a lawn chess set with carved wooden pieces that include a knight with a horsehair tail, an ivy-covered "easy chair" with lace doilies on the green "arms," an antique iron day bed with chipped paint, a large mirror that stands in the middle of the hotel lawn. This whimsical exterior space is the hotel's "outdoor lobby," reached by a series of terraced steps painted red that lead down from the Delano's restaurant terrace. The long narrow interior courtyard has the sense of being walled off from the world here — there's a high fence on the right, a line of hotel bungalows on the left, and a fence blocking the view of the ocean in the back. Rows of tall, dignified palms delineate the outdoor spaces.

The swimming pool, designed after an ancient Roman bath, is filled with water so high that it regularly spills over the sides. Chaise longues, wicker chairs, and hammocks invite lounging around the pool for as many hours as you'd like. Beyond the pool bar is a gate to the beach and the ocean. Not being able to see South Beach from this space is both a drawback and an advantage:

no views of the beautiful turquoise waters this beach is famous for, but also no exposure to prying eyes looking for a glimpse of the rich and famous staying at the Delano.

There is very good service here when anyone gets hungry or thirsty; in general, there are a lot of staff on hand to cater to the needs of guests. During the day, most people staying here tend to stay "close to home," spending most of their time around the pool or on the beach. There's also a 24-hour gym on the property, with trainers and fitness classes that are held on the beach. The hotel's spa is outstanding. It includes a rooftop bathhouse for women only, a solarium with a health bar, and the pampering treatments that spa devotees have come to love, such as massages and aromatherapy. There are also exercise and aerobics classes for the energetic among us.

For dining, most guests at the Delano go out to the cafés and restaurants on trendy Ocean Drive. The hotel offers both indoor and outdoor dining, but the food at the Delano gets mixed reviews. The most common criticism has been that the hotel's creators have cared more about looks than taste. It will be interesting to see if the cuisine catches up to the excellence of the rest of the hotel.

The guest rooms are all that one could hope for. Colors are pale gray and the Delano's ubiquitous white. Furniture is custom-designed. Bathrooms are both sleek and funky, with multi-head showers and freestanding bathtubs. Blackout shades over the windows keep out the early morning sun for those who've been up late clubbing the night before. The rooms on the highest floors have wonderful views of the Atlantic and the beach.

A total of 238 guest rooms includes suites, lofts, and bungalows. The latter are worth looking into for an extended stay. They line one side of the pool and "outdoor lobby" of the Delano and have a large sitting room on the first floor and bedroom and bath on the second floor. Decorated in white and soft cream, they are patterned after the bungalow accommodations of the Beverly Hills Hotel in California. Although the bungalows have a private entrance on the street side the hotel, their one drawback is that when the billowing drapes aren't closed on the pool side, people lounging around the pool can see in. For those who can afford them, these are nice for families, especially those with children who want to spend the day swimming.

For all its chic, the Delano is indeed a good hotel for families, even if all the white provides temptation for small, smudgy hands. There's a supervised playground area and a $1 movie theater on the property. The iron floor lamps and other furniture look pretty indestructible. Owner Ian Schrager originally envisioned the hotel as a "family resort," although the price of rooms has gone up as the Delano's fame has spread, so the average-income family is shut out here.

The owners of the Delano had great courage when they bought this hotel, not just because they chose designers who dared to do the unusual, but also because they bought a property on a block of Collins Avenue that had a long way to go. Only a few years ago, drunks slept on the front steps of boarded-up buildings and the haunted, broken windows of abandoned hotels cast a somber look to this strip of Collins Avenue. The entire area — caught as it was between the stylish small hotels of Ocean Drive and large flashy places like the Fontainebleau farther north on Collins — looked a little like a war zone. Small hotel owners with less to risk had renovated in the 1980s in spite of the financially shaky start to SoBe's rejuvenation, but few projects have been as large as the Delano. Today, the success of this hotel has resulted in the renovation of other hotels as large as the Delano, causing a nice domino effect that can only work in its favor. A few blocks up the street, Lincoln Road, a shopping area that was fashionable in the middle of the century and then declined, has been refurbished, with palm trees planted in the meridian and a new open-air market. This should further enhance the area and reflect well on this exciting hotel.

As they say on the Italian Riviera, the Delano is *multo magnifico*.

Hotel Impala

1228 Collins Avenue
Miami Beach 33139
800-646-7252, 305-673-2021
Fax 305-673-5984
htlimpala@aol.com
www.HotelImpalaMiamiBeach.com

| **A small gem** |

Accommodations: 17 rooms, 3 suites. **Rates:** Rooms $215, suites $300. $25 extra person in room. **Included:** Continental breakfast. **Minimum stay:** Required on holidays and in-season weekends. **Added:** 12.5% tax. **Payment:** Major credit cards, traveler's checks. **Children:** Over 15 welcome. **Smoking:** Allowed. **Open:** Year-round.

➤ **The Hotel Impala is run like an exclusive European hotel, with excellent service, understated elegance in its decor, and fewer than twenty rooms and suites for guests. Originally constructed in 1930, the building went through hard times during the decline of Miami Beach in the 1960s. By the time architect and designer Peter Hawrylecwicz began to work his magic and transform the place, it was an inexpensive apartment building that was rumored to be a crack house.**

Peter Hawrylecwicz, who also designed the late Gianni Versace's oceanfront mansion in South Beach, has created more than a tastefully designed hotel here. The Impala is a haven for those who love peace as well as beauty. Guests can enjoy the beach and the lively nightlife one block away on Ocean Drive, but retreat to the serenity of the Impala when they've had a surfeit of hot sand and hot bands.

The Impala is almost hidden away. New arrivals can easily mistake the restaurant next door for the hotel, especially since so many hotels on Ocean Drive are accessed through a restaurant or café. Like them, the Impala and the adjoining restaurant are right on the street, but the Impala has a separate entrance to the left of the building as you face it. Guests pass through an archway and then along a serpentine walkway of tabby that is landscaped with large ferns and bougainvillea. Under a tropical tree is a small table with two chairs that provide the feeling of a backyard garden. The play of water in a small fountain is very restful.

The entrance to the hotel is near the end of the walkway. Inside is a small lobby made distinctive by a floor mosaic of the man in the moon — or is it the sun, here in this Mediterranean-like escape? The striking floor mosaic is the visitor's first taste of the artwork that graces the hotel. The mosaic was originally intended for Versace's mansion, which Hawrylecwicz was working on at the same time as he was redesigning the space here. Small artistic touches everywhere remind guests that this is a place where extra care was taken. On the hallway wall next to each room is a silk-screened collage with the number of the room in the design, the work of Chicago artist, Jim Faulkner.

Most rooms and suites are accessed by way of the second-floor open-air gallery, one of the most pleasant of the Mediterranean features of this hotel. Each room is quietly tasteful. Colors are soft neutrals. Floors are of cool Saturnia stone. The bathrooms have stone walls and floors, large ironwork mirrors, and custom-made vanities of iron and stone. The television, VCR, and CD player are housed in Mediterranean-style pine armoires. Tab curtains are at the shuttered windows, most of which look out at a cityscape or street scene, a few the landscaped walkway to the hotel. Original artwork adorns the plaster walls. The rather unusual closet doors have a design of iron leaves and vines over muslin shirring.

More important than the interesting decor is that each room is primarily designed for a guest's comfort and includes high-tech convenience. Though imported stone and marble are used generously throughout the hotel, bedrooms and sitting areas are carpeted. Linens on the pine sleigh beds are of soft cotton. Comforters and pillows are goosedown. The bathrooms often have a large soaking tub and walk-in shower. Each room has an overstuffed couch or easy chair to sink into and the balconies of suites have wooden chaise longues with thick cushions.

High-tech conveniences include speakerphones and voice mail and desks that have a retractable desktop with computer hookup. Other amenities are a complimentary morning newspaper, valet parking, and 24-hour concierge service. The Impala's complimentary breakfast of croissants, juice, and coffee is next door at the restaurant, which is not owned by the Impala but provides both breakfast and room service through an agreement with the hotel. The restaurant serves northern Italian cuisine with homemade pasta and bread made daily. The service is usually good, unlike that of so many restaurants in South Beach.

Staff at the Hotel Impala are multilingual and nearly bend over backward to please guests. Quiet and discreet, they contribute as much to the restful atmosphere of this excellent hotel as the soft bed linens and dulcet murmurings of the entryway fountain.

Hotel Ocean

1230–38 Ocean Drive
Miami Beach, FL 33139
800-783-1725
305-672-2579
Fax: 305-672-7665

A French hideaway with small surprises

Owner: Xavier Lesmarie. **Accommodations:** 8 rooms, 19 suites. **Rates:** Rooms $179–$215, suites $235–$515; extra person in room $45. **Included:** Continental breakfast. **Minimum stay:** On major holidays and special events. **Added:** 12.5% tax. **Payment:** Major credit cards, traveler's checks, cash. **Children:** Welcome. **Smoking:** Allowed. **Open:** Year-round.

The Hotel Ocean manages to balance the many worlds of Ocean Drive: the daytime American beach scene, the epicurean European dining scene, the trendy nightlife of young South Beach, and a sheltered night's rest. Even the architecture is a mix: a barrel tile roof, Spanish-style arched doorways, art deco jalousied windows, and an unpretentious stucco exterior accented with carved medallions — all painted in cool gray-blue, white, and sand. The many moods of the Oceanfront are accommodated by its shape — that of an E, with two stylish squares of the building directly on Ocean Drive, an outdoor French café and grape arbor in between, and, farther back in the spine of the E, a small gift shop and the entrance to the hotel.

Guest rooms are on the top floors of the main buildings fronting Ocean Drive and in a four-story addition behind that, which backs onto the alley. Good insulation and double-pane glass assure a good night's rest even though the restaurant and bar fill up during the lively evening hours. There are 27 rooms in all, including a penthouse suite with a balcony and Jacuzzi. The oceanfront rooms are the best, though many guests prefer accommodations in the back of the building overlooking the arbor and little café tables. All rooms have a stereo/CD player, wet bar with fridge, color TV and VCR (videotapes are for rent in the gift shop), a safe with credit card processing, two telephone lines, and voice mail. Beach towels are complimentary, as are bathrobes if you request them. The bathrooms are immaculate and elegant, with pedestal sinks, 1930s-era light fixtures, and chrome-and-glass enclosed showers.

Each room is a little different, and there's a good deal of attention to detail. For example, in many rooms the clean lines of the plaster walls are accented by plaster molding in an attractive leaf pattern. Some rooms have art deco fireplaces and the hotel's original French and English antique furnishings. Beds are covered in white linens and have accent pillows with French button closures. Fine wrought-iron grillwork runs along the bottom of the windows. When these rooms were refurbished, the minimum could have been done, with postage-stamp sameness and just a few cosmetic touches, but the owners chose to attend to details. The care has paid off.

There are small surprises here and there, like the lovely mosaic near the lobby downstairs — until one realizes the "mosaic" is not made of tiles or stone but is stenciled on the wall. Adjacent to the lobby is a little shop. Gift shops in a hotel or B&B can be a turnoff, but this one is done with panache — and useful things are for sale here: fine shampoos and lotions that you might really need to buy.

Both the hotel and the restaurant have a French ambience, furthered certainly by the French accent of the owner, Xavier Lesmarie. The restaurant has won awards for its seafood, and the adjacent raw bar and lounge are popular with the South Beach crowd, so this is a busy place at night. But it is also a cut above the average South Beach café, so the music and voices don't become obtrusive. The restaurant's outdoor seating, which overlooks the Ocean Drive scene, is very open, with potted palms and fountains. Farther back and closer to the entrance to the hotel and its small lobby is an arbor of natural wood. Guests can enjoy the gardenlike ambiance here each morning during the hotel's Continental breakfast, which is included in the price of the room. For a few extra dollars, guests can have a full gourmet breakfast here.

Island Outpost Art Deco Hotels

1330 Ocean Drive
Miami Beach, FL 33139
800-338-9076 or 1-800-OUTPOST
305-531-8800
Fax: 305-672-2881
www.islandoutpost.com

> **A good bet for an enjoyable stay is at one of the Art Deco Hotels**

Accommodations: 234 rooms and suites total in the six Art Deco Hotels. **Rates:** Rooms $100–$450, suites $250–$1,500; rates vary according to individual hotel and season. **Included:** Varies. **Minimum stay:** 3 nights during special events; 2 nights on most weekends. **Added:** 12.5% tax; 10% service charge; free cribs. **Payment:** Major credit cards. **Children:** 12 and under free in room with parents. **Smoking:** Some nonsmoking rooms available. **Open:** Year-round.

➤ **The Art Deco Hotels comprise a group of six hotels on Ocean Drive and South Collins Avenue in the art deco district of Miami Beach, now managed by the Island Outpost. Ocean Drive has become a neon "hot spot," with sidewalk cafés, restaurants, clubs, and refurbished hotels that are hopping night and day. One block from the ocean, Collins Avenue is both urban and urbane. Both streets have some wonderfully funky, sophisticated hotels on them.**

Much has been written about the art deco district, and it is sometimes difficult to separate the actual experience of staying at a hotel here from all the hoopla about the hotels' architecture. The art deco district was the first 20th-century neighborhood to be put on the National Register of Historic Places, and South Beach (SoBe) has more examples of art deco design than any other area in the United States.

Buildings in the art deco, streamline, and modern styles are typically finished in stucco and painted in ice cream colors like raspberry or pistachio and have smooth, streamlined corners and entryways. The architects of the era played with many decorative elements: plaster friezes, shields, panels, borders, and bands. The interior design is usually modern, with terrazzo floors, etched glass, beveled mirrors, and chrome embellishments. The hotels reflect the neighborhood's role as a playground for the rich and famous in the 1930s and 1940s.

In the late 1950s and throughout the 1960s, the area deteriorated. Occasionally, there is still a crime problem on some blocks of

South Collins Avenue. On both Ocean Drive and Collins, hotels have sometimes closed after a great deal of fanfare surrounding their restoration and grand opening. Some art deco hotels written up in the guidebooks of the 1980s were part of the first restoration efforts and are already looking dilapidated. Others look all right on the surface but have indifferent service, soiled furnishings, and harried management. Some get the noise of late-night revelers outside or jazz from nearby clubs through the thin walls. Therefore, travelers to this fascinating neighborhood must pick a hotel carefully.

The Cavalier is right in the middle of the ever-changing scene on South Beach. The suites and rooms in front are the most desirable, overlooking Ocean Drive, Lumus Park (a slightly shabby oceanfront park), and the Atlantic. Though small by today's standards, the rooms have some nice features, such as comfortable, firm double beds with batik bedspreads, interesting artwork, and wooden furniture. Amenities include radio and cable TV, CD and cassette player, VCR, direct-dial phones, vases of fresh flowers, and bottles of Evian water.

In a typical room, walls might be sponged a warm mustard color and the floorboards and doors painted purple and orange or bright turquoise. The furnishings are eclectic, with African, European, and American influences. The service can be nonchalant at times and the outside noise level high on weekend nights. In some rooms, the lights may blink when you turn on the bathroom fan. But if you have a taste for the bohemian and a free and easy attitude about your stay in the art deco district, you can have a great time at the Cavalier.

The Art Deco Hotels also include the Leslie, Kent, Tides, and Marlin, as well as the all-suite Casa Grande. The Leslie, just down the street from the Cavalier, is a standard Ocean Drive hotel/café, in that there are tables on the sidewalk and, a few steps up to a dais-like terrace there are more tables. Up a short flight of stairs in the back is the tiny lobby and crescent-shaped registration desk. The multilevel floor plan of the café and hotel is quite typical for a number of art deco hotels in South Beach, which survive on a combination of room, bar, and restaurant income.

Painted a lemon yellow, the Leslie is more funky in decor than the Cavalier, and its room colors are decidedly tropical. Even the hallways leading to rooms and the exposed heating and water pipes above are colorful. Lopsided diamond shapes are stenciled in deep primary colors on the walls, and the furniture is very 1950s art deco. The beds and easy chairs are comfortable. Bathrooms are small and usually have the original ceramic tile. The Leslie, like most of the Island Outpost hotels, is clean but not immaculate. The bedspread might have a little smudge or the table a waterspot that goes unnoticed by the maids. Standard rooms are small, while the Leslie's more spacious suites are really not much bigger than a standard room in a moderately priced Marriott.

The Kent is in a mid-century streamlined building with purple and ocher trim on yellow stucco — a surprising color combination perhaps, but it's all part of the SoBe scene. The rooms with queen-size beds and two suites are decorated in tropical colors. Rooms have a TV and VCR, CD/radio/cassette player, safe, kitchenette, and fully stocked minibar. The Kent offers conference space and production planning facilities for film crews. Other extras include a video library, valet parking, and in-room massage and aromatherapy for extra fees.

The Marlin is on Collins Avenue, one block from the beach — not necessarily a disadvantage because the hotel is quieter than some of the trendier places on Ocean Drive. The Marlin is one of the most interesting examples of exterior decoration in the art deco district. Its intricately sculpted stucco facade is painted in blues, purple, aqua, and ocher. Inside, the lobby walls are painted like underwater Pollack paintings with drips of paint in murky blues and lavender. The big clay pots of green plants have also been dipped in paint buckets. Sofas are upholstered in fluorescent blues with improbable-looking curves and art deco curlicues. Just below the lobby is a bar and pool table area. Stools at the bar have a cruel-looking but fairly comfortable back of black wrought iron in the shape of what looks like a question mark. Rooms are small but comfortable and cleverly decorated with period furniture.

The Casa Grande is a European-style hotel on Ocean Drive that has studios and one- and two-bedroom suites. Guest rooms are decorated eclectically with Indonesian-style furniture, antiques, and interesting fabrics. All the rooms have kitchens, entertainment centers, minibars, and roomy mirrored closets with safes. Double-sealed doors in the oceanfront suites keep out the noise of the club scene on Ocean Drive. The hotel has room service and a café downstairs. The lobby is decorated in warm tones of beige, brown, and mustard with sponged walls, and large containers of exotic tropical greenery are scattered in the space. Both drama and comfort are found at the Casa Grande.

The Art Deco Hotels often have film production crews and models as guests, since South Beach has become a "hot" location for magazine layouts and film productions. At all these hotels, non-celebrity guests love to people-watch. Fashion photographers and their pouty young models from Los Angeles, New York, and vari-

ous European cities use the district as a backdrop for fashion layouts. Strolling along the sidewalk, you may come upon a photographer with a group of bored-looking models dressed in neon pink.
Sometimes producers rent fin-tailed cars from the 1950s and park
them along Ocean Drive to complete the look for a layout.

Though it's unwise to walk on the beach or in the park late at
night, some young people take evening strolls and visit South
Beach clubs till the early morning hours. It should be noted that, as
in trendy areas of L.A. and New York, visitors should keep an eye
on personal valuables late at night.

Lily Guesthouse Hotel

835 Collins Avenue
Miami Beach, FL 33139
305-535-9900
Fax: 305-535-0077

> This bright yellow art deco
> hotel generates a warmth
> of its own

Owner: Julia Lido. **Accommodations:** 5 rooms, 4 suites, 8 cottages. **Rates:**
Rooms $159–$209, suites $259, cottages $130–$150; extra person in room $20.
Included: Continental breakfast. **Minimum stay:** None. **Added:** 12.5% tax. **Payment:** Major credit cards, traveler's checks. **Children:** Under 12 free in room
with parent. **Smoking:** Allowed; 3 nonsmoking rooms. **Open:** Year-round.

➤ **A wooden deck on the second floor is great for relaxing in the brilliant sunshine.**

The Lily Guesthouse is located on Collins Avenue in South Miami
Beach, one block from the Atlantic and funky Ocean Drive. The
yellow stucco reflects the Florida sun brilliantly, and in every way,
this hotel is a warm, sunlit place.

The Lily was built in 1936 and is a fine example of art deco design. A small porch stretches along the front of the hotel with
white iron railings; large urns of subtropical plants and a few
chaises furnish it. The pillars and trim are painted in pistachio
green, vanilla, and blue. Some of the windows are small-paned and
jalousied. The front door is glass, etched with an exotic bird.

Just inside is a small lobby with a few pieces of cushioned,
wrought-iron furniture where coffee is served every morning after
9 o'clock. The guest rooms are in two low-rise buildings.

Each accommodation has a kitchen or kitchenette with full-size
refrigerators and cable TV. The bathrooms are marble. Each room is

decorated individually but all have beautiful wooden furniture. Many of the armoires have finely wrought metal grills over the glass. The heavy fabrics are in deep colors like forest green or dark mauve. The artwork on the walls has been tastefully selected to complement the colors. The floors are natural wood, accented by fringed rugs. The kitchenettes are a bit austere but modern and clean.

The front building of the Lily has 10 rooms and suites while the back building has eight "cottages." The latter are preferred by returning guests because of their privacy.

Palm Beach

Brazilian Court

301 Australian Avenue
Palm Beach, FL 33480
561-655-7740
800-552-0335 in U.S.
800-228-6852 in Canada
Fax: 561-655-0801
info@braziliancourt.com
www.braziliancourt.com

> **A hotel with a quality that sets it apart from the ordinary**

General manager: Michael Brown. **Accommodations:** 103 rooms and suites. **Rates:** Rooms $140–$360, suites $200–$775; special rates for groups midweek and weekends from June to September. **Minimum stay:** With some packages. **Added:** 10.25% tax; $25 extra person. **Payment:** Major credit cards; personal checks. **Children:** Under 12 free in room with parents. **Smoking:** Nonsmoking rooms available. **Open:** Year-round.

➤ **The courtyards are delightful. Everywhere there are beautiful plantings and the restful sound of splashing fountains. The private pool area has the sense of enclosure and quiet that characterize the entire hotel.**

In a town that considers itself the epitome of style, the Brazilian Court is very, very chic. It is also restful, charming, and colorful. Frequent refurbishings over the years have made it one of the brightest, most beautiful hotels in the area.

A low-rise building of pale yellow stucco with a tile roof, the Brazilian Court is "Old Florida" in architecture. The hotel meanders around two subtropical courtyards. Double doors beneath a canopied entrance open to stunning white marble floors that run the length of the building. A color scheme of cool beige and white accentuates the sunny, airy feeling of the sitting area and lobby. Comfortable chairs are placed in conversational groupings.

This sitting area overlooks the Fountain Courtyard, where there is al fresco dining under umbrellaed tables. Guests enjoy breakfast and lunch during the day here and, in the evening, cool drinks and dinner. Inside is the Chancellor Grille Room, a formal dining room serving classic French meals. A healthy spa menu is also available. The Brazilian Court trio plays here for after-dinner dancing. The Terrace Dining Room is more casual, with French doors and tropical foliage and trees. The hotel also has a small, informal bistro. In addition to its restaurants, the Brazilian Court has a private dining room that can serve up to twelve. Always extremely popular for weddings and receptions, the hotel's Grille Room can accommodate parties of up to 150, and the Fountain Courtyard is large enough for a reception of about 300.

Guest rooms are generous in size; most feel more like an apartment than a hotel room, and even the smallest rooms at the Brazilian Court are spacious. All are beautifully appointed, with wood furniture and a cable TV hidden in a handsome armoire. The neutral walls are a stunning backdrop to splashes of color: brilliantly upholstered chairs or stylish window treatments in vibrant designer fabrics.

All guest rooms have a kitchenette with wet bar, refrigerator, coffeemaker and honor bar, cable TV with remote, a digital clock radio, bathrobes, an iron and ironing board in the walk-in closet, and a telephone with voice mail and a PC data port. The suites have a CD player and personal computer. All of the beds are queen- or king-size; twin beds can be arranged with advance notice. The sofa beds have mattresses that are actually comfortable.

Number 101 is a typical studio accommodation, with a sophisticated beige and white color scheme and a king-size bed. Room 103, around the corner, is a one-bedroom suite with a queen-size bed. Beside the armoire is a period chair upholstered in bold citrus and white stripes. Number 125, a two-bedroom suite, has a bedroom and bath placed at either end of the living room, assuring privacy for all occupants. The living/dining area has a pull-down table for entertaining and dining. Room service is available 24 hours a day.

When guests are not out on the town, which is within easy walking distance, activity centers around the beautiful courtyard out-

side and the stunning lobby/sitting area. There also is a complimentary fitness center, beauty salon/barber shop, and a heated
swimming pool. The Brazilian Court is in a lovely residential section of Palm Beach, nice for a morning or balmy evening walk.
There is also the beach nearby and the galleries and shops of elegant Worth Avenue.

The Breakers

1 S. County Road
Palm Beach, FL 33480
800-833-3141 or 888-BREAKERS
561-655-6611
Fax reservations: 561-659-8403

**A traditional Palm Beach
gathering place**

Accommodations: 572 rooms and 47 suites. **Rates:** Rooms $250–$610, suites
$485–$2,700; Presidential and Imperial suites available; packages available;
prices vary depending on season. **Added:** 10.25% tax; $40 extra person; MAP
rate $67 plus $13 service charge, lower for children. **Payment:** Major credit
cards. **Children:** Under 17 free in room with parents. **Smoking:** Nonsmoking
rooms available. **Open:** Year-round.

➤   **The Breakers offers a variety of activities for many interests and ages,
with outstanding guidance from an energetic professional staff: golf and
tennis clinics, bicycling, croquet, spa services, scuba diving and snorkeling, and historic and garden tours.**

The Breakers is a five-star hotel built by the railroad baron Henry
Flagler and the first oceanfront hotel in South Florida. Unlike so
many other grand hotels in Florida, it has never suffered financial
disaster or neglect. But its early history was not without difficul-

ties. The first hostelry on this spectacular site was the Palm Beach Inn, built in 1895. The inn was so successful it was enlarged three times, but was destroyed by fire in 1903. When it was rebuilt as the Breakers it entered one of its most illustrious periods, when finely dressed ladies and gentlemen, children and nannies would come down to Palm Beach for the season by way of Flagler's famous railroad. At the train depot at the end of Royal Poinciana Way, they were met by donkey-drawn surreys that carried them along the Old Pine Walk to the grand hotel.

When this structure also succumbed to fire in 1925, Flagler's heirs decided to build an invulnerable hotel that would rival Florida's best. The hotel was built in 1926 on a round-the-clock schedule that included over a thousand workers, among them artists and artisans from Europe, most notably Italy. Today, The Breakers is one of the few grand hotels whose beautiful exterior has survived intact through the Depression and two world wars.

Of ivory stucco, the hotel has a red tile roof with belvedere towers at each side, arched, recessed windows on the top two floors, and long colonnades. In 1969 two oceanfront wings were added, in keeping with the architecture of the original. The ceilings of the lobby are vaulted and frescoed; the stucco walls and solid columns have a soft patina. On the walls are 15th-century Flemish tapestries. From the lobby, with its arched loggias, French doors lead out to colonnades and arched courtyards. Fountains are set with richly colored European tiles. Everywhere are palm trees and luxuriant gardens.

The grand ballroom and the dining rooms are equally breathtaking. Circling the palatial Gold Room, just below a ceiling of gold leaf, is a series of portraits of Renaissance rulers and Old World explorers. The ceilings of other dining rooms have intricate carved moldings in teal and gold and are painted with scenes of Italian cities. The frescoes and paintings are lit by chandeliers of Austrian crystal and bronze.

Behind the hotel is the inspiration for the hotel's name: the warm waves of the Atlantic breaking on the narrow strip of sand on the private beach. The resort has a popular beach club and luxury spa overlooking the ocean.

There are 14 tennis courts and two golf courses: the original Ocean course at the hotel and a newer one at nearby Breakers West. It's easy to imagine tennis greats of the 1930s playing here in their whites, or men in plus fours and women in white skirts and middies golfing on the Ocean course. Children's programs include a camp. Worth Avenue, with its elegant boutiques, galleries, antique shops, and restaurants, is just a few miles away.

Accommodations at The Breakers are beautifully decorated and maintained. A recent refurbishment freshened up the hallways and the guest rooms. Wood furniture is lighter, wall colors softer, and marble has been installed in many of the bathrooms. A typical room has plaster walls and deep-pile carpeting. Amenities include two-line phones, jacks for computers, in-room movies, minibars, safes, robes, and irons and ironing boards.

The Breakers has long been thought of as a winter resort, but it has been open year-round since 1971, and many of its most interesting children's programs take place in the summer. In recent years, The Breakers has attracted more and more families, and more rooms are furnished with two beds. Rates during the spring and fall are relatively reasonable, and the staff urge wintertime visitors to try The Breakers in the summer, too, when the temperature is not much higher than it is in northern cities and ocean breezes keep things cool.

The Chesterfield Hotel

363 Coconut Row
Palm Beach, FL 33480
800-243-7871
561-659-5800
Fax: 561-659-6707

A small hotel with the refinements of both Europe and Palm Beach

Accommodations: 53 rooms and suites. **Rates:** Rooms $89–$450, suites $179–$975. **Minimum stay:** None. **Added:** 10.25% tax; $15 extra person in room; $15 rollaway; cribs free. **Payment:** Major credit cards. **Children:** Under 12 free in room with parents. **Smoking:** Nonsmoking rooms available. **Open:** Year-round.

➤ **A traditional English tea is served in the afternoon, with delicate sandwiches and fresh scones.**

The Chesterfield Hotel, just down the street from Henry Flagler's mansion, Whitehall, has a stylish, European feel to it. Built in the Mediterranean style favored by renowned Palm Beach architect Addison Mizner, the Chesterfield is painted pink and has French-style awnings over the front windows. Guests walk through an ornate white iron gate into a pretty courtyard, which also serves as the outdoor dining area for the excellent restaurant. French doors lead into a small but elegant lobby. Fresh flowers are everywhere.

All of the public rooms on the first floor, including the restaurant's dining room and lounge, are richly appointed and decorated. The Leopard Lounge is both whimsical and elegant, with bright red upholstered chairs, a leopard-spotted carpet, and a leopard and floral wallpaper border accenting the walls. The Leopard Room restaurant has seating both inside and out in the courtyard.

A favorite public room for many overnight guests is the beautifully paneled library, which carries national and international newspapers. In the winter, a fire crackles in the fireplace. Just down the hallway is Churchill's Cigar. Again the colors are brilliant: red felt-topped game tables and red lacquered chairs. The floors in this part of the hotel are of marble, hardwood, or plush carpeting, and furnishings are antiques and good reproductions. Churchill's Cigar has a large TV and a computer for guests' use.

The Chesterfield's pool and Jacuzzi are encircled in a pretty aqua tile, and the patio has pink cement paving — very Palm Beach.

The room amenities are above the ordinary: fine English toiletries and a hair dryer in the bathroom, thick bathrobes, bottled mineral water, and a remote control TV with free cable movies. The baths are clean and fresh, some with the original ceramic tile and others with new marble. A variety of room sizes is available, including suites with queen-size sofa beds and two baths. All beds are either queen- or king-size. If you're traveling with children, the best bet is probably a one-bedroom suite with a sleep sofa.

Views from the rooms are usually "cityscape": the building next door, the street, perhaps the pretty courtyard and the pool. Outside, the scene is quiet in the evening as well as during the day, since the restaurant crowd is a gentle group. Ideally located on the corner of Australian Avenue and Coconut Row, the Chesterfield is only a few minutes from Worth Avenue shops. The airport is an unharried 10-minute drive.

The Colony

155 Hammon Avenue
Palm Beach, FL 33480
800-521-5525
561-655-5430
Fax: 561-659-8104
colres@flite.net
www.thecolonypalmbeach.com

One of Palm Beach's oldest and most distinguished hotels

Accommodations: 95 rooms and suites. **Rates:** Rooms $110–$295, suites $199–$695. **Included:** Welcoming champagne cocktail, morning newspaper. **Minimum stay:** With some packages. **Added:** 10.25% tax. **Payment:** Major credit cards, traveler's checks. **Children:** Allowed. **Smoking:** Allowed. **Open:** Year-round.

➤ **Many guests spend as many hours of the day out here relaxing on a chaise longue as they can manage, alternating between sun and shade. The atmosphere is always very peaceful.**

Few places in the town of Palm Beach reflect the best that is Palm Beach in quite the way the Colony does. Located just a few steps from the expensive shops and galleries of Worth Avenue, the hotel caters to "swells," as one might have said in the 1940s. No doubt, some of the social climbers who inevitably flock to Palm Beach every winter alight at the Colony, but generally, clientele are comfortable with themselves and their money, so the atmosphere is low-key rather than condescending or snobby. This is largely attributable to the staff, who are extremely cordial and sensitive; some have been employed here for decades. Service is thus very good, and the staff are obviously proud of the beautiful hotel they have helped to create.

Built in 1947, the Colony was refurbished a few years ago to give it a fresh look while retaining the elegance of old features. The exterior of the five-story main building is cream-colored stucco with white trim on the paned windows and three-story columns out front. A small circular drive curves to the entryway. Inside are light airy public rooms, comfortable sofas, and vases of orchids. Floors are marble or fine hardwood. The reception staff is friendly and thorough in explaining hotel procedures, but never intrusive. They'll tell you as much or as little as you wish about Palm Beach County tourist spots.

The elegant dining room and cocktail lounge are just off the lobby. Innovative chefs assure excellent food, and the service matches the cuisine. The Dining Room serves breakfast, lunch, and dinner and has been named one of the ten best U.S. restaurants by the American Academy of Restaurant Sciences. Local residents as well as hotel guests dine here. Live music is performed three nights a week, and there's a parquet dance floor.

Glass doors lead out to the patio where there's alfresco dining, and to the pool, which is shaped like the state of Florida. Blue and white umbrellas shade some of the tables and give the area a Mediterranean look and an outdoor Tiki bar offers drinks and snacks.

On the other side of the pool, through an ornate wrought-iron gate, is the hotel's conference facility, the Pavillion. Once a Palm Beach mansion, the facility has been beautifully refurbished. Its 3,200 square feet of function space can accommodate up to 210 for banquets, conventions, wedding receptions, and smaller meetings. It has a modern sound system and state-of-the-art lighting for business meetings and presentations. Banquets and small suppers are serviced by its private kitchen. The place itself is gorgeous, with marble floors in some areas, elaborate moldings, murals of fantasy landscapes, and large bouquets of fresh-cut flowers.

Other amenities at the Colony are its hair salon and bicycle rentals. There is no golf or tennis on the property, but the concierge can arrange for them, as well as fishing, boating, and scuba diving nearby. The Colony has packages that include excursions to the golf course or the Kravis Center of Performing Arts. World-class polo is close by in West Palm Beach. The concierge can also arrange rental cars for those who took advantage of the hotel's complimentary transportation from the airport and want to drive themselves to nearby recreation.

The guest rooms are more varied than one might expect in an old hotel, principally because of the Colony's handsome villa suites. These are located in Spanish-style buildings located across the street from the main hotel and are like beautifully furnished small apartments. They are good for an extended stay.

Rooms and suites in the main building have the same attention to detail in designer fabric drapes and bed coverings, as well as bathrooms with the original ceramic tile. Room 505, on the top floor and with an ocean view, is especially attractive. Most of the bathrooms are a bit small for travelers used to modern hostelries, but they are certainly adequate, with a mix of old and new fixtures. Little extras include bottled sparkling water and hair dryers. Suites have a large sofa, a walk-in closet, and a bigger bathroom than the standard rooms. Some of the suites also have wonderful views of the ocean, which is only a couple of blocks down the street.

Four Seasons Resort, Palm Beach

2800 S. Ocean Boulevard
Palm Beach, FL 33480
800-432-2335 in U.S.
800-332-3442 worldwide
561-582-2800
Fax: 561-547-1374

> **A hotel in the tradition of the grand Old Florida resort**

Accommodations: 210 rooms, suites, and penthouses. **Rates:** Rooms $255–$640, suites $775–$2,500; packages available. **Minimum stay:** During holidays. **Included:** Children's program for 3- to 12-year-olds. **Added:** 10% tax, parking fee. **Payment:** Major credit cards. **Children:** 17 and under free in room with parents. **Smoking:** Nonsmoking rooms available. **Open:** Year-round.

➤ **The accommodations at the Four Seasons are so luxurious that most people will be more than satisfied with the least expensive rooms. A standard room with two double beds is large enough for a family of four. Prices tend to go up with height and view.**

From the high ceilings and cut coral columns at the entrance to the great vistas of the Atlantic from its French windows in the back, the Four Seasons is indeed grand. The ground-floor hallways and public rooms are of marble, and fine art adorns the walls.

The hotel has a number of charming sitting areas. Its Living Room lounge is like a French drawing room, with empire furniture. A nearby card room has intricate, inlaid-wood game tables and beautiful wainscoting. The only jarring element is a carpet with a pattern that looks like leopard spots encircling yellow flowers.

The restaurants are elegant, with high ceilings and expansive windows. Even the Bistro café, which is advertised as the least formal, has an upscale air in the evening. The service and the food are quite good at all the restaurants, and the resort's main dining room is the only five-diamond hotel restaurant in South Florida.

Guest rooms are also impressive. Standard rooms have a choice of bed sizes, a large armoire that holds a TV, a bureau, a small desk with a telephone, lots of closet space, a minibar, and a furnished terrace. The marble bathrooms, with a telephone and a mini-TV, are quite beautiful. All rooms have a safe in the bedside cabinet.

The one-bedroom suites have much more space for a family, a pullout king-size sofa, a powder room, balconies off both the sitting area and the bedroom, and a VCR and stereo. A variety of suites and penthouses are also available.

For exercise, there's swimming in the hotel's freshwater pool or the warm Atlantic, tennis on three Har-Tru courts, and golf nearby, which can be arranged at the concierge desk. The Four Seasons has ample facilities for group meetings and banquets to accommodate conferences and executive retreats.

When making reservations, be sure to inquire about packages. The hotel's Grand Getaway is wonderful for a honeymoon or an anniversary weekend. Those who want to splurge might try the spa package, including a facial and massage, manicure, aerobics, a power walk on the beach, and access to all the exercise equipment in the hotel's immaculate spa. Service throughout the Four Seasons is usually excellent.

Palm Beach Historic Inn

365 South County Road
Palm Beach, FL 33480
561-832-4009
Fax: 561-832-6255

A Victorian-style B&B with surprisingly sensible rates

Innkeeper: Jean Charette. **Accommodations:** 9 rooms, 4 suites. **Rates:** Rooms $75–$185, suites $150–$275. **Included:** Continental breakfast. **Minimum stay:** None. **Added:** 10.25% tax; $25 extra person. **Payment:** Major credit cards, personal checks with credit card. **Children:** Under 14 not recommended, ages 14-18 free in room with parent. **Smoking:** Nonsmoking rooms available. **Open:** Year-round.

➤ **In the afternoon, the parlor tea service is warmed up, and tea is served in the small downstairs library and parlor.**

A reasonably priced B&B in downtown Palm Beach? Impossible! This is what anyone would have said about this exclusive enclave before the Palm Beach Historic Inn opened in 1993. But the impossible happened. For under $100, guests can stay in a historic building just a few minutes' walk from chic Worth Avenue and the Atlantic.

Mind you, corners have been cut. The brass beds are not heavy-gauge antiques or reproductions, and the prints on the walls look like the kind of art that one might buy at a discount store. But the attempt to create a Victorian retreat at affordable prices is sincere, and the location at such prices makes the heart stop.

The inn is in the loveliest part of town, across the street from the Spanish-style town hall. Within walking distance are Mizner mansions, the boutiques, art galleries, the flower-draped archways of Worth Avenue, and a beautiful beach. At a small reception desk in the Victorian parlor, the innkeeper welcomes guests. The parlor is a pleasant gathering place where a 1940s Coca-Cola machine still dispenses cold bottles of Coke for a dime. Tea is served here in the afternoon.

Upstairs are rooms and suites decorated with antiques, firm beds, and frothy Victorian touches. All rooms and suites have cable TV and telephones and modern bathrooms with old-fashioned fixtures. The curtains at the windows and festoons above the beds may not be the finest fabric, as one would find in the Breakers or the Chesterfield. But an effort has been made to create a mood. Each room is individually decorated and of a unique shape and size, so there is the feeling of being in a home rather than a motel.

The suites have sitting areas that recall the grace and ease of the upper classes during the Victorian era. Especially nice is Suite 121, done up in pink and ruffles, with a daybed and a queen-size bed in the bedroom and another daybed in the sitting room. A family of four could be quite comfortable here.

Every morning, staff deliver to each room a Continental breakfast that includes hot muffins, Danish pastries, or a bagel and cream cheese, melon or other fresh fruit, yogurt, juice, coffee and tea, plus a morning newspaper. There is no pool or other recreation here, but pretty Palm Beach is just outside the door.

Ritz-Carlton, Palm Beach

100 S. Ocean Boulevard
Manalapan, FL 33462
800-241-3333
561-533-6000

> An elegant beachside hotel
> with all the traditions of the
> Ritz

Accommodations: 270 rooms and suites. **Rates:** Rooms $165–$700, suites $525–$1,000; packages available. **Minimum stay:** With some packages. **Added:** 10.25% tax; $20 for fourth person in double occupancy room. **Payment:** Major credit cards, personal checks. **Children:** 18 and under free in room with parents. **Smoking:** Nonsmoking rooms available. **Open:** Year-round.

➤ **All employees of the hotel are trained in the Ritz-Carlton creed: they are "ladies and gentlemen serving ladies and gentlemen."**

The town of Palm Beach receives so much publicity that visitors to Florida often aren't aware that the island of Palm Beach has many other small communities. Manalapan, just eight miles from the Mizner mansions and exclusive boutiques of Worth Avenue, is one of the nicest. The Ritz-Carlton is on a slight incline above Ocean Boulevard on the southern end of the island. Stately royal palms line the curved drive up to the entrance, where the Ritz-Carlton lion-and-crown emblem is emblazoned on an elegant porte cochere. Everything about the Ritz feels substantial, rooted in the traditions of this world-renowned hostelry and the finer things of Palm Beach life.

The hotel forms an E shape with the prongs of the E facing the ocean, a clever design that makes the most of the Ritz-Carlton's seven acres. The architecture is influenced by the eclectic Spanish style of Palm Beach's seaside villas. Its smooth, buff-colored stucco exterior is embellished with mission bell towers and fine Italianate detailing beneath the terra-cotta-tile roof. On the back of the hotel, iron railings outline the balconies of the rooms, which overlook the Atlantic and the bilevel courtyard and pool patio.

Many rooms have sweeping views of the ocean. Lower-priced rooms look out at landscaped gardens or, on the first floor, have tiled patios next to the pool. All the rooms have a little more space and a few more extras than a standard hotel room. All have three telephones, including one in the bathroom, cable TV hidden in an armoire, a safe, and a mini-fridge stocked with beverages and other treats (there is, of course, a charge for these). Terry robes hang in the closets. French doors lead to the furnished private balconies.

The oversize bathrooms have floor-to-ceiling marble and both a tub shower and a stall shower. All bathrooms have double sinks, a makeup mirror, hair dryer, and bath scale. Suites have a separate dressing room; many suites also have a second bathroom.

It's not just the elegance of the baths that makes the Ritz-Carlton special. Another reason is the service. Staff members nearly bend over backward to give attentive, courteous service. Occasionally they may seem self-conscious, as if they're serving tea sandwiches to Mother's guests for the first time and are nervous about spilling something on the tablecloth. But this is a welcome change from the languid service that visitors to Florida often find in hotels.

The Ritz-Carlton has three restaurants, a lounge, and a poolside bar and café. The food is outstanding. Dinner menus offer appetizers such as wild mushrooms in scallion cream sauce, barbecued shrimp, tomato-leek soup, and oysters on the half shell. Entrées include grilled chops and steaks, North Atlantic salmon, and Colorado lamb chops, and some exotic dishes like Gulf shrimp basted in hazelnuts and almonds and a veal paillard in a pine nut Parmesan crust. Desserts are both traditional American (warm apple pie or bread pudding) and Floridian (Key lime pie and passionfruit sorbet).

The conference facilities include a banquet service that provides the same superlative cuisine. The Ritz-Carlton has a skilled concierge team that arranges the details for large and small meetings. Conference space includes two boardrooms and two ballrooms that can be divided into smaller meeting rooms.

For diversion, there are the Worth Avenue boutiques and galleries and the nearby golf courses. But it is difficult to top the Atlantic Ocean. The breeze from the water can make this expanse of the coast cooler in summer than cities hundreds of miles north. The water is pleasantly warm in the winter without being "bathtub warm" in the hotter months. For freshwater swimmers, there's a pool with a large Jacuzzi overlooking the ocean. Everywhere, there are beautiful plantings of traditional annuals and luscious subtropical plants, creating a feeling of gentility and exotica.

Palm Beach Gardens

Heron Cay Intracoastal Bed & Breakfast

15106 Palmwood Road
Palm Beach Gardens, FL 33410
561-744-6315
Fax: 561-744-0943
www.heroncay.com

An Intracoastal retreat with its own little mangrove island

Innkeepers: Marge Salyer and Randy Burgener. **Accommodations:** 6 rooms. **Rates:** Rooms $105–$180, suites $155–$250 ($10 less for singles); extra person in room $10. **Included:** Full breakfast. **Minimum stay:** 2 nights in winter and on weekends. **Added:** 10% tax. **Payment:** Visa, MasterCard, personal checks, cash. **Children:** Allowed with some restrictions. **Smoking:** Permitted outside only. **Open:** Year-round.

➤ **The real showpiece of Heron Cay is the patio overlooking the Intracoastal. With its handsome tilework, meandering pool, and elevated hot tub, it almost has the ambience of a Mediterranean grotto.**

Turn onto the curving drive of Heron Cay and it's like arriving at an old banana plantation. The landscaping in the front yard is a tamed jungle. However, a few things hint that this is neither a plantation nor an ordinary suburban house, despite the middle-class residential setting. In the middle of the front porch, a tree grows up through the roof, making it immediately obvious that this B&B is going to be a little different.

The house is what you'd expect an island planter to live in: a two-story building faced in cedar clapboards with a big veranda across the front, small-paned windows, and French doors leading past white wicker and pots of subtropical flowers into a breezy entryway. Spacious rooms are on either side of the wide central hallway. Broad steps of terra cotta tile lead down to the sunken dining room and living room. A delicious breakfast is served here at a round glass table, with the cool veranda just beyond. The ceilings are rare pecky cypress; the fireplace is fieldstone. The living room is furnished in Victorian antiques.

Innkeepers Marge and Randy are not immaculate housekeepers. They are too interested in people and good food, as well as working and playing hard. They have an interesting mix of artwork and funky collectibles in the downstairs rooms and along the hallway, like old slot machines, boat wheels, and a jukebox. At the end of the hallway is a bar and den on the left and a kitchen on the right, which Randy uses for his small catering business as well as for themselves and their guests. They create dinners here for special occasions as well as breakfasts for guests. Randy is eccentric, creative, and talkative. Marge is just as outgoing and interesting and has been a well-respected businesswoman in the area for many years. Their elegant cats lounge on the cool tile floors.

The house and garden have been completely redone by Marge and Randy over many years. There are lots of chaises and lawn chairs for relaxing. A sea breeze relieves the summer temperatures, and an overhang by the kitchen and bar area provides some shade in the middle of the day.

Guests can fish off the dock. Those who arrive by boat are welcome to dock here at one of the eight boat slips, free of charge. A floating boardwalk and dock lead to Marge and Randy's tiny private island. The eastern side of this island has a sandy beach. It is quite amazing that this B&B is in a residential neighborhood in conventional Palm Beach Gardens, about half an hour from Palm Beach International Airport. Both the outdoor area and the house itself seem miles from mundane civilization.

A spiral staircase in the middle of the B&B leads to upstairs bedrooms, which are contemporary in decor, almost dramatic. All rooms have a small refrigerator, access to the second floor veranda through glass doors, and gorgeous tiled bathrooms. The upstairs rooms on the back are the best because they have full water views. The southeast corner room, called Nautilus Bay, has a king-size antique bed and a sofa bed in the separate sitting area. The large bathroom has a marble shower as well as an old clawfoot tub. Starfish has a king size bed and an impressive bathroom and can be connected with an adjacent room to create a two-bedroom suite. But the most appealing attribute of the Starfish is that guests staying in this room can walk out onto the veranda overlooking the water.

Rooms overlooking the garden do not have the same impressive views of the pool and the Intracoastal, but they're also decorated in contemporary designer fabrics and some of Randy and Marge's art collection. Since the landscaping is so creative and beautiful, their views are very pleasant. One advantage for those traveling with older children or another couple is that there is some flexibility with rooms at Heron Cay — most can be combined with other rooms or have a sofa bed so that they can sleep four. Randy and

Marge are forever upgrading the rooms, most often expanding a bathroom and adding spectacular tilework.

PGA National Resort & Spa

400 Avenue of the Champions
Palm Beach Gardens, FL 33418
800-633-9150
561-627-2000
Fax: 561-622-0261

A resort where golf is played with intensity, commitment, and humor

Accommodations: 339 rooms and suites, 80 cottages. **Rates:** Rooms $150–$350; junior suites $195–$450; 2-bedroom, 2-bath cottages $295–$450; packages available. **Minimum stay:** 2 nights with packages. **Added:** 10% tax; $15 rollaway. **Payment:** Major credit cards. **Children:** 17 and under free in room with parents. **Smoking:** Nonsmoking rooms available. **Open:** Year-round.

➤ **The breezy manmade beach, overlooking a 26-acre lake, is a favorite spot, especially for families. Aquacycles, kayaks, sailboats, canoes, and aquatic equipment are for rent at the mini-beach.**

The PGA National Resort is, of course, best known for golf. In addition to the formidable PGA Champion Course here, there are four other excellent courses: the Estate; the Haig, named after Walter Hagen; the Squire, named after Gene Sarazen, the first professional to win a Grand Slam, and the General, for Arnold Palmer and his "charges." All these courses challenge pro and amateur alike and are meticulously cared for year-round.

Apart from the outstanding golf, this resort offers an abundance of activities for all ages and interests. The PGA National has an excellent health club, with an aerobic dance studio, racquetball courts, exercise rooms, and sauna and massage rooms. The Spa offers hydrotherapy and many other treatments, massages, a salon, and tanning areas. The resort's restaurants, serving seafood, Mexican, Italian, and mesquite-grilled cuisine, also offer spa meals.

Outdoors, there are whirlpools for soaking well-exercised muscles, as well as swimming pools surrounded by chaises. A jogging path winds under palms and pines past velvety greens. The croquet complex has five tournament-size courts, including one for instruction. The resort does not slack off when it comes to tennis, either. There are 19 clay courts, 12 of them lighted for night play. The resort offers an excellent recreational program for children ages 6 to 13. Activities include sand castle building, cookie decorating, arts and crafts, picnics, and movies.

The standard guest rooms are quite spacious, and the PGA National also has a selection of one- and two-bedroom suites. All rooms have safes and well-stocked minibars. Upstairs rooms and suites have balconies overlooking the fairways or grounds; first-floor rooms have Mexican terra cotta tile in the rooms and patios outside. These ground-floor rooms are perfect for the golfing addict who can't even wait for breakfast before getting out on the course.

Pompano Beach

Palm-Aire Resort & Spa

2601 Palm-Aire Drive North
Pompano Beach, FL 33069
954-972-3300

A spa with more than twenty years of success in helping guests feel healthy

Accommodations: 100 rooms. **Rates:** Room $125–$200, golf and spa additional. **Minimum stay:** With some packages. **Payment:** Major credit cards. **Children:** Under 16 not permitted in spa, children under 12 free in room with adult. **Smoking:** Discouraged; outside only. **Open:** Year-round.

➤ **The landscaping around the buildings and the outdoor recreational facilities is exotic and beautifully maintained. Although there is so much to do here that there is no need (and little time) to go anywhere else, Palm-Aire is located near some beautiful beaches. There's also harness and greyhound racing nearby.**

The Palm-Aire Resort & Spa has two separate but identical spa facilities, one for men and one for women, plus some coed areas. The spa offers a number of different programs and packages: informal lectures on exercise and motivation, skin care, weight control, and cooking demonstrations. Each spa facility has exercise rooms with aerobics machines and weight-training equipment, exercise pools, saunas, steam rooms, whirlpool tubs, and hot and cold plunge pools. There's also a lap pool and a parcourse jogging track with exercise stations. Outdoors, spa guests have access to five championship golf courses and 37 all-weather tennis courts. The recreational facilities are so spectacular because the spa is part of the 1,500-acre Palm-Aire Community. The professionally trained staff are caring without being patronizing. They aim to help clients achieve their weight loss or fitness goals and motivate them to maintain their health after they leave Palm-Aire. Many of the guests are local residents who belong to the Palm-Aire Country Club and come here for exercise and fitness classes and relaxing spa treatments.

When dining, guests can choose between a regular menu and a spa menu. A typical spa menu might offer a seafood or salmon salad, twice-baked potato with Jarlsberg cheese, teriyaki swordfish with ginger relish, or a burger on bagel thins. Food is surprisingly filling and satisfying and includes some clever low-calorie desserts.

Accommodations are extremely comfortable and attractive. Standard rooms have two double beds or one king-size bed, color TV, telephone, a private terrace, and spacious bathrooms with separate dressing areas. One- and two-bedroom suites are available, some with an attractive kitchenette. All of the rooms have two bathrooms, which is especially nice for friends sharing double occupancy.

The Keys

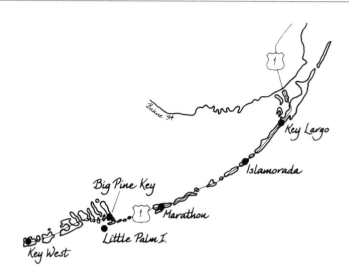

Best B&Bs

Best Beachside Accommodations

Best Budget Finds

Best Island Getaway

Best Resorts and Spas

Islamorada
Pelican Cove Resort, 345
Key Largo
Marina Del Mar, 347
Westin Beach Resort Key Largo, 349
Key West
Hyatt Key West, 365
Key West Hilton Resort & Marina, 369
Ocean Key House Resort & Marina, 379
Pier House Resort & Caribbean Spa, 381
Wyndham Casa Marina Resort, 393
Marathon
Faro Blanco Marine Resort, 399
Hawk's Cay Resort and Marina, 401

Best Small Hotels, Inns, and Motels

Key West
The Banyan Resort, 353
Eden House, 359
The Marquesa Hotel, 374
South Beach Oceanfront Motel, 386
Southernmost Motel in the USA, 387

South of Miami and Key Biscayne are the Keys, the chain of tiny islands that have a reputation for being laid-back and unpretentious, with some of the best fishing in the world. The Keys can be disappointing at first, until you learn where to go to fulfill your particular fantasy or expectation.

Many people who go to **Key Largo,** the first and largest of the Keys, expect the wild, remote beauty they remember from Bogart and Bacall's film *Key Largo.* They are disappointed to find two-lane Route 1 lined with ramshackle food stands, bars, bait shops, souvenir stores, and uninspired accommodations. You have to leave Route 1 to find the real Key Largo. There are interesting, attractive places to stay on narrow roads that end at the water — the Atlantic and Straits of Florida on the east, Florida Bay on the west. Like Fort Lauderdale, Key Largo has many inlets, marinas, and canals. A nature walk at John Pennekamp Coral Reef State Park provides insight into the physical characteristics of all the Keys, with its native vegetation and sandy soil. An excellent staff of rangers and diving experts can take you by boat to the enormous living coral reef several miles offshore. The reef is long, stretching from Key Largo to the Dry Tortugas south of Key West. Divers will see not only the beautiful lacy coral but also many varieties of colorful fish.

The reef is responsible for the lack of natural beaches everywhere but on **Bahia Honda** and Key West. All the Keys on Route 1 are made of dead coral rock. Originally, Key Largo was a series of rock and sand keys that were filled in when Flagler's railroad came in. The railroad was completed with much fanfare in 1912, just a few months before Flagler's death. Though the railroad no longer exists, Route 1, which links all the Keys, was constructed on the old railroad bed, much of it washed out during a hurricane. The railroad was supposed to create prosperity for the Keys by transporting the fruits and vegetables grown on plantations and struggling farms to major markets. Ironically, **Key West** became a distribution center for cheaper South American and Caribbean produce. Eventually, many farms and plantations failed because of this competition and because there wasn't enough topsoil to support their crops. Always beset by economic woes, the Keys survived on fishing. Until recently, the leading industry in Key West was shrimping. Today, of course, it is tourism.

The lack of fresh water and the desolation of the Keys kept them off most tourists' itineraries in the earlier part of this century. There were mosquitoes and deadly hurricanes. The worst of these occurred in 1935, when a train was blown off the tracks in Islamorada, south of Key Largo, and much of the track elsewhere in the Keys was swept away. The Great Depression hit the Keys hard. Although work was begun to convert the railroad into a highway after 1935, the hurricane took the heart out of development for many years. Today, some would say there has been too much development, but tourism has saved the region economically. The Keys have become popular for their informality and funky charm, as well as for the excellent fishing. A swimsuit, a pair of shorts, several T-shirts, and a pair of sandals are all you need to pack unless you plan to go out to dinner, in which case you might want to bring a pair of slacks or a sun dress.

Getting around is pretty easy too. You can fly into Ft. Lauderdale, Miami, Naples, or Key West and rent a car or, if your only destination is Key West, fly there, take a taxi to your guest house, and rent a moped, bicycle, or car in town. If you're staying in Old Town, you can simply walk everywhere and forgo the rentals. If you're driving from a mainland airport, you'll eventually get on

Route 1, the only highway that runs the length of the Keys. Along Route 1, you will notice mile marker signs with an MM followed by a number. These orient people to what's where on the Keys and are used in place of street numbers. Accommodations and restaurants on side streets off Route 1 often use mile markers to indicate their addresses.

Fishing is still important in the Keys, for both food and sport. Tavernier and Plantation Keys and Upper and Lower Matecumbe Keys are popular for saltwater fishing. **Islamorada** is the largest town on the Upper Keys, with big marinas and a nightspot, Holiday Isle, that draws tourists and natives. There are some good restaurants here, a post office, souvenir shops, resorts, and the Theater of the Sea, a dolphin show and marine education center. Occasionally, the Upper Keys and various other Keys in the chain have a problem with water pressure. This usually means only that you might shorten your morning shower by a few minutes, but you should be sensitive to the fact that the natives don't like to see water or other resources wasted in the Keys.

Southwest of Islamorada are several tiny uninhabited islands inaccessible by car throughout this stretch of waterway, many made of mangroves. One Key that has built up over the centuries is Lignumvitae, an unspoiled island of wild vegetation accessible only by boat. Lignumvitae is named after a tree with unusually dense wood that is extremely rare and is reputed to be nonflammable.

The next big community is **Marathon,** at the center of the Middle Keys. Founded as a base camp for railroad workers in 1906, this is a good place to buy supplies and fishing bait and equipment. Marathon is at its prettiest on back roads and beside its long canals.

South of Marathon, the Keys shed their tourist quality and become more rural up to the outskirts of Key West. Pigeon Key is the start of the old Seven-Mile Bridge, Flagler's great engineering achievement and the longest of the Keys' bridges. After 1935, it was widened and became a highway bridge. It was replaced in 1982. Altogether, there are 42 bridges linking the various Keys.

Bahia Honda State Park, adjacent to the Bahia Honda Bridge, is the tail end of the Middle Keys, with the best beach on the Keys and good diving in the deep waters near the bridge pilings. You can see corals and sponges as well as fish. But the current is swift in some areas, and there are stinging fire coral and sea urchins, as well as occasional hammerhead sharks when the tarpon are running. It's best to get advice from state park personnel on spots to avoid off Bahia Honda, or simply stay at the state park for safer swimming.

Many of the islands in the Upper and Middle Keys are elongated, but south of Bahia Honda they broaden out a bit. Beyond the Keys proper, there are dozens of smaller islands. Big Pine Key is the most settled area before Key West, with a big shopping center and a good deal of development. Otherwise there is little commercialism. Tiny Key deer live here, with fawns that weigh less than five pounds at birth. Drive carefully at night and in the early morning hours when they may be out. The National Key Deer Refuge (MM 31) is worth visiting. Though it is tough to spot the deer themselves except in the early morning and late evening when they come out to feed, there are plenty of waterfowl, hawks, and smaller birds in this area.

When Ernest Hemingway first moved to Key West, he said it was "the best place I've ever been any time anywhere." Throughout this century, Key West has had an aura that many visitors find difficult to explain. At the southernmost tip of the continental United States, Key West is closer to Havana than Miami and, both geographically and atmospherically, is a world unto itself. It is a zany, laid-back, tolerant place with an international citizenry that at times delights in the bizarre. Key West is sometimes called the "Conch Republic," and natives are called "conchs." Key West actually declared itself a republic briefly in 1982 in response to roadblocks set up to search cars for smuggled drugs. Key West seceded from the union at high noon on April 23, 1982, raised a quickly designed Conch Republic flag, declared war against the United States, formally surrendered in order to be "eligible for foreign aid," and then held a party that lasted several days. Only in Key West could this happen.

Despite its designation as the southernmost region of the United States, more northerners than southerners live in Key West, as well as Cubans and natives of various Caribbean islands. Except for conchs who own small shops or fish for a living, most people are from someplace else. Many of them, particularly gays, moved here specifically because of the island's openness. A small segment of the population is really down-and-out and probably living here because of the mild climate as well as the tolerance for any lifestyle. There are bag ladies and bag men and a few people who took one too many acid trips and never fully returned. Several famous artists live here and any number of bon vivants and bohemians. At its best, Key West gives a glimpse of what the rest of American society could be in its diversity, tolerance, and sense of fair play. When little kids play in their sandy front yards at dusk, it is not unusual to see children of three or four different racial or ethnic groups together. Many biracial couples from northern cities choose Key

West for their honeymoon. Residents are outside a lot, walking or bicycling to their destinations rather than driving their cars. No one is in a big hurry or makes a big fuss about anything.

At night, some of the tourists and local fishermen get drunk at places like Sloppy Joe's, a favorite hangout of Ernest Hemingway's. Though wild and woolly, the town is really pretty safe. The Key West community is very close, and there is an unwritten rule that tourists are to be protected — largely because they are crucial to the economic health of a place that has seen many precarious times, but also because of the sense of fair play in Key West. There is virtually no violent crime here, and although there are occasional robberies, they tend to be local against locals. It is nevertheless wise to watch your wallet or purse, especially if you are drinking, since out-of-towners sometimes prey on inebriated tourists.

A favorite haunt of visitors is the Old Town, particularly Mallory Square and Duval Street. To orient yourself and decide what attractions to see, take one of the Conch Train tours during the day. The loquacious guides of these toylike trams point out old Victorian conch houses and shotgun houses while providing information about the town's checkered past and its famous residents.

Also worth some time and money is a tour of the Currier Mansion, a marvelous example of Victorian architecture with a bird's-eye view of Old Town from its widow's walk. Lately, maintenance has slipped and the place is not as immaculate as it was when first opened. But it is worth seeing for those who are fascinated by Victorian island architecture and are willing to ignore the dust and air of neglect.

In recent years, Mallory Square and the Duval near Front Street have become extremely commercial, a blatant tourist trap. There are some lovely shops here, but there are also stores selling profane T-shirts and souvenirs at ridiculously high prices. The owners of one of these stores once nearly sold some German tourists four T-shirts for $600; a local resident overheard the swindle and called the police. Avoid these places; there are better shirts and nicer people further up the street. Some of the most interesting shops featuring local craftspeople are several blocks from Mallory Square at the far end of Duval Street and along quiet side streets.

Key West's guest houses and hotels reflect the many qualities of the island and appeal to a wide range of visitors. Some are enclaves for gays and the free-spirited, others for the chic and wealthy, still others for history buffs who love Victoriana and gingerbread. A few, like the Marquesa, have restaurants that have become renowned in their own right. Generally, restaurants in Key West, like so many other things on the island, go up and down. A place that is outstanding one year may be overpriced and mediocre the next, so ask the proprietors of your hotel or guest house for suggestions. Louie's Backyard is dependably good, though expensive. For authentic, cheap Cuban food, try El Seboney on Catherine Street. At the high end of Duval Street is Camille's, also inexpensive and a favorite of locals for breakfast.

For a look at some native wildlife and plant life on Key West that has survived development, visit the Riggs Wildlife Refuge through the Audubon House in town. Although Key West prides itself on its natural beaches, most are privately owned by resorts. One good public beach is Higgs Memorial, at the end of White Street. Be forewarned that most beach sand is of ground coral stone, not soft sand.

Big Pine Key

Bahia Honda Bayside Cabins

Bahia Honda State Park
Route 1, Box 782
Big Pine Key, FL 33043
305-872-2353

A bargain for families and nature lovers

Accommodations: 6 cabins. **Rates:** $100-130. **Included:** All applicable taxes and charges. **Minimum stay:** 2 nights; 14-night maximum stay. **Added:** $6.00 extra adult. **Payment:** MasterCard, Visa. **Children:** Free in room with parent (up to 6 family members allowed per cabin). **Smoking:** Outside only. **Open:** Year-round.

➤ **As one would expect, this environment attracts many birds: roseate spoonbills, reddish egrets, white-crowned pigeons, ospreys, terns, herons, and brown pelicans are among them.**

Bahia Honda State Park is on Bahia Honda Key, near Big Pine Key, with the Bay of Florida on one side and the Atlantic Ocean on the other. Pronounced *bay-ya hahn-da*, the name means "deep bay," and this is one of the deepest natural channels in the Keys. Many people come here for the day because Bahia Honda is reputed to have the most beautiful beach in the Keys. There are plenty of overnighters here, too, camping out or staying in the state park's reasonably priced cabins. From one end of the beach, you can see part of the picturesque old railroad bridge that juts into the water at the farthest point of land, running roughly parallel to a new bridge. A small marina on the bay side of the island has two boat ramps. The marina also has a gift shop and snack bar, barbecue grills, picnic tables, and a parking lot. This is a good place for boaters and families who want to vacation in clean, moderately priced accommodations.

There are many treasures here. This small state park has some of the most diverse terrain in the United States, with coral outcroppings, dunes, berms, mangroves, and, of course, a real sand beach. The beach near the marina has a state park feel, with picnic tables and palm trees. Walk up a bank of old cement steps past the old bridge, and you are on the Atlantic side of the island. This beach, which runs for several thousand feet, has flat areas near the water, dunes and berms dotted with sea oats and other grasses, and an occasional bank of exposed coral. The ocean is warm and has many shallow stretches that are ideal for young children to wade in.

This is also the perfect place to go beachcombing: the gentle waters of Bahia Honda encourage deposits of treasures like pieces of coral, seaweed, and sponges to wash ashore. The color of the water is remarkable — it's pale blue or turquoise near the shore and darker farther out, particularly above seaweed beds, where the water looks almost purple.

One of the park's campgrounds and its cabins are on the bay side of Bahia Honda, overlooking a small inlet; to get to this area, you have to drive under the highway bridge. The six cabins are only a few hundred yards from the highway, so there can be some highway noise when the air conditioning is not on. Each cabin has two bedrooms and a full bath with tub shower — no stumbling through the dark to a campground shower. One bedroom has a double bed and the other a double bed and two twins, so the cabin can sleep four to six people quite comfortably.

The cabins are rustic, with plywood walls, linoleum floors, and drapes at the windows. Furniture is serviceable but attractive; there are nightstands and dressers in the bedrooms and living room furniture in the sitting and dining area. The kitchen has a small refrigerator-freezer and a full set of pots and pans and tableware. The cabins have no telephone, TV, or radio. Clean linens and towels are provided, but you should bring beach towels and soap and shampoo; the little store adjacent to the marina has sundries for sale. On the way to Bahia Honda, it may be wise to stop at the supermarket in the town of Marathon. One of the larger commercial settlements in the Keys, Marathon also has a number of good shops.

Each of the six cabins has a deck overlooking the bay inlet with a barbecue grill and picnic table. The living quarters, on the second floor of the cabins, are constructed on pilings with a wooden staircase along the side that leads to a railed veranda and the entrance. The veranda runs along the length of the cabin and is a wonderful vantage point from which to view the inlet and the peaceful bay beyond. Swimming is not allowed in the inlet because the edge is rather rocky; most people who want to swim drive to the beaches in the main part of the park. Although there are a few places to explore in the bay side of the campground, the ocean side of the park is quite appealing for the nature lover.

A number of wildflowers grow at Bahia Honda that are found nowhere else in the United States. Their seeds were carried here from Caribbean islands by hurricanes, the ocean, and birds hundreds of years ago. An unusual species of morning glory thrives here as well as small-flowered lily thorn, yellow satinwood, silver palm, and a variety of other flowers and trees. Some of the flora are rare or endangered, and visitors are cautioned to step with care when taking nature walks.

Bahia Honda is an ideal place for anyone who loves bird watching, nature walks, beaching, boating, or camping out. One could come back here year after year for a lifetime and never begin to see all that there is in this small, peaceful place.

Barnacle Bed & Breakast

1557 Long Beach Drive
Big Pine Key, FL 33043
800-465-9100
305-872-3298
Fax: 305-872-3863

A breezy, unpretentious
place to stay

Innkeepers: Tim and Jane Marquis. **Accommodations:** 3 rooms, 1 cottage. Rates: $85–$125 rooms, $125–$140 cottage. **Included:** Full breakfast; bicycles and water sports equipment. **Minimum stay:** 2 nights on weekends. **Added:** 11.5% tax. **Payment:** Discover, MasterCard, Visa, traveler's checks. **Children:** 16 and older allowed. **Smoking:** Permitted outside only. **Open:** Year-round.

➤ **After breakfast, guests often lie out on one of the chaises or in the hammock strung between two coconut palms on the Barnacle's private beach. There's also a Tiki hut in a shady spot for very hot days.**

The Barnacle is located in a pleasantly secluded residential area and even has its own private beach. To get there, guests turn off U.S. 1 in Big Pine onto seemingly desolate Long Beach Drive, which is indeed long. After a few miles, the area becomes attractive and residential. A wooden sign on a low stone wall around a curve announces the Barnacle.

Innkeepers Tim and Jane Marquis, originally from Louisiana, decided to keep the B&B's unpretentious ambience and decor when they bought the place from the previous innkeepers. Furnishings are a mix of Caribbean, nautical, and antique. The main house and adjacent cottage are constructed in a contemporary island design of stone and dark-stained wood.

Accommodations are well kept and unintimidating. Each has Bahamian ceiling fans as well as air conditioning, private baths, and queen-size beds. Not one of the rooms has a square corner, an unusual feature that first attracted Jane and Tim to the house. The Ocean Room, on the first floor, has a sitting area as well as its own patio and private entrance. You can see the ocean from your bed. The Blue Heron Cottage, high above thick foliage, is the Barnacle's most private accommodation. There are some interesting nooks and crannies here and a beautiful stained glass window. Roomy and comfortable, the cottage has a fully equipped kitchen.

The main house has a bilevel design. A curved outside staircase leads to the center of the Barnacle and the second-floor guest rooms, the Tarpon and the Dolphin. These have a mix of furnishings, queen-size beds, and mini-fridges. They both open onto the Mexican-tiled atrium on the second floor, which is the heart of the B&B. Here, guests can soak in the hot tub, surrounded by banana trees, palms, and flowers, even a small fountain.

Breakfast is served here every morning at 8:30 at tables overlooking the ocean. Tim and Jane serve a breakfast that is influenced by the Caribbean and down-home America. A typical morning meal might be seafood quiche, tropical fruits, apple cinnamon muffins, hash browns, and hot coffee and tea.

The Marquises have complimentary bicycles, snorkeling gear, and kayaks for guests to use. Excellent snorkeling and diving are available at Looe Key, a beautiful coral reef that is only four miles away. Tim and Jane are happy to arrange for snorkeling and diving there, although guests can do both at the Barnacle. Tim is a scuba instructor, and the Marquises offer dive packages with instruction and certification. Like most of the Keys, Big Pine beaches have shallow, rocky shorelines, although the Barnacle does have a white sand beach. For fishing enthusiasts, there's game and sport fishing in Big Pine as well as in Marathon and Islamorada. The Barnacle has an outdoor barbecue where you can grill your catch of the day.

Bed & Breakfast on the Ocean: Casa Grande

P.O. Box 378
Big Pine Key, FL 33043
305-872-2878

| A standard for Keys guest houses |

Owner: Kathleen Threlkeld. **Accommodations:** 3 rooms. **Rates:** $110; $20 extra person in room. **Included:** Full breakfast; water sports equipment. **Minimum stay:** 2 or 3 nights on some holidays. **Added:** 11.5% tax. **Payment:** Personal checks, cash. **Children:** Not allowed. **Smoking:** In restricted area only. **Open:** Year-round.

➤   Guests have free access to what Kathleen calls her beach junk: wind-surfers, rafts, snorkeling equipment, and kayaks. Bicycles are available for those who want to bike around the neighborhood. The town of Big Pine Key, one of the larger settlements on the Keys, has some small, inexpensive restaurants for lunch.

Bed & Breakfast on the Ocean is so perfect as a B&B, any guest would swear that Kathleen Threlkeld designed this oceanside home with future guests in mind. All the bedrooms, decorated in green, ivory, melon, and other rich colors, have private baths — unusual in a family home. But according to Kathy, who moved to Big Pine Key in 1967, the individual baths were a response to having five teenagers living at home. Several years later, when the teenagers had grown up and gone, Kathleen and her late husband, Jon, started Bed & Breakfast on the Ocean. The design of the house follows that of a traditional hacienda, with a crescent of bedrooms opening onto a garden patio. The screened patio is a focal point, with a hot tub overlooking the water, lawn furniture, and a breakfast table with umbrella.

Bed & Breakfast on the Ocean was one of the first B&Bs to open in the Keys, and it has maintained a consistently high standard throughout the years. Breakfast is superb. It begins with hot tea or coffee and proceeds to juice, fresh tropical and native fruits, and a hot entrée: lobster Benedict, waffles, stone crab quiche, or a special omelet. Kathleen will sometimes serve a true English breakfast: eggs and fish, with local seafood such as tuna, dolphin, or yellow-tail. "I like to serve as much native food as possible," she says. "I also like educating people about seafood or dishes that they might not have had at home."

The patio, where the morning meal is served, is surrounded by subtropical and tropical flowers and profuse greenery. The table is always set with pretty china and flatware, and there is an arrange-ment of tropical flowers and ferns at the center. From the table, guests can see the ocean.

Kathleen's secluded beach, directly behind the house, is a good place to spend a morning. The beach is shaded by trees near the house and also has open stretches closer to the water. It's a pretty, restful spot with a boat ramp and dock for fishing, a chikee hut, and a barbecue grill.

Many people come to the Keys to snorkle. Kathleen has three boats available, one for each guest room at the Casa. These are fun to pedal around in, and with the anchor thrown out they can also be used as a jumping-off spot for snorkeling. The water is clear and warm and offers a variety of underwater sights. Big Pine Key is only about 33 miles from Key West, so there is a balmy feel to the air and a breeze from the water most of the year.

After a morning of swimming and lounging on the beach, a nap under the ceiling fan in the bedroom is always nice. Each room has a small refrigerator for soft drinks and snacks, and there's an attrac-tive sitting room with a fireplace and television. Take some time to look around at Casa Grande: the house makes dramatic use of many natural materials such as coral, pine, terra cotta tile, and ceramic tile. The spectacular fireplace in the sitting room is of rough coral.

Some days, it's nice to take a drive into Key West, stay for din-ner, and then come back for a soak in the hot tub. At night, stars blink above the steaming tub, and the tropical plants around the patio give off a moist, earthy fragrance.

Islamorada

Cheeca Lodge

U.S. Highway 1, Mile Marker 82
P.O. Box 527
Islamorada, FL 33036
305-664-4651
800-327-2888
Fax: 305-664-2083

> A longtime favorite of those
> who can afford excellence

General Manager: Klaus Peters. **Accommodations:** 139 rooms, 64 suites. **Rates:** Rooms $195–$650, suites $285–$1,500; packages available. **Minimum stay:** 2–3 nights on some weekends and holidays. **Added:** 11% tax; $25 extra adult; $25 rollaway. **Payment:** Major credit cards, personal checks with credit card. **Children:** Under 16 free in room with parent. **Smoking:** Nonsmoking rooms available. **Open:** Year-round.

➤ **Cheeca Lodge has plenty of options for those who want to do more than just unwind. There are lighted, all-weather tennis courts; a charming children's playground; a modest nine-hole golf course designed by Jack Nicklaus; sailing and water sports; and great fishing off the 525-foot lighted fishing pier. Deep-sea fishing and various excursions can also be arranged.**

Cheeca Lodge is luxurious yet informal, with the focus on both comfort and natural beauty.

Every accommodation at Cheeca Lodge has been recently refurbished. There are guest rooms and penthouse suites in the main lodge, as well as villa rooms and suites scattered around the property. All the buildings are of ivory stucco, with deep blue tile roofs and blue shutters. The individual villas are on thick concrete stilts — insurance against hurricane damage — with carports below.

All guest rooms have thick carpeting or rugs on marble or tile floors, teak and oak furniture, queen- or king-size beds, minibars, remote control TV, VCR, and bathrobes. The new baths have large double sinks, glass and tile showers or shower baths, and hair dryers. Many of the porches are screened and are a pleasure to sit on in any kind of weather, with their views of the water or the landscaped grounds — both, if you're lucky. With the sliding glass doors drawn open, you can bring the outdoors into your room any time of day.

The most reasonably priced rooms are in the original lodge building overlooking rooftops or, better, the courtyard. These are spacious, and their bathrooms have a tub shower, whereas bathrooms in the new cottages have only a large shower stall. The bathrooms also have a second sink and vanity top outside the bathroom proper, opposite a minibar and countertop. Natural wooden shutters slide over the big windows. Furnishings are similar to that of the cottages: wooden bureaus, double beds, and an oak and bamboo table with wicker chairs. The same type of room in the main lodge is also available overlooking the water, although the rate is a good deal higher.

Cheeca Lodge has always been one of the most beautiful properties on the Keys, with a variety of old mahogany, ficus, orchid, gum, palm, and other trees. These were preserved in the renovation, and areas between the lodge building and the ocean were landscaped with flower beds and small oases of green plants and trees. The lodge grounds are now a greater delight to walk through than ever, night or day.

The recreation area between the main lodge and the ocean is the sort of place where you can linger. There is a lagoon-style swimming pool adjacent to a real lagoon with two springs feeding directly into it from the ocean. Just beyond is the Atlantic, which can always be depended on to provide a cooling breeze. The poolside terrace has a new surface of white concrete and shellstone, which gives the whole area a fresh, clean look. Chaise longues are scattered here and there, and Seminole-built chikee huts give shelter from the sun. You can order a cool drink or a light meal at the snack bar, or call for a waiter from the Ocean Terrace Grill. This patio, with comfortable lawn furniture, a whirlpool spa, and fresh- and saltwater lagoons, provides both fun and rest in the midst of beauty.

For businesspeople, Cheeca Lodge has a versatile 4,000-square-foot conference center that accommodates up to 200 people. It is only 75 miles from the Miami Airport, close enough to be accessible but far enough from civilization to give business executives and professionals a sense of getting away from it all.

It's also one of the best places in the Keys to eat. The two restaurants at Cheeca Lodge are the Atlantic Edge, an elegant, semicircular room overlooking the ocean, and the Ocean Terrace Grille, an airy new dining room with oak casement windows that open onto the poolside terrace and the beach. The lounge is popular with fishermen and other local residents. There are huge mounted fish on the walls, windows overlooking the ocean, a solid teak horseshoe bar, and teak tables.

The lounge, the restaurants, and the lodge's boutiques are all in the main building, just off the lobby. The floors of shellstone and concrete are accented with cobalt blue tiles; above are the original cedar beams. French doors lead out to the courtyard and the archway of the front entrance. The shellstone walkway of the courtyard loggia is lined with big clay pots of bougainvillea and several varieties of hibiscus. At night, the loggia and the paths through the grounds of the lodge are lighted for romantic walks. When it's finally time to walk down the loggia for the last time, it's hard to leave this beautiful, restful place.

Chesapeake Resort

Mile Marker 83.5
P.O. Box 909
Islamorada, FL 33036
800-338-3395
305-664-4662
Fax: 305-664-8595

The kind of place families come back to year after year

Accommodations: 65 rooms and suites. **Rates:** Rooms $105–$150, efficiencies $185, oceanfront rooms $210–$230, oceanfront suites $335–$520, villas $145–$415; packages available; 10% discount for 7 nights or more. **Minimum stay:** 3 nights on holiday weekends and with some packages. **Added:** 11.5% tax; $20 extra person in room. **Payment:** Major credit cards; cash. **Children:** 12 and under free in room with parent. **Smoking:** Allowed. Open: Year-round.

➤ **For those who love to relax in the sun, the resort's saltwater lagoon is wonderful. The lagoon is suitable for swimming, and its far end is accessible to the Atlantic.**

This is not only a winter vacation spot; Floridians and other Southerners stay at the Chesapeake in the summer, mostly for the island breezes and the relaxed atmosphere. The feeling here is informal and unpretentious. People are here simply to enjoy the salty air and the work and fun of boating or fishing. The Chesapeake is not for the sophisticated — room numbers are painted on baby whales, and the restaurant is plastered with shells that look a bit corny. The informality, the friendly staff, and the availability of both bargain accommodations and more expensive waterfront suites are the attraction.

Islamorada calls itself the "sport fishing capital of the world," and you'll find out why. Boat dockage and the resort's launch ramp are available to guests who arrive by water or have their boat hitched to their car. Amenities do not include hookups, and space is limited to boats that are less than 28 feet long. Chesapeake of Whale Harbor charters fishing boats and rents water sports equipment.

The villas are the resort's oldest accommodations. Really more like beach cottages, these are 1950s-style, one-story units. There are small lawns in front, and palm and orchid trees dot the area. Each cottage has a full kitchen, a TV, and a telephone. The furnishings are functional; their ordinariness is relieved by prints on the walls. The cottages are well cared for, freshly painted and extremely clean. For a family planning to cook most meals, these are a real bargain.

Next to the office (and closer to the highway) is a two-story motel. Like the other Chesapeake accommodations, these rooms are extremely clean, and the owners have made an effort to compensate for the motel atmosphere. The units are pleasantly decorated and have small balconies and pretty stenciling in the tile baths. Available to all guests are shuffleboard, two pools, a gym, a whirlpool, tennis, and a child's playground. At night, guests and locals gather at the Whale Harbor Restaurant for drinks, hearty food, and live entertainment.

Overlooking the lagoon and the Atlantic are the Chesapeake's newest accommodations, the oceanfront suites. These are in three-story pink stucco buildings that have tin roofs, in the tradition of old Florida hostelries. The suites are luxury accommodations that have a Jacuzzi right in the bedroom, and railed balconies have unhindered views of the Atlantic. These are the most sought-after accommodations at the Chesapeake for those who are not on a budget — except for families who have been coming for years and have a favorite cottage.

Pelican Cove Resort

84457 Overseas Highway,
Mile Marker 84.5
P.O. Box 633
Islamorada, FL 33036
800-445-4690
305-664-4435

**A small, well-cared-for
waterfront resort**

General Manager: Cathy Salvatori. **Accommodations:** 63 rooms, suites, and efficiencies. **Rates:** Rooms $115–$195, efficiencies $135–$215, oceanfront 1-bedroom suites $195–$285; $20 extra person. **Minimum stay:** 7 nights on holidays and 2 on weekends. **Added:** 11.5% tax. **Children:** Under 16 free in room with parent. **Payment:** Major credit cards. **Smoking:** Allowed. **Open:** Year-round.

➤ **Guests can rent small boats at the resort and explore the warm Islamorada waters.**

The Pelican Cove is on two-lane Route 1, next door to the Theater of the Sea, a dolphin show and educational center. Because the crowds are at the shows during the day, the resort is surprisingly quiet except for occasional highway noise. Activity centers around the swimming pool and a Jacuzzi that overlook the Atlantic. Both are decorated with striking Mediterranean tile. The surrounding patio has light paving stones broken up by little islands of palm trees and other vegetation. The shake-roofed cabana by the pool sells drinks to quench your midday thirst.

Guests arriving by boat can tie up at the Pelican Cove dock. The beach is manmade, like so many in the Keys, where the Atlantic waves have been too gentle over the centuries to turn rock into sand. The white sand of this little beach is dotted with palm trees, and the rock sea wall along the water is picturesque.

The resort arranges backcountry fishing, and guests may also fish off the dock. Islamorada has the largest charter fleet in the

Keys for deep-sea and backcountry fishing. Expert scuba and snorkeling instruction is available at the John Pennekamp Coral Reef State Park, just down the road. The live coral reef is worth diving to see, even if you have never dived before. There is also a tennis court for guests only.

The resort's accommodations can house a family comfortably. All have either two queen-size beds or one queen-size bed and a pullout couch. Deluxe efficiencies have a bed, a sofa bed, and a kitchenette. For couples on a honeymoon, there are luxury one-bedroom suites with Jacuzzi. All the rooms are decorated in soft pastels with deep blue-gray carpeting, oak furniture, light walls, and prints of waterfowl on the walls. The kitchens in the efficiencies include a counter that wraps around to form a breakfast bar.

Railed balconies sweep around the three-story complex. The architecture is Old Florida, with crimped tin roofs and sliding shutters. The palm trees shading the balconies and the pelicans who come to roost on the pilings let you know you're in the subtropics.

Key Largo

Largo Lodge Motel

101740 Overseas Highway, Mile
Marker 101.5
Key Largo, FL 33037-2664
800-IN-THE-SUN
305-451-0424

The real Key Largo is represented here, on a budget

Owner/manager: Harriet Stokes. **Accommodations:** 1 room, 6 duplex apartments. **Rates:** $95–$115; extra person in room $10. **Minimum stay:** 2 nights. **Added:** 11.5% tax. **Payment:** MasterCard, Visa. **Children:** 16 and over permitted. **Smoking:** Allowed. **Open:** Year-round.

➤ **Snorkeling and scuba diving are available at nearby Key Largo National Marine Sanctuary, one of the best places for diving in the United States.**

The Largo Lodge is hidden away several hundred feet off busy Route 1, at the end of a long, narrow driveway canopied with tropical trees and plants. The honky-tonk of the highway is just a funky memory once guests arrive at this unpretentious motel. This is another world, with exotic ibis, ducks, lizards, and squirrels sharing the grounds. It feels almost as if guests are the intruders here.

Largo Lodge has a dock with space for guests' boats and a typical Florida Keys beach: small and manmade. A wide lawn runs directly to the beach, and this is where many of the animals wander, unconcerned with human onlookers. Under small shade trees near the dock are cushioned PVC lawn chairs and chaise longues, unfortunately soiled by some of the animals.

The lodge's accommodations are tucked away in its canopied "jungle." All the apartments are white brick, one-story 1950s duplexes. They have a living/dining room furnished with attractive bamboo furniture, kitchen, bedroom, bathroom with shower, and a screened porch. The appointments are "motel modern," and everything is clean and well cared for. The landscaping around the duplexes has been allowed to grow profusely but not out of control. Pots of colorful hibiscus and poinsettia on the doorsteps accent the green.

The Largo Lodge offers fishing off the dock (bring your own equipment), swimming, and beaching. The small beach is a boon in the Keys, where there are few sandy beaches with open-water swimming.

Marina Del Mar

527 Caribbean Drive
Mile Marker 100
P.O. Box 1050
Key Largo, FL 33037
305-451-4107
800-451-3483
marinadelmar@insn.com

A great place to tie up your boat or just hang your hat

General Manager: Scott A. Marr. **Accommodations:** 48 rooms, 28 suites. **Rates:** Rooms $89–$189, studios $139–$219, suites $139–$219, 2-bedroom villas $199-319, 3-bedroom villas $219–$349; packages available; weekday rates reduced. **Included:** Continental breakfast. **Minimum stay:** On some holidays. **Added:** 11.5% tax; surcharge for some holidays. **Payment:** Major credit cards, traveler's checks, personal checks with credit card. **Children:** Free in room with parent. **Smoking:** Allowed; 38 nonsmoking rooms available. **Open:** Year-round.

➤   **The one-bedroom suites are so well designed and roomy that a family of four can live quite comfortably for many days without feeling cramped.**

At least 40 percent of the Marina Del Mar's guests come for the scuba diving at nearby Key Largo National Marine Sanctuary. But they also come for the fantastic fishing and the resort's excellent deep-water marina. For those who don't own a boat, Marina Del Mar is a low-key, relaxing place with a lively restaurant and lounge.

The hotel is built on coral on the Atlantic side of Key Largo. Because of the reefs offshore, there is no heavy water action, and therefore no sandy beach. The lack of a beach and small waves disappoint some people, but the gentle waves make for great diving. If you're not interested in diving, it is enough to relax on a bench overlooking the marina and watch the boats and the people.

Marina Del Mar succeeds in looking unmanicured and pretty at the same time. Square wooden planters hold a profuse array of bougainvillea and green plants. The swimming pool and expanded sun deck have similar plantings. In the evening, the patio and the railings of the wooden ramps to the resort's restaurant are lit with tiny lights.

A few steps from the patio is Coconuts Restaurant and Lounge, a lively, though never wild, meeting place for fishermen, divers, boaters, and other locals. There's a handsome bar overlooking the boat slips, and clusters of small tables and chairs here and there. The sounds of nightly live entertainment in the lounge float into the adjoining restaurant, which serves lunch and dinner. Food is hearty, and the chef uses his imagination.

The restaurant, pool, and lounge are located well away from the accommodations, to allow guests a good night's rest. Rooms and apartments are in three main buildings of light green stucco, with railed verandas that overlook the water. Lodging types available are standard rooms, marina-view rooms, marina-view studios, one-bedroom suites, two-bedroom marina-view suites, and three-bedroom marina-view villas. All have cable TV, radios, refrigerators, and tiled bathrooms, most with whirlpool tubs.

The studios and two- and three-bedroom suites have completely equipped kitchens with full-size refrigerator, coffeemaker, toaster, dishes, and plenty of pots and pans. They also have a built-in entertainment center in the living room and a dining room set for four. Studio apartments have a couch in the living room and a Murphy bed. The two- and three-bedroom suites are more luxurious, with pretty sofas and love seats and two tiled bathrooms.

In all of the accommodations, an effort has been made to give a feeling of space and airiness. Rates in all the accommodations include daily maid service. There are coin-operated washers and dryers in the corridors leading to rooms.

The marina and the main buildings of Marina Del Mar are on the Atlantic side of Key Largo, but the resort now also has Bayside, a hotel just off Route 1. Standard rooms have two double beds and nice bathrooms. The king standard room has a king-size bed. Suites overlooking the water above the patio have tile floors, a kitchenette with a full stove and refrigerator, small bedroom with a king-size bed, and a dining and living room. Bayside includes first-floor wheelchair-accessible rooms, with a parking space right next to the room's entrance and a sidewalk and ramps up to the door.

Westin Beach Resort Key Largo

97000 S. Overseas Highway
Mile Marker 97
Key Largo, FL 33037
800-539-5274
305-852-5553
Fax: 305-852-5198

A choice getaway spot on Florida Bay

Accommodations: 200 rooms and suites. **Rates:** Rooms $119–$329, suites $289–$419; $15 extra person. **Minimum stay:** With some packages. **Added:** 11.5% tax. **Children:** Under 17 free in room with parent. **Payment:** Major credit cards. **Smoking:** Nonsmoking rooms available. **Open:** Year-round.

➤ **Parrot's Tapas Bar, on the top floor of the hotel, is the place for dancing and music. The gourmet restaurant here is Tree Tops, where the specialty is Angus beef and seafood. Café Key Largo is more casual. Its Sunday brunch, popular with Key Largo residents as well as hotel guests, is a must for anyone staying the weekend.**

Just a little over an hour from the Miami airport, the Westin Beach Resort Key Largo is an ideal hotel for executives who want to work in a businesslike atmosphere removed from the city. The location feels remote, though it's just a few minutes' walk from busy Route 1. With its romantic bayfront location and some convivial nearby watering holes, this is a great place for honeymooners as well as businesspeople, and the outdoor swimming pool and the nature trail make the resort nice for families, too. This is a place where you can leave your troubles behind and play hard or work hard without the hassles of civilization.

The resort has two lagoon-shaped pools on two levels connected by a grotto and waterfalls, one pool for children (and their parents) and another for adults. Beneath the waterfall is a massage table with a masseur at the ready. Bright bougainvillea and other tropical plants spill over the rocks around the grotto and patio. At the upper-level pool, Splashes serves kids and adults light meals and cool drinks.

Across the hotel grounds is the dock, with 21 slips and a man-made beach overlooking Florida Bay. It's too rocky for comfortable swimming until you get out pretty far, but the crescent-shaped beach is a nice place to stretch out in one of the hotel's chaises. Between the beach and the hotel is a boardwalk with wooden stairs to the hotel. These cross a dense hammock (an Indian word for a tropical hardwood forest), with many rare and unusual trees. This is a favorite place for nature walks for children and parents, though it is important to protect the trees by staying on the boardwalk. Just above the nature boardwalk is Tree Tops, a restaurant that commands romantic views of the bay and the leafy treetops in the forest, particularly at dusk and at night.

Accommodations include standard, superior, and deluxe rooms, and spacious Jacuzzi suites. Prices reflect square footage and views; some rooms overlook the bay, others the parking lot and pool. All accommodations are decorated in tropical colors and have light pine furniture and deep carpeting. All have balconies. The bathrooms are surprisingly large, with double sinks, a tile shower bath, and a makeup mirror above the sinks. Standard amenities include minibars, coffeemakers, cable TV, Nintendo, irons and boards, hair dryers, and safes.

The resort has two tennis courts with free tennis clinics on Saturdays. The Keys are a great place for fishing and boating, and the concierge can arrange for both. Snorkeling and scuba diving are nearby at the John Pennekamp State Park, with a storied coral reef that should not be missed. The resort is very proud of its Kids' Club, where seven days a week parents can drop kids off for games and activities supervised by a special staff. In the back of the hotel, the Westin has a recently renovated fitness center. A 14-mile bike and jogging path traverses the Key.

The Westin property itself, landscaped with brilliant flowers and lush greenery, is an enjoyable place to explore. Behind the check-in counter is an unusual coral rock mural. The shells and coral that formed naturally within the rock itself are accentuated with bright enameled tropical fish painted by the artist. Just off the lobby and lounge are the conference facilities, which include a ballroom and a spacious boardroom. French doors lead from the lounge to a patio that can be transformed into a reception area. The larger suites can double as hospitality suites and small meeting rooms for executive work sessions.

Care has been taken by those who operate the resort to provide a restful yet recreational environment. A sense of tropical tranquillity descends as one opens the French doors and steps onto the cool terra cotta tiles of the lobby.

Key West

The Artist House

534 Eaton Street
Key West, FL 33040
305-296-3977
800-582-7882
Fax: 305-296-3210
info@artisthousekeywest.com
www.artisthousekeywest.com

A lavender and white confection

Accommodations: 4 rooms, 3 suites, 7 villas. **Rates:** Rooms $119–$299, villas $139–$299; $10 extra person. **Included:** Continental breakfast. **Minimum stay:** During weekends, special events, holidays. **Added:** 11.5% tax. **Payment:** Major credit cards, traveler's checks, personal checks. **Children:** Mature teenagers with a parent. **Smoking:** Only on balconies, porches, patio. **Open:** Year-round.

➤ **A large Jacuzzi in the garden is surrounded by terra cotta pots of flowering and green plants. A dwarf palm tree shades an ornate iron garden bench on the brick patio. Later in the day, this is the perfect place to unwind after taking in the sights of Key West's Old Town.**

The Artist House is a dream for anyone who loves Victoriana: intricate scrolling on the brackets of the verandas, louvered shutters, etched-glass transoms above doors, a tin-roofed turret, and a black wrought-iron fence enclosing the azaleas in the little front garden. If an art historian — or a movie producer — were looking for the perfect Key West Victorian, this would be it. A recent sprucing up and redecoration have made this B&B into a jewel.

The Artist House is just one block from busy, touristy Duval Street, close enough to be near the excitement but far enough to provide respite from it. Built in 1890 and once owned by Key West painter Gene Otto, the house has been beautifully restored. Guest rooms have four-poster and brass beds, wood floors, wing chairs, new carpets, TVs, and lace curtains at the large double-hung windows. The furnishings are antiques or good reproductions. Appointments include oil paintings and Oriental vases and lamps.

One of the most popular rooms is the Turret Suite on the second floor. It has a sitting room bay, separate dressing room, and bathroom with a clawfoot tub. Floors are the original pine, with a blue and cream Oriental rug on the floor. Through narrow double doors opposite the four-poster king-size bed is a small, enclosed porch. Adjacent to the doors is a winding staircase that leads up to the third-floor turret. From this vantage point, one can look out over Key West.

Anne's Suite is one of the quietest rooms, with a private entrance and stairway as well as a hallway door that separates it from the house. The four-poster is king-size, and there's also a fireplace in this room. The bathroom is original, with a clawfoot tub, horizontal white-painted paneling, and blue and white tile border of festooned ribbons and flowers — very Victorian.

Though each guest room in the main house has individual character, all are in keeping with the Queen Anne Victorian architecture of the house, which includes carved mahogany banisters and crown moldings. But comfort is not sacrificed for authenticity. A telephone and television (hidden in an armoire or wall system) are found in every room. The private bathrooms were replumbed recently, and in most cases, newly tiled.

One block from the main house are the villas, beautifully decorated in island chic. They each have a kitchen with a stove, refrigerator, microwave, coffeemaker, toaster, and cookware and dishes.

All have queen-size beds, queen-size sofa beds, TVs and CD players, and either a private deck or porch. Other amenities are a swimming pool and reserved parking — not minor things in crowded Key West.

The Banyan Resort

323 Whitehead Street
Key West, FL 33040
800-225-0639
305-296-7786
Fax: 305-294-1107
banyan2@bellsouth.net
www.banyanresort.com

A Key West institution

Accommodations: 38 suites. **Rates:** Studios $150–$275, suites $200–$350; weekly rates available. **Minimum stay:** During some holidays, weekends, and special events. **Added:** 11.5% tax; $20 for extra person. **Payment:** Major credit cards. **Children:** Older children preferred. **Smoking:** Allowed. **Open:** Year-round.

➤ **There are a total of 200 varieties of tropical and subtropical flora at the Banyan, in flower beds connected by curving pathways to the swimming pools and the eight houses.**

You spend the first few minutes after arriving at the Banyan Resort gaping and gasping. Spectacular banyan trees dominate the gardens around the white Victorian mansions of the resort. Banyan trees are more like families of trees; over the course of their long lives, tendrils descend to the ground and form new trunks, forming a huge canopy of branches above and a vertical web of tree trunks below.

One of these huge trees stands in the middle of the front garden, greeting guests who enter the brick drive to the mansion whose front parlor serves as a reception area. Next door is another white Victorian house with a lacy veranda that is also part of the complex. These two houses back onto a garden where there are six more Victorian houses and another banyan tree many centuries old.

The resort comprises eight Victorian houses, five of which are on the National Register of Historic Places, and each with its own fascinating features: tin roofs, ornate porch brackets, lacy balustrades, fishtail shingles, leaded glass doors, large bay windows. They're all very pretty, very gracious. Inside are surprisingly fresh, contemporary furnishings and designer fabrics.

There's a great deal to choose from here: studios, one-bedroom suites, and two-bedroom suites with one or two baths. Some of the suites have loft bedrooms, and the spacious studios have Murphy beds. All suites have a furnished kitchen, modern private bathroom, TV, and telephone. The one-bedroom suites have a sleep sofa and can sleep a total of four people; the two-bedroom suites (which also have a dining area) have a sleep sofa and can accommodate six.

Guests who are light sleepers will probably want to be in one of the studios or suites toward the back of the resort, since Whitehead Street can be a little noisy with mopeds and cars roaring along. Many people like the upstairs rooms that have a romantic balcony and a bird's-eye view of the gardens. Other longtime guests think that the best rooms are those on the ground floor with their own little patio area shielded by a high wooden fence.

All accommodations have a private patio or a veranda overlooking the garden flourishing beneath the big banyan tree. It is this backyard area that makes the Banyan feel like a world apart. There are two pools and a Jacuzzi to soak in here, but it is really the shaded tropical garden that creates the mood of a hidden Caribbean retreat. And guests are allowed to use the pool and facilities after they have checked out. You can keep your bags in the little luggage sheds near the pools until you're ready to leave. Parking here is limited and there is a small charge, so many guests don't even bother renting a car.

Although all suite accommodations have a kitchen, many guests do little cooking. A Continental breakfast is served every morning except Sunday from the rustic-looking Tiki bar under the banyan tree. Coffee is complimentary, and croissants, bagels, yogurt, cereal, fruit, juice, and specialty coffees and teas are available at a reasonable charge. Lunch is served "noonish to sometime around five" and includes Caesar salad, grilled chicken, and hamburgers and hot dogs. Most guests take meals at quite a leisurely pace, lounging around the pool or on their private veranda or deck while they eat and drink. The Tiki bar also offers beer, wine, and iced tea.

Bicycles are for rent by the day, although the major Key West attractions and shopping are within walking distance — that is, if you can bear to leave this place.

Center Court

916 Center Street
Key West, FL 33040
800-797-8787
305-296-9292
Fax: 305-294-4104
kwinn@conch.net
www.centercourtkw.com

A small enclave of historic hideaways in Old Town

Innkeeper: Naomi Van Steelandt. **Accommodations:** 17. **Rates:** Rooms $88–$178, suites and cottages $128–$358; $15 extra person; weekly rates available. **Included:** Continental breakfast in accommodations without kitchens. **Minimum stay:** During weekends and special events. **Added:** 11.5% tax. **Payment:** Major credit cards; traveler's checks; personal checks. **Children:** Welcome in most accommodations. **Smoking:** Outside only. **Open:** Year-round.

➤　　**Center Court is not one place but several turn-of-the-century conch houses and cottages on little side streets, just minutes from Key West's main drag, Duval Street.**

Center Street, the location of the office where you check in as well as some of the lodgings, is a narrow dusty lane between Duval and Simonton. Sometimes the street sign for Center is down, so it's easy to drive past Simonton and then hit busy Duval and think, "Hey, where was Center?" Be sure to get specific directions from the innkeeper and owner, Naomi Van Steelandt, when you call for reservations.

Even then, you may wonder if you're in the right place as you turn onto Center Street from Truman Avenue and pass tiny, down-at-the-heels bungalows painted bargain paint colors, with tired wicker on the front porch. But look to the left after two or three houses and you will see the pretty lily pad logo that swings on a sign above the Center Court office. You are in the right place — most definitely. The mix of modest old houses and elegantly restored old houses is all part of the Key West atmosphere.

Naomi's properties, located in the quiet neighborhood of Center, Olivia, and Petronia Streets, have won awards for historic preservation and restoration. They are immaculate but unpretentious and offer some of the best value on the island. Several have a kitchen and are appropriate for a long stay and children. Number 16, the Family House, has a large eat-in kitchen, two bathrooms, one bedroom with a king-size bed, another with a double bed, and a living room with a queen-size sleeper sofa. This is the most expensive Center Court accommodation, but it's worth it if you're traveling with a family or friends.

The main guest house has rooms for under $100 in the summer and fall that are also very reasonable (for Key West) during the winter. These have private baths and queen-size beds and are decorated with charm and verve. Numbers 3 and 4 have private entrances. The rest of Naomi's offerings are suites and cottages. Porchside Paradise, on Petronia Street, is a trim little cottage with an efficient kitchen, pretty bedroom, private bath, and a living room with queen-size sleeper. It can accommodate up to four people. The Treetop Studio on Center Street is often reserved for honeymoon and anniversary couples. It has a galley kitchen, bedroom/sitting room, bath, and a private deck with a Jacuzzi and an outdoor shower — no one can see you when you're in the shower surround, but you can look out and get a treetop view of Key West. Room number 12, in The Eyebrow House, just around the corner from the Center Street accommodations, sleeps up to four and has a beautiful tile kitchen. The big bathroom has a large shower and bidet. All of the rooms are airy and have a feeling of spaciousness.

Many of the suites and efficiencies at Center Court have private verandas, garden courtyards, porches, and private decks — some outfitted with a spa. All are painted in fresh sherbet colors or soft neutrals and are decorated with local art. The porches and verandas have gingerbread detailing that looks freshly painted. Center Court's lily pad logo swings on signs on the front porch of each accommodation.

All guests are invited to enjoy the pleasant pool and patio area, which has a nice feeling of seclusion, surrounded as it is by Center Court guest houses, which screen off the street. Lawn chairs and chaises form a crescent along one side of the pool, while at the other side are headless Ma and Pa Tourist — whimsically painted plywood cutouts of typical tourists, complete with scuba gear and camera. In a niche near the pool is a large Jacuzzi, and adjacent to the Cistern House is another open-air niche that is a small exercise area. In the back of the main guest house, which fronts the pool, is a pleasant sitting room furnished with wicker. Guests staying in rooms and suites without kitchens (about 7 of the rooms) are treated to a complimentary breakfast in this open-air sitting room overlooking the pool. Naomi is a high-energy person who has put heart and soul into her business, and it shows everywhere.

Because Center Court has such a feeling of seclusion and quiet, quirky fun, it is surprising to venture out one morning and realize that the place is a half block from the noise and hoopla of Duval Street. Duval is a good place to spend the evening and, well, the early morning hours, but Center Court is a great place to retreat in the light of day and the gentleness of twilight.

Duval House

815 Duval Street
Key West, FL 33040
305-294-1666
800-22-DUVAL
Fax: 305-292-1701

> **One of Key West's most beautiful and restful guest houses**

Owner: Richard Kamradt. **Accommodations:** 28 rooms and suites. **Rates:** Rooms $110–$235, suites $140–$315; slightly higher during some holidays, lower for weekly stays; $20 for extra adult. **Included:** Continental breakfast buffet; on-site parking. **Minimum stay:** On holidays. **Added:** 11.5% tax. **Payment:** Major credit cards. **Children:** Under 12 discouraged. **Smoking:** Allowed. **Open:** Year-round.

➤ **Restoration was done expertly, always with an eye to comfort and making the most of the Key West breezes.**

Duval Street is essentially the main street of historic Old Town and sees a lot of action; late at night, it can get downright wild. But at Duval House, most guests are oblivious to the Key West rowdies, with whom Hemingway might have hung out at Sloppy Joe's. The Victorian houses that make up the inn are just far enough from Mallory Square and the center of the action that there is little to interfere with a guest's relaxation, night or day. At the same time, the charming historic district and the boutiques and galleries at the high end of Duval Street are at the doorstep, to say nothing of the gulf and the Atlantic at opposite ends of the street.

Guests are an adults-only mix of gays and straights who want to enjoy Key West in an oasislike setting. The feeling of seclusion is largely due to the lovely back garden the houses share, with a huge banyan tree dripping rust-colored roots from its limbs, a variety of palms, and many flowering plants.

Connecting the houses and garden is a pathway and an attractive wooden sun deck. The airy pool lounge overlooking the Spanish-tile swimming pool has a deep green awning that shades the French doors of its entrance. Inside are a comfortable couch and rockers, a communal kitchen, a television, and a small library. A Continental breakfast buffet is laid out here every morning.

The first two houses made into guest quarters were originally tenements for cigar makers in the 1800s. They were vacant and neglected when the previous owners bought them in the early 1980s. Now, with pale salmon clapboard siding, white trim, and dark green wooden shutters, the houses are charming examples of Key West Victoriana. The rooms have lots of windows, and most open onto verandas with white railings and gingerbread detailing. Although all the rooms are air-conditioned, they don't need to be if the windows are open and the paddle fan is whirring overhead.

Duval House now has a number of suites that have private patios and kitchens. Furnishings in all the guest rooms are an interesting mix of West Indies and turn-of-the-century style. The armoires are great fun, with inlaid burled woods and odd curves and moldings. Beds are firm and comfortable, and the bright tropical bedspreads contrast well with the delicate wall colors. Some rooms have high ceilings with intricate crown moldings or stenciling, and all have immaculate baths. Special touches like decorative antiques and small stone carvings placed on a shelf show how much thought has gone into creating the ambience of each room.

For anyone who wants to sample the glories — and the excesses — of Key West, Duval Street is the place to be. But the Duval House has more to offer than that. The historic authenticity of these homes, their charming verandas, and the spectacular jungle garden they overlook are the features best loved by the guests who come back year after year.

Eden House

1015 Fleming Street
Key West, FL 33040
800-533-KEYS
305-296-6868
Fax 305-294-1221

**Varied accommodations
with a talented owner**

Owner: Mike Eden. **Accommodations:** 40 rooms and suites. **Rates:** Rooms with shared baths $65–$85; rooms with semi-private baths $80–$105; rooms with private baths $85–$145; luxury rooms and suites $100–$275; seventh day free in off-season. **Included:** Complimentary happy hour daily; on-site parking. **Minimum stay:** With packages. **Added:** 11.5% tax. **Payment:** Deposit by check only; MasterCard and Visa at check-in. **Children:** Welcome at no additional charge. **Smoking:** Outside only. **Open:** Year-round.

➤ **For those who would rather ride than walk when exploring Key West, Eden House has bicycles for rent.**

The Eden House is another one of those Florida institutions where the out-of-town visitor, with reservations and the glowing reports of friends, drives up and thinks, "Oh, no, this can't be right." The place almost looks like a converted gas station from the 1920s. It sits squarely facing Fleming Street with just a perfunctory sidewalk in front. Its architectural style could maybe be called 1920s art deco "bungalow" Mediterranean, with traces of Aztec. The stucco exterior is painted white, with squarish pillars on the front porch, and a timbered, Spanish-style veranda above. At the top of the hotel is a ziggurat cutout design that looks like something that might surmount a Mexican restaurant. On the front porch are painted metal rockers that have been there since the 1930s, along with some potted and hanging plants, and bicycles resting against the front porch pillars. Everything looks fresh and clean, so there's reason to be encouraged.

Inside are more reasons: a pleasant, cool-looking lobby furnished in white wicker with touches of white lattice and Victoriana gingerbread at the registration desk. A staff person, who seems laid-back but at the same time attentive, hands you a chilled drink while you're registering. You begin to notice whimsical touches in the lobby: funky artwork or tiny claymation figures resting on the top of the communal big-screen TV. Free condoms are in a basket near the front desk. Free books are available to take back to your room and, at the end of your stay, if there's one you're still reading, you can take it with you. The only requirement is that you mail it back.

On the left side of the lobby is a door to the pool patio and garden in back where even the most jaded traveler can get excited. The garden patio is a wonderful space. Three Victorian houses that house luxury accommodations form an enclave with the original art deco hotel. Many guest houses in Key West are composed of several individual houses that back up onto each other, forming a patio and pool area. But the one at the Eden House is especially impressive. Quirky little stairs and bridges crisscross between the houses and go up and down between floors. A small wooden bridge curves over a goldfish pond surrounded by greenery and a slender tree festooned with Spanish moss. A metal gate leading to one area of the Eden House is a beautifully hand-wrought original design. There are lots of unnecessary — sometimes even slightly loopy — but purely wonderful details like this at Eden House. Owner Mike Eden's sense of play and artistry is evident everywhere.

At the same time, the Eden House is a well-run hotel. The patio and boardwalks between the various buildings are well swept and always in good repair. The houses that back onto the pool patio were expertly restored and are largely responsible for the hotel's historic preservation awards. The turn-of-the-century Victorian facing Fleming Street is particularly pretty, with teal clapboards and gingerbread details. All four houses have porches or verandas, most of them overlooking the garden patio and pool. Full meals and snacks are available at the café around the corner.

The three Victorian houses have deluxe rooms and suites with features like queen-size beds, lofts, kitchenettes, oversize showers, and private terraces. The honeymoon suite has an oak spiral staircase that leads to a sleeping loft and balcony above the pool and garden. Accommodations include a roomy apartment that Mike and his growing family lived in for several years.

The original hotel was once a budget hostelry that attracted bohemian residents and visitors to Key West. When Mike bought the place in 1975, he slowly repaired and repainted the place, offering bargain rates to artists and low-budget travelers who would put up with the sawdust and wet paint. As the place became more popular, Mike could have gutted the interior of the original art deco building and converted the old rooms into luxury accommodations. Fortunately for longtime guests and for anyone who is appalled by present Key West room rates, he chose not to do this. As a result, it is still possible to get a basic but attractive room here, with twins or a double bed, a sink in the corner, and a shower and toilet down the hall.

These 10 guest rooms are referred to as "European" and do, in fact, attract a good many Continental travelers who can't understand our insistence on private baths. They're also popular with American students. They are like a miniature conch house in that they have a veranda entrance overlooking the pool and another entrance that opens out into the main hallway. Built in 1924, they have no closets, so guests store things underneath the beds. Similar budget accommodations available are guest rooms that share baths between two rooms. These are particularly good for families and friends who want connecting rooms.

Recent additions to Eden House are a 40-by-15-foot sundeck built above the guest house's parking lot, a poolside gift shop, and a hammock area with not one but several padded hammocks, as well as hammock swings. Adjacent to this area is a luxury suite that is particularly nice, #503. It includes a sleeping loft with a queen-size bed where you sleep beneath a beautiful stained glass window. The smallness of the bathroom is made up for by the large corner shower. The sitting area has a small kitchen with a sink and apartment-size fridge, so it is possible to prepare simple meals and snacks here.

The main activity at the Eden House is relaxing and languorously swimming in the lovely pool when the mood strikes. But the hotel is walking distance from Old Town and the nightlife of Key West.

The Gardens Hotel

526 Angela Street
Key West, FL 33040
305-294-2661; 800-526-2664
Fax: 305-292-1007

> **An elegant haven in zany Key West**

Manager: Jody Smith. **Accommodations:** 14 rooms, 2 suites, 1 cottage/condo. **Rates:** $155–$335 rooms (double occupancy); $385–$675 suites; $295–$465 cottage. No extra person allowed in room. **Included:** Continental breakfast. **Minimum stay:** 2 nights on weekends, longer during special events. **Added:** 11.5% tax. **Payment:** Visa, MasterCard, American Express, traveler's checks, personal checks. **Children:** 12 years and older allowed. **Smoking:** Allowed on porch or designated area outside. **Open:** Year-round.

➤ **The Gardens Hotel provides a pleasant escape from the brassiness and noise of Mallory Square and Duval Street.**

Situated on the quiet corner of Simonton and Angela Street, The Gardens Hotel and its meandering gardens are surrounded by a white stucco wall with a wrought-iron gate at the entrance. The main house faces Angela Street, its picture-perfect front porch furnished in white wicker with green and white cushions. The white clapboards and dark green shutters look as if they must be scrubbed every day. Inside the main house are well-proportioned rooms that almost look more New England than Key West. The genteel sitting room in the main house, open to all guests, has a fireplace, reading lamps, and comfortable sofas. French doors lead out to brick walkways and a patio and swimming pool. Once the estate of one of Key West's first families, the grounds comprise a quarter of a city block — a great deal of land in a place like Key West where old conch houses often have little more than 15 inches between them. The bricks that pave the garden walkways are at least a century old, once serving as ballast for ships that ran between England, and North and South America. The gardens are very lush with palms, black bamboo, banana trees, and a variety of colorful flowers.

Here and there, at a bend in the brick path, are chairs with a table for companionable sitting, a fountain, or a small pool that was once a cistern. The gardens are also accented with large earthenware jugs called Tinajones. These were imported from Cuba by the previous owners in 1950, but their manufacture dates to the late 1700s, and they are quite rare today.

The brick walkways join the five buildings that comprise The Gardens Hotel, two of which are new, but have been constructed to look very much like the original structures, with tin roofs and white balustraded verandas. Guest rooms are in these two buildings and the original main house, carriage house, and Eyebrow Cottage. The interiors of the rooms are a combination of Island and New England decor, with coordinating designer fabrics, soft wall colors, and polished wooden floors. The vibrant paintings are by New Zealand Impressionist painter Peter Williams. Rooms open out onto verandas, decks, porches, or brick walkways, so there is always of a sense of garden lushness just outside.

Those who plan to do a great deal of walking in Key West might want to reserve the hotel's Master Suite, which has a spectacular bath, outfitted with a sauna, steam shower, and large Jacuzzi bathtub for soaking weary bones. All of the bathrooms at the Gardens are of marble and have luxury amenities, and plush cotton robes hang behind the louvered closet doors.

The Eyebrow Cottage located in a quiet corner of the garden has cathedral ceilings and charm — especially nice for couples who want seclusion. The guest rooms in the main house have the advantage of being just upstairs from the sitting room and the gazebo-like breakfast room. All rooms have either a queen- or king-size bed, television, telephone, coffeemaker, and well-stocked minibar.

Rates include a delicious tropical breakfast of fruit, yogurt, cereals, cheeses, breads, and fresh croissants. Guests can enjoy this at one of the garden tables outside, at the pool bar, on the porch, or in the beautiful turreted breakfast room. Guests are friendly, but couples are usually here to enjoy each other in relative seclusion, rather than to have a homey bed-and-breakfast-type experience with other guests. Staff demeanor ranges from cordial to cold, but most guests focus only on relaxing and enjoying each other, rather than staff or other clientele.

The Gardens Hotel is one of the most expensive places to stay in Key West, with suites in the Eyebrow Cottage and carriage house especially expensive during high season. However, "historic" and "garden" rooms are about the same as comparable rooms at the Hilton and Hyatt. The elegance and seclusion of this island enclave are worth it for many who want a romantic Key West hideaway.

Heron House

512 Simonton
Key West, FL 33040
305-294-9227
888-265-2399
Fax: 305-294-5692
www.heronhouse.com

> **A labor of love and a haven
> of rest and beauty**

Owners: Fred Geibelt and Robert Framarin. **Accommodations:** 21 rooms.
Rates: Rooms $119–$349; $25 for extra person in room. **Included:** Expanded
Continental breakfast buffet. **Minimum stay:** Over some holidays. **Added:**
11.5% tax. **Payment:** Major credit cards. **Children:** Under 15 not permitted.
Smoking: Limited to outside decks. **Open:** Year-round.

➤ **Terra-cotta pots of fig trees are placed around the swimming pool
near well-tended beds of bougainvillea, jasmine, and bird-of-paradise.
Orchids and ferns drape down from little wire planters attached to palm
trunks.**

In a town where guest house owners pride themselves on their
gardens, innkeeper Fred Geibelt has one of the loveliest. The entrance to the Heron House is through a pair of large cedar gates set
in a coral stone wall. Inside are brick patios and a garden shaded
with mango and avocado trees and palms.

Fred has also created special accommodations. Three old homes
make up Heron House, their backs or sides opening onto the garden and pool deck. The newest rooms are the best, with walls of
beveled wood, granite vanities, and old-fashioned verandas. The
new rooms upstairs have handcrafted stained glass transoms above
each door. Some older accommodations have walls of the original
pine. Recent changes include wet bars in some of the rooms and
the replacement of queen-size with king-size beds . All guest rooms
have color TVs, robes, telephones, irons and ironing boards, and
safes.

Though some rooms are larger and more spectacular than others,
all are furnished with West Indian–style wicker. Irma Quigley's
watercolors decorate the walls, and thin venetian blinds at the
windows filter the subtropical light. Bathrooms are constantly being upgraded by Fred, who loves to work around the place. Some
attractive recent additions are a state-of-the-art orchid house, a

marble inlaid floor in the office, and a sun deck, built by Fred's talented partner, Robert Framarin.

In the morning, Fred serves an informal, do-it-yourself Continental breakfast under a breezeway. A table near the pool is set with a pitcher of fruit juice, a basket of homemade muffins and other goodies, a toaster, bread, English muffins, butter and jam, tea and coffee. Guests usually eat on chairs and chaises around the pool or in the cool breezeway. Heron House's guests tend to be well-traveled, congenial, and dedicated to the B&B experience, as are the excellent staff.

The swimming pool at Heron House is small, but the deck is so attractive it hardly matters. Beside the pool are oversize coral planters that Fred put in himself along with intricately patterned brick paving. At the bottom of the pool is a mosaic of a blue heron created by Robert. Unusual features like this reflect the mood of this exceptional guest house.

Hyatt Key West

601 Front Street
Key West, FL 33040
305-296-9900
800-55-HYATT
Fax: 305-292-1038

| **A breezy, tropical respite** |

General manager: Chris Aldieri. **Accommodations:** 120 rooms, 2 suites, 8 king salons. **Rates:** Rooms $195–$385, suites $300–$665. **Minimum stay:** With packages. **Added:** 11.5% tax. **Payment:** Major credit cards. **Children:** Under 18 free in room with parent. **Smoking:** Nonsmoking rooms available. **Open:** Year-round.

➤ **The *Floridays* yacht operates from the Hyatt's marina. The hotel also has Yamaha wave-runners for rent and can arrange for snorkeling, scuba diving, and fishing trips.**

The turquoise waters of the Gulf of Mexico provide the setting for one of Key West's most refreshing hotels, the Hyatt Key West. The Hyatt is built in Old Florida style with tin roofs, smooth peach stucco exteriors, and white-railed verandas. Guests enter a small lobby, checking in at a cherry registration counter. A full-time concierge is ready to arrange any Key West activity a guest can conjure up. Many guests simply want to rest between excursions and enjoy the tropical breeze that blows across this pretty corner of Old Town. Just off the lobby, a fishpond and gentle waterfall set the mood for relaxation, while a mosaic wall mural of Key West echoes the vibrancy of the town. The mural and fishpond lead to the Hyatt's airy patio and pool.

Wooden decks and walkways lead guests to the Hyatt's restaurants and bars and the pier and marina on the gulf. Large clay pots of tropical plants and flowers and groupings of palms and native trees accent the patio and decks. All the lawn furniture is sparkling white, kept so by a vigilant maintenance staff. The Hyatt's swimming pool is the centerpiece of the patio, with the Hyatt restaurant and the pier and beach beyond. A gazebo overlooks the Jacuzzi and the pool.

The beach is small and manmade but well maintained, rimmed by large chunks of rough coral called key stone. A 65-foot yacht, *Floridays*, is docked here and can be rented by guests for sailing, snorkeling, or romantic evening cruises.

One of the nicest things about the pier and dock is the deck that leads to them, where there's plenty of room for sunning on chaises. It's pleasant to hear the marina traffic but to be lazily removed from it. Deck service from Scuttles, the poolside bar and grill, makes it unnecessary to get up even for lunch or drinks.

When you do summon the energy to get up, there are a couple of choices for light lunches, drinks, and dinner. Scuttles, which closes at sunset, has an unusual tiled bar and overlooks the water. Serving three meals a day, Nicola's is the resort's seafood restaurant, located downstairs from Nick's Grill. Both restaurants are in a clapboard building with an Old Florida–style tin roof that's reminiscent of turn-of-the-century Key West, and the eateries feature indoor and outdoor dining overlooking a slice of the Gulf, ideal for leisurely meals. In the evenings, many guests start out at Nick's with drinks on the deck above the gulf and watch the sunset.

Accommodations at the Hyatt are in four-floor buildings that include a range of prices, sizes, beds, and views. The Hyatt has five wheelchair-accessible rooms with roll-in showers, and 71 percent of the rooms are nonsmoking. As more families visiting Key West have chosen to stay at the Hyatt, the hotel has increased the number of rooms with two double beds. Most rooms have a view of either the Gulf of Mexico or the pool courtyard. Some views are better than others, and the Hyatt usually compensates for a mediocre view with more space. If you are traveling with children, ask about these larger standard rooms. Also, the Hyatt will usually make an effort to upgrade your room in the low season whenever possible.

The rooms and suites have very pretty decor: tropical prints and a generous use of a sea green in upholstery. Furniture is of light oak or wicker, and some of the floor lamps and entryway tables are of bleached coral stone. The tiled bathrooms have oversize tubs, with hair dryer, makeup mirror, and complimentary toiletries. Other amenities are irons, safes, and minibars. Suites have double sinks and a little more room in the bathroom.

All the rooms have large balconies with a small table and two chairs; the suites have double balconies furnished with chaises and a table and chairs. The higher-priced suites on the top floors have a large sitting room with tile floors and an area rug, a desk and two phones, and sliding glass doors out to the large balcony. Views of the gulf and the small islands beyond the marina will take your breath away, especially at sunset.

The Hyatt offers a lot more for visitors of all ages. Bicycles and mopeds are available for rent, and water sports at the Hyatt marina include deep-sea fishing, sailing, diving, and wave-runners. Excursions can be arranged through the Hyatt's helpful concierge. All of the activities and shopping in Key West's Old Town are within easy walking distance.

Throughout the year, the Hyatt staff organize a number of conferences and executive retreats. The resort has meeting and banquet facilities, with a 448-square-foot executive boardroom overlooking the gulf and a larger meeting facility that can accommodate up to 60 people. The clientele at the Hyatt Key West is varied, with many businesspeople, vacationing couples, and families. The clientele is also international, with many visitors from the United Kingdom, Canada, Germany, and South America.

The Hyatt offers more privacy than most hotels in Key West, many of which are open to outsiders. Except for the businesspeople who come to Nicola's for power lunches, the Hyatt is here for its guests alone.

Island City House

411 Williams Street
Key West, FL 33040
305-294-5702
800-634-8230
Fax: 305-294-1289
www.islandcityhouse.com

**Three historic houses
clustered around a tropical
garden**

Innkeepers: Stanley and Janet Corneal. **Accommodations:** 24 suites. **Rates:**
Studios $115–$175, 1-bedroom suites $135–$240, 2-bedroom suites $185–$315;
packages available. **Included:** Continental breakfast. **Minimum stay:** 2–6
nights during some holidays and special events. **Added:** 11.5% tax; $20 for
extra person in room, no charge for crib. **Payment:** Discover, Carte Blanche,
American Express, MasterCard, Visa. **Children:** Under 12 free in room with
parent. **Smoking:** Outside only. **Open:** Year-round.

➤   **The tropical garden is shaded by large trees, while the deck that surrounds the Jacuzzi and pool is sunny. Brick pathways connect the three
houses and the little office cottage. Under one tree is a brick patio with a
covered breakfast bar, where fruit and danish pastries are served each
morning.**

The main house of this B&B is a tall, narrow Victorian trimmed
with gingerbread and graced with breezy verandas on all three
floors. Its top floor, capped with a pediment and four improbable-
looking wedding cake spires, was added in 1912. The original
owner, Samuel Lowe, heard that Flagler's railroad was coming and
added the third floor to turn his family home into a hotel. The
Lowes also owned an intriguing place called the Arch House on
Eaton Street. Eaton is perpendicular to Williams, so the rear of the
Arch House property joins the back yard of the Williams Street
House. The Arch House is like a double house, with an ornate gingerbread archway between the two buildings through which a
horse and carriage could drive to reach the cigar factory behind. It
is the only extant carriage house on the island. The third house
that makes up Island City House is a replica of a cigar house that
stood on the same spot.

Those who call early in the season or come during off-season get
their choice of one- and two-bedroom suites. The rooms in the
Island City House are Victorian, with wonderful dark antiques,
lace and rose bedspreads, old-fashioned curtains, and memorabilia.

The spindled verandas onto which the rooms open are charming. The Arch House has a Caribbean atmosphere and is decorated in rattan and wicker and bright colors.

The Cigar House was built in the 1980s by the previous owners, who were preservationists with a keen interest in Key West history. This replica of the Alfonso Cigar Factory is constructed of natural cypress, with louvered doors and hardwood floors. All the suites have a spacious sitting area, separate bedroom, full kitchen, and roomy bath. The decor is contemporary, with bright tropical colors. The first-floor suites open onto the pool and sun deck, while those on the second and third floors have a balcony overlooking the pool and Jacuzzi.

The Island City House is the sort of place where you can feel at home right away. Unlike some guest houses in Key West that cater only to adults and have a large gay clientele, here there are guests of all ages and lifestyles, including many families.

Key West Hilton Resort & Marina

245 Front Street
Key West 33040
800-221-2424
305-294-4000
Fax: 305-294-4086

A busy marina resort in Old Town

Managers: Steve Robbins and Rick Konsavage. **Accommodations:** 151 rooms, 27 suites, 37 cottages. **Rates:** Rooms $169–$325 suites $250–$650, cottages $400–$1,295; extra adult in room $20 (no extra charge in cottages). **Included:** Continental breakfast in cottages. **Minimum stay:** 1–3 nights. **Added:** 11.5% tax. **Payment:** Major credit cards, traveler's checks. **Children:** Allowed, under 18 free in room with parent. **Smoking:** On porch and designated area outside; some rooms accommodate smoking; all cottages nonsmoking. **Open:** Year-round.

➤ **Located on Front Street near Mallory Square and Duval Street and overlooking a busy waterfront scene, the Hilton is no shrinking tropical violet.**

The Key West Hilton Resort is right in the middle of it all. There is something for everyone here and everyone is welcome. Brick and cement walkways lead up from the street along the side of the hotel to the boardwalk-like atmosphere of the marina behind the hotel. Docked here are cruise ships, a casino ship, fishing and deep-sea diving boats, motor boats, catamarans, and private yachts. Along the sides and back of the Hilton are boutiques and shops, and there's even an ice cream parlor. On the broad brick expanse between shops and water are benches and iron lampposts — a romantic spot in the evening.

The excursion boats and other attractions here are a scene of activity day and night. The Hilton also has 7,000 square feet of meeting space and conference services for business groups. But there is still time to enjoy the languidness that Key West is famous for. The Gulf of Mexico is an exquisite turquoise blue here, and one of the Hilton's major draws is the complimentary shuttle that crosses the Gulf to Sunset Key, a tiny island just beyond the marina where Hilton guests enjoy a private beach. Because the marina can sometimes seem a bit hectic, it's nice to go to Sunset Key for a few hours. It's also home to the Hilton's best accommodations — the Sunset Key Guest Cottages, which have two to three bedrooms and fully equipped kitchens. The cottages feature a living and dining area with TV, VCR, and CD player. Other amenities on Sunset Key are the CD, video, board game, and literary lending library; a grocery shopping service; a deli market; a lagoon-style pool and whirlpool; tennis courts; and a romantic café on the water.

The architecture of the hotel is island- or Caribbean-style, with tin roofs, gables, and white-railed balconies and verandas. Key West bans high-rise hotels, so the Hilton is no more than four floors. Hilton's best rooms in the main hotel also look out over the beautiful turquoise water. If you can afford a room or suite with a Gulf view, do so, but be sure to request a full view when making reservations: occasionally a guest room deemed "water view" has only a partial side view. Balconies are small yet adequate for two people to relax on. Some of the higher-priced suites have two balconies. All the rooms and baths have the usual Hilton amenities and attractive tropical furnishings.

The Hilton's restaurant continues the island theme with outdoor dining, lending an air of a sidewalk café, overlooking the Gulf. There is also indoor dining on cool and breezy nights in the off-season or when the al fresco seating is at capacity in-season. At the hotel's pool and at the beach on Sunset Key, there is also casual food and bar service. Hilton's shops and attractive restaurants are open to the public. The Hilton's rooftop cocktail lounge has live music at night and is a popular gathering place earlier in the evening — for the famous Key West sunset. This is a lively place to view it.

La Mer Hotel and Dewey House

504 and 506 South Street
Key West, FL 33040
305-296-5611
Reservations:
Old Town Resorts
1319 Duval Street
Key West, FL 33040
305-296-5611
800-354-4455
Group sales and information:
305-296-6577
Fax: 305-294-8272

> **The Victorian charm of Key West with the amenities of a resort motel**

Accommodations: 19 rooms. **Rates:** $130–$315. **Included:** Continental breakfast and afternoon tea. **Minimum stay:** 3-5 nights during holidays and winter. **Added:** 11.5% tax. **Payment:** Major credit cards. **Children:** Under 18 not permitted. **Smoking:** Allowed. **Open:** Year-round.

➤ **The front and side gardens are extremely pretty, boasting a variety of flowering and green plants as well as mature trees. The back porch of La Mer looks out at the palm trees of South Beach — a stretch of sand with wave-smoothed rocks, the calm ocean beyond.**

La Mer and the Dewey House are owned by Key West's Old Town Resorts. The other two resorts are the Southernmost Motel in the USA and the South Beach Oceanfront Motel. La Mer, the Dewey House, and the South Beach Motel both front South Street, with the Atlantic and tiny South Beach in back. The Southernmost Motel is across the street, straddling South and United streets, which run perpendicular to busy, bizarre Duval Street. Actually, Duval Street becomes relatively sedate here, making this location ideal — close enough to the Key West action for younger guests and quiet enough for older guests.

La Mer was built at the turn of the century and is a wonderful example of Key West conch house architecture, with a gabled tin roof, white clapboards with gray trim, double-hung windows, and spindle balusters on the gingerbread veranda. Rooms open out onto balconies upstairs and verandas and wooden decks downstairs. There is a low white wall at the front of the house and lattice fences. A stone walkway joins La Mer to the Dewey, its Victorian next-door neighbor, which is also a charmer.

All the Old Town Resorts have color cable TV and modern private baths and share swimming pools and other recreational facilities. For swimming, guests can choose the Atlantic, just out the back door, one of the swimming pools at the Southernmost Motel, or the South Beach Motel pool across the parking lot. The Southernmost Motel offers water-sports rentals and mopeds, and the South Beach Motel has its own dive shop.

Rooms vary in size and shape, as one would expect in old Victorians, but they share the same decor and modern amenities. Entrance to some of the rooms is from the pretty verandas, which have views of the side garden or water, usually both. The rooms are immaculate, with traditional touches like paneled doors, bay windows, paddle fans on the high ceilings, and wood venetian blinds.

Among the rooms, spacious #407 is particularly nice, with a queen-size bed and pullout sofa. Windows look out over treetops to the street and the pretty fountain and front garden. At one end of the room is a kitchenette with a refrigerator and small stove, hardwood cabinets, and a tiled breakfast bar. The efficient room has a small sitting area so that a family won't feel too cramped.

Continental breakfast is served each morning. Guests can take their pastries and coffee up to their room, or — the preference for most — have breakfast on their private deck, looking out at the palm trees and the water. For brunch and dinner, visitors enjoy Louie's Backyard on Waddell Avenue and Antonia's at 615 Duval Street.

La Pensione

809 Truman Avenue
Key West, FL 33040
800-893-1193
305-292-9923
Fax: 305-296-6509
lapensione@aol.com

**An inn that offers
no-nonsense hospitality**

Innkeeper: Carl Lopez-Porter. **Accommodations:** 9 rooms. **Rates:** $98–$168; holiday and weekend rates slightly higher; AAA and other discounts. **Included:** Expanded Continental breakfast. **Minimum stay:** 2 nights on weekends, 3 nights on holidays. **Added:** 11.5% tax. **Payment:** Visa, MasterCard, Discover, personal checks with 10-day advance. **Children:** No children. **Smoking:** Allowed; preferred outside. **Open:** Year-round.

➤ **The Italian word *pensione* means a room in a private home, and there is certainly that feeling of hominess in this B&B.**

La Pensione is owned by a family from Dallas, Texas, whose daughter, Monica Wiemer, lives in Key West. It was originally operated by two veteran Key West innkeepers, Vince Cerrito and Joe Rimkus, who owned another B&B in Key West before buying this 19th-century clapboard structure. They therefore knew how to preserve the physical beauty of an old house and at the same time provide the modern amenities that vacationers want. Monica, her partner Jane Rodriguez, and Carl are carrying on the traditions of preservation and no-nonsense hospitality that Vince and Joe began at La Pensione.

A strict preservationist, knowing that the house dates back to the late 1800s, might express surprise that the old pine floors aren't exposed in the bedrooms or that there aren't clawfoot tubs in all the baths. However, in their experience, Vince and Joe learned that wooden floors are noisy floors and that old tubs strung up with gerrymandered showerheads can lose their charm quickly. Consequently they endeavored to preserve important interior and exterior features of the house while providing modern amenities like new bathrooms and a pool area that includes a modern bathroom and a Coke machine hidden away.

The guest rooms are more spacious than many rooms in historic guest houses in Key West, and they are immaculate. Each room is furnished in Ethan Allen furniture (no sticky antique bureau drawers here) and has a firm king-size bed. The designer fabric spreads often match upholstered loveseats that are set in a corner or before a bank of windows. Rooms have attractive transoms above the doors in clear and green-stained glass. New plush carpeting is on the floor and lace curtains at the windows. The tile bathrooms have new sinks and fixtures in traditional styles that nicely blend appropriate Victorian design with modern dependability.

Room number 7 on the second floor is perhaps La Pensione's best accommodation. It has a grayish-teal color scheme, an interesting pine wall behind the king-size bed, and a dressing area, which makes it a bit larger than the average room. A sofa stands before the three windows of number 7, which is often called La Pensione's Turret Room. The bathroom has a pedestal sink and a shower. Number 9 has a spindle bed, pine furniture, and two pairs of doors that lead out to the second floor veranda, which 7 and 8 also share.

On the first floor is La Pensione's wheelchair-accessible guest room, which has an outside entrance via a ramp.

Also downstairs is a front parlor that serves as a reception area and, behind that, a small dining room. Breakfast can be taken here or out on one of the verandas. The Wiemers have greatly expanded the standard La Pensione breakfast so that it is now a small feast. The innkeeper usually serves a main dish like quiche or raspberry waffles, fresh tropical fruit, homemade muffins and breads, orange juice, coffee, tea, and decaf. Food is served buffet-style on the counter of the kitchenette where Carl cooks up the French toast to order. The fragrances waft up the hallway from the kitchen — no need for a wake-up call. In the dining room there are books for guests to borrow and photo albums of old Key West to look through.

La Pensione, built in 1891, is certainly a part of the history of Old Town. The house is on Truman Avenue, a fairly busy street since it's the main route of arrival for tourists but also a great location for getting to know Key West on foot. The 100th anniversary of the house in 1991 was also the year that the previous innkeepers, Joe and Vince, completed its restoration. They preserved the fluted moldings around the windows and repaired the newel post at the foot of the front stairway, which was composed of more than 200 pieces of wood. They painted the clapboards of the exterior a deep yellow. The trim and the veranda banisters are white and the louvered shutters green, a typical Victorian color scheme. A modern amenity is the swimming pool with patio on the east side of the house, enclosed by a wooden fence for privacy.

The Marquesa Hotel

600 Fleming Street
Key West, FL 33040
800-869-4631
305-292-1919
Fax: 305-294-2121

A Key West reprobate that's been polished into a beautiful gem

Accommodations: 27 rooms and suites. **Rates:** Rooms $150–$250, junior suites $190–$295. **Minimum stay:** During holidays. **Added:** 11.5% tax; $15 for extra person. **Payment:** Major credit cards. **Children:** Under 16 discouraged. **Smoking:** Allowed. **Open:** Year-round.

➤ **Each room has something special: a dhurrie rug in soft pastels, original pine walls, a pillowed window seat, an antique secretary, a private veranda on the street, or an extra-large deck overlooking the pool. Flowers are in every room, and turndown service includes Godiva chocolates. A newspaper is at the door of each room in the morning.**

On the wall near the front parlor of the Marquesa Hotel is a framed collage of before-and-after pictures. Anyone visiting the Marquesa is impressed by its restful charm, and seeing these photos, one can appreciate how far the old rooming house has come. More than $2 million was spent on the original restoration by the owners, Richard Manley and Erik DeBoer. For their work on the Marquesa, Manley and DeBoer were presented with the Master Craftsmanship Award of the Historic Florida Keys Preservation Board. Since then, additional late-nineteenth-century houses have been restored and added to the Marquesa's mix of Victoriana and chicness.

When this elegant yet laid-back hotel was a rooming house, called the Q-Rooms, it was frequented by rowdy drunks. Now it attracts a quiet crowd who come here to relax in luxury and to enjoy the creative atmosphere of Key West. The Marquesa is beautifully run, offering 24-hour service, as one would expect at a fine city hotel. A concierge is always on hand to make suggestions for daytime excursions in Key West and give excellent advice about restaurants and entertainment.

The staff are polite and professional, knowledgeable about the Key West scene without succumbing — or allowing unwary guests to succumb — to its flashier trendy side. They will do everything possible to save guests from a wasted morning or a bad meal. The staff is one of the many assets that puts the Marquesa in a class by itself in the growing guest house market of Key West's Old Town.

The Marquesa is at the corner of Simonton and Fleming streets (just one street over from famous Duval), four blocks from the gulf, and 11 blocks from the Atlantic. The hotel comprises three fine old clapboard homes, two facing Simonton and one facing Fleming, as well as two additions. Listed on the National Register of Historic Places, the 19th-century buildings were meticulously restored after a shoddy history as boarding houses and an auto dealership. Three of the buildings were added in December 1994 and house the junior suites. Two are renovated Conch houses and another is a new building with rooms on the second floor that is beautifully blended into the others. On the first floor of one of the Simonton Street houses is the Café Marquesa, an excellent restaurant.

The hotel is painted turquoise with slate blue shutters and white trim, an unusual combination that works. Handsome double mahogany front doors and long windows face the front porch. There's also a gingerbread-embellished veranda on the second floor of the house.

Some of the standard rooms overlook the pool, while deluxe rooms overlook the front yard and historic Key West streets. The junior suites all have private balconies that open onto pool and garden areas by way of graceful French doors. These suites have two televisions and a sitting room with a pull-out sofa as well as a king-size bed. Most rooms and suites are a generous size, but smaller rooms have some compensation, such as a large deck. Rooms are reached by white-railed stairs or, in the main house, a polished mahogany staircase. Many rooms on the back of the hotel have French doors that open onto a private deck and brick walkways.

The hotel's decor makes the most of the interesting configurations of each room. Baths have floors of green-veined marble or white tile and pedestal sinks. Terry robes hang in the closets. Even the brass and enamel European-style telephones are special. Framed Key West prints and ceiling fans add a tropical feel to the Victorian elegance. Furnishings in the rooms are eclectic, with a mix of mahogany reproductions, bamboo and wicker, country pine armoires, restored furniture, and authentic antiques.

The lobby of the hotel was probably the front parlor of the original house. It has lovely proportions, floor-to-ceiling windows, and fine moldings. The juxtaposition of different styles or textures can be exciting but not entirely successful: a dolphin-footed glass table with walnut club chairs rests next to a mahogany reproduction table and chairs; opposite is an easy chair of woven grass next to a traditional sofa with a large, abstract painting above.

The hotel has two swimming pools, one of them heated. The unheated pool has a bell-shaped fountain that produces an arc of water, creating the sound of a gently flowing waterfall. Old-fashioned striped awnings hang above some of the windows and French doors. The second kidney-shaped pool is ringed by chaise longues and catches the afternoon sun. There are glass-topped tables scattered throughout the garden where guests can enjoy their complimentary wine in the afternoon. Most people eat breakfast here, too, although guests can also eat in their rooms or on their private verandas.

A Continental breakfast is prepared for all hotel guests by the chef at Café Marquesa, and it is delicious: grapefruit with wildflower honey, homemade granola, muffins and croissants, tea and freshly brewed coffee, espresso, or cappuccino. The beautifully presented breakfast includes fresh tropical fruits as well as traditional

Florida orange juice and grapefruit. In the afternoon by the pool, guests can order from the bar at the Café or sip a complimentary glass of iced tea.

The Café Marquesa is a whimsical, unpretentious place with Cuban tile on the front stoop, rough plaster walls inside painted a deep marigold, and a variety of seating. The food appeals to a sophisticated palate: snails and shrimp and corn for appetizers, fried tomato salad and duck breast salad, homemade pasta, and delicious entrées like salmon, pork loin, Delmonico steak, fresh shrimp, and dolphin fish. Guests staying at the hotel can make arrangements to use the restaurant for meetings of up to 20 to 30 people.

The Mermaid and the Alligator

729 Truman Avenue
Key West, FL 33040
800-773-1894
305-294-1894
Fax: 305-295-9925
mermaid@joy.net
www.kwmermaid.com

Here is "Old Key West," right down to the walls of Dade County pine

Innkeepers: Dean Carlson and Paul Hayes. **Accommodation:** 7 rooms, 1 cottage with 3 separate rooms. **Rates:** Rooms $75–$200; extra adult in room $20. **Included:** Full breakfast. **Minimum stay:** 2 nights. **Added:** 11.5 % tax. **Payment:** Visa, MasterCard, American Express, traveler's checks. **Children:** Young children not allowed; under the age of 16 free in room with parent. **Smoking:** On outside patios only. **Open:** Year-round.

➤ **The walls of the front parlor and dining room are indeed sheathed in Dade County pine, a honey-colored wood impervious to termites that was used extensively in turn-of-the-century construction in Florida. This rare, rather rustic wood no longer exists in Florida — or the world — and it is one of the many things that make The Mermaid and the Alligator special.**

Located on busy (well, busy for Key West) Truman Avenue, the Mermaid is on one of the main commercial streets of the town, with funky bookstores, cafés, B&Bs, a few private homes, and, of course, the Margaret Truman Launderette, on the corner of Truman and Margaret. When the Mermaid first opened as a B&B a few years ago, its beautiful exterior was almost hidden from the street with jungle-like growth in the front yard. The new owners, Dean Carlson and Paul Hayes, have done a wonderful job of clearing and pruning. The landscaping is a pleasant mix of broad-leafed tropical plants, palms of varying heights, and traditional flowering plants. The building itself is typical of early-20th-century Key West architecture, with a transom above the front door, double-hung windows, a crimped tin roof, varnished wooden shutters offsetting the light-colored clapboards, and, best of all, first- and second-floor verandas.

Guest rooms are imaginatively decorated and very comfortable. The first-floor Garden Room has a bedstead of verdigris iron, with a queen-size bed covered with a quilted comforter. The floor is of cool terra cotta tile. Three of the plastered walls are sponged in a soft ocher color and one, surprisingly, is sponged in pale green. The cathedral ceilings is also quite interesting, with part of the wall beneath one peak glassed in so that guests can see the leafy tree-tops outside. A leaded-glass transom is above the double French doors that lead out to a back garden.

The Sun Room on the second floor overlooks this same garden, which has brick walkways and a small pool. At night, the trees that overhang the patio sparkle with tiny white lights, making this room seem rather magical. By day, five large windows make the room both sunny and breezy. The tile bathroom, as in all Mermaid accommodations, is modern and attractive.

The Caribbean Queen Room has a four-poster bed and looks out over the front garden. If the windows are open, this room can be just a bit noisy with scooter traffic on Truman Street, but its wrap-around veranda is a great place to view the Key West scene. The bathroom has elegant grey tile and a large whirlpool tub, great for soaking in after a day of exploring Old Town.

The Conch Cottage is behind the main house. Two of its rooms share an attractive bathroom while a third, the Allamanda, has a private bath. There's a choice of a queen-size bed or twin beds, and the three rooms (the Allamanda, the Papaya, and the Key Lime) have private outdoor entrances. Anyone staying in the conch cottage can, of course, enjoy the pool and patio behind the main house. The multileveled patio is furnished with chaise longues and umbrellaed tables and chairs. Very relaxing.

Dean and Paul run the Mermaid as "a traditional B&B," serving a full gourmet breakfast in the morning and a glass of wine in the evening. A typical breakfast is quiche or French toast followed by a variety of fresh fruit. This is a filling, delicious meal that can "hold you" for more than half the day. It can be enjoyed out in the garden or in the downstairs parlor and dining room, which are imaginatively decorated and full of books. There is a TV in the parlor, and it is the only television in the whole place. Enough said.

Ocean Key House Resort and Marina

Zero Duval Street
Key West, FL 33040
305-296-7701
800-328-9815
Fax: 305-292-7685

> **A friendly resort in the middle of Key West's waterfront scene**

Accommodations: 100 rooms and suites. **Rates:** Rooms $145–$160, 1-bedroom suites $495–$525, 2-bedroom suites $600–$700. **Minimum stay:** 2 nights on weekends and some holidays. **Added:** 11.5% tax. **Payment:** Major credit cards. **Children:** 17 and under free in room with parent. **Smoking:** Nonsmoking rooms available. **Open:** Year-round.

➤ **Guests at the hotel can take advantage of the offerings of the marina for an active vacation or simply spend their time lounging by the hotel's Gulfside swimming pool or people-watching on a bench at the marina.**

The Ocean Key's address, Zero Duval Street, is where Front Street, Mallory Square, and Duval (Key West's "Main Street") come happily, chaotically together. Boats for fishing charters, snorkeling, cruising, and diving are docked here, with colorful signs advertising their excursions. On Mallory Square, people gather every evening to watch the sunset and the goings-on of jugglers and musicians. Close — but not too close — to this scene is the quiet and luxury of the Ocean Key House.

Although there are a few double and single rooms available with a choice of a queen-size bed or twin beds, most of the accommodations are one- and two-bedroom suites. The two-bedroom suites are quite spectacular; the master bedroom has both a king-size bed and a Jacuzzi, which is on a raised tiled platform and mirrored on two sides, with a dramatic flower arrangement on a tiled counter. Guests can soak in the Jacuzzi and look out past the big bed and over the balcony to the Gulf of Mexico.

The other rooms of the suite are a master bathroom next to the Jacuzzi, a spacious living and dining area decorated in designer fabrics, a bedroom with twin beds and a tiled bathroom, and a separate kitchen. The attractive kitchen has everything from pots and pans to a microwave. Guests can buy their food in a supermarket in Marathon or Key West on their way in or purchase treats at the Ocean Key's Café Duval, just off the lobby. A minibar in the living room is stocked with drinks and snacks for sundowners. The balcony could be considered another room, one where guests spend a good deal of time. It extends across three rooms: the master bedroom, living/dining room, and part of the second bedroom.

With the Ocean Key's corner location on two bodies of water, some suites afford a view of the sun setting over the gulf and rising over the Atlantic. Daytime views of the yachts docked below, the fishing boats setting forth, and a variety of people coming and going are fun, too.

The two-bedroom suite has a sofa that pulls down into a double bed so that this suite can accommodate six. The Ocean Key House also has what they call a "convertible two-bedroom, two-bath suite" that can accommodate up to six people. In this slightly different floor plan, the second bedroom shares the master bath instead of having a separate bath. This is a good choice for a family with two or three children but is not as good as the larger two-bedroom suite if you are traveling with another couple or with grandparents.

The Ocean Key's one-bedroom suite accommodates four and has a well-equipped kitchen, a living/dining area with a double pull-out sofa, and a king bedroom with a spacious bath and Jacuzzi. The balcony is accessible from both the bedroom and the living room. When making reservations, be sure to ask about views. The "Island-view" suites are less expensive than the "Gulf-front" suites, but ask for one with a balcony that overlooks a lot of "gulf" and a little "island," which can translate into "street."

Guests staying at the Ocean Key House in the summer need not feel that they'll stay in their air-conditioned room most of the time. Temperatures here are pleasant in the warmer months because of the breezes that sweep over the marina during the day.

The one problem at the Ocean Key House is that since there are no elevators from the lobby to the rooms, guests must traverse the ground-floor garage area to get to the elevator taking them to their rooms. To put it bluntly, the garage is ugly — coming and going, inside and out.

Pier House Resort and Caribbean Spa

1 Duval Street
Key West, FL 33040
800-327-8340
305-296-4600
Fax: 305-296-7568

A warm, uninhibited atmosphere in the middle of Old Key West

General Manager: Joy Smatt. **Accommodations:** 128 rooms and 14 suites. **Rates:** Rooms $205–$460, suites $335–$1,600, spa rooms $310–$415 (spa services/treatments at added charge); packages available. **Minimum stay:** 2 nights on weekends. **Added:** 11.5% tax. **Payment:** Major credit cards. **Children:** Under 18 free in room with parent. **Smoking:** Nonsmoking rooms available. **Open:** Year-round.

➤ **Though the Pier House does a good business in conferences and corporate retreats, it's definitely a place that encourages play.**

Duval Street is Key West's spirited main street, and the Pier House is where a lot of the action begins. It has what most consider Key West's premier restaurant, and four of its liveliest bars. It also has one of the few beaches on the island — small, but still a beach. The atmosphere is sophisticated and uninhibited. Some old Key Westers feel that too many units have been crammed onto the resort's five acres, but the overall design has been well executed. Land is at a premium, and the Pier House has done all that it can with its first-rate location.

The Pier House is made up of Old Florida–style buildings with peaked tin roofs and railed porches, and more contemporary buildings with dramatically angled roofs. All cluster around the center of activity: the beach and the palm-studded deck and pool.

The beach is one of the few places in Key West where you can actually swim; there are no jagged or slippery rocks, just fine sand. One small section is designated for topless sunbathing. Facilities by the beach include a dock several yards offshore with wide benches, a good place to take a breather. There's freshwater swimming in the Pier House's swimming pool, partly shaded with palms, partly open to the brilliant sunshine. The concierge staff is happy to arrange for off-property fishing, diving excursions, and sunset sails.

Accommodations are expensive, but they're also luxurious. All rooms and suites have a minibar and refrigerator, cable TV, and a private balcony or patio. A variety of views are available, and rooms are priced accordingly. Best are deluxe rooms overlooking the courtyard garden or pool, the "harbor-front" rooms, and the suites. No two are exactly alike, but all are decorated in fresh, tropical colors with wicker furniture and Key West artwork.

Some of the most appealing rooms are in the Pier House's Caribbean Spa building. These have hardwood floors, Bermuda shutters on the windows, and oversize bathrooms with a whirlpool or a Euro-habitat, a bathtub that can be enclosed to create a sauna. The spa program provides a full schedule of classes and treatments such as aromatherapy facials, body facials, loofah Salt-glo, herbal peels, and massages. Facilities include a workout room with the latest fitness equipment, sauna, steam room, and Jacuzzi, and a full-service salon.

The Pier House Restaurant has an imaginative menu of American and Caribbean cuisine and an extensive wine list. The restaurant has won a number of culinary awards, including a top-ten designation in a rating of all Florida restaurants. You can eat inside or on the deck overlooking the harbor. The restaurant serves both lunch and dinner and has a good champagne brunch on Sunday. The resort's Harbour View Café is a good choice for day or evening, with a real Key West menu of fresh shrimp, conch chowder, and conch fritters.

Everybody who comes to the Pier House soon has a favorite bar, but the best for a sundowner is Havana Docks, where ships for Cuba once departed. The lounge's Sunset Deck has a great view over Key West's old harbor. If it's an especially impressive sunset, everybody has another drink.

Sheraton Suites Key West

2001 S. Roosevelt Boulevard
Key West, FL 33040
800-45-BEACH
305-292-9800
Fax: 305-294-6009

A Caribbean-style resort on Key West's only natural beach

Accommodations: 180 suites. **Rates:** $129–$359; extra person in suite $10. **Added:** 11.5% tax. **Payment:** Major credit cards, travelers' checks. **Children:** Under 17 free in room with parent. **Smoking:** Nonsmoking rooms available. **Open:** Year-round.

➤ **The hotel's complimentary trolley to Old Town is the best way to get an overview of the historic Key West, and some guests spend part of every day on old Duval Street.**

The Sheraton has done a wonderful job of capturing the Caribbean ambience of Key West in this all-suite resort built in 1993. The three-story buildings are painted in pastel shades of cantaloupe, raspberry, and aqua with tin roofs and Bermuda-style wooden shutters that lift up to let in the breeze. Palm fronds sway. The entrance to the lobby is paved in cool sea green and white ceramic tile, and the tropical color combinations of the appointments are festive and whimsical.

The property sits across the street from the beach and adjacent to a nature preserve. The Sheraton has always catered to the family market, especially during the summer months; so don't feel this is an exclusive adults-only resort. The price is high for a family, although there is a lot of value here. All the accommodations are roomy suites with three separate areas: sitting room, bedroom, and bath/dressing area.

Lots of freebies and little extras are included: coffeemaker with complimentary coffee and tea, newspaper delivered to your door, iron and ironing board, hair dryer, two phones with voice mail and computer ports, two remote control televisions, wet bar with a small refrigerator, minibar, and microwave oven. The king suites have whirlpool tubs. All guests can take advantage of the free shuttle service to Old Town Key West and free transportation to and from Key West International Airport. There are also coin-op laundry facilities.

The guest rooms carry out the theme of the lobby and reception area with lots of seafoam green, white wicker, white woodwork around the windows, and splashy tropical designs in the fabrics. Each suite has a king-size bed or two doubles and a sitting area with a sofa and coffee table, reading lamps, a table with chairs for those who want to have snacks in the room, and a TV. Pool and oceanview suites have a little balcony furnished with a small table and two lawn chairs. Garden-view rooms have no balcony.

The resort has an indoor-outdoor restaurant just off the lobby, an exercise room, a gift shop, and 1,100 square feet of conference space that can be equipped with an overhead projector and screen, TV/VCR, flip charts, and an erasable board. This is a good hotel for meetings and executive retreats because there is plenty to do for spouses both on and off the property during business meeting time. The hotel can arrange group rates and also has corporate and incentive travel planning services.

The staff at the hotel can arrange bicycle and scooter rentals as well as fishing and diving charters, parasailing, snorkeling, sailing, and sunset cruises. Just across the street from the resort is a long stretch of beach, although it is composed of ground coral, not soft sand. Take a big towel to sit on. Behind the Sheraton is the pool and patio area. A conical gazebo bar is perched near the swimming pool's waterfall, with plantings of subtropical flowers, ferns, and palms along the pool patio. The free-form pool also has a whirlpool that's great to soak in.

Simonton Court

320 Simonton Street
Key West, FL 33040
800-944-2687
305-294-6386
Fax: 305-293-8446
www.simontoncourt.com

An enclave of historic Key West buildings

Host: Terry Sullivan. **Accommodations:** 25 rooms and cottages. **Rates:** Rooms $125–$295, cottages $195–$450; extra person $25. **Included:** Continental breakfast. **Minimum stay:** 4 nights during high season and on certain holidays. **Added:** 11.5% tax. **Payment:** American Express, Discover, MasterCard, Visa. **Children:** Under 18 not allowed. **Smoking:** Allowed. **Open:** Year-round.

➤ **There are four pools here and a 10-person hot tub. The most interesting pool has a border of ebony tile at the top and a black coating on the sides and bottom, giving it the look of a dark pool in the depths of the tropics. Guests spend a great deal of time around the pools, and the atmosphere is relaxed and happily indolent.**

One of the first guest houses in Key West, Simonton Court is an adults-only inn that prides itself on a free and easy atmosphere. The main house facing Simonton was a Cuban cigar factory in the 1880s; the row of modest, peak-roofed cottages behind it were the workers' quarters. Simonton Court's Townhouse, Manor, and Mansion were, until recently, private homes. A trim, landscaped gravel path connects the buildings and the garden settings of the four swimming pools.

The owners of Simonton Court respect the integrity of these buildings and have not tried to alter their 19th-century exteriors. Some rooms have the original pine on the walls and floors. Several of the suites have an open floor plan, with lofts. The decor is contemporary, Victorian, tropical, or "old cigar factory," depending on the building.

The poolside Manor House is an authentic Key West "conch" house. It has two rooms, both rustic and down-to-earth, as befits this "shotgun"-style southern house. The Mansion, which faces Eaton Street and backs onto Simonton Court, is a big white Victorian with hardwood floors and high ceilings. It has six rooms (three with marble bathrooms) and is furnished with four-poster beds and other period antiques and good reproductions. The Townhouse has two suites by a swimming pool, one upstairs and one downstairs. This interesting little place has a mansard roof and coral exterior stucco. Skylights and a Jacuzzi, as well as a private arched gate to the house, make this a wonderful place to stay.

The various accommodations share a secluded back garden, a major drawing point for Simonton Court. The 2-acre area is lush with flowering shrubs and green vegetation. A wooden deck covers several hundred square feet. In one corner is a canvas-draped cabana. Chaise longues and small tables are placed in groups on the deck, and there are big wooden planters of tropical trees. It would be easy to settle in here and stay a long, long time.

South Beach Oceanfront Motel

508 South Street
Key West, FL 33040
305-296-5611
Fax: 305-294-8272
Reservations:
Old Town Resorts
1319 Duval Street
Key West, FL 33040
800-354-4455
305-296-5611
Group sales and information:
305-296-6577

A small inn with a fountained pool and access to the Atlantic

Accommodations: 47 rooms. **Rates:** $99–$220; extra person $10–$15. **Minimum stay:** 3–5 nights during holidays and high season. **Added:** 11.5% tax. **Payment:** Major credit cards. **Children:** Under 18 free in room with parent. **Smoking:** Allowed. **Open:** Year-round.

➤ **All rooms in the two-story lattice-trimmed building have an ocean or pool view.**

In the high season, rooms at the South Beach Oceanfront Motel are slightly more than those at its sister hostelry, the Southernmost. But the rooms and the motel itself are usually quieter, and this is *the* spot to be for ocean lovers. One side of the motel faces South Street, diagonally across from the parking lot of the Southernmost. The motel stretches southeast toward the Atlantic, with rooms overlooking La Mer Hotel, South Beach, an Olympic-size pool and deck, and the ocean itself.

Guests reach first-floor rooms by way of a covered wooden walkway that has sunken flower beds and clay pots of palms on each side of the louvered guest room doors, though the doors leading to the rooms look worn and have chipped paint. Upstairs rooms are generally the best, for they are quiet and have wonderful views through the sliding glass doors that lead to the verandas. But there is one first-floor room that is very desirable: at the ocean end of the motel, it has its own little beach and looks directly out at the pier and the Atlantic. The room above it is also quite good, with a spacious veranda that hangs over the beach.

All rooms have tropical decor with bamboo and rattan furnishings, similar to that at La Mer and the Southernmost Motel. The tiled baths are modern and immaculate. The rooms at the Atlantic end of the motel have easy access to ocean swimming, a sunning pier and deck, and a manmade beach. The rooms at the South Street end of the motel may be slightly less quiet in the evening.

The motel has a dive shop that will provide information on diving and snorkeling. Just across South Street, the Southernmost Motel has water sports and moped rentals, two swimming pools, and two poolside bars. Guests at South Beach Motel are free to use the facilities at the Southernmost; they are part of the Old Town Resorts complex and are included in the room rate.

Closer to home there is more activity, particularly for those who like ocean or lap swimming. Next to South Beach Motel is its namesake: South Beach. This small, palm-studded municipal beach is a little rocky along the water's edge, but it's the closest choice for guests who love the beach. Monroe County Beach and Smathers Beach — longer, bigger beaches — are a bike ride away. For anyone who prefers freshwater swimming, South Beach Motel has one of the nicest pools in Key West — it's Olympic-size, rimmed by wood decking and red pavers, with pretty landscaping. Mounted just below the second-floor veranda balusters are two duck heads that spout water into the pool. It's a whimsical touch that adds fun to the relaxing beachside scene.

Southernmost Motel in the USA

1319 Duval Street
Key West, FL 33040
800-354-4455
305-296-6577
Fax: 305-294-8272
Reservations:
305-296-6577
Group sales and information:
305-296-6577

Unusual accommodations at the very tip of the U.S.

Accommodations: 127 rooms. **Rates:** Rooms $95–$220. **Minimum stay:** 3–5 nights during holidays and high season. **Added:** 11.5% tax. **Payment:** Major credit cards. **Children:** Under 18 free in room with parent. **Smoking:** Allowed. **Open:** Year-round.

Calling the Southernmost a motel doesn't do it justice; it looks more like an expanded Florida-style inn. The Southernmost is on the corner of Duval and United streets, stretching down a small Key West city block to South Street, which borders the Atlantic. This glorified motel is the largest and most diverse of the four Old Town Resorts.

The Southernmost is a collection of two- and three-story buildings finished in buff stucco or in clapboards with white or gray trim. The buildings are tied together with a lush garden and a central poolside recreation area. Most buildings have tin roofs and pretty upstairs verandas with latticework balustrades and touches of gingerbread; the general feeling is very Key West.

All rooms have views of one of the swimming pools, the garden, or both. Most rooms are doubles; there is some variation in size and configuration simply because the motel is made up of several different buildings. There is also one spacious penthouse.

The poolside patio seems to be the center of activity — or inactivity. Various types of flowering plants and vines spill over the wooden fences, and the white verandas overlook the main pool. The tropical profusion and the laid-back atmosphere also make the pool popular for La Mer and South Beach motel guests who share facilities. Guests can swim, lounge by the pool, soak in the Jacuzzi, or have a drink at the Tiki Bar. There's also a smaller pool in the center of the South Street parking lot. The location is certainly odd, but this pool has privacy because it's bordered by a cement wall and thick tropical vegetation. Some prefer it to the central pool because fewer people use it.

There are snacks at poolside bars but not much for the gourmand at the Southernmost. However, one of Key West's most venerable restaurants, Louie's Backyard, is a walk away. Another restaurant opened by the owner of Louie's, the Café Marquesa, is a 10-minute walk.

The only other drawback to the Southernmost is the registration office by the main pool: in the middle of the morning it becomes a noisy center of activity. Outsiders come here to rent mopeds or inquire about various excursions. There may also be people using the vending machines by the pool or walking through the breezeway to get back to their rooms. But the Southernmost is more than just a motel — it's an active, fun place. It is not a resort for the reclusive.

Travelers Palm

815 Catherine Street
Key West, FL 33040
800-294-9560
305-294-9560
Fax: 305-293-9130
www.travelerspalm.com

> **A serene retreat so
> secluded you can easily
> miss it**

Innkeeper: Brigid Hensley. **Accommodations:** 4. **Rates:** $95–$350; 10% discount
for 7 nights or more when booked directly. **Minimum stay:** Usually 5 nights.
Added: 11.5 % tax; $25 extra person in the room. **Payment:** Major credit cards;
traveler's checks. **Children:** Older, well-behaved children welcome. **Smoking:**
Outside only. **Open:** Year-round.

➤ **Although Travelers Palm has a wonderfully secluded feeling to it,
guests are actually close to everything.**

Travelers Palm describes itself as "Key West — The Way It Was."
There's more than one reason this is true. Travelers is quiet, as Key
West once was everywhere but in its rowdiest bars. Key West was
known for its brilliant winter sunshine before most people had the
wherewithal to fly to the Caribbean or take a cruise. And there is
plenty of warm sunlight around the pool and patio at Travelers. But
there is also shadow under the low, natural-wood ceilings of the
open-air pavilion adjacent to the pool. Dark, shaded rooms, both
indoors and out, were once the only way to keep cool in Key West
during the pre–air conditioning era. Key West was also once so difficult to get to, it had an atmosphere of retreat and anonymity.
With its walled-in enclosure, Travelers Palm has the feeling of a
hideaway. Finally, Key West has always been unconventional and
creative, but, as the town and island have become more trendy and
wealthy in recent years, they seem merely self-consciously bizarre
at times. At Travelers Palm, the pink bicycle and the church pew
that furnish the pool patio celebrate the genuinely offbeat.

With its slightly inelegant location, the Travelers is very easy to
miss. To find it, drive south down Truman Avenue (US Rte. 1) and
turn left on Margaret Street at the Margaret Truman Launderette.
Go two short blocks to Catherine Street and turn right and then,
quickly, right again. Travelers Palm is on the corner of Catherine
and tiny Royal Street, surrounded by thick vegetation. Royal looks
more like the driveway to an auto body shop than a street, and the

name "Royal" stenciled on the corner telephone pole is barely visible after all these years. On the stucco wall surrounding the guest house is a small wooden sign that says "Travelers Palm." Anyone not knowing what this designates might think the sign is for a travel agency or a restaurant — there's really no indication that there's a guest house here, and, although the owners have a Web site, they don't advertise much. So there are some Key West residents who've never heard of the place.

Above the low stucco wall is a closely slatted wooden fence intertwined with bright bougainvillea and other tropical vines and plants. This wall and fence combination ensure privacy and quiet. Guests enter through a wooden gate on the Royal side of the guest house and are immediately in a brick courtyard that is shaded above by latticework roofing. An immaculately kept cage of tropical birds is on your right, the old wooden registration desk is on your left, and a sunlit pool and patio are just beyond a shadowy garden. Soft, ephemeral music plays in the background, often Irish harps. Innkeepers Brigid and Clyde Hensley or one of their capable assistants help you settle in.

The four accommodations are very clean and have modern amenities. The best is the Captain's Quarters Poolside, with its large, ceramic-tiled kitchen, two bedrooms and two baths, and eclectic Asian art. More modest are the Conch House Suite, with two bedrooms and a bath, and the One-bedroom Apartment and Studio Apartment. These have practical floors of gray and white vinyl tile, stucco or pine walls, and attractive wicker and wooden furnishings. The Conch House has its own deck with a chaise and a table and chairs for four, and the One-bedroom Apartment has a small patio. These three accommodations have kitchens or kitchenettes with full-size refrigerators and either full-size or apartment-size stoves. Ask the Hensleys for complete descriptions when calling for reservations, or visit their Web site.

The Travelers Palm has a 5-night minimum and caters to people who want to soak in the sun and relax for several days rather than come in fast, see the Key West sights and freaks, and then take off. However, the Hensleys often "fill in" between five- or six-night stays with one- or two-night reservations.

Truman Avenue is one of the main streets in town and has a number of offbeat shops. Diagonally across the street from Travelers is El Siboney, a very reasonably priced Cuban restaurant. Other restaurants are within easy walking or driving distance. Bars and clubs and shops are located on Duval, a few blocks west of Travelers, and the beach is a few blocks to the south.

Watson House

525 Simonton Street
Key West, FL 33040
800-621-9405
305-294-6712
Fax: 305-294-7501

A restful guest house with a hideaway garden

Innkeepers: Ed Czaplicki and Joe Beres. **Accommodations:** 3 suites. **Rates:** $110–$370; extra person $15. **Included:** Continental breakfast. **Minimum stay:** 2 nights; longer during holidays. **Added:** 11.5% tax; 10% surcharge for holidays and special events. **Payment:** Visa, MasterCard, American Express, traveler's checks. **Children:** Not allowed; adults-only environment. **Smoking:** Limited. **Open:** Year-round.

➤ **The gentility of Watson House is focused in the garden patio — you hear it before you see it, in the form of the soft trickling of flowing water. The centerpiece is a heated spa with a waterfall that gently cascades into the swimming pool below.**

The Watson House is one of the best examples of Key West architecture on the island. Although most of us would call it a Victorian, and certainly it has many romantic 19th-century touches, it is really what is known as Bahamian architecture, with airy verandas on the first and second floors, a crimped tin roof, long windows with louvered shutters, and solid plain pillars supporting the front porch. Brick flowerbeds border tropical plants on each side of the front steps to the Watson House, and a delicate wrought-iron fence encircles the property. When first-time visitors make their way up the neat brick walk and through the front door with its oval of etched glass, they are sometimes disconcerted to find that the Victorian front parlor they expect inside is a realty office full of computers and ringing phones. But this is also the registry for the Watson House. Once guests sign in, they can enter their cabana suite by a separate entrance in the back.

The Susan Suite is the smallest but has the greatest Victorian charm. All the furniture is white wicker, accented by old-fashioned prints on the wall and white lace on the queen-size bed. The floor is polished pine with area rugs; above is a wooden paddle fan. Modern amenities include a shower bath, small fridge, coffeemaker with complimentary coffee, cable TV, and telephone.

The William Suite has three rooms and a full bath. Its private veranda overlooks the pool and garden. The bedroom has a queen-size four-poster, an armoire, and other period furnishings. The sitting/dining area is decorated with attractive Haitian artwork and wicker furniture. The kitchen is fully equipped, so the suite is more like an apartment than simply a room. The Susan Suite and the William Suite are on the second floor of the main house and can be combined to form the Watson Suite.

The Cabana Suite is in a one-story building located behind the main house and adjacent to the pool and sundeck. It also has a full kitchen, sitting/dining area, and bedroom. The bedroom has a king-size bed and art deco furniture and appointments. French doors lead out onto a private covered deck furnished with white iron lawn chairs and table. As in the other rooms, there is a modern bathroom, telephone, cable TV, and paddle fans to supplement the air conditioning.

Complimentary breakfast of fresh fruit, pastries, bagels, juice, and coffee or tea is delivered to the suites in the morning at the time that guests request the evening before.

The names Susan, William, and Watson refer to Susan and William Watson, who built the main house in 1860. Little is known about them except that they later sold the house, at which time it was remodeled as a southern mansion. The house then fell into obscurity until the mid-1980s, when it was restored and opened as a guest house. In 1987, the Historical Florida Keys Preservation Board recognized the Watson House with an Excellence in Rehabilitation designation. The house has an ideal location — walk one block and you're in the middle of Key West's Old Town, walk a block or two along Simonton in the opposite direction and there are a number of funky little shops and more examples of fine old Bahamian residential architecture.

Wyndham Casa Marina Beach House

1435 Simonton Street
Key West, FL 33040
305-296-5000
800-996-3426
Fax: 305-296-2830

A beachside resort with an airy, fresh feeling

Hotel Manager: Joe Shurmur. **Accommodations:** 150 rooms and suites. **Rates:** Rooms $150–$370, suites $250–$600; packages available; rates lowest on weeknights. **Minimum stay:** On holidays and some weekends. **Added:** 11.5% tax. **Payment:** Major credit cards. **Children:** Under 18 free in room with parent. **Smoking:** Allowed. **Open:** Year-round.

➤ **With its fantastic location, the Beach House could have coasted by with second-rate decor and design; the original owners chose not to, much to the pleasure of their guests.**

The Beach House faces one of the few real beaches on Key West, and takes full advantage of its prize location. Guests can sail, windsurf, parasail, snorkel, and scuba dive. There are sailing lessons for beginners and old hands. Swimming is in the freshwater pool or in the ocean, and there's also a well-equipped health club. Nearby are fishing and charter boating, which the energetic staff can help you arrange. Guests at the resort have access to the facilities of the Wyndham's other resort in Key West, the Casa Marina.

The restaurant at the Beach House also takes advantage of the beachside location, with windows overlooking the water and a dining terrace where people like to sit and gaze out to sea, even when they're not eating. The resort also has banquet facilities and a pool bar.

The resort is pale peach stucco accented with lots of white: white trim around the small-paned windows and the French doors, white Victorian-style railings and pillars on the verandas. The architecture is a mix of Old Florida style with a few touches of Key West Victorian gingerbread. There are a surprising number of rooms in the five-story buildings, but because of the open-air walkways leading to rooms, guests never feel crowded.

Amenities at the Beach House include a conference center, unusual for Key West. The space includes a boardroom, five meeting rooms, and a larger room with French doors leading onto a balcony overlooking the ocean.

Accommodations are in a variety of room types, from Tropical Guest Room (read standard room) to rooms and suites overlooking the water. All are attractive, with tile floors, ceiling fans, minibars, refrigerators, and immaculate bathrooms. The suites have sleeper sofas, kitchenettes, and a dining table and chairs.

Wyndham Casa Marina Resort

1500 Reynolds Street
Key West, FL 33040
800-626-0777 or 800-996-3426
305-296-3535

Henry Flagler's last grand hotel

General Manager: Michael P. Proimos. **Accommodations:** 311 rooms and suites. **Rates:** Rooms $180–$370, suites $345–$695; seasonal packages. **Minimum stay:** With packages. **Added:** 11.5% tax. **Payment:** Major credit cards. **Children:** Under 18 free in room with parent. **Smoking:** Nonsmoking rooms available. **Open:** Year-round.

➤ **Swimming was once rather dangerous here because of a shelf of rocks by the beach, but Wyndham has added a dock and a long pier that goes beyond the rocks, making swimming a real pleasure. The dock is also an excellent spot to push off for snorkeling, a favorite pastime of Casa guests. The Keys' waters are home to plenty of colorful fish and other marine life.**

Built at the terminus of Henry Flagler's Florida railroad line and completed in 1921, several years after his death, the Casa Marina shone throughout the 1920s, 1930s, and early 1940s as Key West's premier hotel. The Casa was a gathering place for writers, statesmen, and movie stars, and its style was indeed grand. The rich and famous posed with their friends and rivals on the terrace behind the Mediterranean-style hotel, with its elegant arched loggia and cool Spanish tile roofs. They sunned themselves on chaises overlooking the picture-perfect grounds and the ocean beyond, and delighted in the pampering of a solicitous staff.

World War II changed all that, when the Casa Marina was leased to the U.S. Navy for housing. The Casa became a hotel again in 1945 but was taken over by the Army in 1962 during the Cuban missile crisis.

In the late 1970s, new owners bought the hotel and spent $13 million renovating it. They enlarged and refurbished accommodations in the original 1920s building, giving odd but interesting angles to the accommodations and making for bigger, more comfortable rooms and suites. The new owners also modernized the bathrooms and added new fixtures throughout the hotel. They restored the Mediterranean exterior and the lobby, always two of the hotel's strongest points.

Today, the old pine floors in the lobby are polished and beautiful. Overhead, the black cypress beams of the vaulted ceiling stretch across the big room to French doors with fanlights above. The doors open out onto the loggia and terrace and to the swimming pools and beautiful grounds beyond. The mood of the era has been captured best here in the lobby.

However, there have been some mistakes. In the first renovation, the intricately molded fireplace and the original brass and wood registration area were restored. But during a later renovation the registration desk was replaced with a large, paneled front desk without the old brass detailing. This new front desk was constructed right up to the side of the handsome fireplace, which used to dominate the lobby from a central position on the front wall.

Some people are also bothered by the west wing that was added to the original building, a flat-fronted, charmless, modern building. Walls are a bit thin, but the rooms are well proportioned, and many have wonderful views of the Casa loggia and courtyard as well as the water.

The guest rooms are attractively decorated, with light stucco walls and bleached oak furniture. There's a good variety of accommodations, including standard and oceanfront balcony rooms, junior suites, corner suites, and two-bedroom loft suites. As in all Wyndham hotels, the baths are well designed and are equipped with many extras.

Service is efficient and friendly throughout the hotel. The service at Flagler's Steak House, the main restaurant, is quicker than average for laid-back Key West, and the food is good. This restaurant, with the original coffered mahogany ceiling and French windows, has recently been lightened and brightened with lots of polished brass and wood. Flagler's serves all three meals. The Sun pavilion, right on the water, with weathered decking and a West Indies look, serves lunch outdoors. Service is sometimes slow here, but the view is great, making this a wonderful spot for a leisurely lunch.

Besides swimming off the pier, Wyndham offers many other diversions, including boating, sailboarding, tennis, and fishing. The Wyndham has a great many rentals available, including mopeds and bicycles. The pool terrace, which is beautifully planted and maintained, has a whirlpool to soak in. This outdoor area, with its

relaxed Riviera ambience and backdrop of Mediterranean archways, is still the Casa Marina's greatest draw.

Little Palm Island

Little Palm Island

28500 Overseas Highway
Little Torch Key, FL 33042
800-343-8567 or 800-3-GET LOST
305-872-2524
www.littlepalmisland.com

> **A favorite honeymoon and anniversary destination**

General Manager: Heinrich Morio. **Accommodations:** 30 suites. **Rates:** Cottages $550–$1,500, houseboat suites $425–$800 per couple plus 10% service charge; $100 for extra person. Ask Reservations for cost of meal plans. **Included:** Water sports equipment. **Minimum stay:** 2 nights on weekends; 3 nights on holidays; 7 nights at Christmas and New Year's. **Added:** 11.5% tax. **Payment:** Major credit cards, personal checks. **Children:** Under 16 not permitted. **Smoking:** Allowed. **Open:** Year-round.

> ➤ **Couples come to Little Palm Island to mend their souls and get reacquainted.**

A recent guest described Little Palm Island succinctly: "When you come here for vacation, you better like the person you're with, because there's nothing here but palm trees and water." Escaping to beautiful surroundings to do almost nothing has been reason enough for hundreds of people to come to this island retreat since it opened in 1988. Admittedly, it's an extremely expensive place, but it is also a superlative resort, and its location is very private. It should be added that the cuisine and accommodations are outstanding, transporting guests to the indolence of the South Seas.

The restaurant, which has won a number of culinary awards, is a building of pecky cypress constructed in 1938 as a fishing lodge. Guests may dine on its deck, looking out at the ocean and the setting sun. Tables are set with white napery, stoneware, and hand-blown glassware from Mexico. Food served by the executive chef and his staff is meticulously prepared and exotically presented. The delicate sauces and soups are flavored with herbs from the island's own garden.

Guests with small appetites who don't wish to have two or three gourmet meals a day can pay for their meals à la carte rather than taking the full or modified American plans. All the meals are full-course events, so many couples request only breakfast and dinner, or lunch and dinner if they sleep in. Those who stay for several days sometimes take the launch to Little Torch Key and then drive to restaurants during a day's excursion on other Keys. For the most part, though, this is the kind of place where people stay put.

A jogging track rims the island's five acres, and there are complimentary sailboats, canoes, and Windsurfers. Other activities are backwater excursions to other Keys, off-island fishing, and snorkeling and scuba diving at the coral reef at Looe Key National Marine Sanctuary. The resort has scuba instructors, fishing guides, and backcountry guides for excursions to nearby Keys. There's also a spa offering massages, including aromatherapy massage, loofah treatments, and facials.

At the Quarterdeck, a dockside administrative building, a 24-hour switchboard responds to guests' room buzzers. The staff's quick response to any need has given the resort an excellent reputation for service.

The owners of Little Palm Island like to call it a "passive resort." They enjoy giving people "a chance to think about what life is all about. So no tennis and no telephones or TVs." In fact, guests can rent a TV or VCR if they are so moved. But the emphasis is on rest and relaxation. Hammocks are strung between palm trees; chaises and lawn chairs form a small cluster on the sand. Many people spend the day simply lying on a chaise on the small, pretty beach, one of the few natural beaches in the Keys.

Children under 16 are not allowed on Little Palm, although there are some families with older children. Except on weekends, when people from the mainland frequently come over for dinner, there is very little noise.

A few steps up from the beach is a meandering path to the pool and bar. This is not to say, however, that you ever have to fetch your own drinks. Just raise the pink flag on the pole by your beach chair and an attendant will come running. The bar and poolside patio are convivial places: the swimming pool is one of the loveliest in Florida — palm trees draped with brilliant bougainvillea arch over it and a tiny waterfall sparkles and spills into a coral pond. Behind the pool is the Great Room, which houses the island's library.

The pool bar prepares a number of tropical rum drinks served in coconuts grown on the island. The staff at Little Palm Island make use of many island resources. Tropical flowers are used as garnishes for food and drinks, and palm fronds are ground up and used for mulch around plants. Also, every effort is made to encourage the wildlife that make their home among the Newfound Harbor Keys, the string of islands of which Little Palm Island, often called LPI, is a part. Everyone is particularly fond of the waterfowl that congregate on the pier by the beach and the tiny Key deer who swim over at night to nibble on the hibiscus.

While the thatched cottages look basic from the outside, they are quite luxurious inside. Each cottage contains two suites, named after Little Palm birds. The suites have a sitting room and bedroom at each end and a spacious bath between. The sitting room is furnished with British colonial pieces. Each suite has a safe and a minibar stocked with pâtés and other good things.

In the bedroom, the plaster walls are painted white or soft peach. Louvered windows look out over the water, and one can relax in a chaise in the corner. Tabletops are deep green marble. Bedrooms have a king-size bed draped with nylon mosquito netting — purely for effect, as guests worried about mosquitoes are assured.

Overhead is a high thatch roof supported by thick pine beams. It takes many different types of palm fronds to make this thatching. Those who have stayed here during a tropical rainstorm say the sound of the raindrops on thatch is wonderful, and there's no chance of any water seeping in.

The bathrooms in the suites deserve a paragraph of their own. Perhaps they are so nice because of the rustic plumbing of the past. (The outhouse Harry Truman used on his visits has been preserved and is now a telephone booth.) Every suite has a large whirlpool in the bathroom and a dressing room with louvered closet. The big tub has custom-made tiles of palm trees and turtles. And on the deck of each suite is an outdoor shower with a bamboo enclosure.

The decks that wrap around each thatched cottage have an authentic South Seas look. They are a nice spot to watch birds swoop over the island. They are also a favorite place to rest and talk for the many couples who come here to get away from work and family responsibilities and renew the friendship in a marriage. One frequent guest remembers the first time his wife surprised him with a long weekend here. "It was time to finish packing and get to the launch and I started searching for the passports. I couldn't find them and started to panic. Then I remembered we didn't even have to leave the country for this!"

Marathon

Faro Blanco Marine Resort

1996 Overseas Highway
Marathon, FL 33050
800-759-3276
305-743-9018
Fax: 305-743-2918

A Marathon mainstay for fishing and boating

General Manager: Greg Kenney. **Accommodations:** 125 cottages, lighthouse apartments, condos, houseboats. **Rates:** Cottages $79–$185, houseboats $99–$109, lighthouse apartments $145–$185, suites $178–$198, condos $215–$327. **Minimum stay:** 3 nights during holidays and special events. **Added:** 11.5% tax; $10 extra person. **Payment:** Major credit cards. **Children:** Free in room with parent. **Smoking:** Allowed. **Open:** Year-round.

➤ **Everyone in the resort's office is very friendly. There is information here and at the dock office on fishing.**

Faro Blanco is most famous for its two full-service marinas and a wonderful lighthouse, its most interesting accommodation. If you come by boat, its whitewashed stucco pinnacle and many-paned windows are the first thing you see. Boat slips are spread out on either side of the lighthouse. Behind these, a long pier stretches out to the Gulf of Mexico.

Guests climb up a narrow flight of stairs to each apartment, with a length of boat line serving as the staircase "railing." The entrance door is cut at an odd angle and leads to a small sitting area with a built-in sofa and a fully equipped kitchen that, appropriately, reminds one of a ship's galley. The walls are of whitewashed paneling with knotty pine accents. A tiny bathroom with whale-handled brass faucets in the miniature sink, a small shower, and a toilet just fits into a corner off the kitchen. A stairway leads off the sitting room to a bedroom with a king-size bed, a window seat, and a clawfoot bathtub near the bed. Under the stairs leading to the bedroom above is a separate vanity, toilet, and chrome sink, with towel racks and shelves screwed into the back treads of those stairs. One is constantly reminded that this is, after all, a lighthouse, and modern conveniences are tucked in wherever they fit.

Thankfully, there has been no effort to standardize the rooms; there isn't a true square angle in either apartment.

The room on the next floor is the kids' room (they're young, they can climb more stairs). It has twin beds and a built-in sofa between two windows. The views of the water get more spectacular with each flight, and they make the odd little rooms seem bigger and brighter than they really are. Guests can see boats coming and going, the waters of the Atlantic, the Gulf of Mexico, and Florida Bay, the pretty grounds of the Faro Blanco resort, and waterfowl sunning themselves on the coral jetty. It would be easy to stay here all day, and, with the little twinkling Christmas lights that encircle the beacon in the evening, maybe all night, too.

The lighthouse apartments are ideal for a honeymoon or anniversary couple or a family, though very young children might find the steep stairs a problem. The drawback to this fascinating accommodation is that the apartments are not maintained as well as they could be. For example, the rug on the floor in the bathroom may be badly soiled, and some of the curtains could do with replacements.

The other offerings at the marina are condominiums and cottages. The Island Condominiums have three bedrooms, two full baths, modern kitchens, and terraces that look out over the grounds and the water. These luxury condos are set back from the water and are within a short walking distance of the resort's Olympic-size swimming pool and tennis court.

The Garden Cottages are the resort's budget and kidproof accommodations. These little stucco houses, painted in ice cream colors, have a 1950s look to them, and some of the three-generation families staying in the cottages have indeed been coming here since the '50s. Inside, furnishings are simple but functional, with a mix of reproduction wood furniture and Formica-topped tables. The modest but comfortable lodgings are clean and well maintained, and are surrounded by trees and lawns. Just across the narrow "street" (this does have the feeling of a neighborhood) that runs between the groups of cottages is a picnic and recreation area, and beyond that, toward the marina, is the pool. On the other side of the resort by the condos is the tennis court. A family could stay in the cottages and not leave the property for days. And for those who can't bear to leave the family pet, Faro Blanco allows animals in the cottages for a small fee.

Although many people familiar with this resort think of Faro Blanco as occupying only a stretch of land from Highway 1 to the marina, there is more dock space, a dock office, and a laundry facility and shower on the Atlantic side of the highway. There is also another interesting group of accommodations here: Faro Blanco's floating stateroom suites. These houseboats cost more than the cottages but have many of the same advantages. Relatively new, they have tile and porcelain baths and comfortable sitting and dining areas. Queen-size beds are new and firm. The floors are either varnished pine or wall-to-wall carpeting. Most units have an attractive kitchenette and a breakfast bar with stools, a coffeemaker, toaster, cooking utensils, and plates and flatware. Units that don't have a kitchenette have an expanded sitting room with a foldout queen-size sofa. Guests go across decking or up a flight of stairs and then enter the staterooms through curtained French doors that give a feeling of modest elegance to the accommodations. The houseboats don't bob because they are fixed to a concrete slab. All have two units, one above the other. A deck in back looks out over the water.

The units all have vertical siding with a weathered gray finish. The high-numbered houseboats are closer to the open water and have the best views. But they are also closer to one of the resort's four restaurants and the marina and so might be slightly noisy on weekend evenings. The low-numbered units look out at houseboats on the other side of the dock; the water views are not as nice, but it's a quieter spot for those with small ones who go to bed early.

Those who stay at this end of the resort can, of course, take advantage of all the recreation available on the Gulf side of Faro Blanco. If you are coming by boat, call ahead to get dockage rates and other information about the marina. This marina is one of the few in the Keys that offers marine engine repair service. There is also a dockmaster's office, ship's store, tackle shop, and charter service.

Hawk's Cay Resort and Marina

U.S. Highway 1, Mile Marker 61
Marathon, FL 33050
800-432-2242
305-743-7000

A cool, breezy private island

Accommodations: 160 rooms and 16 suites. **Rates:** Rooms $150–$350, suites $245–$615; packages available. **Minimum stay:** 2 or 3 nights with packages and on holidays. **Added:** 11.5% tax. **Payment:** Major credit cards. **Children:** Under 12 free in room with parent. **Smoking:** Allowed. **Open:** Year-round.

➤   **Best of all for those who love marine life are the dolphins. The resort is a year-round training center for many sea animals, and one of the pleasures of a stay here is the dolphin show presented every afternoon. This is a private show, open only to resort guests, who sit up on the porch overlooking the water or at a curve of white sand by the lagoon.**

About two hours south of Miami on Route 1, just across a long bridge, is an enclave of low-rise and conical buildings spread out along a crescent-shaped sandbar and turquoise lagoon, with a channel beyond of deeper turquoise. It looks like a great place to unwind, surrounded by natural and manmade beauty. And so it is: it's Hawk's Cay, on its own private island on the five-island formation of Duck Key.

The covered entrance to the resort, landscaped with banana trees and other tropical plants, continues the mood. Beveled, small-paned glass doors lead into the lobby and lounge area. The lobby is cool, with lazy ceiling fans and terra cotta floors. French doors lead to an enclosed terrace, where there are club chairs and small tables. Outside are the poolside restaurant, the Cantina, and the recreational area.

This is the focal point of the resort. There's a large swimming pool with a couple of Jacuzzis, clay pots of brilliant bougainvillea, cushioned chaise longues and lawn chairs for lazing around. Near the pool is a wide expanse of lawn popular for volleyball games, and there is a basketball court and shuffleboard. Softball games start up whenever a few people feel like playing.

The average temperature in the winter at Hawk's Cay is 72 degrees; in the summer, 82, with a strong breeze. The water off Duck Key covers a wide range of blues and blue-greens, depending on the weather. At Hawk's Cay Resort, it is a lovely shade of turquoise, largely because of the underlying white sand of the resort's manmade beaches. Except for a few areas of Key West, there are no natural beaches on the Keys. The "sand" at the lagoon is beautiful but scratchy, so watch out for little ones' tender feet when they are playing and wading here. Various small sailboats and Windsurfers can be rented for sailing on the lagoon. Guests who want to sail larger boats in the wide channel outside the lagoon can rent them at the marina.

Built into a hammock of tropical trees between the palm-studded lagoon and the marina is the "tennis garden," with eight courts, including two clay courts lighted for night play. On the lawn that surrounds the tennis garden is a jogging trail with exercise stations accommodating three levels of fitness. Although Hawk's Cay lacks a golf course, there is free shuttle service to an 18-hole course at the nearby Sombrero Country Club.

At the marina, guests can charter boats for deep-sea, bottom, or backcountry fishing. This is a 60-slip, full-service facility with a marina store that stocks fishing tackle, equipment, maps, books, compasses, and clothing. Adjacent to the marina store is a dive shop that includes the services of a PADI-certified diving instructor. The two dive boats include a 40-foot glass-bottom boat. The Keys offer some of the best scuba diving and snorkeling in the world, with the largest living coral reef in the continental United States just four miles offshore.

The recreational offerings at Hawk's Cay include an excellent children's program. The kids swim and fish, play on the playground, go on nature hikes, and participate in outdoor games. For older children, there is a game room off the lobby with Ping-Pong tables and video games.

Mindful of the beauty that surrounds Hawk's Cay, the resort also offers ecological raft tours of the waterways of Duck Key. Experienced guides describe the beautiful vegetation, waterfowl, and history of this unique region. The free dolphin show is enjoyable and educational.

Hawk's Cay Resort includes convention facilities removed from the rest of the hotel in a center overlooking the water and the dolphin training pool. Meeting rooms include four large boardrooms and four adjoining caucus rooms for smaller meetings. The conference rooms are soundproofed and have very good audiovisual equipment and lighting. Large windows in the conference rooms overlook the water, with French doors that open onto wooden decks. These decks are ideal for receptions and parties.

Guest accommodations are in the main building and in low-rise wings, all recently redecorated and repainted. Rooms have bleached oak furniture and walk-in closets. There is a separate vanity and sink by the closet as well as one in the bath. All rooms have terraces with lawn furniture and have views of the water or garden greenery. A drawback is that the maintenance sometimes isn't as good as it should be and staff turnover is sometimes high, with many college-age employees going back to school or moving on to new adventures. This results in inconsistent service — if you luck out, it's fine, and if you don't, service is inadequate or indifferent.

Though Hawk's Cay is expensive and there are service glitches, you'll probably get your money's worth. The conical, pavilion-style restaurant offers a complimentary buffet breakfast near the dolphin pool, which most guests love. The atmosphere is a little like summer camp, with cheery waitresses filling your coffee cup, soft rock playing, and, in certain seasons, lots and lots of kids. The buffet has 60 hot and cold choices, including cereals, yogurt, a large selection of fresh fruits, brisket of beef, scalloped potatoes, sausage, bacon, and a variety of egg dishes, including eggs Benedict. There is a large selection of pastries, muffins, sweet breads, and éclairs.

During the day, most guests have lunch at the Cantina near the pool or the Ship's Galley, a seafood restaurant at the marina. In the evening, the Water's Edge, off the terrace, offers a variety of American and continental offerings. The salads are interesting here, and there are some good entrées, but service is inconsistent. During the winter season, Porto Cayo, the resort's formal Italian restaurant, is open. For part of their stay, many guests have dinner off the property at one of the fine restaurants elsewhere in the Keys. Key West, romantic and fun at night, is only an hour and a half from Hawk's Cay.

The Gulf Coast

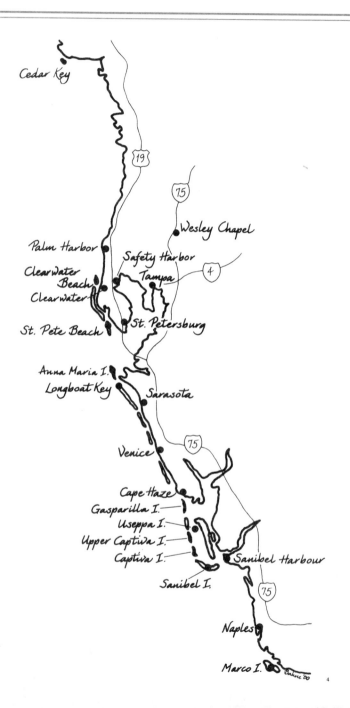

Best B&Bs

Anna Maria Island
Harrington House Beachfront B&B, 416
Cedar Key
Cedar Key Bed & Breakfast, 427
St. Petersburg
Mansion House B&B and The Courtyard on Fifth, 465
Sarasota
The Cypress, 480
Venice
Banyan House, 496

Best Beachside Accommodations

Anna Marie Island
Bungalow Beach Resort, 414
Clearwater Beach
Clearwater Beach Hotel, 432
Longboat Key
Colony Beach & Tennis Resort, 436
The Resort at Longboat Key, 438
Wicker Inn, 440
Marco Island
Marco Island Marriott Resort & Golf Club, 442
Naples
Edgewater Beach Hotel, 444
The Naples Beach Hotel and Golf Club, 447
Ritz-Carlton, Naples, 451
St. Pete Beach
Don CeSar Beach Resort & Spa, 458
TradeWinds Resort on St. Pete Beach, 463
Sanibel Island
Caribe Beach Resort, 471
Casa Ybel Resort, 472
Sanibel Inn, 474
Song of the Sea, 476
Sundial Beach and Tennis Resort, 478
Sarasota
Half Moon Beach Club, 483

Best City Stops

Tampa
Hyatt Regency Westshore, 485
Wyndham Harbour Island Hotel, 486
Wyndham West Shore Hotel, 488

Best Island Getaways

Cape Haze
Palm Island Resort, 419
Gasparilla Island
Gasparilla Inn, 434
Upper Captiva Island
Safety Harbor Club, 456
Useppa Island
Useppa Island Club, 492

Best Resorts and Spas

Captiva Island
South Seas Resort, 421
'Tween Waters Inn, 425
Naples
The Registry Resort Hotel, 449
Palm Harbor
Westin Innisbrook Resort, 454
Safety Harbor
Safety Harbor Resort & Spa, 456
St. Pete Beach
TradeWinds Resort on St. Pete Beach, 463
St. Petersburg
Renaissance Vinoy Resort, 467
Sanibel Harbour (Fort Myers)
Sanibel Harbour Resort and Spa, 469
Wesley Chapel
Saddlebrook Resort-Tampa, 497

Best Small Hotels, Inns, and Motels

Cedar Key
  Island Hotel, 430
Naples
  Lemon Tree Inn, 446
St. Pete Beach
  Island's End Cottages, 461

With its unhurried pace and long string of islands, the Gulf Coast has become increasingly popular in the last few years. The tourism industry on the gulf reports that about a third of the visitors to Disney World travel to another part of Florida during their stay.

Many of these people wind up just 90 minutes west in **Tampa** or **St. Petersburg.** The two cities are on Tampa Bay, a large natural harbor. They share some similarities to Minneapolis and St. Paul, with Tampa reputed to be the livelier city and St. Petersburg considered a staid city of old people — not exactly accurate, according to official demographics. Tampa is a financial and commercial center, while St. Petersburg is less urban, with a wide range of neighborhoods, from the deteriorating to the elegant. **St. Pete Beach** is a residential and recreational town, with a "strip" on the beach similar to Ft. Lauderdale's. Of the attractions near Tampa and St. Petersburg, one of the most worthwhile is Busch Gardens, with more than 2,500 birds and 3,000 animals on the well-kept grounds. The Museum of Science and Industry in Tampa is the largest museum in Florida, and there is interesting shopping at Franklin Street Mall and Harbourside. Ybor Square, in East Tampa, is a Latin neighborhood where you can visit antique and crafts shops, dine at Cuban restaurants, and see cigars being hand-rolled.

St. Petersburg, affectionately known as St. Pete, has an interesting waterfront area and three excellent museums: the Museum of Fine Arts, the Florida International Museum, and the Dali Museum. North of Tampa Bay are a great many beach towns and fishing villages along the Gulf of Mexico that reach up almost to the mouth of the Suwannee River in northern Florida. Tarpon Springs, a Greek enclave that was once a sponge diving center, is the most famous and the most popular with tourists. Halfway between Tampa and Tallahassee is the island of **Cedar Key.** It was once a commercial center for lumber and fishing but is now a sleepy little retreat that has a firehouse and city hall in weathered, unpainted buildings and a population of crusty old-timers and arty newcomers, who are proud of the fact that there are no traffic lights on their main street.

Some of the towns along the coast from Apalachicola to Fort Myers are charming, others are run-down. But the beach they front is generally the same: soft, powdery sand with sea oats and other grasses growing on the gentle dunes, countless seashells, and warm, emerald green water lapping the shore.

Just south of Tampa is the city of **Sarasota,** with a rich offering of theater, music, and art. Interesting historic buildings include the Ringling Museum and Ca'D'Zan, the 1920s mansion of Ringling himself. Sarasota also offers excellent shopping and dining at St. Armand's Circle.

One of the most impressive features of the southwestern coast is the number of islands just offshore. Some are little known outside Florida, because once people find a chunk of authenticity here, they are not always willing to share it. Sarasota Bay has a string of small islands or keys, most notably Lido Key, Siesta Key, and **Longboat Key.**

Farther south, the islands adjacent or just south of Charlotte Harbor have a legend-laden history of pirates, treasure, and treachery. Some of these islands, including **Captiva, Sanibel, Gasparilla,** and Pine Island, are accessible by causeway or bridge, off I-75 near Fort Myers. Others, such as Cabbage Key, **Palm Island, Upper Captiva, and Useppa,** are accessible only by boat. There are also many smaller keys, some of them formed by mangroves, whose roots extend into the water, catching sand and sediment to create islands.

Captiva Island and its larger sister island, Sanibel, were once accessible only by boat. Now a causeway links Fort Myers to Sanibel, and from Sanibel a two-lane highway reaches the tip of Captiva Island and South Seas Resort. Many longtime residents on both islands grumble about the traffic on this little road, and it is slow-going during holiday and vacation times. Of the two islands, Captiva is the least crowded with day visitors, largely because it takes longer to drive up to Captiva from the Sanibel–Fort Myers causeway.

If you can rent a boat on the mainland and travel through the Intracoastal Waterway to see some of these islands, do so. If not, book a room at one of the resorts on Sanibel, Captiva, or Gasparilla. South Seas Resort on Captiva has a boat excursion to Cabbage Key, a favorite haunt of past and present sailors, and to Useppa.

Farther south, near **Naples,** is **Marco Island,** accessible by means of curved, Venetian-style bridges. Both Naples and Marco Island are wealthy communities with few inexpensive accommodations. Old

Naples has a wonderful shopping district on Third Street South. Prices are high, but the area is charming, with excellent restaurants and bistros.

Less well known is the Rookery Bay National Estuarine Research Reserve, a sanctuary and research facility for the study and protection of pelicans, ibis, herons, egrets, and other birds. On an estuary at a turnoff just before the State Road 951 bridge to the island, it has beautiful marshes and mangrove forests. About two thousand birds roost here every night. Like Wakulla Springs, south of Tallahassee, the reserve gives visitors a taste of the richness of Florida's wildlife as it was before man tamed it.

Marco Island is less than an hour's drive west of Everglades City, the "gateway to the Everglades." A drive from the Naples–Marco Island area to the Everglades on Highway 41 (also known as the Tamiami Trail from Tampa to Miami) is worthwhile. Much of the Everglades is inaccessible exccpt by boat, and some areas have grasses that would clog any outboard motor. But on the Tamiami Trail you can see many types of waterfowl in the wet gullies along the road and, in the lagoons, the occasional gnarled hump of an alligator. Along the road is the Indian Village and Culture Center, a commercialized but interesting Indian enclave where you can learn about the Miccosukee Seminole Indians' way of life.

Though Floridians and longtime visitors decry the destruction of native wildlife and plants unique to Florida, there is a greater interest in preserving the environment today than ever before. Legislation passed in the 1980s supports rigorous protection of the environment. Because of such legislation, many hotels, like the Ritz-Carlton, Naples, also have hammocks — forests of native trees — that serve as buffers between the hotel grounds and the shoreline. These harbor a variety of waterfowl and occasional alligators.

Outside Gulf Coast cities, the unique waterfowl and other wildlife of the state can easily be seen by a casual observer. Though their numbers have been greatly depleted and sightings of once-common fauna, like flamingos, are rare today, some animals are making a comeback. Herons and egrets sometimes make their homes near the water hazards of golf courses or on the banks of a shopping center's manmade lagoon.

Alligators are both tolerated and protected in Florida. It is illegal to shoot them, and most residents, understandably, stay out of their way. The most important thing to remember about gators — adult or infant — is never to feed them.

The best way to see wildlife unique to Florida is to make an excursion to one of the state's wildlife sanctuaries, such as the Ding Darling Wildlife Refuge on Captiva Island. For information about these and other sanctuaries, write to the Florida Department of Natural Resources, Office of Communication, 3900 Commonwealth Blvd., Tallahassee, FL 32399.

Anna Maria Island

Bungalow Beach Resort

2000 Gulf Drive North
Bradenton Beach, FL 34217
800-779-3601
941-778-3600
Fax: 941-778-1764
bungalow@bungalowbeach.com
www.bungalowbeach.com

A beachy yet elegant retreat on unpretentious Anna Maria Island

Managers: Bert and Gayle Luper. **Accommodations:** 14 bungalows. **Rates:** $90–$250; less by the week. **Included:** Continental coffee and tea; bicycles. **Minimum stay:** During some weekends and holidays. **Added:** 9% tax. **Payment:** Major credit cards. **Children:** Welcome. **Smoking:** Outside. **Open:** Year-round.

➤   **Anna Maria Island is just south of Tampa and north of Sarasota, at the northern tip of a string of islands off the Gulf Coast.**

Unlike some of its island neighbors to the south, Anna Maria has not been gussied up with wide swaths of water-thirsty lawns and high-rent high rises. Anna Maria is definitely "the beach," and the early-20th-century motels and small resorts that line the two-lane roadway are unpretentious and easy-going. Many of these places were very plain motels that had begun to deteriorate and look passé in recent years. But several of them, including the Bungalow Beach Resort, have been fixed up so that they have many delightful amenities, as well as a sand-between-your-toes informality.

The resort is laid out on each side of Gulf Drive in the manner of an old-fashioned "court" motel, with individual bungalows just a few feet off the road, swimming pools in the center, and the beautiful water beyond. Built in the 1930s, the yellow clapboard buildings have touches of white trim; some have a small patio with an umbrellaed table and chairs. Rather than being only superficially, cosmetically refurbished, the resort has been thoroughly updated, cleaned, and painted, but with an adherence to old features like shuttered or jalousie windows and what appear to be original five-paned cottage doors. The small pools on each side of Gulf Drive are outlined by white picket fences. White chaise longues and lawn chairs are laid out on the pool patios. The grounds include many beautiful subtropical trees and flowers, as well as coconut palms. Guests park beside their bungalow, and white sand and shell paths meander through the property, making everything seem cooler on a hot day.

Each accommodation is a bit different and there's a nice choice: studios (some poolside) are furnished with a king- or queen-size bed. One-, two-, and three-bedroom bungalows have queen-size beds and a sleeper sofa in the sitting room. All accommodations have either a full or efficiency kitchen. Views are of the gulf or the bay, a swimming pool (one has a waterfall), or the gardens. Modern amenities include cable TV, a hair dryer in the bathroom, free local telephone calls, attractive new bathroom fixtures, and a microwave in the kitchen.

Some bungalows have whirlpool bathtubs, cathedral ceilings, hardwood floors, or French windows. The decor is beige and white with wicker and rattan furniture. Decorative pillows with botanical embroidery and ceiling fans contribute to the natural, authentic atmosphere.

Although accommodations are lovely on both sides of Gulf Drive, those on the gulf rather than the bay are more desirable if you're a fan of the more spirited gulf waters. The grounds and courtyards on both sides of the roadway are beautifully kept, but on the gulf side they lead out to a curve of sea oats and white sand dunes and, finally, to gentle aqua waves.

Harrington House Beachfront B&B

5626 Gulf Drive
Holmes Beach, FL 34217
941-778-5444
Fax: 941-778-0527
harhousebb@mail.pcsonline.com
www.harringtonhouse.com

As in a New England Inn, the large common room is the heart of this B&B on the beach

Innkeeper: Jo Davis. **Accommodations:** 8 rooms. **Rates:** $129–$239. **Included:** Full breakfast. **Minimum stay:** During some weekends and special events. **Added:** 9% tax. **Payment:** Major credit cards. **Children:** Age 12 and older welcome. **Smoking:** Outside only. **Open:** Year-round.

➤ **There are many things about the Harrington House that remind one of New England: homey but elegant guest rooms, hearty gourmet breakfasts, the warmth of the hosts, and the broad fieldstone fireplace and hearth in the common room. But the water at the beach just minutes from the door is warmer. Much.**

This B&B is truly a find because it combines so beautifully the best of the traditional New England B&B and the best of Florida's 1920s architecture and informal beach atmosphere. The Harrington is on the upper end of Anna Maria Island in Holmes Beach, set back from the road by a few hundred feet. A berm of grass and flowers serves as a buffer between the narrow road and the B&B. The Harrington itself is almost obstructed by the colorful vegetation that grows in front of this three-story house — at one time the only three-story home on the island. Guests park in the shaded driveway in front and then walk through an archway to the little walkway leading into the Harrington.

Inside, the first room guests step into is the one they'll probably spend a lot of time in when not on the beach. Once the spacious living room of the house, it is now a common room for everyone to enjoy. Walls are of plastered coquina stone, a building material frequently used in houses during the early days of Florida. The natural woodwork is of pecky cypress, resistant to saltwater and now quite rare in Florida construction. The hearth is of rough-cut flat stone in pale earth tones with a pecky cypress mantel. The upholstered sofa and chairs are deep cushioned and very comfortable. Two transomed doorways that once led to the sun porch have been converted into double bookcases. Books are for guests to enjoy while they relax on the sofa. The high cathedral ceilings of this living room originally were part of all early Florida architecture because they kept a house cooler in the summer. Now they afford an airy, spacious feeling to the room.

Just beyond the old living room area are the dining room and a stone-faced enclosed porch. Both of these rooms are set up for breakfast in the morning. In keeping with the best of a New England B&B, breakfast is full rather than Continental. Typically, there's an egg dish or fruit and pancakes accompanied by fresh berries and citrus fruits, cereals, juice, and coffee and tea. Guests who have special dietary needs can be accommodated as long as the Harrington staff is alerted ahead of time.

Host Jo Davis and her staff are extremely skilled at making your stay all that you want it to be in a very unobtrusive way. Guests are invited to use the B&B's kayaks, bicycles, water equipment, and games at no extra charge, first come, first served. Because of the antiques in the Harrington House, those with children under age 12 stay at one of the B&B's other two beachfront properties that are a short walk away: the Suncay Villas or the Beach House. These accommodations also include a full breakfast and use of all the facilities at the Harrington House.

The bedrooms at all three locations are quite individual. The focus is on creature comforts such as wall-to-wall carpets and modern bathrooms combined with old style elegance: floral spreads and quilts, ruffled bedskirts, lace curtains, comfortable wing chairs, dried flower sprays and other Victorian touches above some beds or on the walls. The Veranda Room on the third floor has a larger than average bathroom, a luscious green and cream color scheme, and a deck overlooking the gulf. The Sunset Room, also on the third floor, has interesting angles to the ceiling and a lovely old armoire. The Renaissance Room on the first floor has French provincial decor, a large bathroom, and easy access to the common room and the pool and beach. Some of the rooms have whirlpool bathtubs or a fireplace. All have a small refrigerator, cable TV, and private telephone.

In inclement weather, the individual guest rooms and the sitting and dining areas of the Harrington House are all a treat to relax in for hours. But this isn't New England, after all, so inclement weather is rather rare. Even in the summertime, there is usually a breeze from the gulf that makes being in the out-of-doors pleasant. Just outside the stone porch of the Harrington House is a small rectangular pool and a patio deck furnished with chairs and chaises. There's also a small side yard with a gazebo adjacent to the Harrington's one cottage accommodation.

A picket fence separates the pool area from the beach — a beautiful, beautiful beach with medium-size waves, white sand, and sea oats. The Harrington House is surrounded by many different trees, including tall pines, so there is a sense of privacy here. There is the sound of the breeze flowing through the trees, the murmur of just a few people, and the gentle splashing of the waves on the soft sand.

Cape Haze

Palm Island Resort

7092 Placida Road
Cape Haze, FL 33946
800-824-5412
941-697-4800
Fax: 941-697-0696
www.palmisland.com

A true getaway

Accommodations: 160 suites and villas. **Rates:** At Marina, 1-bedroom villas $95–$150; on Island, 1-bedroom villas $170–$285, 2-bedroom villas $195–$390, 3-bedroom villas $250–$515; packages and weekly rates available. **Minimum stay:** 2 nights; 3 nights during holidays and high season. **Added:** 10% tax. **Payment:** MasterCard, Visa, American Express. **Children:** Under 6 free in room with parent. **Smoking:** Allowed. **Open:** Year-round.

➤ **Guests can rent bicycles, fishing tackle, windsurfers, tennis racquets, swim fins and masks, glass-bottom paddle boats, canoes, and small sailboats.**

Northern escapees from ice and cold could, on waking up at Palm Island their first morning, look out at the beach and think for a minute that they're seeing snow, not beach — that's how pale the sand is. The water is a blue-green so clear you can see several feet down. Best of all, this pristine beauty is just a few miles out from the coast.

Palm Island was developed by some of the same people who did such a superlative job restoring nearby Useppa Island. It is accessible only by boat. Once on the island people walk, ride bikes or golf carts, or take trams to get from place to place. Utility lines are underground, and trash is conscientiously disposed of by residents and visitors. Few day-visitors make it to the island, so there are no crowds.

Palm Island is actually two resorts in one: the island itself and the marina on the mainland, where there is a ship's store, a marina complex, and the white stucco buildings that house the marina villas. The marina accommodations are ideal for anyone arriving by boat who wants to enjoy a night's sleep on land, or for those vacationing on the island and wishing to stay over before taking the launch to the island. The marina villas have a full-size kitchen, a separate bedroom, a pullout sofa in the living and dining room, and a screened porch overlooking the water. Their decor and floor plan are similar to the accommodations on the island.

Vacationers staying on Palm Island take the resort's ferry or, for late arrivals, the water taxi. Ferries run on demand, with a 15-minute (or less) wait, and the cost is figured into the room rate. Once on the island, there is tram service. At the end of a long ramp leading from the island's dock are a casual restaurant, resort recreation, and a general store. Here guests can stock up on food instead of lugging groceries from a mainland supermarket (though prices are higher on the island). Guests can also call ahead and order from the "Island Shopper," a list of food staples, produce, household cleaners, and wines and liquor. For a small fee, the Palm Island staff will stock rental cottages with items guests order from the list before their arrival.

Accommodations are in square-rigger-shaped buildings with an Old Florida look: tin roofs, gray vinyl siding with white trim, double-hung, small-paned windows, French doors, some with fan lights above, white-railed porches, and latticework. The homes are built high on concrete pilings, with storage underneath and pretty lattice concealing the concrete. All are attractively decorated, with wall-to-wall carpet and attractive, easy-care furniture.

Space is well designed, with open living and dining areas, loft bedrooms in the one-bedroom units, breakfast bars, kitchens with full-size refrigerators and stoves, spacious baths, washer/dryers, telephones, satellite cable TV, large closets with mirrored doors, and screened porches with views of the gulf. The two- and three-bedroom units have a bathroom for each bedroom. Some of the spacious beach villas also have dens with pullout couches. The resort has a reasonably priced Continental breakfast at the recreation center and two restaurants for lunch and dinner.

Accommodations are built in clusters, with barbecue grills and foot-washing spigots on the landing of each villa. There are tennis courts and a swimming pool with a whirlpool spa at each cluster, as well as a nature center, clubhouse, 60-slip marina, and tennis center and pro shop at a central location. There are 11 courts on the property, and a full-time tennis pro provides free clinics. Resort rentals include canoes, kayaks, and snorkeling equipment as well as the golf carts and bicycles that guests use to get around. Massage therapy is available by appointment. A scheduled children's program and a safe, wooden climbing and sliding playground keep kids busy. Deep-sea fishing is available by charter at the marina. On the mainland, there is golf at various courses near Sarasota and Fort Myers.

The two-and-a-half-mile beach has been carefully preserved. In the beautiful pale sand, there are more than 400 varieties of shells, as well as petrified sharks' teeth that are four or five million years old. Graceful sea oaks sway on the dunes, and the waters of the gulf lap quietly. After a few nights without city noise and glaring lights, you rest easy, and the sand doesn't look like snow in the morning.

Captiva Island

South Seas Resort

P.O. Box 194
Captiva Island, FL 33924
800-CAPTIVA
941-472-5111

A full-service resort with an informal, South Seas atmosphere

Accommodations: 600 rooms, suites, and villas. **Rates:** Rooms $115–$210, junior suites $215–$365, 1-bedroom villas $205–$420, 2-bedroom villas $295–$710 (1- and 2-bedroom villa rates for 1–4 people; rates higher for 5–6 people). 3-bedroom villas $405–$885 (3-bedroom rates for up to 6 people); $20 extra person; packages available. **Minimum stay:** Varies according to accommodation and season. **Added:** 9% tax; first crib free, second $20; $8 service charge per day. **Payment:** Major credit cards. **Children:** Under 12 free in room with parent. **Smoking:** Nonsmoking rooms available. **Open:** Year-round.

➤ **Captiva Island is famous for its shells, with over 400 varieties, including black sharks' teeth and paper fig shells. It was on Captiva and**

Sanibel that Anne Morrow Lindbergh started the shell collection that became the inspiration for her book *Gift from the Sea.*

In the early part of the century, this island was a plantation that produced key limes and coconuts. Today it's a resort, with so much to do, for any age and interest, that you just can't get bored. But if you want simply to relax, there's no place better than the white sand beach on Captiva Island.

South Seas is a large resort with a busy marina, but it is so well designed that guests are not immediately aware of its vastness. At certain times of the year, there may be as many as 2,000 guests staying here, but the resort never feels crowded. Accommodations are clustered near the golf course, along the beach, and at the marina among beautiful native trees. Parts of the plantation are junglelike, giving a sense of seclusion to the various accommodations and activity centers.

This is a wonderful place for children, not only for the range of children's activities but also because of the resort's setup, right down to the speed bumps in the road and "slow" signs everywhere. Many guests don't drive at all once they get here. Dependable trolleys take guests from one part of the resort to another. This allows older children to go from place to place without needing parents to chauffeur them.

There are various recreational programs for children aged 3 to 17. All programs have age-appropriate activities like arts and crafts, kite making, games, shelling, and sand sculpture for the little ones, and canoeing, sailing, and hiking for the older kids. The programs are provided seven days a week, for half or three-quarters of a day, depending on the season. An enthusiastic, full-time naturalist gives intriguing talks on shells for school-age kids and leads them on shelling expeditions.

Organized family activities include crab races, nature walks, and scavenger hunts for adults. Companies that hold conventions at the resort and want spouses and children to come along get special attention, with adventure trips, theme parties, and competitions that can involve anything from pie eating to an obstacle course.

Corporations can reserve space at the northern end of the island for their family activities and for small meetings at the Harbourside Meeting Center, or gather at the resort's conference center, a spectacular facility at the southern end of the resort for groups of up to 500. The conference center is state of the art, with a concealed projection booth running the length and breadth of the grand ballroom, theatrical lighting, and enough room for vehicle drive-ons.

South Seas has been called a resort within a resort. Guests enter through the security gates at the South End of the property. At this part of the resort are the Bayside Marina (and boat launch), the Nature Center and aquarium, fitness club, the salon, the Tennis Center, the Conference Center, several small boutiques at Chadwick's Square, Mama Rosa's Pizzeria, the steakhouse, and Chadwick's, a restaurant and lounge open to the public. The North End of the plantation has a larger marina, Cap'n Al's Seafood Grill, rentals of bikes, boats, Windsurfers, and jet skis, a sailing school and a game room.

At the North End of the property are some of the original clapboard buildings that made up the plantation. King's Crown, named after a crown-shaped shell common to Captiva, is the resort's fine dining restaurant. Housed in the original commissary building with a wall of small windows overlooking the water, it has a distinctly Old Florida feel. Both the wine list and the menu, which emphasizes fresh seafood, are excellent. Cap'n Al's is still more informal and one of the best places to take children on the property. It is a cool, pavilion-like building, with outside dining at umbrella tables overlooking the marina. Food is not as outstanding here as at the King's Crown, but more than adequate for family meals. Another informal restaurant, Chadwick's, is at the South End, just outside the plantation grounds. Mama Rosa's Pizzeria, near Chadwick's, features unusual combinations that can be eaten in, taken out, or delivered to your room.

Accommodations are in one- and two-bedroom villas. These are no more than four stories high and feature well-equipped kitchens, a living/dining area, and a private porch. Amenities include a private swimming pool and views of the tennis courts or the water. The North End has deluxe hotel rooms and two-bedroom villas within walking distance of the 9-hole golf course and Yacht Harbour. Harbourside hotel rooms, overlooking Pine Island Sound and the Yacht Harbour marina, have two queen-size beds, a king, or a junior suite arrangement with a sitting area. Marina villas have two bedrooms, two baths, a kitchen, a screened porch overlooking the harbor, and a private pool. The two- and three-bedroom condos at Land's End Village look the most like Old Florida, with gray wooden siding, white trim, and tin roofs. These accommodations are the most luxurious and the most expensive (about $100 more than the regular villa prices). They feature separate living and dining rooms, a well-equipped kitchen, two bathrooms, a screened porch with water views, and a pool for Land's End guests with a hydro-spa and a poolside lanai.

The interiors of all accommodations are nicely decorated with carpets and light oak furniture. The bathrooms are particularly large and well designed. Even the hotel rooms have big bathrooms with a closet area, dressing room, and separate vanity at one end and a toilet and oval tub at the other. Above the tub is a cord for hanging wet clothes. When outfitted with two queen-size beds, the hotel rooms are quite adequate for a family. Another good choice for a family, particularly if you want to save money by cooking your own meals, is a one-bedroom villa at the South End. These villas aren't inexpensive, but the guests who come back each year seem to feel they're getting their money's worth.

A major draw at South Seas Resort is the excellent tennis program. The resident pro and his teaching assistants give excellent instruction. Of the 18 courts, seven near the Tennis Center are lighted for night play, with the remainder scattered about the property near villa accommodations. So, except for a lesson or clinic, guests don't have to go to the tennis complex to play a game.

The resort also has 18 swimming pools. Like the tennis courts, they are near the villas, and their varied locations contribute to the uncrowded ambience of the plantation. For those who love the beach, the beachside villas are the best choice. Water sports abound. Canoes, kayaks, sailboats, and power boats are all available for rent.

'Tween Waters Inn

P.O. Box 249
Captiva Island, FL 33924
800-223-5865
941-472-5161
Fax: 941-472-0249
resv@tween-waters.com
www.tween-waters.com

> **Informal old cottages and
> suites for families**

Accommodations: 137 rooms, suites, and cottages. **Rates:** Rooms $170–$260, suites $225–$330, cottages $140–$320; $25 extra person. **Minimum stay:** None. **Added:** 9% tax; $5 rollaway. **Included:** Continental breakfast buffet. **Payment:** American Express, MasterCard, Visa, Discover; personal checks; cash. **Children:** Under 12 free in room with parent. **Open:** Year-round.

➤ **The tennis courts, pool, and Oasis pool bar are tucked away in the middle of the property, where lush greenery and palm trees enhance the hideaway feeling of the place.**

'Tween Waters Inn was once accessible only by boat. Visitors now reach it by the island's main road, an extension of a narrow thoroughfare that begins on Sanibel Island, the first island past the bridge from Fort Myers. The road winds through Captiva under a canopy of wispy pines. The Gulf of Mexico is shallow here, and the white sand lends the water a turquoise color.

Where the road bends to the east a little, a gray wooden sign marks the 'Tween Waters Inn. With Pine Island Sound on one side and the Gulf of Mexico on the other, the name is apt. Here you can watch the sun set over the sea in the evening and turn around the next morning to watch it rise over another beautiful body of water.

The Inn is a collection of several old cottages painted in shades of pink and salmon and newer apartment buildings constructed on supports with carports underneath. The inn started with just one cottage in 1926 and was operated by the same family until 1969. The atmosphere is nautical and beachy — very informal. Dress is a swimsuit or shorts and a shirt during the day, and casual dresses and pants for dinner.

Attractive paving stones and planters are at the entrance that leads to a small reception center. Sandy paths, boardwalks, and curved wooden bridges connect all the inn's buildings to the tennis courts and swimming pool complex, the marina, the conference meeting room, and the resort's popular restaurant and bar. 'Tween Waters has been added to several times in forty years, so there's a wide choice of accommodations for a place this small, with standard rooms, cottages, apartments, and efficiency rooms.

The old cottages are spacious and reasonably priced, and some families have been coming to the same cottage for years. But they are not necessarily the best choice for everybody. Some of them are close to the road and restaurant and can be a bit noisy. The suites in the inn's new buildings would be better for the average family or for vacationing friends. These have a modern kitchen, a spacious sitting area with a sofa bed, two queen-size beds in separate bedrooms, and a screened balcony.

The smaller, waterview rooms are good for families that don't want to do much cooking. These have one large room with two queen-size beds, a mini-refrigerator, and a screened balcony overlooking the water. A new building has one-bedroom suites and three-bedroom suites, all with bay views.

Two of the buildings have laundry facilities that are available to all guests. Rates include daily maid service, but people renting accommodations with kitchens must do their own kitchen cleanup. When making reservations, have the staff send you the inn's rate sheet, which has full descriptions and a map showing locations and water views.

Recreation includes shuffleboard, boating, fishing, shelling, sailing, kayaking, tennis, bicycling, swimming in the Inn's large freeform pool, and a fitness center. Pelican's Roost, the marina store, sells everything from beer to sportswear to bait. The staff rents canoes, sailboats, bicycles, tennis rackets, and fishing gear. They can arrange for fishing and sightseeing excursions and will provide shelling supplies and information on bird watching.

The Inn's Old Captiva House restaurant has been around for years and is immensely popular with locals and guests. The dining room has been cited as one of the 200 best restaurants in Florida.

Also at the Old Captiva House is the Crow's Nest, a smaller dining area and lounge that serves lunch and dinner and has nightly entertainment. Behind the Crow's Nest is the Ding Darling Room — J. N. "Ding" Darling was a conservationist and cartoonist who stayed at the Inn for thirty years. His exuberant sketches and cartoons decorate the walls, and the wildlife refuge nearby is named for him.

It is understandable why 'Tween Waters has been so loved by so many. With luck and love, it will survive another sixty years.

Cedar Key

Cedar Key Bed & Breakfast

Third Street and F Street
Cedar Key, FL 32625
877-543-5051
352-543-9000
Fax: 352-543-8070
bob@cedarkeybedbreakfast.com
www.cedarkeybedbreakfast.com

> **A gingerbread Victorian a block from the gulf and a world away from Florida glitz**

Innkeepers: Bob and Lois Davenport. **Accommodations:** 7 rooms. **Rates:** $75–$120; $20 extra adult in room. **Included:** Full breakfast. **Minimum stay:** 3 nights for special events. **Added:** 7% tax. **Payment:** Discover, MasterCard, Visa, traveler's checks, personal checks. **Children:** Please inquire. **Smoking:** Allowed outside only. **Open:** Year-round.

➤ **In the back yard is a replica of an old island "cracker house."**

Residents of Cedar Key are proud of the fact that the town has a permanent population of 800 and not one traffic light. There have been times in its past when the island was prosperous, with pencil factories, lumber mills, commercial fishing, and sponge harvesting, and the population had risen to a whopping 4,000. But those times are gone, and most folks on Cedar Key are just as glad. They like the quiet and the slow, slow pace.

In places like Palm Beach and Miami, the island has the reputation for being redneck — if it's known at all. But it is a mistake to dismiss Cedar Key as if it were just a quirky place with good fishing. A number of well-educated, well-traveled, creative people have retreated from big cities throughout the country to settle in Cedar Key. There are two museums in this little place and an annual arts festival. The offbeat creativity is evident in some of the shops downtown and on the waterfront, or during a walk from Second Street (Cedar Key's main street) to the Cedar Key B&B at Third and "F" Streets. Some of the old clapboard houses are painted three or four whimsical colors, and many homes have little gardens with odd pieces of rusting "found art" and some genuine art sculpted by the owners or friends. The island's funky charm grows on the observant visitor after only a day or two.

The Cedar Key B&B is in a residential neighborhood on the southern tip of the island. It's an ideal location, a half block to the water. Mostly frequented by fishermen, this part of the gulf, called Goose Bay, has a small, quiet beach outlined by a sweep of green marsh grass. The view between the Cedar Key B&B and the water is marred by a blocky, one-story apartment building. It's too bad, but just avert your eyes when walking by and concentrate on the blue-green water.

The B&B was built in 1880 to house employees of the Eagle Pencil Company. Like so many nice old Victorians in Florida towns that survived economic downturns in the early 20th century, the house fell into neglect until it was partially restored by the previous owners. Since then, Bob and Lois have invested thousands of dollars and tremendous energy into creating a turn-of-the-century retreat. An outgoing, middle-aged couple, they enjoy maintaining the restored building and garden but also like spending time with their guests.

Two of the rooms in the Cedar Key B&B are named after women who grew up in the house. Miss Ida's Room is quite Victorian, with dark wood and lamps of multicolored glass. There's a comfortable wingback chair here, a king-size bed, and a collection of pewter soldiers. The bathroom has a small clawfoot tub-shower. Miss Verona's Room has a king-size bed and a daybed, both covered in down comforters. The private bath has a large clawfoot tub with a European-style handheld shower. These rooms are on the first floor in the main house. One of the two new upstairs rooms has a king-size bed and a private porch overlooking the gulf and 300-year-old trees.

Downstairs are two more rooms, which were created out of the old summer kitchen; these open onto the side veranda overlooking the gulf. Both are fairly small — 10 by 13 feet — and have small bathrooms, but the walk-in showers help make up for this. Both have a queen-size bed. These rooms are also decorated in a charming Victorian style with interesting collectibles and pretty needlework by Lois's mother. The bleached hardwood floors are covered with Oriental rugs.

The Honeymoon Cottage, formerly a separate building in the back of the house, is one of the B&B's most impressive rooms. Walls are sparkling white, and the furniture is white wicker. Lace swags are at the windows and the brass king-size bed is covered in white lace. The bathroom has a large clawfoot tub with shower. All the rooms with soaking tubs have complimentary bath salts.

On the side of the house is a long, narrow breakfast room that looks out on the lawn and a centuries-old oak tree. The food is filling and wonderful: homemade breads and pastries, fresh fruit, yogurt, cereals, juice, and an egg casserole, quiche, or French toast. Just off the breakfast room is a porch where guests can sit with their coffee. There are also benches out on the lawn and a hammock, all overlooking a slice of the gulf.

Island Hotel

Second and "B" Street
P.O. Box 460
Cedar Key, FL 32625
352-543-5111
800-432-4640
ishotel@islandhotel-cedarkey.com
www.islandhotel-cedarkey.com

> **An old-time hotel with its own funky character**

Innkeepers: Dawn and Tony Cousins. **Accommodations:** 13 rooms. **Rates:** $75–$110; $20 extra person in room. **Included:** Full breakfast. **Minimum stay:** 2 nights on some weekends. **Added:** 7% tax. **Payment:** MasterCard, Visa, traveler's checks. **Children:** Over age 12 welcome. **Smoking:** On porches, in downstairs lobby, and in bar only. **Open:** Year-round.

➤ **From any point in town, the water is within walking distance. Cruises to the barrier islands just offshore are offered by locals for dolphin sightings, shelling, and bird watching. Boats are also available for deep-sea fishing.**

The Island Hotel's history goes back to 1859, when it was built as a general store. Later, the owners apparently converted the upstairs into a boarding house and added a restaurant. Constructed of heavy oak timbers and 10-inch-thick tabby walls of limestone and oyster shell, the building was built to last. While many other businesses and houses on the island have been felled by various disasters, the Island Hotel has survived the Civil War, hurricanes, floods, fires, and the Great Depression.

Once visitors turn off Route 19/98 onto little Highway 24, more than 20 miles of road, three bridges, and a lot of salt marshes have to be crossed before they finally reach Cedar Key, but it's worth it. The island of Cedar Key has had a great many economic ups and downs, especially as part of the lumber industry that once thrived in this area. Cedar Key is regarded by some urban Floridians as "redneck," and in some cases the description is not far off the mark. But the town has an independent, down-to-earth character that is rarely found at a Gold Coast golf resort.

Island Hotel owners Dawn and Tony Cousins want the hotel to be a place where people can get away from the stress of contemporary life, read a good book, and watch the sun set. The Island Hotel has been a restaurant and B&B since 1992. Although a previous owner had an outstanding chef and the restaurant gained a reputation for fresh, natural ingredients and excellent seafood, the hotel itself had become run-down.

Each room has its own quirks and character, its advantages and disadvantages. A front room with scuffed floors and furniture may have a great view of the gulf, while a room in the back might have a feather bed or a clawfoot tub. All rooms have private baths; many have porcelain sinks and tubs from the 1880s that have been refinished. Room 28 has the best bathroom, though it's across the hall from the room. Ask Dawn or Tony for a description of individual rooms when you make reservations.

Ten of the rooms are on the second floor but there are also three newly refurbished rooms on the ground floor of the Annex. One of the most unusual comforts of the hotel is the upstairs sitting room, which many of the guest rooms open onto and all share as a place to relax and congregate. Its wall murals are its most intriguing feature. These and the Neptune mural in the bar downstairs were painted decades ago by a guest in exchange for room and board. The scenes, mostly of cypress trees and palms and water, are almost ethereal in mood. Painted on the original cedar planks of the wood paneling, the colors have faded to sepia tones of brown and pale tan.

The eclectic grouping of furniture fits in with the mood of the murals: an aging Empire-style sofa, a writing desk and English settee, a Victorian rocker, a long bookcase, a chess set, and various collectibles. This is a very relaxing place to spend the evening, and since there are no telephones or televisions in the rooms and no flashy nightlife in town, there's no reason not to. The hallway behind the sitting room leads to the veranda, a wonderful place to watch the sun set over the gulf.

Dinner is in the hotel dining room or adjacent lattice-trimmed porch. Weather permitting, the porch is preferable (and usually, on the gulf, the weather does permit). The hotel dining room has recently been restored to its 1950s grandeur, with pictures of Cedar Key landmarks by local artists lining the walls. The porch overlooks the passing scene on Cedar Key's main street and a side street.

Food is definitely four-star cuisine — the Island Hotel restaurant is the best place to eat for many miles around. As much as possible, the chef uses ingredients grown or caught in Cedar Key. A typical meal might begin with artichoke hearts with sautéed shrimp or the restaurant's famous heart of palm salad, and move on to bouillabaisse, Cedar Key soft-shell crabs, or stone crab claws. The poultry and meat dishes are imaginative enough to make up for not coming straight from nearby waters: pork tenderloin sautéed with grapes and mushrooms, rosemary lamb chops, chicken sautéed in cream and rosemary. Vegetarian cuisine is offered as well. The wine list is extremely good — again, the best for miles around.

Clearwater Beach

Clearwater Beach Hotel

500 Mandalay Avenue
Clearwater Beach, FL 34630
800-292-2295
813-441-2425
Fax: 813-449-2083

| **A Clearwater Beach tradition** |

Accommodations: 157 rooms and suites. **Rates:** Rooms $110–$199, suites $169–$249, kitchen suites $135–$249, efficiencies $100–$155; $8 for extra bed. **Minimum stay:** During some weekends or special events. **Added:** 11% tax. **Payment:** Major credit cards. **Children:** Welcome. **Smoking:** Allowed. **Open:** Year-round.

➤ **With Clearwater's brass-studded lounge and restaurant and the beach out back, guests need not even leave the hotel grounds during their stay.**

The words "casual elegance" have been used in so many Florida and Caribbean resort brochures that they have become a cliché, but these words do epitomize the Clearwater Beach Hotel. The original hotel was built in the early part of this century and added to over the years to include beachside apartments and cottages and quarters for the hotel staff. Over the years, both luminaries and unknowns have stayed at the hotel. The wealthiest families from the North would arrive in winter by private railway car.

For many years, the hotel stood alone on the beach and was the only place to stay here. Then, as Clearwater Beach became more and more developed, the strip of highway along the beach became more and more commercialized and honky-tonk. The loyal clientele of the hotel aged, and young people stayed away from a hotel that was beginning to deteriorate. But today, the Clearwater Beach Hotel rises above the "strip" that is reminiscent of Ft. Lauderdale or Daytona. When guests enter the elegant hostelry, they leave it all behind. There is both energy and graciousness here and a growing clientele of young couples, families, and retirees. If you call ahead, the hotel will even arrange to pick you up at the Tampa or Clearwater airport.

The main hotel building was razed a few years ago and replaced with a brand-new building that has the decor and ambience of the original — guests who aren't told think the place is at least fifty years old. In addition to the main building, the Clearwater has beachside efficiency apartments and the Gulf Court Building. All the accommodations have pleasant views of the gulf, the bay, or the pool and gardens. Unless you need a great deal of space, a room in the main building is probably your best bet. These have a private balcony, a small refrigerator, and cable TV.

The main building has some common rooms behind the reception area that wouldn't be found in a conventional modern hotel. There is a library for all guests to use and a banquet and function room called the Oval Room, which has an oval wall of windows at one end and is decorated in rich fabrics. The nearby Dining Room and Schooner Bar hark back to a gracious era when service was better than it is now at the average South Florida hotel restaurant. The Dining Room serves all three meals and specializes in local fresh seafood. At poolside, there is also a casual bar for drinks and snacks.

The courteous staff can arrange for off-property tennis, water sports, and fishing, although for most guests, the hotel's pool and private beach are the focal points of their stay. The Clearwater manages to make guests feel they can relax and "beach it" in elegant, Old Florida surroundings.

Gasparilla Island

Gasparilla Inn

5th and Palm Streets
Boca Grande
Gasparilla Island, FL 33921
941-964-2201

An Old Florida inn with a rich past

Accommodations: 140 rooms and cottages. **Rates:** Rooms $125–$200, adjoining parlor $175–$254; off-season packages available; meal plans available. **Minimum stay:** On certain holidays and weekends. **Added:** 9% tax; charges for extra person; $15 cribs; per person daily service charge. **Payment:** Personal checks. Credit cards not accepted. **Children:** Welcome. **Smoking:** Allowed. **Open:** Winter and spring.

➤ **The island is a lovely place to stroll, particularly along the water, where sea oats grow on the sand dunes.**

The Gasparilla Inn has such a loyal following of retirees and others (85 percent repeat business) that it doesn't advertise. Consequently, not everybody knows about the inn, and lots of folks want to keep it that way.

To those who do know the island, Gasparilla is famous for tarpon fishing and a history of colorful pirates. The island and its namesake hostelry are named after the most famous of these, José Gaspar, an 18th-century Spanish courtier who made for the high seas when he got into trouble at court. Boca Grande, then called High Town, was his headquarters. He is reputed to have entertained his most beautiful captured women and — perhaps — to have buried treasure here.

The village of Boca Grande, the only town on the island, was exclusively a fishing port until the railroad came in at the turn of the century, after which it survived on phosphate shipping as well. By the 1920s, it was a winter enclave for industrialists, and even today, the DuPonts, Swifts, and Oscar Mayers have winter homes here. But the inn staff and the villagers make little of this; an effort is made to protect the privacy of those who stay here.

The inn has a history and character of its own. Built as the Boca Grande in 1912 by Barron Collier, who developed so much of the Gulf Coast, the inn was added to over the years. Its main building is a Greek Revival inn with yellow vinyl siding and white trim and a brick courtyard out front. Inside are common rooms furnished in wicker and chintz, and an old dining room in white and pale yellow with a white brick fireplace and wooden floors. All meals are prepared from scratch, even the ice cream.

Standard hotel rooms are available in the main inn building, while cottage accommodations are spread throughout the inn grounds and the town of Boca Grande. Rooms are motel-comfortable, with ceiling fans, linoleum floors, and a mix of old wooden furniture, wicker, and Formica. Bathrooms may have tubs only, and some rooms come with twin beds. Cottages are roomier, with kitchenettes and porches furnished with rockers. The homey yellow cottages have grassy front yards and are usually fenced.

The basic accommodations are a disappointment to those who envision luxurious resort suites. People come here for the creaky, Old Florida ambience, the natural beauty of the island, and the funkiness of the little town of Boca Grande.

Although it calls itself an inn, the Gasparilla is also a resort. The 18-hole golf course is particularly nice, with a clubhouse built in 1926 that includes a handsome widow's walk. A split-rail fence encircles the course, and pretty flower beds adjacent to the fence include oleander trees and bougainvillea. The Gasparilla Inn closes down in June for the summer, and the old course is groomed and improved upon each year.

The Beach and Tennis Club is located two blocks from the main inn building at the beach. The clubhouse is new, with gray wood siding and a shake roof. There are eight courts and a resident pro on hand to help guests improve their game. The facilities include two swimming pools, an exercise club with saunas, a restaurant and bar, and a Great Hall for parties and receptions.

Every April, the town of Boca Grande is taken over by a passion for sport fishing. The inn keeps a list of dozens of local fishing guides who take guests out for deep-sea excitement. April is also the best time for families to come to the Gasparilla Inn; the atmosphere is more festive and casual than it is in the winter, when the inn tends to have an older, wealthier crowd that is more sedate or, some might say, staid.

The town itself is fun to walk around in or bicycle through. The old railroad bed leading to Boca Grande from the mainland has been converted into a bicycle path, and the inn has bikes to rent. The bicycle path ends at the old depot. Now the Loose Caboose Restaurant and Ice Cream Shop, it's a whimsical place, with 1910 vacuum cleaners and other turn-of-the-century gadgets decorating the original matchstick paneled walls and a Lionel train zooming above patrons' heads on an overhead track.

Longboat Key

Colony Beach and Tennis Resort

1620 Gulf of Mexico Drive
Longboat Key, FL 34228
800-426-5669
941-383-6464
Fax: 941-383-7549

**An island resort for sports
and beachside indolence**

General Manager: Katherine Moulton. **Accommodations:** 235 suites. **Rates:** 1-bedroom suites $195–$495, 2-bedroom suites $245–$645, clubhouse suites $465–$575, lanais and beach suites $505–$665, beachfront house $750–$1,195; holiday, weekend, and sports packages; special rates for month-long stays. **Minimum stay:** On some holidays and with certain packages. **Added:** 10% tax; $15 one-time charge for crib or rollaway. **Payment:** Major credit cards. **Children:** Under 18 free in room with parent. **Smoking:** Allowed. **Open:** Year-round.

➤ **On the beach, a short walk from the accommodations, the water sports center has sailboats, windsurfers, and aqua bikes. Swimmers and sun worshipers can also enjoy the heated pool just a step away. After a swim, have a drink at the Colony's patio bar.**

This resort really does have the feeling of a colony, an enclave of low-rise villas clustered together only a few hundred feet from the beach. And what a resort for tennis buffs. With five-star ratings from tennis magazines, this is one of the outstanding tennis resorts in Florida. There are 21 courts, with two lit for night play — 11 hard surface and six with a soft Hydro surface. A professional staff of nine is on hand to teach; they also will play with guests whenever an appropriate match isn't possible. Court time is free for guests, although reservations are required. Special programs include Tiny Tots Tennis, for kids six and under; a Junior Clinic, hourly instruction for beginners and intermediates; and special tennis packages. The Colony will find partners for guests who wish to play with someone at their own level.

The owner of the Colony, "Murf" Klauber, is a fitness buff, so this is an excellent resort for the health-conscious. The complimentary fitness center has a range of workout equipment and free weights. The health spas have saunas, whirlpools, and steam rooms. The wide array of activities includes low-impact aerobics, "better back" classes, introductory weight training, yoga, water aerobics, and nature walks. There is also a full-service salon.

For a gourmet dinner overlooking the water, there's the Colony Restaurant Dining Room. This restaurant and its wine cellar have garnered well-deserved awards over the years, and the staff is personable, fun, and efficient. This is an excellent place for lunch as well as dinner, with some interesting hot entrées and imaginative salads and dressings. The crisp, flavorful vegetables are organically grown. Desserts are as sinful as one might expect at an award-winning restaurant.

The other main restaurant, the Colony Bistro, serves Floridian specialties and traditional American fare. A private dining room for up to 14 people is ideal for small parties and family reunions. Tastebuds, a gourmet market and wine shop, caters to those who cook in their suites. It stocks pâté, sandwiches, and salads made by the Colony Restaurant. Tastebuds' offerings can be ordered ahead of time and delivered to your suite.

Shopping at the resort includes the Patio Shop for sundries, the Colony Beach Sports Shop, and Le Tennique, with a selection of handcrafted gifts, antiques, and designer clothing. Most guests simply walk to the shops as well as to various activities. The resort is gated and has speed bumps and "slow" signs everywhere. Older kids will walk confidently from place to place.

The many amenities of the resort make it attractive to companies for corporate retreats and meetings. An expert conference staff helps corporate groups organize meetings of up to 200 people. Groups can opt for fitness breaks — several minutes of exercise and motivation scheduled in the middle of a conference — as well as the regularly scheduled activities at the fitness center. The conference center has a landscaped deck for breaks and outdoor buffets.

Some corporate groups rent the spacious beachfront executive houses or the adults-only lanais and clubhouse suites. These have many extras such as designer furniture, oversize marble bathrooms, cathedral ceilings, skylights, and oceanfront decks. Other suites popular with vacationing families are the standard one- and two-bedroom suites: they have a living room with twin Murphy beds or pullout sofa, a fully equipped kitchen and dining area, an attractively decorated bedroom (or bedrooms), and a marble bathroom with a separate mirrored dressing room, a whirlpool bath, and a steam shower. Some of the suites have balconies with wonderful views of the gulf.

The Resort at Longboat Key

301 Gulf of Mexico Drive
Longboat Key, FL 34228
941-383-8821
800-237-8821

> **The Gulf of Mexico is on one side, Sarasota Bay is on the other.**

Accommodations: 232 suites. **Rates:** Club suites $180–$475, 2-bedroom suites $345–$965; packages available. **Minimum stay:** 2 nights with some packages. **Payment:** Major credit cards. **Added:** 10% tax; $15 for rollaway. **Children:** Free in room with parent. **Smoking:** Nonsmoking suites available. **Open:** Year-round.

➤ **At the 277-slip marina on Sarasota Bay, you can rent sailboats and arrange for group cruises, marine ecology wading trips, and fishing expeditions. If you're planning to arrive in your own boat, reserve dockage in advance.**

The Resort at Longboat Key, like its neighbor just down the boulevard, the Colony, is very private, with facilities open only to members, residents, and overnight guests. It's also a gated residential community and a wildlife sanctuary. Some first-time visitors are surprised to find that the resort is so large and that accommodations open to the public are in high-rise condos. However, the suites are very pleasant and command fantastic views of the gulf or the golf course and the Sarasota skyline. Even the parking lots are pretty, with landscaped barriers and arborlike carports.

Despite the resort's high-rise look, there is a surprising variety of accommodations. These include guest rooms with twin beds; club suites with a king-size bed, a kitchenette, and living/sleeping area; one-bedroom suites with king-size beds and a spacious living/dining room next to the kitchen; two-bedroom suites with a king-size bed in the master bedroom and twin beds in another; deluxe suites with two bedrooms, a kitchen, and a generous living/dining room. All suites have a washer and dryer and twice-daily maid service, which includes dishwashing. All accommodations have balconies overlooking the gulf or Sarasota and the golf course lagoons. Bathrooms include a separate dressing area with a vanity and a makeup mirror.

Gastronomic needs — and temptations — are taken care of at the resort's restaurants, with both indoor and outdoor dining. There are also a number of excellent restaurants in Sarasota at St. Armand's Circle. The concierge will offer dining suggestions and directions. Recently, there have been complaints from guests that the staff at the desk are not as gracious as they could be. However, the conference staff service is more praiseworthy. The resort's John Ringling Room covers 3,000 square feet and can be divided into two rooms for conferences or banquets. In addition, there are four smaller rooms that can accommodate 10 to 50 people. Anyone here for a conference or executive retreat can, of course, enjoy all that the resort has to offer.

With championship courses, Longboat's most important offering is golf. The Islandside Course was designed by Billy Mitchell, with views of the Gulf of Mexico and long, winding fairways situated among small lakes and lagoons. One of the delights of this course is that the lagoons are frequented by various species of waterfowl, who lounge along the banks.

Tennis at Longboat Key is challenging, with 38 Har-Tru courts — six lit for night play — and a tennis center and pro shop.

In addition to golf and tennis, the resort has a number of activities organized by an activities coordinator: swimnastics, aerobics, arts and crafts, tennis and golf clinics, movies, shopping trips, and Ringling Museum tours. Special performing arts packages take advantage of Sarasota's concert series and theater productions.

Apart from fishing, golf, and tennis, most guests find that they can easily fill most of a day with beach activities. The resort offers a number of waterfront amenities, from snorkeling gear to sailboards to tandem bicycles to a double chaise longue with umbrella, all available for rent at the beach. Sailing lessons are also offered for a reasonable fee, and boats can be rented by the hour, half-day, or full day. The waters of the Gulf of Mexico are warm, with gentle waves — especially good for children. The beach is famous for soft white sand and shelling, and sunsets over the gulf are impressive.

Wicker Inn

5581 Gulf of Mexico Drive
Longboat Key, FL 34228
800-881-2244
941-383-5562
Fax: 941-383-9780
wickerinn@mail.org
www.wickerinn-longboatkey.com

> **Wicker on the porch and
> the Gulf of Mexico just
> beyond**

Accommodations: 8 suites (with more at Arbors by the Sea). **Rates:** Weekly
$833–$2324; call for nightly rates. **Added:** 10% tax. **Minimum stay:** 3 nights.
Payment: Major credit cards. **Children:** Welcome. **Smoking:** Outside. **Open:**
Year-round.

➤   The Wicker Inn is exactly what is sounds like: informal and relaxing,
hearkening back to a slower pace of life. A narrow strip of lawn, flowerbeds with both tropical and old-fashioned varieties, and a low white
picket fence introduce this pleasant beachside resort. White wicker rockers are on the porch of every clapboard cottage, and purple bougainvillea
drapes luciously over a white arbor.

These one- and two-story cottages are vinyl-sided clapboard
painted in several Mediterranean colors, with gingerbread-trimmed
verandas, white railings, and tin roofs. Each first-floor patio has a
barbecue grill. White shell paths wind around the cottages and
down to the beach and the gulf. Brightly colored bougainvillea,
hibiscus, and other tropical flowers grow everywhere. A white, tin-
roofed gazebo leads to the pool and white-paved patio. A bit further

on is the white archway that leads to a buffer of natural vegetation and then the uncrowded beach and the Gulf of Mexico.

All the rooms are suites, and each suite is named after a flower. The Orchid, Primrose, Magnolia, and Sunflower are two-bedroom, two-bath accommodations. The Bougainvillea is a two-bedroom, one-bath cottage. Morning Glory is a two-bedroom, one-bath suite, while Camellia, Periwinkle, Hibiscus, Gardenia, and Oleander have one bedroom and one bathroom. Some suites have porches or decks with black iron patio furniture. When you make a reservation, you can ask for a specific suite and inquire about the views and individual amenities.

Each suite has light plaster walls accented with seascapes, paddle fans above, white wicker and cushioned rattan furnishings, and tile and hardwood floors. Kitchens are well equipped for any couple or family wishing to stay a week or longer. All have full-size refrigerators, ranges, dishwashers, and microwave ovens. Amenities include the Water Lily laundry room near the pool — not a small consideration with all the wet towels and suits that accumulate for the average family at the Wicker Inn.

Although this is called an inn, there is no breakfast or other food offered, as at a New England inn. Most people here are staying for a week or more, and families typically cook in their suite and then go out for some meals to restaurants and cafés at nearby Armands Circle or in Sarasota.

Just south of the Wicker Inn is another small resort, Arbors by the Sea, owned by the same people who run the inn. The accommodations at the Arbors are also extremely attractive: small cottages of wooden clapboards, scalloped shingles, and white trim and latticework. Also named after flowers, these accommodations are mid-century refurbished units with shuttered, double swing-out windows, wicker-furnished patios and decks, flower boxes, small individual gardens, and handsome views of the gulf. The efficiencies and one- and two-bedroom suites here have lacy wicker and rattan furniture with floral and pastel cushions, hardwood floors, cable TV and VCR, a private patio with a grill, and a nice kitchen. The Rose and Azalea cottages can be rented as a three-bedroom, two-bath unit at a weekly rate. Like the Wicker Inn, all of the accommodations are set back from the highway and joined by white shell pathways, which also meander out to the quiet beach.

Marco Island

Marco Island Marriott Resort & Golf Club

400 S. Collier Boulevard
Marco Island, FL 34145
800-GET-HERE
941-394-2511

> **A relaxed resort for people of many interests**

Accommodations: 735 rooms. **Rates:** Rooms $120–$350, 1-bedroom suites $309–$629, 2-bedroom suites $479–$899, lanais $265–$879, villas $379–$679; packages available. **Minimum stay:** With packages and during holidays. **Added:** 9% tax. **Payment:** Major credit cards, personal checks with credit card. **Children:** Free in room with parent. **Smoking:** Allowed. **Open:** Year-round.

➤ **The sand is fine near the water, coarser and full of interesting shells near the walkway to the resort. Shell gathering is so popular here that there is a little shell-washing station with a sink and spigot at the edge of the beach.**

Marco Island lies between Everglades City and Naples, accessible by small bridges. One of the first things that strikes a visitor is how many people are outdoors: walking, jogging, bicycling, whacking tennis balls. It's no wonder, with an average year-round temperature of 74 degrees and miles of shoreline. The Marco Island Marriott Resort is one of the friendliest places on the island.

Rooms and suites at the resort are some of the best in the Marriott chain. Extras include a minibar, color cable TV, a small refrigerator, a coffeemaker, spacious closets, and a little balcony overlooking the water. Rooms in the two high-rise towers offer king-size beds or two doubles. All rooms have a view of the water, with the best — and most expensive — directly on the beach. Additional accommodations at Marco Island include six penthouse suites in the tower with wraparound balconies overlooking the gulf, lanai suites right on the beach, and private villas. Ask about package rates.

Dining options include the Voyager restaurant and lounge, offering such Florida delicacies as stone crabs and conch chowder. The Ristorante Tuscany is more formal, with an excellent wine list and Northern Italian cuisine. Other offerings for food and drink are decidedly casual: Quinn's on the Beach, Café del Sol (a good place for children), the poolside Tiki Bar & Grill, and the Pizzeria.

Shopping includes seven boutiques off the lobby and a pro shop by the tennis courts. Amazingly for a resort, the shops have reasonable prices and even some sales.

The self-contained quality of the resort makes it popular for conventions. Facilities include two ballrooms, three conference rooms, and four boardrooms. Corporations and professional groups usually choose this Marriott with the participants' families in mind. Kids Klub, the well-supervised program for children aged 5 to 12, includes storytelling, arts and crafts, field trips, sand castle building, video games, and scavenger hunts. Recreation for older children and adults includes three swimming pools, whirlpools, two miniature golf courses, a health club, tennis, volleyball, sailing, water skiing, parasailing, and golf.

If there were nothing else on Marco Island, it would be worth coming here just for the three and a half miles of beach in the resort's back yard. Sunsets are spectacular and are especially pleasant over a cool drink at the beachside Tiki Bar.

The hotel is beautifully landscaped and thoughtfully designed. Guests staying on the upper floors of the north and south towers can dress for swimming and take an elevator directly to the pool on the first level, bypassing the second-level lobby. The atmosphere in the pool and recreation area between the hotel and the beach is relaxed, and convention groups often have evening receptions and buffets on the patio.

The lobby has the same relaxed ambience despite its elegant decor — terrazzo floors, large planters of coral stone, and West Indies-style wicker and rattan furniture. But no one wants to take the elegance too seriously: a big green stuffed alligator sometimes holds court in the lobby.

Naples

Edgewater Beach Hotel

1901 Gulf Shore Blvd. North
Naples, FL 33940
800-821-0196
941-262-6511
Fax: 941-262-1243

> **An all-suite beachside hotel with an American and European clientele**

Accommodations: 124 suites. **Rates:** 1- bedroom suite: $140–$650, 2-bedroom suite: $260–$1,500; packages available. **Minimum stay:** 3 nights during holiday weekends. **Added:** 9% tax. **Payment:** MasterCard, Visa. **Children:** Under 18 free in room with parent. **Smoking:** Nonsmoking suites available. **Open:** Year-round.

➤ **Later in the evening, when the kids have gone to bed, the patio walkway and softly lit garden are ideal for a romantic stroll.**

The Edgewater Beach Hotel is on lovely Gulf Shore Boulevard. Once the playground of the wealthy, the Edgewater makes this beautiful location accessible to ordinary folks who want to splurge for a weekend or the winter season. Though some of the accommodations are expensive, the amenities of this all-suite hotel can make it a good value.

The atmosphere is unpretentious. Many retired people bring their grown children and grandchildren for part of their stay, coming here generation after generation; the Edgewater is not the enclave of any one age or economic group. Activities include an excellent children's program. The pleasant young staff is attentive and ready to arrange outings and golf excursions if you want more recreation than the hotel offers. And they are also sensitive to the fact that most people are here just to enjoy the beach and each other's company.

The Edgewater rests on a slight rise several yards back from Gulf Shore Boulevard. A bilevel patio has bright flower beds, palm trees, a lovely fountain, swimming pool, and a pleasant patio, where musicians play Caribbean music. Beyond that is Flippers, a poolside snack and beverage bar, and the walkway to the beach. The Naples beach is famous for its peachy-pink sand and warm water. Although this is a public beach, the hotel is bordered on the north and south by other quiet hotels and condominiums and by expensive private residences, so there is rarely a problem with beer-swilling teenagers or loud radios. Nearby is outstanding golf at the 18-hole Naples Grande, designed by Rees Jones.

The original hotel was built in the 1960s and had a multimillion-dollar renovation in 1985, which added 2,600 feet of conference space and turned the rooms on the upper floors into large suites. Now there are several buildings at the Edgewater in a mix of styles. Altogether, there are 124 one- and two-bedroom waterview suites and nine penthouse suites, some of which are occasionally used as conference rooms.

The suites are beautifully decorated and have a variety of bed sizes. Kitchens include a full-size refrigerator, good counter space, a microwave, and a double sink; some have a breakfast bar with padded stools. Daily dishwashing is included in the maid service. In each suite, one of the two sofas in the living room opens out into a bed. Two-bedroom suites are large enough to accommodate three generations if there are only one or two children in tow. All have gulf views from balconies or patios.

When the sun sets, the atmosphere at the Edgewater changes a bit. Young professionals, members of the Club at Edgewater, stop by for a sundowner in the Crystal Parrot. This sixth-floor lounge and award-winning restaurant is famous for its view of the gulf sunset — and, in Naples, watching the sun go down is an important ritual.

Lemon Tree Inn

250 Ninth Street South
Naples, FL 34102
888-800-LEMON
941-262-1414
Fax: 941-262-2638
www.lemontreeinn.com

> **The best value in Naples —
> bar none**

Innkeeper/Manager: Stephen Sbertoci. **Accommodations:** 35 rooms and suites. **Rates:** $99–$189. **Included:** Continental breakfast. **Minimum stay:** 2 nights during some weekends and special events. **Added:** 9% tax. **Payment:** Major credit cards, cash, traveler's checks. **Children:** Welcome. **Smoking:** Nonsmoking units available. **Open:** Year-round.

➤ **The low-rise accommodations are on either side of a beautifully landscaped lawn and pool patio.**

After viewing the Lemon Tree's Web site, some people are a bit surprised when they first drive into the place and find that it is not a quaint inn on a quiet Naples street. The Lemon Tree does indeed have an Old Florida look, with small cupolas on the crimped rooftops, gingerbread embellishments, and windows accented by white trim and green shutters. But if you look closely, you realize that the building material is just cinderblock painted yellow. And, although the address on the brochure says "9th Street South," 9th street is also busy Route 41, a highway on the Gulf Coast. Thus the Lemon Tree could accurately be described as a glorified motel — but what a motel; what a location; what a buy! The Lemon Tree is within walking distance of both Old Naples and the beach. Rooms are comfortable, the facilities are beautifully cared for, and the staff couldn't be nicer.

Once you enter the Lemon Tree's courtyard, there is almost the sense of being at a Florida country inn because there is so much greenery masking the road. There's a small Victorian-style gazebo, green canvas market umbrellas above the lawn tables and chairs, and lots and lots of flowers and green plants. There are also some thoughtful and practical amenities: for example, just off the pool patio is a guest bathroom that includes a baby changing table. Everything is immaculate and has the fragrance of lemons.

Several of the guest rooms near the pool are enclosed with a small screened-in patio accessible through a white iron gate. These are the queen accommodations and are worth asking for specially. All rooms have a direct-dial telephone, TV, a queen-size bed or two double beds, and either a private lanai or patio overlooking the courtyard. The furniture is mostly of light blond wood and bamboo. Colors are light and fresh, and on the ceiling above are paddle fans. One-bedroom suites have a sitting room and full kitchen, while deluxe rooms have refrigerators and microwaves. A Continental breakfast is served at the Lemon Tree every morning, usually in the gazebo, and nearby are excellent restaurants if you don't feel like cooking in your suite.

As at any place, it is the people who can make a big difference in your vacation. Lemon Tree staff are upbeat and helpful. They are happy to steer you in the right direction for elegant shopping on Fifth and Sixth Avenue or for a day at the beach or the city dock. Because the Lemon Tree is within walking distance of both Old Naples and the gulf, it is possible to dispense with a car altogether when staying here. The staff can arrange ahead of time for transportation to and from the airport.

If you have a car, you can enjoy some of the natural attractions nearby, such as the Corkscrew Swamp Refuge and the Conservancy Nature Center. Nearby are also various boat rental services for fishing and charter rentals by the day. However, there's much to be said for lazing around the Lemon Tree's pool during the day and enjoying a stroll along the streets and lighted fountains of Old Naples in the evening.

The Naples Beach Hotel and Golf Club

851 Gulf Shore Boulevard North
Naples, FL 34102
800-237-7600 (Reservations)
941-261-2222

A family-owned resort with a range of accommodations

Owners: The Watkins family. **Accommodations:** 318 rooms, suites, and efficiencies. **Rates:** Rooms $120–$340, suites $160–$475; efficiencies add $30 per day in high season; packages available; meal plans available in high season. **Included:** Children's program. **Minimum stay:** With some packages. **Added:** 9% tax; $15 extra adult. **Payment:** Major credit cards. **Children:** Under 18 free in room with parent. **Smoking:** Nonsmoking rooms available on request. **Open:** Year-round.

➤ **Naples Beach Hotel has recreational space right on the Gulf of Mexico that includes a swimming pool and facilities for water sports: pedal boats, a sunfish sailboat, a Hobie Cat, paddle cruisers, and inflatable floats and rafts. A concierge can make arrangements for field trips and fishing off the property.**

The Naples Beach Hotel and Golf Club is for those who want the combination of golf and the beach — it is the only resort in Naples that has both right on the property. The staff is friendly and down to earth, and the grounds and accommodations are pleasant rather than slick. This is the sort of place where you see many three-generation families having lunch together after the adults have had a vigorous morning on the golf course and the kids have built sand castles on the beach.

The club's 18-hole, par championship course has large greens and tees and some challenging traps and water hazards. Many who play here have been coming back year after year since the course was bought and restored in 1946 by Henry B. Watkins, whose grandson is now the president of the resort. There's also an award-winning tennis center and full-service spa here.

The beach in itself is worth the trip to Naples. Sandpipers scurry along the water's edge and gulls cry overhead. The white sand has the texture of sugar, and the water is a deep blue-green. The crescent-shaped Sunset Beach Bar serves drinks and salads and sandwiches. In addition to the Sunset Beach Bar is HB's on the gulf, a casual dining room overlooking the water, and the Broadwells, overlooking the tenth tee. The Everglades Room overlooks the Gulf of Mexico and is open for breakfast and Sunday brunch. The Seminole Store features a gourmet deli located off the main lobby and has outdoor seating. Guests staying in efficiencies usually prepare some of their own meals, and all guests may take the hotel's meal plan at an additional cost.

There are many restaurants and trendy cafés in Old Naples for guests who wish to explore a little, and wonderful, if expensive, shopping on Third Avenue. The boutiques and internationally known stores are Mediterranean in style, and the immaculate streets and sidewalks are graced by palm trees and bright flowers. For those who want to get a sense of the area's natural environment, there's the Naples Nature Center and the nearby Corkscrew Swamp Sanctuary, operated by the National Audubon Society.

The hotel has a free Beach Klub for Kids, for children 5-12, which is excellent and one of the reasons this is such a great family hotel.

Rooms and suites at the hotel have recently been refurbished, as has the attractive meeting space. The orchids one sees throughout the hotel and club are grown in a special orchid house in the center of the golf course and are part of a collection of 5,000 plants.

Lodgings are in six midrise buildings on the property. They include standard rooms, which have wicker or bamboo furniture, TVs, large closets, and attractive baths; deluxe suites, with one bedroom and a living room with bar and refrigerator; and efficiencies, with one bedroom and a kitchenette. The majority have striking views of the Gulf of Mexico or the golf course.

The Registry Resort Hotel

475 Seagate Drive
Naples, FL 33940
941-597-3232
800-247-9810 or 800-9-NAPLES
Fax: 941-597-9151

**A luxury hotel near
Vanderbilt Beach**

Accommodations: 474 rooms and suites. **Rates:** Rooms $144–$395, suites $239–$1,190; packages available. **Minimum stay:** With packages. **Added:** 9% tax; $30 extra person. **Payment:** Major credit cards. **Children:** Under 18 free in room with parent. **Smoking:** Nonsmoking rooms available. **Open:** Year-round.

➤ **The Registry is not right on the gulf, but guests can take the board-walk across the nature preserve or hop on the open-air tram to get to the**

water. The resort's private beach club offers snorkeling, parasailing, sailing, and other water sports. The beach itself has fine, pale sand near the aqua water and a wide strip of shells at its edge.

Seagate Drive cuts through a plush Naples development called Pelican's Bay, which includes a golf course called the Pelican's Nest. The Registry, at the end of Seagate, has an atmosphere of informal luxury. There's courteous valet parking, as well as a convenient lot where you can park yourself. Most guests begin to unwind the minute they hear water flowing from the little manmade stream in a faux grotto at the entrance to the hotel.

Inside are floors of Italian marble, hand-woven rugs from the Orient, and more water, this time from waterfalls tumbling over tiers of marble. The Registry fits in well with upscale Naples. The restaurants and lounges, frequented by Naples residents as well as hotel guests, are dramatically decorated with polished wood or marble.

The management and staff here are eager to take care of any minor glitch or inconvenience — no small achievement, since the hotel has become extremely busy in the last couple of years with both vacationers and executives. The management has worked hard to be true competition for the Ritz-Carlton in Naples; both hotels set a high standard for the area.

Lobby elevators whisk guests up to one of rooms that overlook either the gulf or the canals and greenery of Naples from private balconies. Thick carpeting in the hallway is a foretaste of the decor in the rooms — no antiques here, just modern comfort. Standard rooms have queen- or king-size beds, deep-pile carpeting, minibars, built-in desks, cable TV and movie channels, and luxury baths with a large dressing area, makeup mirror, telephone, and hair dryer. The suites have similar appointments, along with Jacuzzis and large balconies.

The Registry has 49 tennis villas arranged in two clusters with Jacuzzis and patios off the bedrooms. The tennis center and courts are a draw for visitors from out of state who come to Naples to improve their game. Guests can also improve their aerobic capacity here. The Registry has an excellent spa, with dozens of treatments, an exercise and aerobics room, tanning beds, a whirlpool, and sauna, steam, and massage rooms. Golf is at the Pelican's Nest or, more often, at the Naples Grande course. Excursions to both courses are arranged by the hotel's staff.

Two of the Registry's three swimming pools are at the tennis center; the most exciting is behind the hotel tower. This is a fantastic free-form pool, with a grotto surrounded by tropical greenery and a waterfall. The rocks are fake, and the whole production is a little like Disney's Fantasyland, but kids love it.

Ritz-Carlton, Naples

280 Vanderbilt Beach Road
Naples, FL 33963
800-241-3333
941-598-3300

A palace hotel with superb service

Accommodations: 463 rooms and suites. **Rates:** Rooms $200–$595, suites $365–$4,000; packages available. **Minimum stay:** With some packages. **Added:** 9% tax. **Payment:** Major credit cards. **Children:** 18 and under free in room with parent. **Smoking:** Nonsmoking rooms available. **Open:** Year-round.

➤ **Between the beach and the large free-form swimming pool is a nature preserve of mangroves and other native trees. A weathered boardwalk leads to the gulf shore.**

The sumptuous beauty of the Naples Ritz-Carlton makes some people feel guilty, even decadent, at first. But it takes only about five minutes to get used to the decadence.

The Ritz-Carlton is reminiscent of the palace hotels of the Riviera and of the resorts Flagler built in Florida in the 1920s. Set on 19 acres in upscale Pelican Bay, the Mediterranean-style hotel has a pale stucco exterior and spare, understated lines, almost austere in the Florida lushness. At the cobblestoned, fountained entry, a bellman in top hat and tails greets you. Everywhere, service is attentive but unobtrusive. The ratio of employees to guests is almost two to one.

In the two-level lobby, guests are surrounded by beauty: deep-cushioned brocade sofas and chairs, English oil paintings, high ceilings and richly carved moldings, marble floors covered with fine Oriental rugs, and museum-quality antiques. It is especially pleasant in the afternoon, when tea and an array of pastries are served and the rays of a setting sun slant through the Palladian windows.

The "playground" behind the hotel has tennis courts, a Jacuzzi, two pools, and the beach. A long stretch of the Ritz's property fronts on Florida's "Platinum Coast." Here the sand is a pale peach, the shoreline ankle-deep in shells. The hotel rents out a variety of sailboats as well as kayaks and Waverunners. The staff can arrange scuba diving, water skiing, and deep-sea fishing. There are covered cabanas on the beach, chaise longues, and beach towels. The pleasant patio around the heated pool and Jacuzzi is furnished with chairs and umbrellaed tables. A pool bar provides food service between the two pools. The Ritz's large rose garden, located in a quiet side yard, is a rarity in Florida.

Overlooking the rose garden is the aerobics room in the hotel's fitness center, with the best in equipment. There are saunas and massage rooms in both the men's and women's locker rooms. The center also includes a game room with a pool table and a juice bar. "Ritzercise" classes are held several times a day. Scrubs, wraps, and several types of massage are available.

The six tennis courts are excellent, with hard and clay surfaces and lights for night play. A covered pavilion overlooks the courts, where spectators can sit at tables and chairs to watch a game and sip drinks. Golf is available at Tiburón, a 27-hole course designed by Greg Norman, just 10 minutes from the hotel. This is a beautiful course, with native habitat bordering the fairways. Tiburón also features the Rick Smith Golf Academy. The academy has a video computer that videotapes a player's swing, which player and pro can then analyze.

The Ritz has a children's activity program, with swimming and outdoor games, sand castles on the beach, and movies in the afternoon and evening. Charges range from half a day to a full-day schedule of recreation.

The hotel is popular for conferences and corporate retreats. Meeting space includes a 10,000-square-foot ballroom, a second smaller ballroom, and 12 meeting rooms. All of these rooms are exquisitely appointed with beautiful carpets, mahogany-paneled walls, leather chairs, and museum-quality etchings and oil paintings. The facilities include teleconferencing, audiovisual equipment, and lighted lecterns. Secretarial service is also available.

Luxurious accommodations for corporate groups are the Club Level guest rooms on the twelfth and fourteenth floors. The Club itself is a large, private room with comfortable seating where guests can enjoy a Continental breakfast, tea and pastries in the afternoon, and complimentary hors d'oeuvres in the evening.

All of the suites and rooms at the Ritz have water views; most have a small terrace with European-style railings. Bathrooms are of marble, with polished chrome fixtures, a large shower-tub, and a hair dryer and personal toiletries. The suites that overlook the gulf have a bedroom and sitting area separated by French doors, while royal suites have a large parlor and a separate bedroom. The two presidential suites are elegant and spacious, with working fireplaces. Twice-daily maid service for all accommodations includes turndown service.

Though young waiters and waitresses may sometimes be a bit slow (as everywhere in Florida), the service is generally very good at the resort's restaurants. In high season, there are 124 people on the kitchen staff alone. The Dining Room, open for breakfast, lunch, and dinner, is the most formal of the three. Floor-to-ceiling French windows look out over the gulf. A separate wood-paneled dining room seats twenty for private occasions. Cuisine is French and quite creative. Desserts are excellent, with a particularly good Key lime pie. The wine list is 20 pages long and has some outstanding offerings.

The Terrace, the most casual of the restaurants, serves breakfast, lunch, dinner, and midnight and afternoon snacks in its informal dining room or on the terrace near the pool. Located just off the walkway to the pool and recently refurbished with a matte-finish tile floor in earth tones, it is informal but handsome in decor and ambiance. It features rotisserie-cooked entreés and outstanding buffets.

The Grill has a clubby atmosphere, with bronze sculptures of hunting scenes, Honduran mahogany paneling, and an unusual carved fireplace. The specialties are Florida seafood, roasts, and grilled steaks and chops. A pianist plays softly at the Steinway grand and a fire sometimes roars in the grate.

The Ritz-Carlton, Naples, has consistently won accolades for its beauty, graciousness, and service. After just one day sunning on the beach, walking the lovely grounds, or savoring a perfect meal, it is easy to understand why.

Palm Harbor

Westin Innisbrook Resort

36750 U.S. Highway 19 North
Palm Harbor, FL 34684
800-228-3000
813-942-2000

A famous golf resort near a historic town

Accommodations: 1,000 suites. **Rates:** Club suites $120–$200, 1-bedroom suites $150–$228, 2-bedroom suites $200–$390; packages available. **Minimum stay:** 2, 3, or 5 nights with some packages. **Added:** 11% tax. **Payment:** Major credit cards. **Children:** Aged 17 and under free in room with parent. **Smoking:** Non-smoking rooms available. **Open:** Year-round.

➤   **At Innisbrook you can be dead serious about your golf game and devote many hours to it, or you can hit a leisurely round each day with a business associate or family member. The Innisbrook Golf Institute specializes in small-group instruction to enable all levels to improve.**

At Innisbrook Resort, excellent golf is accompanied by tennis and other recreation, as well as good accommodations, food, and service. The lawns look like green velvet, and there are sweeping beds of brilliant flowers everywhere. The golf courses and tennis courts are well cared for, and the service is usually attentive yet nonintrusive.

Innisbrook has won just about every golfing award that exists. Its Copperhead course ranks among the top 100 in the world, and it has often been ranked the number-one course in Florida. The Copperhead, par 71, is made up of three nines and totals 7,031 yards. The Sandpiper, 6,006 yards, is the shortest of the three championship courses. The 6,999-yard Island course, par 72, is fraught with bunkers and lake hazards and demands some long tee shots. All three are dotted with loblolly pines and other native trees and large free-form flower beds. Occasionally, there are unusual hazards: elegant — and slow-moving — blue herons who do not understand the frustrations of an impatient golfer.

Tennis hardly takes a back seat here. The 18 tennis courts include 11 of clay and seven of Laykold, with seven lighted for night games. The head pro and the instructors of the Australian Tennis Institute offer private and group lessons, a junior program for children of all ages and levels, and a videotape training center. The tennis center has four indoor racquetball courts, an observation deck, whirlpool spas, a pro shop, and a cocktail lounge and snack bar.

Innisbrook also has six swimming pools, a Parcourse jogging trail, bicycling, lakeside fishing, and a racquetball and fitness center with saunas and whirlpools. There is plenty to see and do off the property, with Busch Gardens and Cypress Gardens nearby, and great deep-water fishing and sightseeing in the Greek fishing village of Old Tarpon Springs.

Innisbrook has had great success in organizing meeting and golf packages for corporate retreats. There are three conference centers here. The Carnelian Conference Center is the most impressive, with a spectacular ballroom where a massive crystal chandelier hangs from a brass ceiling.

Innisbrook has four restaurants, serving fresh Florida seafood, American, and Continental fare. These restaurants are popular not only among corporate and vacationing guests at Innisbrook but also in the Tarpon Springs and North Tampa area.

Accommodations are in low-rise stucco and wood villas, which blend nicely with the stands of tall loblolly pines along the fairways. Club suites have twin bedrooms separated from the spacious living and dining room by sliding doors, a well-equipped kitchen with a built-in bar, and a balcony or patio. One-bedroom suites have a living room, a separate bedroom, a kitchen with bar, and a balcony. Two-bedroom suites can sleep up to six, with a much larger living and dining room, a kitchen and built-in bar, and a balcony overlooking the fairways or landscaped grounds.

Safety Harbor

Safety Harbor Resort & Spa

105 N. Bayshore Drive
Safety Harbor, FL 34695
888-BESTSPA
727-726-1161
Fax: 727-726-4268

**A reasonably priced spa
with plenty of pampering**

Accommodations: 193 rooms. **Rates:** Typical 2-night/3-day plan $532 per person in season single occupancy; other plans available; rates vary according to spa plan. **Included:** Meals with some plans. **Minimum stay:** None **Added:** 11% tax; 17.5% service charge. **Payment:** Major credit cards. **Children:** Under 16 not permitted in spa. **Smoking:** In restricted areas only. **Open:** Year-round.

➤ **A hot soak in one of the small elevated tubs that surround the oval indoor pool is a wonderful experience after a demanding exercise class.**

In 1539, Hernando de Soto proclaimed the mineral springs along the subtropical shore of a New World bay to be the Fountain of Youth. For centuries, men and women have come to these mineral springs, insisting that the waters possessed rejuvenating and curative powers. In 1926, a high-domed pavilion was built over the main spring. Today, the New World territory is called Florida, the bay is called Tampa Bay, and the enclosure over the springs has been made into the dining room of the Safety Harbor Resort.

Once a spa that catered to retirees, Safety Harbor now has a clientele of fitness-minded men and women of all ages. And it's not just a place for the Beautiful People. This is the kind of spa where you can feel comfortable with a suburban wardrobe and generic jogging shoes. The staff is down-to-earth, low-key, and friendly.

A number of programs are available at this 50,000-square-foot facility. They include facials, herbal wraps, five kinds of massage, manicures, and pedicures. Some plans may have a greater emphasis on exercise, with aerobics, dancercise, yoga, and water exercise.

The fitness center has 20 fitness classes a day. Like the other gymnasiums, it has Super-Gym aerobic flooring. All of the equipment is excellent, and there is everything anyone could want for a thorough workout, weight loss plan, or training program. Safety Harbor has Florida's highest-rated water fitness program.

The mineral water that de Soto called *espiritu santo* (holy spirit) is used in all the water at the spa, and when heated, it does have a silky, refreshing quality. Besides indoor and outdoor swimming pools, there are men's and women's saunas and whirlpools and Jacuzzis for coed groups. All spa guests have access to Safety Harbor's shuffleboard courts, nine tennis courts, weight room, cardio room, and golf practice range.

Fueling all the hard work is a varied and healthy array of delicious food. A typical lunch is a salad of spinach and other greens, grilled or poached seafood, lightly cooked vegetables, and fresh fruits. For snacks during the day there are raw vegetables and fruits and freshly squeezed fruit juices at the lobby juice bar. A second restaurant, the Café, features a non-spa menu of New American cuisine.

Accommodations are in rooms at the spa. All deluxe rooms feature a sitting area and a large bathroom with a dressing area, separate vanity, and two closets. All of the spa guest rooms have been recently redone and are quite attractive. Some have patios or balconies with views of the swimming pool or Tampa Bay. All are comfortable and have private bathrooms, telephones, and color TV.

The lobby and reception area of the spa has recently been refurbished, with new carpeting and new countertops and desks. The look is one of clean lines and airiness, reflecting Safety Harbor's commitment to update its image and attract more young fitness buffs.

St. Pete Beach

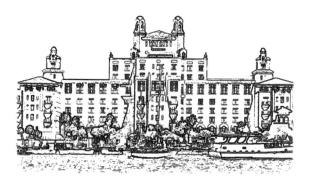

Don CeSar Beach Resort & Spa

3400 Gulf Boulevard
St. Pete Beach, FL 33706
800-282-1116
727-360-1881
Fax: 727-367-6952
Reservations: 800-637-7200

> A landmark hotel where
> F. Scott and Zelda danced
> in the ballroom

Accommodations: 275 rooms, suites, and penthouses. **Rates:** Rooms $140–$265, suites $230–$600; penthouses and packages available. **Included:** Shuttle service to golf course; KIDS Ltd. program. **Minimum stay:** With some packages. **Added:** 11% tax; $15 extra person; $15 rollaway. **Payment:** Major credit cards; personal checks. **Children:** Under age 18 free in room with parent. **Smoking:** Nonsmoking rooms available. **Open:** Year-round.

➤ **Sunsets at the Don are legendary, largely because of the backdrop, an Italianate terrace set with tropical trees and bright flowers overlooking the water. Dramatic white balustrades curve from the terrace garden and pool to double stairways that ascend to the French doors of the lobby.**

First-time visitors to this resort don't have to worry that they won't be able to find the hotel in the crowd of hotels and motels on St. Petersburg Beach. The grand pink palace is visible for miles. In fact, it's such a distinctive landmark that the National Maritime Association charts it on their maps as a navigational aid.

Opened in 1928, the Don, as it's now referred to, hosted such celebrities as F. Scott Fitzgerald, Franklin D. Roosevelt, and Al

Capone. When the banks failed in 1931, the founder of the resort, Thomas Rowe, rallied his close-knit staff, and together they managed to survive the Depression, often working for half pay. When Rowe died in 1940, having finally gotten the hotel out of debt, there were still troubles ahead. After the bombing of Pearl Harbor, the Don rented out fewer than 100 rooms during the entire winter season. The resort was sold to the Army and converted into a hospital. The penthouses became operating rooms, the third- and fourth-floor rooms dental clinics, and what is now the Marathon Grille served as a morgue.

After the war, the resort became an Air Force convalescent center, a hurricane shelter, and a Veterans Administration office, and whatever had thus far been preserved of the hotel's grandness was almost totally destroyed. Oriental rugs, expensive furniture, and elegant drapes were loaded onto government trucks and carted away. The walls were stripped of their bronze light fixtures and painted a drab green.

When the Veterans Administration moved out in 1967, there was talk of tearing the hotel down and building a public park. A "Save the Don" committee was formed, and the property was bought by the hotelier William Bowman, Jr., who was determined to return the Don to its former glory. The hotel reopened in late 1973 and has been on the National Register of Historic Places since 1975. In 1988, during the 60th anniversary of the St. Petersburg Beach landmark, some of the old fixtures bought by St. Pete residents in the 1940s were returned to the hotel.

The Don's architecture is Mediterranean, with a red tile roof, white trim accenting the pink stucco exterior, bell towers, and archways on the gulf side that lead to terraces and curved white balustrades. A stately vehicular ramp has been built over the highway in front of the hotel, so guests can disembark at the elegant second-floor lobby entrance. Inside are pale marble floors, Axminster rugs, high ceilings, tall arched windows with fanlights, and tapestries, etchings, and original paintings.

All rooms have thick carpeting and French country furniture that are kept scrupulously clean. There are arched doorways to many of the rooms and bathrooms, and the walls have interesting angles accented by brightly painted moldings. The bathrooms are of delicately veined Carrara marble.

The duplex penthouses are impressive, with spiral staircases and access to enormous rooftop terraces overlooking the gulf and St. Petersburg. The indoor-outdoor carpeting on the terraces is worn and a little buckled, but the penthouses are a fine place for a party or a corporate reception.

On the terrace, pink stucco shelters with arched doorways and tile roofs provide poolside drinks and light meals; you can almost see Fitzgerald sitting here in a white linen suit, ordering a drink.

Downstairs, in what was once the original lobby of the hotel, is an old-fashioned ice cream parlor and sundries store. The red broken-tile floors are the same that Zelda and F. Scott Fitzgerald trod when they visited. If you ask the staff behind the counter, they may show you the original staircase, now a storage area, that is hidden behind a door.

Though service has slipped a little recently, especially at the front desk, the overall performance is good. Particular attention is given to the children's program so that both parents and kids will enjoy themselves. A huge room in the basement is set up like a nursery school, and every kind of activity imaginable is offered. The program is headed by a former schoolteacher who constantly thinks up creative things to do.

Visitors who poke around the basement and the restored fifth floor will notice some of the hotel's eccentricities. In parts of the Don, there are funny angles and odd little platforms, many of them built to hide the heating and air-conditioning ducts.

In the middle of the marble reception room off the ballroom is an unusual fountain, a touching remnant of the Don's past. Originally on the fifth floor, it was moved here to replace one that was apparently destroyed or carted away. At its base is a ring of monklike figures, their hands folded piously and water shooting out of their mouths in a most undignified way. This charming piece is a taste of the humor, as well as the beauty, that still graces the Don.

Island's End Cottages

1 Pass-A-Grille Way
St. Pete Beach, FL 33706
727-360-5023
Fax: 727-367-7890
www.islandsend.com

> A rustic group of private
> cottages

Hosts: Jone and Millard Gamble. **Accommodations:** 6 cottages. **Rates:** 1-bedroom cottages $70–$120, 3-bedroom cottages $185; $15 extra person; weekly rates available. **Included:** Continental breakfast Tuesdays, Thursdays, Saturdays. **Added:** 11% tax. **Minimum stay:** 10% surcharge for 1-night stay in 3-bedroom cottages. **Payment:** MasterCard, Visa, personal checks, traveler's checks. **Children:** Welcome. **Smoking:** Allowed. **Open:** Year-round.

> ➤ **The boardwalk is punctuated by sandy flower beds and Florida greenery. Everything looks very natural and informal, yet pretty.**

Although the address of Island's End is St. Pete Beach, this island location is thought of by locals on the west coast as a separate, very special place. Pass-A-Grille is a historic town and has some preserved cottages from the early part of this century that residents are especially proud of. The town is on the southernmost tip of the peninsula that makes up St. Pete Beach, so you can stand at that tip and see the bay on one side and the gulf on the other. Island's End is on the southeast corner, more bay than gulf, but you can walk to the gulf's public beach. The beach is a freewheeling place, with a mix of people — everyone from elderly widows taking a morning constitutional to gay couples sunbathing and picnicking. The area is not well known to tourists.

Like Pass-A-Grille, Island's End is a real find. The street side of the place looks like the back of a small motel. But tucked away behind the subtropical foliage are six hidden cottages connected by weathered boardwalks and lattice-trimmed porches. Each cottage in this rustic enclave is slightly different, with weathered gray vertical siding on the outside and knotty pine or plaster walls inside. Furnishings include a king, two twins, or queen-size bed in the bedroom and pullout double or queen-size sofas. All have full kitchens, cable TV, and telephones. Laundry facilities and barbecue grills are available for everyone to use.

A special guest house, referred to in the office as "A," has three bedrooms. The kitchen includes a dishwasher and microwave. The house has its own heated pool. It's directly on the water; a wall of glass doors looks out over the gulf.

All the cottages have access to porches and decks of weathered wood and lattice. These are furnished with lawn chairs and tables. There's also a wood gazebo at the water's edge. Many guests enjoy the complimentary breakfast of orange juice and croissants on a covered porch or in the gazebo.

Most guests spend their time right here: in the sand and sunshine of the little beach or in the shade of the porches. But you can also fish off the pier on the property, and there's the public beach adjacent and beaches all along the St. Pete coast. Along the bay side is a sea wall (where people also fish) and park benches that are pleasant to sit on in the evening. This end of St. Pete Beach seems to be safe and is quieter than the "strip" farther up on the peninsula at night. Most guests don't wander too far afield, however; at night, the boardwalk and flower beds are softly lit, making the place look even more like a hideaway.

TradeWinds Resort on St. Pete Beach

5500 Gulf Boulevard
St. Pete Beach, FL 33706
727-562-1212
Reservations: 800-237-0707

A lively beach resort

Accommodations: 577 rooms. **Rates:** Rooms $179–$325, 1-bedroom suites $227–$399; packages available. **Minimum stay:** 2–5 nights with some packages. **Added:** 11% tax. **Payment:** Major credit cards. **Children:** Under 12 free in room with parent. **Smoking:** 5 nonsmoking floors. **Open:** Year-round.

➤ **There's paddleboating on the waterways that meander through the resort, and guests love to sail and windsurf on the gulf.**

With paddleboats on the narrow waterways, railed verandas, and white gazebos overlooking the beach, there is some romance to this busy resort. Yes, the little streams are manmade, and maybe it's all a bit much, but after a few hours it doesn't matter. Here you can leave your practical self behind.

TradeWinds caters to families and has a variety of accommodations. Guests choose among hotel rooms, one- to three-bedroom suites, and penthouses. Rooms are decorated in what the proud employees call a "Floribbean style," with whitewashed furniture and colors of coral and teal. Amenities include TV, coffeemaker, toaster, wet bar, and, in the suites, full kitchens and sitting rooms.

TradeWinds offers dining and dancing in the evening and live entertainment till late at night. Dining is in the Palm Court, a casual Italian bistro, or Burmudo's. Indulge in a refreshing drink at Reflections, the resort's waterside piano bar. You can also get a drink and a light meal at the Flying Bridge, which floats on the waterway along with the white ducks.

The chefs can create large buffets for groups, and TradeWinds is a popular place for gatherings. Its 8,400-square-foot ballroom can be divided into smaller meeting rooms. A total of 21 meeting rooms and outdoor function space make TradeWinds a good choice for events.

A supervised children's activity program, play areas, kiddie pool, life-size chess set, paddleboats, and an electronic game room assure time for adults to pursue their own activities. There's tennis on four Har-Tru courts with a tennis pro, racquetball, croquet, and a putting green; golf is nearby. Deep-sea charter fishing can be arranged. TradeWinds has four pools, as well as beachfront whirlpools, a health center, and a full-service salon. Families can spend time together and apart.

Although the town of St. Pete Beach is a little tacky (and TradeWinds is on the main drag), the resort is worth visiting for its beachside location alone. Here, there is pale peach sand, millions of shells, and a warm, rolling surf.

St. Petersburg

Mansion House B&B and The Courtyard on Fifth

105 Fifth Avenue, N.E.
St. Petersburg, FL 33701
800-274-7520
813-821-9391
Fax: 813-821-9391
mansion1@ix.netcom.com
www.mansionbandb.com

> A pleasant B&B a short
> walk from the bay

Innkeepers: Robert and Rose Marie Ray. **Accommodations:** 6 rooms. **Rates:** Rooms $100–$150, weekday and weekend/seasonal rates, $25 for extra rollaway bed. **Included:** Full breakfast, and wine or soft drinks and cheese. **Minimum stay:** None. **Added:** 11% tax. **Payment:** American Express, Diners Club, MasterCard, Visa. **Children:** One child per room welcome with parent. **Smoking:** In outdoor areas only. **Open:** Year-round.

➤ **Though the place may look vintage, the Rays are thoroughly up to date.**

Reputedly the home of the first mayor of St. Petersburg, the Mansion House B&B is an Arts and Crafts house built in 1904. With awnings that give it an almost jaunty look, the place sits on the corner of two moderately busy city streets.

Innkeepers Robert and Rose Marie Ray bought the original B&B in 1995 from a Welsh couple who had purchased the house as a somewhat dilapidated property. They spent almost a year renovating and redecorating the place, and the Rays have continued to make improvements. The Mansion House has won a number of beautification awards. Robert and Rose Marie recently purchased a mirror-image house next door and created a beautiful garden courtyard between the two properties, providing guests with some additional amenities: a swimming pool with a Jacuzzi, a second porch to relax on, a small conference facility, and a new library/TV room.

All of the guest rooms and common rooms are immaculate, yet still have the homey feel of an old house. The guest rooms have traditional wallpapers and are furnished with period furniture. The private baths are modern but have some old-fashioned touches.The Carriage House suite, accessible by a private stairway, is located above the garage and has a cathedral ceiling, hand-painted four-poster bed with a mosquito-netting canopy, TV, stocked refrigerator, roomy bath, and Jacuzzi.

The six new rooms in the Courtyard are furnished with handmade linens, canopy beds, and attractive antiques and reproductions. Most of the rooms have desks, and the telephones in both houses have data ports. The Rays have made an effort to make a stay pleasant and efficient for business travelers. For those who've forgotten a toothbrush or razor, the Rays have extras on hand. Additional amenities are terry robes, fresh flowers, Godiva chocolates, cable TV and VCR, guest barbecue, and a well-stocked refrigerator.

Breakfast is delicious, with selections like blueberry pancakes, French toast, fluffy omelets, home-baked muffins, whole-grain bread, fresh fruit, juices, and steaming hot drinks. Cookies, fresh fruit, soft drinks, and wine are available throughout the day in the open kitchen, dining room, and library. Guests enjoy the morning meal under a paddle fan on the screened porch, in the courtyard, or in the dining room, which can seat as many as 28 people. Guests are encouraged to invite family and friends to breakfast, for a small charge. The courtyard has a barbecue for guests' use.

The Rays are currently appealing to the business traveler who wants to get away from big city hotels when doing business in the St. Pete–Tampa area, as well as leisure travelers. They also are marketing their place especially to women travelers.

There are plenty of activities and places to see nearby. Just down the street is the bay, a marina and city pier, a park, and a spectacularly restored grand old resort, the Renaissance Vinoy. Also within walking distance are the Florida Cultural Museum and the Dali Museum. The pier is quite an active place, with live music, boat trips, fishing, and a tropical fish display. Certain neighborhoods in old St. Pete are still somewhat derelict, but this area of restored homes has made a genuine recovery, and the Mansion House is certainly contributing to the revitalization of the neighborhood.

Renaissance Vinoy Resort

501 Fifth Avenue, N.E.
St. Petersburg, FL 33701-2644
727-894-1000
800-HOTELS-1
Fax: 727-822-2785
TDD for hearing impaired:
727-821-7010

A recently restored grande
dame

Accommodations: 360 rooms and suites. **Rates:** Rooms $140–$325, suites vary according to season and night requested; special weekend rates and packages. **Included:** Coffee and newspaper; meals and recreation with some packages. **Minimum stay:** With some packages. **Added:** 11% tax; $20 per extra person. **Payment:** Major credit cards. **Children:** Welcome. **Smoking:** Nonsmoking rooms available. **Open:** Year-round.

➤ **The restoration of the Vinoy is one of the most meticulous ever done on a Florida hotel. What was preserved has been cleaned up and polished; what had to be replaced has been historically researched and duplicated with great concern for detail.**

This fine old hotel, a Mediterranean Revival building, is on the National Register of Historic Places. The restored hotel had a slow start, but it is now taking off, to the delight of both residents and Tampa Bay visitors. This lovely place has helped to revitalize the whole neighborhood.

Guests enter the hotel and walk along an arched loggia-style reception area. Floors are the original European terra cotta tiles with accents of figured tiles in primary colors. Chairs are upholstered in rich tapestries and ivory brocades with a deep silk fringe. Pecky cypress beams above are stenciled with geometric figures and flowers. Vases of fresh tropical flowers and large pots planted with ginkgo trees create a gardenlike freshness.

Just beyond the arched loggia is the Grand Ballroom. The Vinoy has more than 45,000 square feet of meeting space, including the Grand Ballroom and the Sunset Ballroom. The resort has an attractive boardroom and 11 breakout rooms for smaller meetings. There is also function space outside, and a professional convention services staff attends to all the details of catering and audiovisual needs.

At one end of the loggia is the main restaurant, really a lounge and two restaurants in one. The floors are of Brazilian cherry, and the wainscoting is mahogany. On one side of this large, long room is the Terrace Room, which serves three meals a day. On the other is Marchand's, for more formal evening dining. In the middle is the new bar, all polished wood and brass. Informal dining and imbibing are at the poolside Alfresco. Overlooking the resort's golf course on pretty Snell Island is the Clubhouse Restaurant, serving three meals a day.

The golf course and clubhouse are worth the short trip from the hotel to Snell Island. The island is an upscale residential area in St. Pete with many fine examples of early-20th-century architecture. The hacienda-like clubhouse has an ivory stucco exterior, barrel tile roof, and interesting little turrets and towers. The golf course is new, designed for the hotel by Ron Carl.

The tennis facilities are perhaps even more impressive. The 14 courts have four different surfaces: Deco-Turf II, clay, Har-Tru, and grass. The pro shop is larger than most and carries fitness clothing as well as golf and tennis attire. Next to the shop is the fitness center, with excellent equipment in the exercise room, steam rooms, saunas, and spas, and an aerobics room. The Vinoy also has a 74-slip marina.

Other recreational facilities at the Vinoy include a well-maintained croquet court, whirlpools, and two swimming pools, one with a waterfall. The main swimming pool is rather too contemporary in design for this old hotel: the tiles are cobalt blue and pistachio green, and a sheet of water tumbles down at the waterfall end.

Originally built in 1925 and called the Vinoy Park Hotel, the main hotel has 258 guest rooms, with 102 rooms in an adjoining new tower building. In each room an armoire hides a TV; a second television is in the marble bathroom. Most rooms have a sitting area and desk and chair. There are telephones at the desk, in the bathroom, and on the night table. First-floor rooms in the new tower have outdoor patio whirlpool tubs, while other rooms have small private balconies, many overlooking the bay and marina. Additional amenities include a hair dryer and a double-sink vanity in the bathroom, a minibar, bathrobes, and a complimentary newspaper and coffee with a Vinoy wake-up call.

Except for the two dozen or so suites, the rooms are quite similar (and similar in price), so if a view of the bay and the resort's marina is important to you, ask for a bay-view room on a top floor. Inquire about the resort's "Breakations" and other special packages. Some of these offer wonderful pampering for a special occasion. The honeymoon package is particularly lavish and includes a tower room with a patio spa, champagne and roses, and limousine service.

Sanibel Harbour (Fort Myers)

Sanibel Harbour Resort and Spa

17260 Harbour Pointe Drive
Fort Myers, FL 33908
800-767-7777
941-466-4000
Fax: 941-466-2150
www.sanibel-resort.com

A secluded resort only 20 minutes from the airport

Managing Director: Brian Holly. **Accommodations:** 347 hotel rooms and suites, 80 2-bedroom condos. **Rates:** Rooms $145–$345, suites $165–$375, 2-bedroom condos $199–$549. **Included:** Fishing privileges off resort dock; admission to spa and fitness center; free shuttle to selected area attractions. **Minimum stay:** With packages. **Added:** 9% tax. **Payment:** Major credit cards, personal checks. **Children:** Under 18 free in room with parent (2 children maximum). **Smoking:** Nonsmoking rooms available. **Open:** Year-round.

➤ **The recreational area behind the hotel is one of the most spectacular in Florida, with a three-tiered waterfall, a large pool with a cascading waterfall, and a thousand-foot beach overlooking the bay. One could easily spend every day of a vacation relaxing here.**

Sanibel Harbour Resort is located on Punta Rassa Peninsula in San Carlos Bay, an idyllic site. The resort overlooks several tiny outlying mangrove islands in the gulf as well as popular Sanibel Island, which is just a few minutes away via a causeway. Lately Sanibel Island has become a bit congested and, especially during the holidays, the causeway traffic at toll booths can become a bottleneck. The revitalized city of Fort Myers, in the opposite direction, is also a busy place. At this resort, guests have views of the island and the gulf but none of the congestion.

Initially a tennis resort, Sanibel Harbour now has a number of other amenities that make it popular with both locals and out-of-state vacationers and businesspeople. The spa is particularly impressive. Two floors in an attractively decorated facility just opposite the hotel and adjacent to the tennis center include exercise rooms, four racquetball courts, 10 whirlpools, a lap pool, hot and cold plunge pools, Swiss showers, sauna and steam rooms, a suspended Batar Bed with vibrating stereo speakers — the list goes on and on. Services include personal training sessions, aerobics classes, and more than 60 beauty and health treatments.

Tennis facilities include 8 lighted fast-dry clay courts, an impressive tennis center, and a 5,500-seat stadium. Guests receive top-notch instruction from the pro staff, with private and group lessons, courtside video instruction, round robins, and clinics. Services include a player-matching service and restringing, a ball hopper, and ball-machine rentals.

Guests can fish and enjoy water sports from the private dock. The staff at the dock can also arrange for more ambitious fishing charters off the property. The Sun Princess package includes shelling, beach, and wildlife and dolphin cruises daily. The *Sanibel Harbour Princess*, a 100-foot luxury yacht, offers nightly sunset dinner cruises and Sunday brunch cruises.

Like any large resort, Sanibel Harbour has restaurants that appeal to a range of tastes, and there are two lounges with nightly entertainment. Extensive meeting facilities include two small ballrooms, several conference rooms, and two full-service banquet kitchens.

Sanibel Harbour's two- and three-bedroom condominiums, in high-rises built several years ago, are particularly good for an extended stay. These are spacious, with full kitchens, living/dining areas, two bedrooms, and screened balconies overlooking barrier islands and the bay.

But the hotel, constructed on the site of a 19th-century inn, is the resort's showcase. The architecture is Old Florida, with a stucco exterior, understated brackets under the roof, white and green balconies, and a conical tin roof on the main lounge that overlooks the water.

The spacious rooms are attractively decorated with real wood furniture, mini-bars, color cable TV, and a king- or queen-size bed. All accommodations have balconies that provide spectacular views of the resort's 85 acres and the turquoise water of the San Carlos Bay.

The two-bedroom, two-bath condos have a washer and dryer, a king-size bed in the master bedroom, and a queen-size or two twin beds in the smaller bedroom. The master bedroom and the living room have sliding glass doors to the screened balcony. Each condominium group has its own pool and Jacuzzi. The new Inn at Sanibel Harbour is a low-rise building of 107 units, a boutique-style hotel overlooking the causeway and water. it has its own pool and whirlpool.

Sanibel Island

Caribe Beach Resort

2669 W. Gulf Drive
Sanibel Island, FL 33957
941-472-1166
Fax: 941-472-0079
Reservations: 800-330-1593
tkenoyer@aol.com
www.travelbase.com/destinations/sanibel-captiva/caribe

> **A nice little place on the quiet side of the island**

Accommodations: 40 studios, efficiencies, apartments, and cottages. **Rates:** $67–$240. **Minimum stay:** None. **Added:** 9% tax. **Payment:** Major credit cards. **Children:** Welcome. **Smoking:** Allowed. **Open:** Year-round.

➤ **This is a small, well-kept place that is somewhat reminiscent of a 1950s family resort in the modest pleasures it offers. The pace is very slow and the people are friendly.**

Caribe Beach Resort is located on West Gulf Drive, on the other side of the island from the more commercial Periwinkle Way. This is a modest but very pleasant family resort. The white-washed two-story accommodations, from a distance, look like ordinary motel units, but they are clustered along each side of an attractive pool patio and outdoor grassy area. At the Caribe, families splash in the pool; play shuffleboard, horseshoes, or volleyball; birdwatch under the Australian pines; barbecue; or go shelling on the beach. Near the Victorian-style pergola overlooking the pool, there's also a lawn with a swing set and slide for young children. On the other side of the pool is a small shelter with bikes that guests can use during their stay.

Since most guests staying at the Caribe are here for at least a week, they stay in an efficiency or a one-bedroom apartment. The efficiencies are one large, long room with a double pull-out sofa and a queen-size Murphy bed. It's furnished with a table and four chairs and various built-ins and has a well-equipped kitchen. The one-bedroom apartments are L shaped and have similar amenities. The resort also has a cottage near the beach. It has gray vinyl siding and white-railed porches furnished with a table and chairs and chaise longues — modest but very relaxing and, again, reminiscent of a quieter, mid-century time. All accommodations have attractive paint colors and wallpapers, tiled and carpeted floors, hardwood furniture, cable TV, video player, refurbished bath, and nice kitchen. The first-floor patios and second-floor terraces of the efficiencies and one-bedroom apartments have a couple of lawn chairs and, though unscreened and small, are quite adequate for a couple to enjoy a drink in the evening.

The Caribe is a bit unusual for a beachside resort — or any resort — in that it has devoted a good deal of space between the beach and the pool to a large grassy area instead of cramming in more motel units. Large trees grow overhead and lots of birds chirp. There are picnic tables and barbecue grills and just . . . grass. Along the edge of the grassy area is a shell and sand path that leads to a buffer of sea oats and then the gulf. This particular stretch of beach on the island has the advantage of being fairly quiet. The pool area at the Caribe is a little noisier, but pleasantly so, with lots of kids and moms and dads splashing in the water. Tropical plantings and white chaise longues and chairs around the pool make this a pleasant place for both adults and kids.

The resort has both large and small bikes for guests to use during their stay, and it's only a 15-minute bike ride to the shops and restaurants of Periwinkle Way. But there is definitely an away-from-it-all feeling to the Caribe — and maybe an away-from-time feeling too, since it does indeed feel a lot like retro-1955 here.

Casa Ybel Resort

2255 W. Gulf Drive
P.O. Box 167
Sanibel Island, FL 33957
941-472-3145
Reservations: 800-276-4753
941-472-3145

An all-suite waterfront resort

Accommodations: 114 suites. **Rates:** 1-bedroom suites $190–$405, 2-bedroom suites $230–$450; weekly rates only during winter season; packages available. **Minimum stay:** In winter and with some packages. **Added:** 9% tax; maid service $30–$60 in 2-bedroom suites. **Payment:** Major credit cards. **Children:** Welcome. **Smoking:** Allowed. **Open:** Year-round.

➤ **Latticed gazebos and lighted barbecues invite old-fashioned community closeness.**

To get to Casa Ybel, guests take the causeway from Fort Myers to Sanibel Island. The entrance to the resort is a bumpy wooden bridge, which must be traversed slowly. The slowness is a good introduction to Casa Ybel. Here you can unwind and just lie on the beach, or you can play a sharp game of tennis — and then lie on the beach.

The resort was opened years ago as the Thistle Lodge, a Queen Anne–style Victorian that was the island's first inn. The old inn is now a restaurant and lounge.

Accommodations are one- and two-bedroom villa suites in two-story Florida cottages with gray wooden siding and dormers. Like many homes in this region, the suites are built on stilts as a precaution against hurricanes. All the suites have kitchens, making them ideal for those who prefer to eat in. The two-bedroom suites have galley kitchens with a full-size refrigerator, stove, microwave, double sink, cutting board, coffeemaker, toaster, and full set of dishes and pots. The master bedrooms have king-size beds, good wicker and oak furniture, and a private tile bath. The open living and dining area has a comfortable sofa and easy chairs, and a dining room table with four chairs. Upstairs is a bedroom with two twin beds and another bathroom. Bathrooms on both floors have a Roman tub and shower.

The one-bedroom suites are modest, with a small kitchen along one wall and a basic bath with tub and shower. The bedroom is large enough for two double beds and an ash bureau. There are some welcome touches here. All of the suites have screened porches that overlook the water and carpeting or ceramic tile floors.

Behind the suites is a patio with a poolside bar, a large swimming pool with water slide, a children's pool, and a whirlpool. Beyond is the beach and the emerald gulf. The tennis center, with six courts, is across the parking lot on Gulf Drive and includes a lounge area.

Casa Ybel's fine restaurant is in the old Thistle Lodge, a recreation of the Victorian cottage built by the original settler for one of his daughters. The lodge has a number of dining rooms on the first and second floors, each decorated differently. Many people watch the sun set over the water with drinks and then have dinner in the attractive dining room with an intimate, turn-of-the-century setting.

A nature walk on the property runs past a lagoonlike fishing pond where an island gazebo is reached by a wooden bridge. Parts of the grounds have been allowed to grow naturally, making a hospitable environment for waterfowl and other wildlife. A sign in the middle of the pond reads "Feeding Alligators Prohibited by Law." You know you're on a subtropical island.

Sanibel Inn

937 E. Gulf Drive
Sanibel Island, FL 33957
941-472-3181
Fax: 941-472-5234
Reservations: 800-237-1491
941-481-3636
www.sanibelinn.com

A garden and gulf retreat welcoming butterflies and people

Accommodations: 95 rooms and suites. **Rates:** $159–$475. **Included:** Trolley transportation; recreation program for children. **Minimum stay:** During some holidays and special events. **Added:** 9% tax. **Payment:** Major credit cards. **Children:** Welcome; under 16 free in room with parent. **Smoking:** Outside. **Open:** Year-round.

➤ **Some of the stone pavers of the driveway into the Sanibel Inn form the design of a butterfly and the resort sometimes refers to itself as "Butterfly Crossing." There are indeed many butterflies here, as well as dragonflies and many varieties of birds.**

In addition to ruminating on a bench in the butterfly garden or floating in the warm waters of the gulf, there's quite a bit to do here. The resort has two tennis courts with several more at its bigger sister resort, the Sundial. There's also a large swimming pool area, and kayaks and bicycles available for rent. Fishing and golf are close by. Although some complexes in Florida call themselves "inns" but offer no food, there is gourmet dining here at the Portofino Restaurant as well as casual food at the poolside bar and grill.

Located on East Gulf Drive, this small resort is set back a bit from the road. Although it is an easy trolley or bike ride to the small shops and eateries on Periwinkle Way — the more commercial part of Sanibel Island — guests have a sense of being "away from it all" here. The flower-fringed reception cottage sets the tone, with a tiny goldfish pond beside the steps up to the entry doors.

Guest rooms are in several low-rise stucco buildings painted in pastel colors and named after flowers. There are white veranda railings and latticework on the front of the buildings. In the back of each unit is a screened-in porch that looks out over the gulf or the gardens. This is not a small consideration in Florida — certain times of the year can be buggy. While there is always bug spray, it is nice to avoid slathering oneself with the stuff and instead enjoy views of the out-of-doors from the comfort of one's back porch. White shell paths join the units to the reception area, tennis courts, topiary and butterfly gardens, outdoor grills, and pool area.

The Sanibel Inn's standard rooms are spacious and include a small refrigerator and coffeemaker. The efficiencies have a separate bedroom, sitting area, and a kitchenette with a small refrigerator, microwave, and coffeemaker. The resort's two-bedroom "condominiums" offer the most space and choices, with a full-size kitchen and a washer and dryer. All accommodations have screened-in back porches, which are referred to by the Hawaiian term *lanai*.

During the day, the recreation of guests can be divided among the pleasures of swimming in the gulf or pool, shelling, playing tennis, and lounging around the swimming pool. The free trolley service takes guests to The Dunes Golf and Tennis Club, "related" island resorts such as the larger Sundial Resort, and boutique shopping on Periwinkle Way. For children, the Sanibel Inn offers their Nature and Discovery Programs.

This is one of those places where adults don't have to work too hard once they are ensconced on the pool patio. A tiki bar serves drinks and light lunch fare, attendants at a towel bar give out generously sized terry towels, and there's both blazing sun and, under the tropical plantings, dappled shade. There are some nice communal extras here: newspapers in the lobby in the morning and nature videos in the loan library. The maids resupply rooms with coffee for the coffeemaker each day.

Those who love the wildlife of southwest Florida are often rewarded here. The butterfly garden has iron-and-wood benches where anyone can sit indefinitely watching birds, butterflies, and other winged creatures alight on the flowers or the topiary "animals." Now and then, white herons delicately pick their way along the buffer of dunes and grasses between the resort and the beach.

Song of the Sea

863 East Gulf Drive
Sanibel Island, FL 33957
800-231-1045
941-472-2220
Fax: 941-472-8569

**A European-style B&B
overlooking the gulf**

General Manager: Linda Logan. **Accommodations:** 22 studios and 8 suites. **Rates:** Studios $169–$330, beachfront suites $225–$410. **Included:** Continental breakfast, bicycles, beach chairs. **Minimum stay:** With some packages. **Added:** 9% tax. **Payment:** Major credit cards. **Children:** Older children welcome. **Smoking:** Allowed. **Open:** Year-round.

Sanibel Island has become quite popular, and there are now so many places to stay lining Gulf Boulevard that it is difficult to choose. Song of the Sea is special in that its American informality is coupled with an eclectic Continental–West Indies decor and European sophistication. The result is a beach retreat where honeymooners, retirees, and young families all feel comfortable.

Song of the Sea was built by a Frenchman in 1969. Guests driving in first see a low-slung, pale pink stucco building with a barrel tile roof and a porte cochere. This is the lovely reception center where visitors register at a French country desk. In the living room, a lending library of bestsellers and videotapes is arranged on bookshelves opposite the deeply cushioned sofa. A Continental breakfast buffet is set up here each morning.

The staff explains how to borrow books or bicycles, sign up for golf or tennis, use the laundry room and barbecue grills, or anything else about the island or the inn that guests need to know. The staff is unobtrusive but helpful so that visitors can have as much time on their own as they wish. Many couples come here for both honeymoons and anniversaries.

Just outside the French doors of the reception center is a brick terrace with lawn chairs and glass tables shaded by green-and-white-striped umbrellas. Small Greek statuary pieces, white plaster urns filled with greenery, and pots of flowers are placed near the tables and at the little fountain in the center of the terrace. Citrus trees, palms, and other greenery screen the area, giving it privacy from the resort next door. During the day, guests can sun and read on the terrace. In the morning, most people enjoy their breakfast here, which consists of croissants, cheese Danish, apple turnovers, yogurt and fruit, and fresh bread, bagels, and muffins.

Accommodations are in two-story stucco buildings painted light pink with white trim and small green shutters. Each room has a European name, like Milano or Danzig. A water cooler provides spring water for those who find the taste of Sanibel water a bit sour. All accommodations have kitchenettes with a full-size refrigerator, microwave, and small stovetop. The bathrooms are small but pretty, with hair dryer, single sink, and tub-shower.

Suites have a bedroom with a king-size bed, TV, and small bureau. There is no closet in the bedroom, but there is good closet space in the entryway. The living/dining room has an armoire hiding a television and VCR, a small wood table with four chairs, and a queen-size sofa bed. Rollaways are available. A screened balcony or patio provides a view of poolside gardens and, in second-floor accommodations, the gulf waters beyond.

Studio accommodations have two queen- or king-size beds rather than a separate bedroom, but they are not too crowded. There is room for a kitchenette and small table in the entryway as well as a table and four chairs in the room itself. The studios have the same attractive balcony and carpeting. Fresh flowers are placed in the bedroom and the bath, and a bottle of wine sits on the little kitchen table, compliments of the innkeeper.

Cement sand dollar steps and brick paving lead from the accommodations to the pool and Jacuzzi and a patio furnished with chaise longues. Beyond the patio is a lawn with barbecue grills, a shuffleboard court, and, at the end of the property nearest the beach, chaises and lawn chairs where guests can sit and watch the sun set over the gulf.

All the beaches on Sanibel Island are famous for excellent shelling, and most people on the beach in the morning have a bucket or plastic bag for collecting. The best time to look is in the early hours after a storm. There are, of course, many other things to do here in addition to Sanibel's famous shelling. Guests can sign up for complimentary bicycles to ride into town or down to the light-house. Tennis is complimentary at the nearby Sanibel Inn Resort. Then there is the beach, relatively uncrowded along this stretch, and the warm waters of the gulf.

In town, there are a number of restaurants and boutiques, fine food shops, and ice cream parlors along Periwinkle Way. For those who wish to do most of their own cooking, Jerry's is the place to stock up on groceries. This supermarket and shopping center is an event in itself, with a subtropical garden where a waterfall tumbles over fern-draped rocks and cockatoos and parrots squawk from their cages.

In spite of all the grumbling of locals about the onslaught of big-city life, Sanibel Island remains one of the safest, most relaxing places to vacation in Florida.

Sundial Beach and Tennis Resort

1451 Middle Gulf Drive
Sanibel Island, FL 33957
941-472-4151

| A large, happy, busy resort |

Accommodations: 270 suites. **Rates:** 1-bedroom condo $155–$450, 2-bedroom condo $239–$585, 2-bedroom/den condo $249–$635; $20 extra person; meal plans & packages available; special group rates. **Minimum stay:** With some packages. **Added:** 9% tax. **Payment:** Major credit cards. **Children:** Age 12 and under free in room with parent. **Smoking:** Allowed. **Open:** Year-round.

➤ **This is a place where everyone can successfully combine an appreciation of natural island beauty with vigorous activity and periods of relaxation.**

Sundial is Sanibel Island's largest and most complete resort, with tennis and extensive meeting facilities for large groups. For those who want a quiet retreat, this is not exactly it, though the Sundial may surprise visitors with its quiet side during spectacular sunsets in the evening and the peaceful waters of the gulf in early morning.

The resort has 10,000 square feet of meeting space, including two ballrooms and a number of conference rooms. The conference services staff has a reputation for excellent service no matter what the size of the meeting. Audiovisual equipment includes slide, movie, and overhead projectors, tape recorders, large-screen TV, VCRs, blackboards, flip charts, and sophisticated sound systems.

Banquet catering for large functions seems to be quite professional. Children and spouses staying during a conference are well taken care of, with plenty to do day and night.

An extensive recreation program has activities for both children and adults conducted by recreational professionals. The resort has 6 clay and 6 hard tennis courts, with a matching service, pro clinics, lessons, and round robin tournaments. Golf privileges are at an 18-hole course at the Dunes Golf and Country Club. Boats, catamarans, and sea kayaks are also available, and deep-sea fishing can be arranged. In addition to swimming in the gulf, there are the five heated pools. The main pool, junior-Olympic size, is in a large patio area behind the reception center along with a 10-person Jacuzzi.

Near the patio restaurant is the Environmental Coastal Observatory Center, which acquaints kids and adults with the wildlife and vegetation of Florida. This room has changing exhibits dealing with endangered species, mangrove forests, the predatory habits of various fish, and dangers to the saltwater environment. In the "touch tank," kids can actually hold some sea animals and watch as mollusks lay eggs or crabs crawl out of their shells. The center's aquarium holds various sea creatures from west coast waters that are frequently exchanged with new animals, so there is always something new to see during an extended vacation. An "adoption" program lets kids take home a hermit crab.

Kids and adults can learn a great deal about the environment by simply shelling on the beach. More than a dozen species are relatively easy to find, and there are so many individual specimens that walkers frequently crunch them underfoot. The gentle waves on the gulf make this an ideal place to wade with toddlers and help older children learn to swim. After the beach, guests can wash up in the poolside bathrooms, which have showers for those who don't want to track sand and seaweed into their room.

Accommodations are in one- and two-bedroom condos in the resort's rental pool. A typical two-bedroom condo has a master bedroom with a king-size bed or two double beds, a twin-bedded room, two baths, a living room, dining area, and, in larger units, a den. Kitchens are equipped with full-size appliances and dinnerware and cookware. All accommodations have access to a private swimming pool. Large, screened porches have views of the gulf, a swimming pool, or the grounds. The nicely landscaped lawn and garden areas include fountains at each accommodation cluster.

The Sundial has a lounge bar overlooking the gulf and three restaurants: Windows on the Water, specializing in Flor-Asian and gulf shore cuisine; Noopie's Japanese Seafood and Steakhouse, where chefs prepare the meal as guests watch; and Crocodial's, a poolside bar and grill. The walls opposite Crocodial's are painted with mischievous crocodiles and bright green palm fronds. It's a whimsical touch that reminds people not to take anything too seriously at the Sundial.

Sarasota

The Cypress

621 Gulfstream Ave., South
Sarasota, FL 34236
941-955-4683
Fax: 941-906-8952
www.bbonline.com/fl/cypress

Truly, the best place to stay in Sarasota

Innkeepers: Vicki Hadley and Nina and Robert Belott. **Accommodations:** 3 rooms, 1 suite (also available as 2 rooms). **Rates:** $150-$210. **Included:** Full breakfast, afternoon and evening refreshments. **Minimum stay:** For some special occasions. **Payment:** American Express, Discover, MasterCard, Visa. **Added:** 10% tax. **Children:** No. **Smoking:** Outside. **Open:** Year-round.

➤ **Robert Belott prides himself on his ability to avoid repeating a breakfast menu during a two-week stay: "fourteen entrées and fourteen muffins."**

The Cypress is indeed constructed of cypress. It is a somewhat odd-looking house at first glance, with the left side of this big white house jutting out a bit and surmounted by a tiny, two-foot by three-foot railed balcony that almost looks like the lookout on a ship. The right side of the house looks more traditional, with small-paned windows framed by stained wooden shutters. A white railed porch sweeps along the entire front of the house overlooking Sarasota Bay and Gulfstream Avenue. A solid wooden door opens into the beautiful interior.

To the left of the entryway is a glassed-in breakfast room where guests relish the B&B's delicious breakfasts. One of the owners, Robert, a talented artist and photographer, is also a gifted chef. A typical breakfast starts outs with fresh-squeezed orange juice, fresh fruit, and muffins followed by an entrée such as omelette stuffed with Canadian bacon, tomatoes, and avocado or French toast stuffed with blueberries. Both the entrées and the muffins often feature food from the gardens at the Cypress. The lime tree provides the lime glaze on one of the muffins and a mango that rolls down the tin roof of the house might land eventually in an elegant sauce for breakfast crepes. Robert's wife, Nina, and her friend Vicki grow herbs and edible flowers, which also wind up incorporated in gourmet breakfast dishes or as a garnish. The breakfasts are complemented by fine china and crystal and bouquets of flowers from the front and back gardens.

There is also a feast in the surroundings. Vicki and Robert and Nina are all art collectors, and when they decided to open their B&B they amassed furnishings and accessories that span three centuries and several countries, thus creating an exotic amalgam of fine paintings, Victorian English and Castillian furniture, sculpted figures, opera glasses, and ladies' compacts. Not content to simply slap on fresh coats of paint when they refurbished the house, the three partners took a year and a half to create distinctive rooms in which to display their treasures. The downstairs sitting room, where the most interesting artwork resides, was a labor of love for Robert, who did most of the renovations throughout the house. He refinished the heart-pine floors as a backdrop for the Oriental rugs, faux-finished the walls in a shell color, and added pickled moldings and chair rails. Since this circa 1940s house was constructed of cypress, he went to the trouble of making the moldings and chair rails out of cypress.

Although the guest rooms in the Cypress haven't been quite as lavishly refurbished as the downstairs sitting room, they come close. Each one has individual furnishings that are quite impressive: a brass and pewter bedstead, a roll-top desk, an armoire of bird's-eye maple, or a marble-topped chest of drawers. There are also interesting finishing touches: pretty shells on a guest room wall, a pottery weed vase, or a papier-mâché fish in a bird cage. Each room has soft linens on the queen-size beds, swags and curtains in designer fabrics or wooden Venetian blinds at the windows, and Oriental rugs on the wooden floors. Modern amenities include cable TV and elegant new bathrooms. A cordless phone for all guests is available in the library/sitting room, off the kitchen.

The Cypress B&B's one first-floor guest room, the Essie Leigh Key West Room, has a private entrance and its own small porch and garden area with a hammock. A small floral Oriental accents the deep gold of the pine floors. The furnishings include an antique oak chest and Spanish side tables. No curtains obstruct the view of the bay: the window has only 1940s-style wooden blinds. The bathroom in this room is especially nice. Above the chair rail and grasscloth wallcovering, Robert washed the walls with three different colors to mirror a bay sunset: pink, aqua, and yellow. White tile in the shower-bath and a white pedestal sink offset the soft pastel of the walls.

Upstairs are the other three — to four — guest rooms, depending on how you count. The Elizabeth Brittany Suite has two bedrooms. Both the Elizabeth and the Brittany are very Victorian, furnished with some lovely period pieces. The Martha Rose, decorated in maroon, green, and white, has a pleasant sitting area and sliders to the B&B's odd little balcony overlooking Sarasota Bay. The big wooden mansion bed and wooden armoire made by Nina's grandfather make this a very elegant room. This also has a luxurious bathroom. Kathryn's Garden Room has views of trees, and the sound of the B&B's fountain is just audible. There's only one window here, but the room is sunny and the elaborate window treatment matches the botanical bedspread on the wicker bedstead. The Jacuzzi tub (with a handheld shower) has a pine frame and the floor of the bathroom is also pine, so even the bathroom has a woodsy, garden feeling to it.

The Cypress is a long, thin house surrounded by towering modern condos. The lot is very deep, running from Palm Avenue in the back to Gulfstream Avenue, a main thoroughfare, along the bay. So, although the Cypress fronts Gulfstream, most people enter the B&B from the back, where there is ample parking and a quiet residential feeling to the city street. The back yard has a barbecue grill and a wooden table and chairs on the deck shaded by a green market umbrella. In some ways, the front yard of the Cypress feels more like most people's back yard even though there's a busy boulevard beyond the lawn. This is where people rock on the porch while reading the paper or swing in a hammock under the mango trees while looking out at the bay. In the late afternoon, guests can enjoy warm hors d'oeuvres and drinks in either the front or back garden.

Although both Gulfstream and Bay Front Drive have car and bus traffic, it's fairly easy to cross both and stroll down to Sarasota Bay and Bayfront Park. Nearby are the Opera House, the Film Society, and Marie Selby Botanical Gardens. Also within easy walking distance are the art galleries and antiques shops of Old Sarasota, on Palm Avenue and Main Street. Sarasota is a cultural mecca in the state, so there is no end to the offerings in the arts in this small, livable city. Fashionable St. Armand's Circle, well known in Florida for both shopping and restaurants, is a 10-minute drive. The beach is also just a few minutes away — or rather beaches, since there are several to choose from on the barrier islands that fringe the gulf.

Half Moon Beach Club

2050 Ben Franklin Drive
Lido Beach
Sarasota, FL 34236
800-358-3245
941-388-3694
Fax: 941-388-1938
info@halfmoon-lidokey.com
www.halfmoon-lidokey.com

An unpretentious beachside resort

General Manager: Chip Parmelee. **Accommodations:** 84 rooms and suites. **Rates:** Rooms $105–$259, suites $189–$259. **Included:** Complimentary breakfast with summer and fall packages. **Minimum stay:** During some holidays and special events. **Added:** 10% tax; $15 for extra person; rollaways $15. **Payment:** Major credit cards. **Children:** 17 and under free in room with parent. **Smoking:** Allowed. **Open:** Year-round.

➤ **Half Moon Beach Club is a host hotel for the Sarasota Cine-World Film Festival in January and the Sarasota Music Festival in June. It is also one of the sponsors of the Jazz Festival and the Winefest in April.**

The west coast of Florida is dotted with more than a thousand islands. The cluster of small islands or keys along Sarasota Bay are some of the loveliest. With the considerable cultural offerings of Sarasota just across the bridge, these islands are ideal for vacationers who want more than a beach. There is a chic quality to the area, especially along the boulevards and elegant shops of Armand's Circle.

Located at the lower end of the key, near a wooded beachside park, the Half Moon has a getaway feel. Although the word "Club" in its name might sound as if this is one of the many private west coast resorts where overnight guests are just an afterthought, this is not the case here. Part of the unassuming, friendly atmosphere is due to the staff, who are genuinely cordial and service-oriented.

The exterior is of white stucco and glass bricks, a modern version of Florida Art Deco. Inside, green plants and tropical flower arrangements are set against the white stucco walls of the common rooms. Behind the crescent-shaped building are the pool and patio, landscaped in palms and tropical flowers and greenery. A short walk beyond is a beach deck, furnished with chaise longues and tables and chairs, and the beach itself, with powdery sand and gentle waves. There's also golf and tennis off the property that can be arranged by the staff.

All the rooms and suites have been thoroughly refurbished. The deluxe beachfront rooms, with a king-size bed and kitchenette, are good for couples; so are the less expensive standard rooms, with a king-size bed and small refrigerator. Ideal for families are poolside accommodations with two queen-size beds or rooms in the Seaside building with two double beds or a king-size bed and sofa bed. These have kitchenettes with a stovetop, microwave oven, and small refrigerator. The one-bedroom suites are the most spacious for a family, with two queen-size beds, a living room with a sofa bed, and a kitchenette. All accommodations have coffeemakers, direct-dial telephones, color TV, and a patio or balcony. Furnishings have a Caribbean flavor.

The kitchenettes at the Half Moon Beach Club are adequate for preparing simple meals, but most guests eat at least some of their meals in the resort's Seagrapes Restaurant, which serves American and Continental food with what the chef calls a "Floribbean flair." There are also expensive but excellent restaurants and bistros at St. Armand's Circle. For regional theater that sometimes approaches the caliber of New York's, ask the concierge about the Asolo Center for the Performing Arts.

Tampa

Hyatt Regency Westshore

6200 Courtney Campbell Causeway
Tampa, FL 33607
800-233-1234
813-874-1234
Fax: 813-281-9168

> **One of Tampa's most appreciated business hotels**

Accommodations: 445 rooms. **Rates:** Rooms $129–$240; packages and weekend discounts available. **Minimum stay:** With special packages. **Added:** 11.75% tax. **Payment:** Discover, MasterCard, Visa. **Children:** Under 18 free in room with parent. **Smoking:** Nonsmoking available. **Open:** Year-round.

➤ **Off-hours relaxation centers around the Hyatt's four lounges and three restaurants. The rooftop restaurant, Armani's, serves northern Italian cuisine, while Oystercatchers has mostly seafood. Both are frequented by discerning Tampa residents as well as hotel guests.**

Just four minutes from the airport and a few minutes' drive from downtown Tampa, the Hyatt Regency Westshore has much to recommend it. Its location is perfect for the business traveler, yet its 35-acre nature preserve and Old Tampa Bay location give it a relaxing, secluded ambience. With two excellent restaurants, both on Tampa's Five Best Restaurants list, and 22,000 square feet of conference space, the Hyatt is ideal for meetings. Although the hotel is in a section of the city that was for years a marshy territory of cheap honky-tonks and struggling businesses, Hyatt and other developers are doing their best to change that image.

Tampa's recent surge in hotel construction has resulted in some interesting high-rise architecture. The Hyatt Westshore has a serpentine design built of glass and concrete. Its 445 guest rooms and suites have some lovely views of the bay and the hotel's nature preserve.

Both the villas and the hotel rooms are decorated in soothing pastels and French provincial or traditional furniture. The best rooms for business travelers are those on the Regency Club floor. These are quite spacious, well organized for work, and include concierge service.

There are two freshwater swimming pools on the property, as well as a health club, tennis courts, and whirlpool spas. Cruises and golf can be arranged through the hotel.

The Hyatt's lobby is another favorite gathering place. It is a pleasure simply to walk across the floors, which are made up of different kinds and colors of marble laid out in patterns and borders. Throughout are sitting areas of light French provincial chairs, and sofas upholstered in pastels. With massive pillars and archways and a trompe l'oeil ceiling of leafy ferns, this lobby takes your breath away.

Wyndham Harbour Island Hotel

725 S. Harbour Island Boulevard
Tampa, FL 33602
800-996-3426
813-229-5000
Fax: 813-229-5322

> **An excellent meeting place for business groups**

Accommodations: 300 rooms and suites. **Rates:** Rooms $179–$259; weekend and other discount rates available. **Minimum stay:** None. **Added:** 11.75% tax. **Payment:** Major credit cards. **Children:** Free in room with parent. **Smoking:** Allowed. **Open:** Year-round.

➤ **The 300 guest rooms and executive suites are geared primarily toward businesspeople, though they are spacious enough for a family.**

Harbour Island in Hillsborough Bay is a 177-acre complex of businesses, condominiums, restaurants, boutiques, a marina, and a luxury hotel — the Wyndham Harbour Island Hotel. But since Hillsborough Bay is right in the middle of Tampa–St. Pete, the island is essentially in downtown Tampa. Thus, views from the upper floors of the hotel are of both the city and the water.

Harbour Island is accessible by car or trolley. The complex has brick walkways, exuberant fountains, and a festive mix of boats, shops, and busy people. Just across the bridge from Harbour Island is the impressive Tampa Convention Center.

The hotel itself is beautifully furnished and decorated and has some outstanding amenities. The floors of the lobby are dark green marble with deep-pile rugs, furniture is upholstered in rich green wool or tapestry, and Oriental vases with dramatic flower arrangements accent the tables. The massive doors into the ballroom are tiger maple. The design and craftsmanship are excellent, with interesting recessed areas, wooden moldings on the ceilings, and large wooden pillars.

A standard room has two double beds or a king-size bed, with traditional mahogany furniture, an armoire hiding the TV, substantial drapes, and wall-to-wall carpeting. Bathrooms have marble countertops and tiled tub-showers.

Executive suites have dark-stained traditional or Oriental furniture and a comfortable sofa and chairs. The bedroom and parlor are separated by double glass and louvered doors. Luxury suites are even more lavishly appointed and have a dining room table and chairs. The spacious bathrooms include hair dryers and a vase of fresh flowers. All suites have panoramic views of the waterfront, downtown Tampa, Davis Island, and the convention center.

The restaurants at Wyndham Harbour Island Hotel have become increasingly popular with Tampa residents over the years, and the Sunday brunch at Harbourview Room is now frequented by both locals and guests. With its spectacular views of the harbor, the Harbourview Room, which serves American cuisine, is also popular for breakfast meetings during the week. The atmosphere and dress code are casual, though sometimes the service is a little too casual. For cocktails, Garrison's Bar is the favored meeting place. It has a tropical feel, with potted palms and terrific views of the water.

The Wyndham's large pool, surrounded by chaise longues and tables with umbrellas, overlooks the marina. For those who want more vigorous activity, the hotel has an affiliation with the Harbour Island Athletic Club. State-of-the-art facilities include lighted, all-weather tennis courts, racquetball and squash courts, Nautilus and Hydra Fitness weight training systems, and an aerobics studio.

These upscale attractions provide some enjoyable distractions, but the Harbour Island Hotel is also an excellent place to get business done. The attractively appointed ballroom can accommodate up to 500 people for banquets, or it can be divided into smaller meeting spaces. There are seven conference rooms connected by a spacious foyer. Services for conferences and small conventions include professional planning and catering.

Wyndham West Shore

4860 W. Kennedy Boulevard
Tampa, FL 33609
800-996-3426
813-286-4400
Fax: 813-286-4053

**A functional and
inspirational place to
work and play**

Accommodations: 324 rooms, 23 suites. **Rates:** Rooms $150–$175, suites $270;
discounts available. **Minimum stay:** None. **Added:** 11.75% tax. **Payment:** Major
credit cards, personal checks. **Children:** Free in room with parent. **Smoking:**
Nonsmoking rooms available. **Open:** Year-round.

➤ **A staff member is always on hand to give directions to downtown
businesses, make arrangements for theater tickets, suggest places to eat
downtown, and otherwise make a guest's stay hassle-free.**

Connected to Tampa's Urban Centre offices by two 11-story atri-
ums and only a few minutes' drive from downtown and the airport,
the Wyndham West Shore is an excellent convention and business
hotel. Convention and conference facilities are functional and
beautiful, with a professional planning staff on hand. The 5,000-
square-foot grand ballroom, which can be divided into three separate rooms, opens into a reception area with a spectacular atrium
view. Other amenities are a theater, a boardroom, and eight executive meeting rooms.

The Sheraton is also a good place to unwind and play. The heated
outdoor pool has a deck that overlooks Tampa Bay. Windows in the
rooms and suites have double drapes to block out the sun on those
mornings when you want to wake up late or slowly. Standard
rooms include a desk, and the lighting is good. Furniture is dark-
stained bamboo or traditional. Suites have a comfortable, elegant
parlor with deep-cushioned chairs and a sofa, ideal for a small conference or for relaxing.

Accommodations include a Grand Club Floor, which caters to
the business traveler. The club room has a home-away-from-home
ambience and elegant decor, with vases of orchids and other exotic
flowers on the glass tables. A complimentary Continental breakfast is served here every morning, and cocktails are offered in the
evening.

For unwinding in a lounge setting, the bar is intimate, with rich,
dark woods, soft lighting, and pool tables and big-screen TV for
watching sports events. Those who want a little more action and

people-watching will find the lobby lounge a favorite spot, with piano music and the soothing rush of waterfalls and fountains from the gardenlike atrium.

The hotel's Courtyard Café has the same airy, garden feel, with a view of the fountains and green plants in the adjacent patio. French doors open for alfresco seating in balmy weather. Sunday brunch here is popular with Tampa families. The hotel's other restaurant is a steakhouse.

Upper Captiva Island

Safety Harbor Club

Safety Harbor Club, Inc.
P.O. Box 2276
Pineland, FL 33945
800-472-7866
941-472-1056
Fax: 941-472-1381
sharborclub@aol.com
www.safetyharborclub.com

> **A secluded resort on an island sanctuary**

Rental manager: Louis Volpe. **Accommodations:** The number of villas available varies. **Rates:** $900–$3,015 per week. **Included:** All club facilities; golf carts. **Minimum stay:** 3 nights. **Added:** 9% tax. **Payment:** Personal checks. **Children:** Free in villa with parent. **Smoking:** Nonsmoking rooms available. **Open:** Year-round.

➤ **The woods are so dense and jungly in places that it's easy to see what the west coast of Florida must have looked like when DeSoto and other explorers hacked their way through it.**

The journey to Pine Island and the launch for Upper Captiva Island is a journey through Old Florida. The back roads have names like Burnt Store and Stringfellow, and part of the trek is through a Florida fishing village called Matlatcha, where the scene hasn't changed much in the past fifty years. The road has expanses of pine woods and what can only be called palmetto fields. Finally, there's the bridge to the island and the tiny Pine Island post office, a curving stretch of road with a few houses and a religious retreat settlement, and the Mattson's Marina at Pineland, which offers a glimpse of the wildlife that thrives on Upper Captiva (also known as North Captiva Island). So many pelicans roost in the mangroves at the marina that it looks as if the trees might collapse under their weight. Little fish and crabs dart in the shadows of the moored boats.

After the allotted passengers, luggage, and foodstuffs are loaded onto the launch, it takes off, passing Useppa Island, Cabbage Key, and small mangrove islands. Several minutes later the boat arrives in small Safety Harbor, barely ruffling the feathers of the cormorants sunning on the dock and the ospreys nesting on the observation tower at the wharf.

No cars are allowed on the island. Houses face either the Intracoastal Waterway and dock or the gulf. The best and most expensive are on the beach. Houses near the dock and the Intracoastal side of the island can be a little noisier because of the "traffic" from golf carts whisking by on the little sand paths.

The villa accommodations are all privately owned, mostly by members of the Safety Harbor Club, which owns 35 acres of land on the island. Rentals are handled by a club office a few hundred feet from the dock. It provides small maps of the enclave that will help you get oriented.

The two- to three-bedroom villas built on stilts are contemporary or Old Florida in architecture. Carpeted stairs lead up to a second-floor living room with a dining room and fully equipped kitchen. Usually there are one or two bedrooms with a king-size bed and bath behind the living room and two or three bedrooms and bathrooms on the dormered second floor. All the villas have washer/dryers and plenty of extra towels. There's also generous closet space. Ceiling fans and screened porches make it possible to do without air conditioning for all but the hottest months of the year.

Most couples and families stay for at least a long weekend, buying food at the supermarket near Pineland Marina. For years, both vacationers and island residents had to do their own cooking except for an occasional lunch at Barnacle Phil's restaurant, but now the island also has the Mango Café and Marketplace Deli. The Mango Café has natural clapboard siding, a tin roof, and wicker-furnished verandas. Herbs growing in clay pots on the back porch attest to the freshness of the chef's ingredients. The Marketplace Deli has a general store that sells some food and sundries: juice, soda, sunscreen, T-shirts, tennis balls, and, at the Mango, fresh cream and Häagen-Dazs ice cream. Two little boutique shops, Coconut Connection and Upstairs at Barnacle Phil's, offer island clothing and small gifts for an impromptu purchase.

The stores also stock insect repellent, which is often a must, since most of the 700-acre island is a sanctuary operated by the state of Florida. The rest is owned privately by Safety Harbor Club members and by other private landowners who have a great respect for wildlife and a desire for privacy. Safety Harbor itself feels like a wildlife sanctuary, with lots of birds winging across the perfect skies and tiny lizards darting across the sandy paths. Small animals scurry under the palmetto leaves and fall silent when someone approaches.

Sandy golf cart paths meander from the restaurants to the guest villas to recreational facilities: an attractive pool and patio, two well-maintained tennis courts, and a clubhouse with a lending library and a nifty observation deck overlooking forest, beachfront, and a small pond where herons fish. The narrow golf cart paths also lead to the beach, a peaceful expanse of sand and shells that the sandpipers love as much as kids and adults.

It's really more fun — and more in keeping with the slow pace of Upper Captiva — to dispense with the golf carts altogether. Walking also has the advantage of providing a closer kinship with the island's wildlife and plant life. Bougainvillea and other exotic plants have been planted around the villas, but elsewhere the natural vegetation still grows wild. One of the most beautiful plants on the island is a sea grape with yellow hibiscus-like flowers that turn orange and then red before cascading to the forest floor.

Useppa Island

Useppa Island Club

P.O. Box 640
Bokeelia, FL 33922
941-283-1061
Fax: 941-283-0290

> Some of the most exotic
> scenery in Florida

General Manager: Vincent Formosa. **Accommodations:** More than 25 suites, duplexes, and cottages. **Rates:** Rooms $100–$250, suites $135–$310, cottages $215–$415, houses $160–$685; lower rates on weekdays. **Included:** Afternoon sherry and tea; Continental breakfast. **Minimum stay:** 2 nights on weekends, 3 nights on holidays and long weekends. **Added:** 9% tax. **Payment:** Major credit cards. **Children:** Free in room with parent. **Smoking:** Nonsmoking rooms available. **Open:** Year-round.

➤ **The island offers tennis, croquet, shuffleboard, saltwater and freshwater swimming, lawn chess, and fishing. There's even a small museum of island history.**

After a stay on Useppa Island, you might think back and wonder why it was so special. Was it the beach or the seclusion or the fishing or the sunsets or the atmospheric old Collier club? Or is it really true that Useppa Island has a mysterious and indescribable aura?

Most visitors would say it's all of these things. Useppa is an island several miles off the west coast of Florida that can be reached only by boat or seaplane. The subtropical flora has been allowed to grow naturally — though it is restrained from completely taking over — and is profuse and almost primeval. Many of the palm trees leaning over the Old Florida-style homes are draped with long ribbons of cactus that look like spiny green snakes. Ancient banyan trees form massive canopies over the pink shell walkway that links the clubhouse and residences. The roots that flow from the limbs to the ground of one of these enormous banyans have spawned a miniature forest of middle-aged and baby banyans.

Useppa Island is the oldest continuously occupied land mass on the Gulf Coast. From about 3500 B.C., the Caloosa Indians fished its abundant waters. Sometime in the 1700s, the Indians disappeared, and the history of the island became linked with the Spanish. Prominent among them was the pirate José Gaspar, who imprisoned his love, Joseffa de Mayorga, on the island. Because she spurned him, he had her killed, and her ghost supposedly haunted him until he later killed himself. Legend says she still haunts the island named after her, "Joseffa" altered over the years by fishermen to "Useppa."

In the early 1900s, New York millionaire Barron Collier bought Useppa and built a mansion for himself and tin-roofed cottages for his friends. The main attractions were tarpon fishing and the beach. After Collier died in 1939, Useppa passed into neglect until the mid-1970s, when the island was bought by Garfield Beckstead. With his wife and partners, Beckstead brought it back to its former beauty. Under 10 feet of vegetation, he found a winding pink pathway of crushed conch shells and cement that links the cottages to Collier's mansion, where the resort's two dining rooms and some of its most impressive accommodations are now located.

The old cottages were restored and new ones built. Today, Useppa is a private club and residential community of mostly winter homes, with a few cottages available for rent as well as individual suites. The interiors of the cottages are attractively decorated and well laid out, with modern bathrooms and kitchens. All have screened porches. Houses are scattered throughout the island, but all must conform to strict design guidelines — 10 pages of them. Their architecture follows the 1920s Old Florida style of the original Collier bungalows: crimped tin or gray asphalt roofs, large porches, latticework, and usually clapboard siding that is stained or painted gray or white.

Gasparilla Cottage and Collier Inn, original buildings constructed by Collier's craftsmen, were converted into B&B-style accommodations for visitors here for a short stay. The old two-story Gasparilla Cottage has been beautifully restored. The suites are furnished with comfortable sofas, polished wooden floors underfoot, and paddle fans above. Gasparilla Cottage is both a private cottage (in the front of the house and on the second floor) and a guest accommodation with four individually decorated suites. The Sunrise has paneled walls and ceiling, an attractive sitting area with sofa, TV, desk, and its own little porch. Area rugs are on the pine floors. An archway leads to the bedroom, which has a king-size bed. The high-ceilinged bathroom has the original cottage bathtub and a fluted pedestal sink. The suite has two closets, a small fridge, and a view of the water through the vegetation. Miniblinds are at the three windows and there are no curtains to obstruct the view.

Another suite, the Gasparilla, does not have a water view but makes up for it in drama, with a cathedral ceiling, bookcases on either side of a massive fireplace and chimney, wood paneling, and, in the sitting area, an imposing settee and matching chair made of dark ebony wood. An entertainment center is opposite the king-size bed, and a Japanese ceremonial costume is suspended on a rod above the bedstead. The suite has lots of windows and a pleasant side porch.

The suites in the Collier Inn, on the second and third floors of the original mansion, are more formal and luxurious. The grandest is the Centennial, which is the Useppa's honeymoon suite. Furnishings are Victorian: a mahogany four-poster bed with a plethora of frothy pillows, stained-glass lamps, a marble-topped Eastlake table, and oversize gold-tasseled lamps, which you turn on and off by pulling on the tassel. A large painting of white peacocks stands on an easel, a vase of peacock feathers behind it. The spacious bathroom has double sinks and an extra-large Jacuzzi tub. Most wonderful is the bank of floor-to-ceiling windows and the french doors that lead out to a wooden deck overlooking the water. During the course of a day spent rocking on this wonderful porch, the views are invigorating or relaxing, depending on the time of day and one's mood. While the suite itself is ornate and elegant, this little perch above the water reminds one that Useppa Club is really quite unpretentious.

Another impressive inn suite that combines the elegant and the rustic is the Barron Collier Room, which has the original pecky cypress paneling and fireplace. The pine floors are covered in rich red Orientals and the leather sofa and upholstered armchair in the sitting room are quite handsome. This suite includes a small table before the fireplace and a desk. As in all Useppa Island accommodations, there is plenty of light coming through the windows and the transomed French door that leads out to the railed balcony. Guests staying in both the Gasparilla and the Collier Inn are treated to a complimentary Continental breakfast in the mansion's waterfront tea room. Woodwork is painted white, and miniblinds at the small-paned windows let in lots of sunshine. The Collier Inn suites, in the original neo–Greek Revival mansion, are elegantly appointed and have many extras: sherry in the afternoon, a welcome potpourri package, aromatherapy oils in the bath, and a gourmet breakfast and dinner for two.

Automobiles are prohibited on Useppa, except for a few trucks used by the island maintenance crew. Most people get around by walking, bicycling, or driving a golf cart. Club activity is centered on the first floor of the mansion, with a lounge that feels like the living room of a summer cottage, an informal bar, and two dining rooms. Food is good here, with a nouvelle cuisine menu, excellent service, and a great key lime pie.

Joseffa's General Store, near the marina boat dock, sells some canned goods and other staples as well as the morning newspaper. The place has a summer camp atmosphere, friendly and unpretentious. Kitchen staff, corporate millionaires, and boatmen talk and joke easily together.

The island can feel so relaxing and pleasantly remote that one forgets that there are a number of facilities for recreation: a beautiful pool, a fitness center, bicycle and boat rentals, tennis courts, and even croquet courts. Fishing has traditionally been a major activity here, especially tarpon fishing. In the winter, the mansion is the scene for cooking classes as well as microbrew- and wine-tasting parties. From November to April there are monthly wine dinners that include a reception out on the terrace, where the wine maker is introduced to guests.

Perhaps because the island is also a residential community for those who live here all or most of the year, Useppa Island has a small lending library for residents and visitors, as well as a museum. The museum traces the history of the island back several centuries to the Calusa Indians, who had a sophisticated trading system in the gulf that included canals to what is now Cape Coral and a well-traveled route to Cuba. The island has recently become a destination for small groups on eco-tours and a favorite of birders and members of the Florida Audubon Society.

Useppa is only half a mile long and a third of a mile wide, so many of the paths and trails have views of water to east and west. In many of the cottages, you can see Pineland Sound from windows or a porch on one side of the house and the Gulf of Mexico from a room on the other.

Venice

Banyan House

519 South Harbor Drive
Venice, FL 34285
941-484-1385
Fax: 941-484-8032
relax@banyanhouse.com
www.banyanhouse.com

> **B&B rooms hosted by
> cordial innkeepers**

Innkeepers: Chuck and Susan McCormick. **Accommodations:** 2 rooms, 3 efficiencies, 5 apartments. **Rates:** Rooms $89–$99, efficiencies $109–$129; $15 for extra adult; discounts for longer stays. **Included:** Expanded Continental breakfast. **Minimum stay:** None. **Added:** 10% tax. **Payment:** MasterCard, Visa, cash, traveler's checks. **Children:** Over age 10 welcome. **Smoking:** On patio only. **Open:** All months except August.

➤ **One of the best things about breakfast at the Banyan House is eating in the solarium, overlooking the back garden and the big laurel tree.**

Venice, Florida, offers just what one might hope from its name: warm waters and sunshine, Mediterranean homes and charming shops, palm trees and tropical flowers. The group that had the vision to create Venice, Florida, in the 1920s was the Brotherhood of Locomotive Engineers. One member of that group, Robert Marvin, had a beautiful Mediterranean-style house built for himself that, happily, is now the Banyan House.

To get to residential South Harbor Drive, visitors drive over a bridge to the historic section of Venice, called "the island," part of the city that was originally planned by the Brotherhood in the 1920s. The stucco Banyan House is one of the most distinctive homes in the area, with a brick drive and subtropical landscaping accenting the Italian Mediterranean architecture. It's easy to find the place; just keep an eye out for the trees — huge, spreading trees. The one at the end of the drive is a wonder. In the back of the house another amazing tree, a Cuban laurel, picturesquely hangs over a bilevel patio.

Next to the patio is a tree-shaded whirlpool and swimming pool, the first one constructed in Venice. Closer to the house is a terrace that leads to a solarium. Here guests enjoy an expanded Continental breakfast: one day it's crêpes, another day it's French toast stuffed with cream cheese and strawberries. There's always a generous offering of homemade muffins or bread, fresh fruit, and steaming coffee. It's as filling as any "full" breakfast.

Behind the solarium is the living room, furnished in Victorian antiques, with elaborate valances above the windows. At one end of the room is a piano. Above is a beamed cypress ceiling. Guest rooms are upstairs. The Palm Room, the original master bedroom, has a king-size bed. Decorated in shades of pink, it has hardwood floors and area rugs and a fine fireplace and mantle. This room has a kitchenette and an original bathroom, which has a special step up to the tub, built for the former lady of the house, who was only four feet seven. The Laurel Room has a queen-size bed and a detached private bathroom.

During the day, guests enjoy exploring the historic district of Venice, shopping, or spending time on one of the nearby beaches.

Wesley Chapel

Saddlebrook Resort — Tampa

5700 Saddlebrook Way
Wesley Chapel, FL 33543-4499
800-729-8383
813-973-1111
Fax: 813-973-4504

A village with spacious villa accommodations and a friendly, knowledgeable staff

General Manager: Richard Boehning. **Accommodations:** 800 rooms and suites. **Rates:** $160–$332; packages available. **Minimum stay:** With packages. **Added:** 8% tax; $20 extra person. **Payment:** Major credit cards; personal checks. **Children:** Under 12 free in room with parent. **Smoking:** Allowed. **Open:** Year-round.

➤ **The Sports Village and luxury spa are equipped with exercise rooms, men's and women's spas, whirlpools, saunas, steam rooms, and massage rooms. Guests can have fitness programs set up for the duration of their stay.**

There is a sense of community at Saddlebrook, even if one is at the resort for a short stay. This, no doubt, is due to the fact that vacationers and conference participants walk nearly everywhere.

Saddlebrook has earned its reputation as a mecca for golf enthusiasts and is the world headquarters of the Arnold Palmer Golf Academy. Staff and management insure that golfers want for nothing. Rather than simply having soft-drink machines at shelters on the courses, a snack cart makes daily rounds for those with a mid-game thirst. The two golf courses have been ranked among Florida's best for years. Designed by Arnold Palmer, with cypress trees and lagoons a part of the beauty and challenge, the Saddlebrook and the Palmer provide hours of excitement. Special putting greens, a practice range, and an excellent pro shop complete the picture.

The resort's reputation for tennis is largely derived from its Hopman International Tennis Program. This program has trained thousands of young athletes and touring professionals from all over the world, including many Davis Cup winners. Instruction involves well-focused clinics, individual and private lessons, round robins, and amateur tournaments. The courts themselves — 45, with five surfaces lighted at night — are immaculate and are in a beautiful setting. Small islands between the courts are sheltered by awnings and have tables and chairs for spectators. The tennis center includes a well-equipped pro shop and match services.

Golf and tennis are often incorporated into conference activities at Saddlebrook. Apart from this temptation, Saddlebrook is popular for meetings because of its impressive facilities and services: two ballrooms, several seminar and board rooms, catering, and a professional conference-planning staff. Meeting space includes the Lagoon Pavilion, accessible by a wooden bridge over a lagoon and worth seeing even for nonconventioneers. The pavilion's unusual design won awards for its architects. It can be used as an open-air facility or enclosed. The pavilion has lovely views of the lagoon and the tropical waterfowl that winter here or reside year-round.

Saddlebrook's 480 acres have so many species of wildlife and vegetation, including mysterious and beautiful cypress swamps, that it could be designated as a wildlife sanctuary. But accommodations are a good deal more luxurious than the usual state-park digs. The hotel rooms and suites are all privately owned and rented out by the resort. Both the rooms and one- and two-bedroom villas feature kitchens, combination or separate living and dining rooms, and balconies. The bathrooms have mirrored closets and tile or marble shower baths. Luxury extras include terry robes.

Rooms are decorated with Asian artwork, and brass chandeliers hang over the dining room tables. For the most part, the low-rise villas are well constructed, with extras like marble window sills. In some of the rooms, however, the soundproofing is weak, and guests can hear creaking and muffled noises from the upstairs floors. Light sleepers might prefer a top floor or an end room.

Most guests stay in Saddlebrook's "walking village" accommodations, but there are also weekly, monthly, and annual rentals available in Lakeside Village. This development includes the resort's presidential suite, with a sunken living room, a spiral staircase, three bedrooms, three and a half baths, a private swimming pool and whirlpool just outside the door, and spectacular views of the pond and the golf course. The villa facades are buff-colored stucco with Tahitian-style shake roofs.

The reception center is the site of the resort's "superpool," a huge, lagoonlike pool that holds half a million gallons of water, has 25-meter racing lanes, and hosts water basketball and volleyball games. Adjacent are two whirlpools, a swim shop, and a children's playground. Saddlebrook has a well-supervised children's program that runs year-round.

For those as interested in good food and wine as in staying fit, the Cypress Restaurant has an impressive gourmet menu. The Cypress Room is large enough to be used for banquets, but room dividers lend intimacy. A row of windows overlooks cypress trees draped with Spanish moss that emerge from a lake. Adjacent is the three-level Polo Lounge and sports bar. With polished brass railings, soft candlelight, and a fireplace, this is clubby in the early evening and lively later on, when the band gets going.

Outdoor dining is at Terrace on the Green. Other spots for dining and convivial libation are the greenhouse-style lounge and steakhouse; the alfresco Little Club Patio, for light meals and drinks; the Hunt Room, an elegant oak and brass dining room for small groups; a poolside café; TD's Sports Bar; and Halfway House on the golf course, serving light refreshments.

All the major facilities blend in with the scenery of Saddlebrook, rather than compete with it. Much use has been made of fieldstones in construction. Wherever possible, bridges and walkways are made of wood. Native and imported trees and plants have been allowed to grow naturally. The cypress trees, with their Spanish moss dangling over lake and swamp waters, are the most impressive. But there are also several varieties of palm and oleanders, and small evergreens originally imported from China that now thrive in Florida.

Recommended Guidebooks

These books are excellent sources of information for fishing, camping, sightseeing, and restaurant suggestions.

Birnbaum's Walt Disney World. Edited by Stephen Birnbaum, Alice Gerard, and Jill Safro. Hyperion Press, 1999, 256 pages, paper, $13.95. This is the official guide to Walt Disney World, and the emphasis is on information rather than a more critical appraisal of each ride and attraction. Copious information is provided in this easy-to-read large-format book. The sheer volume of up-to-date information on every nook and cranny of this delightful place makes this guide well worth the price, even though ratings of many attractions are unclear. The maps are excellent.

Camper's Guide to Florida Parks, Trails, Rivers, and Beaches, second edition. Mickey Little, Gulf Publishing, 1995, 185 pages, paper, $15.95. Regionally organized and comprehensive in its coverage, this camping guide provides the essential details on camping sites, as well as maps showing campsites, trails, parking, and so on. Special features and riding and hiking trails are clearly marked.

Cruising Guide to the Florida Keys. Frank Papy, Frank Papy Publishing, 1998, 240 pages, paper, $19.95. Although a bit cluttered with ads, this book contains a lot of information on places to go, things to see, weather, marinas, and more, as well as several aerial satellite photos. Numerous charts (an "artist's sketch, not for navigation") are provided to orient travelers. The book is updated every two to three years.

Diver's Guide to Florida and the Florida Keys. Jim Stachowicz, Windward Publishing, 1990, 64 pages, paper, $5.95. This is a very useful collection of the best diving and snorkeling spots along the Florida coast, complete with charts, rules, and laws to consider, and a review of hazardous marine life to keep an eye on.

Fish Florida: Saltwater. Boris Arnov, Gulf Publishing, 1991, 232 pages, paper, $12.95. A top-notch guide that tells you where, when, and how to catch Florida's abundant marine fishes. It includes maps, tips on lures, baits, and riggings, and illustrations of fish species.

Florida: Off the Beaten Path, fifth edition. Bill and Diana Gleasner, Globe Pequot Press, 1998, 256 pages, paper, $12.95. Full of unusual and delightful things to see and do, this guide takes you to some of those wonderful, less-discovered spots that most tourists just don't know about. Included are good descriptions, directions, general location maps, and other helpful details.

Florida Island Exploring: 57 Tropic Islands and the Keys. Joan Scalpone, Great Outdoors Publishing, 1987, 64 pages, paper, $6.95. This book contains myriad day-trip ideas. Also authored by Joan Scalpone are the Let's Go Somewhere booklets for southwest Florida, northwest Florida, and Tampa to Big Bend, Florida, published by the same publisher.

The Florida Keys: A History and Guide. Joy Williams, Fodor's Travel, 1999, 240 pages, paper, $14.95. An irreverant but loving look at the Keys' checkered past and ecologically endangered present. It includes maps and descriptions of worthwhile attractions as well as a few restaurant reviews.

Florida Parks: A Guide to Camping in Nature, sixth edition. Gerald Grow, Long Leaf, 1997, 255 pages, paper, $15.95. This is an excellent guide to the vast selection of parks in Florida. It is arranged regionally, with each park nicely described and camping options and other important facts discussed. The latest updates are added to the back of each regional section. A clear emphasis on the environment and man's impact on it make this a particularly good guide for natives and visitors alike.

Florida's Historic Restaurants and Their Recipes, revised edition. Dawn O'Brien and Becky Roper Matkov, John F. Blair Publisher, 1994, 204 pages, cloth, $16.95. This is a fantastic series of inexpensive hardback books combining the best recipes of the historic restaurants of each state with informative descriptions and reviews, including the practical details. Of course, the emphasis is on the recipes, so some of the titles are a bit old to be absolutely reliable on the current state of affairs at any particular restaurant. Nonetheless, they are a good way to start the selection process. For those who like to look over the recipes before they choose their restaurant, this series is just plain great.

Fodor's Exploring Florida, Third Edition. Emma Stanford and Fodor's Travel Publications/Random House, 1998, 288 pages, paper, $21.00. Practical information, many detailed maps, excellent photographs.

A Gunkholer's Cruising Guide to Florida's West Coast, eleventh edition. Tom Lenfestey, Great Outdoors Publishing, 1997, 158 pages, paper, $17.95. This excellent, large-format book covers in great detail all the specifics of sailing/cruising the waters of Florida's west coast from the Everglades to Pensacola. The charts are exact and usable for navigational purposes. The text is specific as to routes, anchorages, fuel, food, and every other need. This title is updated every one to two years.

What's What

Best B&Bs

Amelia Island
Addison House, 34
Anna Maria Island
Harrington House Beachfront B&B, 416
Big Pine
Barnacle Bed & Breakast, 336
Bed & Breakfast on the Ocean: Casa Grande, 338
Cedar Key
Cedar Key Bed & Breakfast, 427
Daytona Beach
Coquina Inn B&B, 55
Gainesville
Magnolia Plantation, 176
Sweetwater Branch Inn B&B and the McKenzie Home, 179
Green Cove Springs
River Park Inn, 61
Jacksonville
Cleary-Dickert House B&B, 66
House on Cherry Street, 68
Plantation Manor Inn, 72
Key West
The Artist House, 351
Center Court, 355
Duval House, 357
The Gardens Hotel, 362
Heron House, 364
Island City House, 368
La Mer Hotel and Dewey House, 371
La Pensione, 372
The Mermaid and the Alligator, 377
Simonton Court, 384
Travelers Palm, 389

Best Beachside Accommodations

Naples
Edgewater Beach Hotel, 444
Naples Beach Hotel and Golf Club, 447
Ritz-Carlton, Naples, 451
Palm Beach
The Breakers, 307
Four Seasons Resort, Palm Beach, 313
Ritz-Carlton, Palm Beach, 316
Ponte Vedra Beach
The Lodge & Club, 92
Ponte Vedra Inn & Club, 94
St. Pete Beach
Don CeSar Beach Resort & Spa, 458
TradeWinds Resort on St. Pete Beach, 463
Sanibel Island
Caribe Beach Resort, 471
Casa Ybel Resort, 472
Sanibel Inn, 474
Song of the Sea, 476
Sundial Beach and Tennis Resort, 478
Sarasota
Half Moon Beach Club, 483
Seaside
Seaside, 157

Best Budget Finds

Big Pine
Bahia Honda Bayside Cabins, 333
Daytona Beach
Sunny Shore Motel, 60
Jupiter
Jupiter Waterfront Inn, 81
Key Largo
Largo Lodge Motel, 346
Kissimmee
Wynfield Inn — Main Gate, 186
Orlando
Wynfield Inn — Westwood, 234
St. Augustine
International Haus, 114

Best City Stops

Coral Gables
Omni Colonnade Hotel, 260
Jacksonville
Omni Jacksonville Hotel, 70
Miami
Grand Bay Hotel, 284
Hotel Inter-Continental Miami, 286
Hyatt Regency Miami, 287
Mayfair House Hotel, 289
Orlando
Orlando Marriott Downtown, 229
Palm Beach
The Colony, 311
Pensacola
Pensacola Grand Hotel, 155
Tallahassee
Cabot Lodge, 161
Governors Inn, 162
Tampa
Hyatt Regency Westshore, 485
Wyndham West Shore, 488

Best Eclectic Finds

Lake Wales
Chalet Suzanne, 205
Miami Beach
Colony Hotel, 292
Island Outpost Art Deco Hotels, 301
Vero Beach
The Driftwood Resort, 133
Wakulla Springs
Wakulla Springs Lodge, 165

Best Island Getaways

Cape Haze
Palm Island Resort, 419

Best Resorts and Spas

Best Small Hotels, Inns, and Motels

New Smyrna Beach
  Riverview Hotel, 85
Orange Park
  The Club Continental on the St. Johns, 87
Palm Beach
  Brazilian Court, 305
  The Chesterfield Hotel, 309
Pensacola
  New World Inn, 154
St. Augustine
  Old City House Inn, 118
St. Pete Beach
  Island's End Cottages, 461

Dockage Available with Advance Notice

Aventura (North Miami)
  Turnberry Isle Resort & Club, 249
Big Pine Key
  Bahia Honda Bayside Cabins, 333
Boca Raton
  Boca Raton Resort & Club, 253
Captiva
  South Seas Resort, 421
  'Tween Waters Inn, 425
Destin
  Sandestin Golf & Beach Resort, 145
Flamingo
  Flamingo Lodge, Marina & Outpost Resort, 262
Fort Lauderdale
  Fort Lauderdale Marina Marriott, 266
  Riverside Hotel, 271
Gasparilla Island
  Gasparilla Inn (limited), 434
Grenelefe
  Grenelefe Golf & Tennis Resort, 182
Howey-in-the-Hills
  Mission Inn Golf and Tennis Resort, 184
Hutchinson Island
  Indian River Plantation Marriott Resort, 63
Islamorada
  Pelican Cove Resort (limited), 345

Fishing

Amelia Island
Amelia Island Plantation, 36
Big Pine Key
Bahia Honda Bayside Cabins, 333
Bed & Breakfast on the Ocean: Casa Grande, 338
Boca Raton
Boca Raton Resort & Club, 253
Captiva
'Tween Waters Inn, 425
Daytona Beach
Indigo Lakes Holiday Inn, 57
Destin
Sandestin Golf & Beach Resort, 145
Flamingo
Flamingo Lodge, Marina & Outpost Resort, 262
Fort Lauderdale
Lago Mar Resort, 267
Grenelefe
Grenelefe Golf & Tennis Resort, 182
Hutchinson Island
Indian River Plantation Marriott Resort, 63
Islamorada
Cheeca Lodge, 340
Chesapeake Resort, 343
Pelican Cove Resort, 345
Jupiter
Jupiter Waterfront Inn, 81
Key Largo
Largo Lodge Motel, 346
Marina Del Mar, 347
Key West
Hyatt Key West, 365
La Mer Hotel and Dewey House, 371
Ocean Key House Resort and Marina, 379
South Beach Oceanfront Motel, 386
Southernmost Motel in the USA, 387
Wyndham Casa Marina Resort, 394
Lake Buena Vista
Walt Disney World Resorts, 191
Marathon
Faro Blanco Marine Resort, 399

Golf

Pets Allowed with Advance Notice for a Fee

Tennis

Index

Best Places Report

Authors of the Best Places to Stay series travel extensively in their research to find the best places for all budgets, styles, and interests. However, if we've missed an establishment that you find worthy, please write to us with your suggestion. Detailed information about the service, food, setting, and nearby activities or sights is most important. Finally, let us know how you heard about the place and how long you've been going there.

Send suggestions to:

> The Harvard Common Press
> Best Places to Stay Suggestions
> 535 Albany Street
> Boston, Massachusetts 02118

NAME OF HOTEL_____

TELEPHONE_____

ADDRESS_____

_____ ZIP _____

DESCRIPTION_____

_____

_____

_____

_____

_____

_____

YOUR NAME_____

TELEPHONE_____

ADDRESS_____

_____ ZIP _____

Best Places Report

Authors of the Best Places to Stay series travel extensively in their research to find the best places for all budgets, styles, and interests. However, if we've missed an establishment that you find worthy, please write to us with your suggestion. Detailed information about the service, food, setting, and nearby activities or sights is most important. Finally, let us know how you heard about the place and how long you've been going there.

Send suggestions to:

> The Harvard Common Press
> Best Places to Stay Suggestions
> 535 Albany Street
> Boston, Massachusetts 02118

NAME OF HOTEL_____

TELEPHONE_____

ADDRESS_____

_____ ZIP _____

DESCRIPTION_____

_____

_____

_____

_____

_____

_____

YOUR NAME_____

TELEPHONE_____

ADDRESS_____

_____ ZIP _____

Best Places Report

Authors of the Best Places to Stay series travel extensively in their research to find the best places for all budgets, styles, and interests. However, if we've missed an establishment that you find worthy, please write to us with your suggestion. Detailed information about the service, food, setting, and nearby activities or sights is most important. Finally, let us know how you heard about the place and how long you've been going there.

Send suggestions to:

> The Harvard Common Press
> Best Places to Stay Suggestions
> 535 Albany Street
> Boston, Massachusetts 02118

NAME OF HOTEL _____

TELEPHONE _____

ADDRESS _____

_____ ZIP _____

DESCRIPTION _____

_____

_____

_____

_____

_____

_____

YOUR NAME _____

TELEPHONE _____

ADDRESS _____

_____ ZIP _____

Best Places Report

Authors of the Best Places to Stay series travel extensively in their research to find the best places for all budgets, styles, and interests. However, if we've missed an establishment that you find worthy, please write to us with your suggestion. Detailed information about the service, food, setting, and nearby activities or sights is most important. Finally, let us know how you heard about the place and how long you've been going there.

Send suggestions to:

> The Harvard Common Press
> Best Places to Stay Suggestions
> 535 Albany Street
> Boston, Massachusetts 02118

NAME OF HOTEL_____

TELEPHONE_____

ADDRESS_____

_____ ZIP _____

DESCRIPTION_____

_____

_____

_____

_____

_____

_____

YOUR NAME_____

TELEPHONE_____

ADDRESS_____

_____ ZIP _____

Best Places Report

Authors of the Best Places to Stay series travel extensively in their research to find the best places for all budgets, styles, and interests. However, if we've missed an establishment that you find worthy, please write to us with your suggestion. Detailed information about the service, food, setting, and nearby activities or sights is most important. Finally, let us know how you heard about the place and how long you've been going there.

Send suggestions to:

> The Harvard Common Press
> Best Places to Stay Suggestions
> 535 Albany Street
> Boston, Massachusetts 02118

NAME OF HOTEL _____

TELEPHONE _____

ADDRESS _____

_____ ZIP _____

DESCRIPTION _____

_____

_____

_____

_____

_____

_____

YOUR NAME _____

TELEPHONE _____

ADDRESS _____

_____ ZIP _____

Best Places Report

Authors of the Best Places to Stay series travel extensively in their research to find the best places for all budgets, styles, and interests. However, if we've missed an establishment that you find worthy, please write to us with your suggestion. Detailed information about the service, food, setting, and nearby activities or sights is most important. Finally, let us know how you heard about the place and how long you've been going there.

Send suggestions to:

The Harvard Common Press
Best Places to Stay Suggestions
535 Albany Street
Boston, Massachusetts 02118

NAME OF HOTEL _____

TELEPHONE _____

ADDRESS _____

_____ ZIP _____

DESCRIPTION _____

_____

_____

_____

_____

_____

_____

YOUR NAME _____

TELEPHONE _____

ADDRESS _____

_____ ZIP _____